TRANSFORMATIONAL LEADERSHIP IN NURSING

Elaine Sorensen Marshall, PhD, RN, is currently professor and Bulloch Healthcare Foundation Endowed Chair at the School of Nursing at Georgia Southern University. She served as dean of the College of Nursing at Brigham Young University and as a member of the Board of Trustees of Intermountain Healthcare in Utah. She has served in national elected and appointed leadership positions for the American Association of Colleges of Nursing (AACN), the American Association for the History of Nursing (AAHN), and the Western Institute of Nursing. She has published two books and more than 50 professional and public articles and book chapters. Her work has been noted by the New Professional Book Award from the National Council on Family Relations, the Lavinia Dock Award from the American Association for the History of Nursing, and the Jo Eleanor Elliott Leadership Award from the Western Institute of Nursing.

TRANSFORMATIONAL LEADERSHIP IN NURSING
From Expert Clinician to Influential Leader

Elaine Sorensen Marshall, RN, PhD

SPRINGER PUBLISHING COMPANY

NEW YORK

Springer Publishing Company, LLC
11 West 42nd Street
New York, NY 10036
www.springerpub.com

Acquisitions Editor: Margaret Zuccarini
Project Editor: Peter Rocheleau
Project Manager: Amor Nanas
Cover Design: Mimi Flow
Composition: The Manila Typesetting Company

ISBN: 978-0-8261-0528-8

E-book ISBN: 978-0-8261-0529-5

10 11 12 13/ 5 4 3 2 1

The author and the publisher of this work have made every effort to use sources believed to be reliable to provide information that is accurate and compatible with the standards generally accepted at the time of publication. Because medical science is continually advancing, our knowledge base continues to expand. Therefore, as new information becomes available, changes in procedures become necessary. We recommend that the reader always consult current research and specific institutional policies before performing any clinical procedure. The author and publisher shall not be liable for any special, consequential, or exemplary damages resulting, in whole or in part, from the readers' use of, or reliance on, the information contained in this book. The publisher has no responsibility for the persistence or accuracy of URLs for external or third-party Internet Web sites referred to in this publication and does not guarantee that any content on such Web sites is, or will remain, accurate or appropriate.

Library of Congress Cataloging-in-Publication Data

Transformational leadership in nursing : from expert clinician to influential leader/Elaine Sorensen Marshall.
    p. ; cm.
  Includes bibliographical references and index.
  ISBN 978-0-8261-0528-8 — ISBN 978-0-8261-0529-5 (e-book)
    1. Nurse administrators. 2. Leadership.
  I. Marshall, Elaine S.
  [DNLM: 1. Nurse Administrators. 2. Leadership. 3. Nursing, Supervisory.
  WY 105 T7723 2010]
  RT89.T733 2010
  362.17'3068--dc22

                                                                    2010026128

Printed in the United States of America by Bang Printing

The true professional is one
Who does not obscure grace
With illusions of technical prowess,
The true professional is one
Who strips away all illusions to reveal
A reliable truth in which
The human heart can rest.

Margaret Wheatley

Contents

PART I: BECOMING THE TRANSFORMATIONAL LEADER

PART II: CONTEXTS FOR TRANSFORMATIONAL LEADERSHIP

PART III: DESIGNING NEW CARE DELIVERY MODELS

PART IV: POWER, POLITICS, AND POLICY

Foreword

What would you do in the next three to five years if you absolutely know that you cannot fail? If you cannot answer that question spontaneously, you have probably let your dreams sit on the back burner for way too long. Throughout my career journey, I have had the privilege of assuming multiple leadership roles in healthcare systems, professional organizations, and academia. In those roles as well as through reading the biographies of many leaders who have made a phenomenal impact in the world, one of the most important things I have learned is that to be a transformational leader, you need to have a big dream or vision for what you want to accomplish and an ability to inspire that vision in others. Any successful initiative needs to begin with the end or dream in mind. However, there are far too many leaders who do not realize the importance of the team vision or dream and, instead, are overly focused on processes instead of outcomes. These types of extreme "process-driven" leaders have a challenging time keeping people motivated, especially when the going gets tough. Although process is important, it should never be the main driving force in realizing a vision.

When individuals are inspired with a common vision by a transformational leader, they are intrinsically motivated to accomplish that vision instead of satisfied with the status quo. Transformational leaders recognize that a clear consistent focus on the vision by the team and an ability to keep the dream bigger than any fears are a key ingredient to success, especially when the journey gets tough or "character-building." However, having a dream and inspiring it in others is not enough by itself. Transformational leaders must believe in their abilities to accomplish their dreams and enhance that belief in others. They also must provide ongoing support and encouragement to others throughout the journey.

Transformational leaders are innovators, positive deviants, and "movers and shakers." They typically see things before others, use creative strategies to problem-solve challenges, and are not afraid to take risks in order to accomplish their dreams. These types of leaders also have the ability to anticipate and overcome barriers as well as mobilize resources and people to accomplish the vision. They are comfortable with uncertainty and thrive on change. Transformational leaders also have high integrity; their followers trust them, and they invest in the people on their team, especially through mentorship and encouragement. They strive for continuous quality improvement by using and generating evidence to inform best practice and organizational policies as well as use evidence to influence health policy. Finally and very importantly, transformational leaders persist through the "character-builders" until their dreams are realized in contrast to many individuals who give up on their dreams, right before they would have come to fruition. Transformational leaders go from one failure to the next with enthusiasm, knowing that they are one step closer to the realization of their dreams.

With so many daunting challenges in the current healthcare system, there has never been a greater need for transformational leaders. Although many individuals are recognized as leaders because of their titles, a title does not make a transformational leader. I have seen clinicians who are informal leaders often make a bigger impact and influence more people than leaders with titles. Therefore, do not wait to be promoted or receive a new title to spearhead efforts that result in a higher quality of care and improved patient outcomes. You are needed *right now* to step up to the plate and lead pioneering change for the better in our struggling healthcare system.

This outstanding and engaging book by Dr. Elaine Marshall will provide you with the knowledge and skills you need to become a transformational leader in today's healthcare system. Elaine's own expertise as a transformational leader has resulted in a unique book that is relatable to the reader and especially mindful of the qualities necessary to provide great leadership in today's healthcare world. The content in this book covers all salient points for becoming a transformational leader and includes exciting chapters on cultivating habits of a transformational leader, understanding contexts for transformational leadership, and practice design and management. The chapter on economics and finance is especially useful in today's healthcare system, which is driven by costs.

Knowledge alone is typically not enough to change behavior. Many health professionals have a lot of knowledge, but do not use that knowledge to lead needed change in our healthcare system and improve outcomes for patients and their families. It is my hope that, as you read this book, you will make a firm commitment to use the knowledge and skills gleaned from these chapters to lead transformational change in our healthcare system for the ultimate purpose of improving the health, safety, and quality of life for people throughout the United States.

I ask again, what will you do in the next three to five years if you absolutely know that you cannot fail? In the words of Les Brown, remember to "shoot for the moon, even if you miss, you will land amongst the stars!"

Warm regards,

Bernadette Mazurek Melnyk, PhD, RN, CPNP/PMHNP, FNAP, FAAN
Dean and Distinguished Foundation Professor in Nursing
Arizona State University College of Nursing & Health Innovation

Preface

This book is written for future leaders. It is directed specifically to future leaders in health care, from the solo practice clinic to the most complex system, from an isolated rural community to a health sciences center. If you are reading this book, you probably already have some level of clinical expertise. You are an expert clinician in patient care practice, in management or administration, or you teach clinical nursing. Your challenge now is to enhance your skills and stature to become an influential leader. If that "becoming" is not a transforming experience, it will not be enough to lead in a future of enormous challenges. The future of health care in the United States and throughout the world requires leaders who are transformational in the best and broadest sense. It requires a thoughtful, robust sense of self as a leader. It requires an intellectual, practical, and spiritual commitment to improving clinical practice and leading others toward their own transformation. It requires courage, knowledge, and a foundation in clinical practice. It requires an interdisciplinary fluency and the ability to listen, understand, and influence others across a variety of disciplines. It requires vision and creativity.

Many who use this book will be students in programs of study for a clinical doctorate. The book specifically references the *Essentials of Doctoral Education for Advanced Nursing Practice* (*DNP Essentials*; American Association of Colleges of Nursing [AACN], 2006). The *DNP Essentials* and the position statement on the doctor of nursing practice (DNP) of the AACN (2004) call for a "transformational change in the education required for professional nurses who will practice at the most advanced level of nursing" (AACN, 2004, 2006, p. 4) and "enhanced leadership skills to strengthen practice and health care delivery" (AACN, 2006, p. 5). Expert and advanced clinicians who become transformational leaders focus not only on direct care, but also on health care for entire communities.

This work is not meant to be a comprehensive encyclopedic text for healthcare leadership, nor is it a traditional text in nursing management. Rather, its purpose is to identify some key issues related to leadership development, to the contexts for transformational leaders in health care, and to the arena in which healthcare leaders work. The work is meant to introduce you, as the clinical expert, to important current issues in the transition to leadership. It is meant to accompany and to lead you to more focused current literature and experts on all issues that face leaders in health care. It is meant to launch you into the literature and evidence on many topics of leadership and current issues in health care.

You will read about transformational leadership. Although there are some formal theories called "transformational leadership," this work refers to the concept in its best and broadest sense without adhering only to a specific theoretical perspective. The book is heavily referenced not only to provide usual citation, but also to lead you to a vast range of literature. The appendix further provides examples of classic books for your library as a transformational leader.

Finally, this work is meant to be taken personally. If your journey toward transformational leadership is not a deeply personal one, then you will not be the leader that you must be or the leader for which the future pleads. Alongside many references from professional literature is the occasional personal story. I did not begin to write a personal story, but the more I saw you, the reader, and myself as a leader wanting more than literature reviews, the more I wanted to reach out and connect on a personal level. While working on this book, I was traveling home from a professional meeting when I was fortunate enough to be upgraded to a first-class seat on the plane, seated next to the wife of a famous writer whose name you would recognize. Noticing my absorption in the manuscript, she asked about what I was writing. When I told her it was a textbook on leadership for advanced practice nurses and other healthcare providers, she pleaded in a very personal way, "I hope you share yourself. It won't be any good if you don't share your own story." My first response was that she did not understand the language of academic textbooks. They simply are not personal. But the more we talked, and the more I contemplated, I was drawn to sprinkle a bit of myself and other leaders whom I have known on a personal level. I extend to you my personal encouragement. The world waits for you and the good you will do.

Thomas A. Stewart (2004, p. 10), editor of the *Harvard Business Review*, mused:

> Academic leadership studies grew out of historians "great man" theories, which explain events by examining the role of highly influential individuals . . . . In portraits, great men (and a few women) are heroic, larger than life; often they're on horseback. Their strength and vision inspire us. We don't know much about what they feel, however. We don't know their doubts or their secrets.

As you become the transformational leader in your own future, I hope you might share your secrets and leave the legacy we so need in the future of health care.

REFERENCES

American Association of Colleges of Nursing (AACN). (2004). *AACN position statement on the practice doctorate in nursing*. Washington, D.C.: AACN.

American Association of Colleges of Nursing (AACN). (2006). *The essentials of doctoral education for advanced practice nursing*. Washington, D.C.: AACN.

Stewart, T. A. (2004, January). The leader's secret self. *Harvard Business Review*, 10.

To the leaders in my life:

To Margaret Zuccarini, for her trust and patience.

To Brenda Talley, who wrote Chapter 10, lending her own experience and leadership.

To the courageous future leaders, my students, who have endured my thinking and who might recognize some of their own thinking in this book.

To my first doctor of practice class (DNP) in "Leadership and Management in Practice Transformation": Della Brown, Myron Faircloth, Carmen Hill-Mekoba, Lee Hunter-Eades, Kim Lingerfelt, Kay Lynn Olmstead, Susan Riley, Joy Scarborough, Michael Scott, Janet Smith, and Linda Upchurch. This is the text you requested. You inspired it.

To Jean Bartels and Donna Hodnicki, for inviting me to the adventure, with friends at Georgia Southern University, and to dear colleagues at Brigham Young University.

To John, for love.

To Rulon and Jean Shaw, for life.

To Janene and Leonard Dabb, LaDawn and Bob Cox, Ryan and Jan Shaw, for inspiration.

To Brian and Jeannie Sorensen, Chad and Amy Sorensen, Johanna Sorensen and Alex Hart, and Todd, Rachael, Blake, Derek, Aaron, and the babies coming in the summer who remind me of what is most important—for everything.

1

Expert Clinician to Transformational Leader in a Complex Healthcare Organization

> The very essence of leadership is that you have to have a vision.
> It has to be a vision you articulate clearly and forcefully on every
> occasion. You cannot blow an uncertain trumpet.
>
> — *Theodore Hesburgh*

The world needs visionary, effective, and wise leaders. Never has this statement been more true than it is for health care today. Leadership matters. Perhaps, every generation of leaders "believes their challenges are greater than the ones of the previous generation" (Yoder-Wise & Kowalski, 2006, p. 1), but the current state of health care creates unprecedented challenges for individuals, families, the nation, and the world. Health care continues to grow more complex, corporate, and costly. In the United States, we face urgent problems of system complexity, financial shortfalls, poor distribution of resources, shortages of clinicians, issues of errors and patient safety, and controversy regarding future directions for healthcare reform (Institute of Medicine, 2000, 2001, 2003). Furthermore, we meet a host of health problems such as greater incidence of chronic illnesses, epidemics of new infectious diseases, and growing numbers of vulnerable, underserved, and aging populations. Meanwhile, the society impatiently waits with waning confidence in the current healthcare system. Dialogue becomes more strident; positions become more polarized. Where are our leaders?

The healthcare needs of past decades focused on clinical practice and educational preparation for practice. The society demanded clinical experts to master the burgeoning body of clinical information and skills. Nurses and physicians responded to that challenge; they became clinical experts. They devoted learning and practice to clinical excellence. The nursing profession continues to provide an army of advanced practitioners who continue to effectively meet healthcare needs for thousands of individuals and families. You responded; you prepared yourself to offer care at the highest levels of evidence-based practice and human compassion. We continue to need expert clinicians. But our greatest need is for leaders. Your clinical expertise, whether it is in direct patient care, management or administration, or clinical education, is now needed as a foundation for leadership. We need nurse leaders who can draw from their roots in clinical practice to collaborate with leaders in other disciplines, with policy makers, and with members of the community to create new solutions to the problems facing health care, to improve quality of life, to transform healthcare systems, and to inspire the next generation of leaders. Preparation at the highest level of practice must include preparation for leadership. The world needs expert clinicians to become transformational leaders. The world needs you to become the leader to transform health care for the next generation.

WHAT IS TRANSFORMATIONAL LEADERSHIP?

Leadership

First, what is leadership and who are leaders? Leadership is one of those difficult concepts that is sometimes readily identified but never easily defined. Simply put, leadership is the discipline and art of guiding, directing, motivating, and inspiring a group or organization toward the achievement of common goals. It includes the management of people, information, and resources. It requires commitment, communication, creativity, and credibility. It demands the wise use of power. "Leadership is ultimately about creating a way for people to contribute to making something extraordinary happen" (Keith, A., personal communication, quoted in Kouzes & Posner, 2007, p. 3). Leadership is succinctly described as the following:

> In its essence, leadership in an organization role involves 1) establishing a clear vision, 2) sharing (communicating) that vision with others so that they will follow willingly, 3) providing the information, knowledge, and methods to realize that vision, and 4) coordinating and balancing the conflicting interests of all members of stakeholders. A leader comes to the forefront in case of crisis and is able to think and act in creative ways in difficult situations. Unlike management, leadership flows from the core of a personality and cannot be taught, although it may be learned and may be enhanced through coaching or mentoring. (Business Dictionary, 2009a)

Leadership is the ability to guide others, whether they are colleagues, peers, clients, or patients, toward desired outcomes. A leader uses good judgment, wise decision making, knowledge, intuitive wisdom, and compassionate sensitivity to the human condition, to suffering, pain, illness, anxiety, and grief. A nursing leader is engaged and professional and acts as an advocate for health and dignity.

Leaders "are people who have a clear idea of what they want to achieve and why" (Doyle & Smith, 2009, p. 1). They are usually identified by a title or position and are often associated with a particular organization. Leaders are the resource for confidence, assurance, and guidance. "We look to them when we don't know what to do, or when we can't be bothered to work things out for ourselves" (Doyle & Smith, 2009, p. 10). Leaders are known for qualities that set them apart. A leader influences others. A leader has followers. Individual, solitary vision cannot take the leader so far ahead that followers, left behind, lose the light.

Perhaps some people are born leaders, or some leaders grow out of crisis or being in the right place at the right time. Most leaders are neither born, made, nor found by luck but emerge when preparation, character, experience, and circumstance come together at a time of need. Leaders are most often ordinary people demonstrating extraordinary courage, skill, and "spirit to make a significant difference" (Kouzes & Posner, 2007, p. xiv). In any case, a leader cannot lead without preparation. An old professor once said, "Good luck is that sweet smile of fortune that comes so often to those who are well prepared." No one can teach you to be a leader; not this book nor your professor. But you can prepare yourself and you can learn to be a leader. Others can support, coach, and mentor. The purpose of this text is to help you as an advanced clinician to prepare to become a transformational leader.

Transformational Leadership

A simple definition of transformational leadership is a "style of leadership in which the leader identifies the needed change, creates a vision to guide the change through inspiration, and executes the change with the commitment" of others (Business Dictionary, 2009b). Transformational leadership "taps into the emotional and spiritual resources of an organization" (Tracy, 2004). It is a process of developing the leadership capacity of an entire team. Transformational leaders inspire others to achieve what might be considered extraordinary results. Leaders and followers engage with each other, raise each other, and inspire each other. Transformational leadership includes value systems, emotional intelligence, and attention to the spiritual. It connects with the very soul of the organization and honors its humanity. It raises "human conduct and ethical aspirations of both the leader and the led and, thus has a transforming effect on both" (Burns, 1978, pp. 4, 20). Transformational leaders are charismatic, visionary, and inspiring. They are role models for trust. Their leadership is based on commitment to shared values. For over a decade, nurses have described and promoted transformational leadership in practice (see Bowles & Bowles, 2000; Loeffler, 1994; Marriner-Tomey, 1993; Sieloff, 1996), although it still may not be clear where and how leadership is truly "transformational" in nursing and health care (McKenna, Keeney, & Bradley, 2004). But there is no question that it is now so much needed.

The original concept of transformational leadership is attributed to James MacGregor Burns, who proposed the idea in 1978. Other leadership scholars continue to build on the principle. Bernard Bass (1985) developed the idea of a continuum between transactional and transformational leadership, and Robert Kegan added a list of developmental stages of leadership traits toward transformational leadership (Kegan, 1982; Kegan & Lahey, 1983). Goleman, Boyatzis, and McKee (2002) further advanced the perspective to include aspects of emotional intelligence, such as self-awareness, self-management, social awareness, and relationship management. Since this text does not embrace a sole theoretical perspective, transformational leadership is considered here in its best and broadest sense, as a context and backdrop for leadership development.

Characteristics of Transformational Leadership

The transformational leader must make the conscious decision to lead (Heathfield, n.d.). Often, competent nurses are given opportunities to supervise or manage, but successful leaders *choose* to lead. I remember the first "official" day I was required to be a leader. I had been out of nursing school for less than a year, working on the job I loved as a staff nurse on a medical-surgical unit in a large flagship hospital. The nurse manager, then referred to as the team leader, called in sick. One by one, calls to all the other usual suspects to take her place were in vain. The house supervisor came to me and said, "You are *it* today, you are in charge. I will be available if you need anything." I was left in charge of a unit staff of one other registered nurse, two practical nurses with more bedside experience than I had in years of life, two nursing assistants, and 22 very sick patients. My heart raced simultaneously with the surge of excitement and panic. I will not violate privacy regulations here to tell you all the near-death adventures that day, but I can say that it was probably not the ideal first step on a path toward transformational leadership. I did learn, almost immediately, what worked and what did not work to inspire or influence others. Eventually, over a lifetime, I gained knowledge, insight, and experience as a transformational leader, but I always return to that summer day when I learned the "sink or swim" theory of leadership. I learned that my heart was in the right place, that I wanted to care for others, that I had some innate abilities to influence others for good, that I was a natural goal setter, that I had fairly good judgment in making decisions, and that others trusted me. But I had no specific knowledge on how to lead, no preparation for leadership, no coach or mentor, little confidence, and not much insight on organization of resources to meet what came next. I knew only that I was in a situation that needed a leader.

Some more effective, specific aspects of transformational leadership are outlined below. Transformational leadership theorists have developed some foundational concepts or characteristics of transformational leadership (Bass & Riggio, 2006):

Charisma or Idealized Influence

A transformational leader is a role model of values and aspirations for followers. He or she inspires trust and commitment to a cause. Charisma refers to the ability to inspire a vision. The current preoccupation with celebrity charisma in popular culture has tarnished its meaning. Unlike narcissistic charisma, which focuses on self, often with some sensationalism, the charisma of idealized influence finds its success from a primary belief in others. It is the ability to influence others, to inspire not only a willingness to follow, but also an expectation of success, an anticipation of becoming part of something greater than self. Charismatic leaders know who they are and where they are going. They have themes and personal mantras to their lives. I know one leader who keeps a file called "Dream" that holds ideas about future opportunities, and another who keeps a hand-drawn diagram of her "Tree of Life" showing the roots, trunk, and branches of her life and future. Charismatic leaders, grounded in a commitment to ethical values, influence others to make a positive difference in the world. Healthcare needs such leaders. Indeed, one study demonstrated higher satisfaction and greater happiness among workers who follow a charismatic leader (Erez, Misangyi, Johnson, LePine, & Halverson, 2008).

Charismatic leaders often emerge in times of crisis. They exhibit personal qualities that draw people to believe and follow them. If they are wise, they inspire followers in a synergistic manner that provides safety, direction, beliefs, and actions that exceed the expectations of either follower or leader.

Charismatic leaders are not necessarily flamboyant. Indeed, the most successful leaders "blend extreme personal humility with intense professional will...." They are often "self-effacing individuals who display the fierce resolve to do whatever needs to be done to make the [organization] great" (Collins, 2001, p. 21). Drucker (1996, p. 9) noted that great leaders possess "a belief in oneself, self-confidence to step into the unknown, and persuade others to go where no one has gone before... coupled with humility that you can be wrong on occasion, that others may have better or great ideas, and that listening is more important than talking." One such leader was heard to say, "I never stopped trying to become qualified for the job" (Collins, 2001, p. 20, from Wicks, 1997, p. 10). Charisma may refer to a quality of authenticity, transparency, and trust that draws others to you to share the vision and the will to work toward the goal. Kouzes and Posner (2007) pointed out that such leaders may be ordinary people who accomplish extraordinary results by being a role model, being an example, and leading by behavior that authentically reflects the behaviors expected of others.

Inspiration and Vision

Bass (1985, 1990, 1997) noted that authentic transformational leadership must be grounded in the moral character of the leader, a foundation of ethical values, and collective ethical processes. Goal orientation is also critical. From an ethical foundation, transformational leaders create a compelling image of a desired future. Kouzes and Posner (2007, p. 17) explained, "Every organization, every social movement, begins with a dream. The dream or vision is the force that invents the future." Transformational leaders influence others by high expectations with a sight toward the desired future. They set high standards and instill others with optimism, a sense of meaning, and commitment to a dream, goal, or cause. They extend a sense of purpose and purposeful meaning that provide the energy to achieve goals. They inspire from a foundation of truth.

Intellectual Stimulation

The transformational leader is a broadly educated, well-informed individual who looks at old problems in new ways. He or she challenges boundaries, promotes creativity, and applies a range of disciplines, ideas, and approaches to find solutions. This involves fearlessness and risk taking. The transformational leader reads broadly, takes lessons from many disciplines beyond clinical practice, and engages as an interested citizen in public discourse on a full range of topics from ballet to baseball, from ecology to economics. The transformational leader may find strategies from the arts and literature, humanities, business, or other sciences. Such leaders ask questions and nurture independent and critical thinking. The transformational leader assumes that people are willing and eager to learn and test new ideas.

Individual Consideration

The transformational leader has a kind of humility that looks beyond self to the mission of the organization and the value of the work of others. He or she uses many professional skills, including listening, coaching, empathy, support, and recognition of the contributions of followers. The transformational leader enables others to act toward a shared vision. The effective leader recognizes and promotes the contributions of others and creates a culture of sharing, celebration, and unity within the entire team. Who gets the credit is less important than how team members affirm the work of each other.

Transformational leaders effectively build on these characteristics and integrate principles from a variety of leadership theories and pragmatic approaches to advance, enhance, and expand clinical expertise from a focus on direct individual patient care to a focus on the care of groups, aggregates, and entire populations in a variety of environments. They consider the individual and the aggregate at once.

Although there has been considerable discussion of transformational leadership in a variety of settings including those of nursing practice (Bowles & Bowles, 2000; Porter-O'Grady, 1992; Trofino, 1993), there has been little actual study of the outcomes of transformational leadership in nursing and health care. We know little about how it works, what it ultimately means to patients, and precious little concerning who are the models. Such models must emerge from the next generation of leaders. It is your job to envision and articulate the prototypes for transformational leadership in health care.

Management and Leadership

In their zeal to promote charismatic transformational leadership, some writers make unfortunate distinctions between managers and leaders, as though managers are undesirable and leaders are better in all situations. Jennings, Scalzi, Rodgers, and Keane (2007) reviewed the literature to find a growing lack of discrimination between nursing leadership and management competencies.

Nevertheless, Bennis (2009) asserted that managers "do things right," and leaders "do the right things." Managers are thought to control and maintain processes with a focus on the short term, relying on authority rather than influence, while leaders are visionary, insightful, and influential. Managers minimize risk and leaders maximize opportunity. Bennis (1989, p. 45, adapted) made the following further distinctions between managers and leaders:

> Managers administer; leaders innovate. Managers ask how and when; leaders ask what and why. Managers focus on systems; leaders focus on people. Managers maintain; leaders develop. Managers rely on control; leaders inspire trust. Managers have short-term perspectives; leaders have long-term perspectives. Managers accept the status-quo; leaders challenge the status-quo. Managers have an eye on the bottom line; leaders have an eye on the horizon. Managers imitate; leaders originate. Managers emulate the classic good soldier; leaders are their own person. Managers copy; leaders create.

Transformational leadership theorists refer to the manager style as transactional leadership. Transactional leaders motivate by systems of rewards and punishments. Their power lies largely in the authority of their position. A manager may be referred to as the "laissez faire" supervisor who provides little direction or motivation for change, leaving most decision making with the followers. Leaders, on the other hand, develop, innovate, focus on developing others, inspire and create trust, and hold a long-term, big-picture futuristic view.

The reality is that anyone in charge of a group of people working toward effective goal achievement needs the wisdom to develop and use the qualities of both manager and leader in different situations. Indeed, Millward and Bryan (2005, p. xii) proposed that "the reality of clinical leadership must involve a judicious blend of effective management in the conventional sense with skill in transformational change in order to make real difference to the care delivery process." Thus, the terms *manager* and *leader* may be used interchangeably in this text, not for lack of precision but with the view that the characteristics of each are needed in effective leadership. Effective leaders (and managers) rely on a broad repertoire of style, rather than specialization of techniques. You must be able to distinguish when incentive/punishment motivation is needed versus when charismatic inspiration will achieve the desired results, or even when "well enough" is left alone. The next generation of leaders will be required to blend techniques of artistic management and wise leadership all "on the run" in a rapidly changing health care environment (Bolman & Deal, 1991; Garrison, Morgan, & Johnson, 2004). Indeed, some studies of actual military platoons in combat (the ultimate fast-paced and stressful environment) showed both transformational and transactional leadership to be positively related to group cohesion and performance (Bass, Avolio, Jung, & Berson, 2003). Researchers have compared the effects of transformational leadership and other leadership styles and have found high correlations among all styles with organizational outcomes and employee satisfaction (Molero, Cuadrado, Navas, & Morales, 2007), confirming the idea that a variety of leadership styles and approaches is effective in differing roles and circumstances.

THE ROLE OF THE DOCTOR OF NURSING PRACTICE IN ORGANIZATIONAL AND SYSTEMS LEADERSHIP

You have taken a step toward innovation in leadership by pursuing the doctor of nursing practice (DNP) degree. From the beginning of the development of the degree, leadership development has been a high priority (Lenz, 2005). Indeed, the need for leaders prepared in advanced clinical practice was a precipitating factor in the earliest discussions of the DNP. Carryer, Gardner, Dunn, and Gardner (2007) observed three components of advanced clinicians such as nurse practitioners: dynamic practice, professional efficacy, and clinical leadership. Draye, Acker, and Zimmer (2006, p. 123) called on DNP programs to prepare expert clinicians with "enhanced leadership" skills. Other leaders in the discipline (Marion et al., 2003; O'Sullivan, Carter, Marion, Pohl, & Werner, 2005, p. 6) have boldly announced that "educational programs need to prepare clinicians with increased leadership and management skills in order to better understand and master the emerging complex health care systems."

Nursing joins other practice disciplines, such as medicine, optometry, pharmacy, physical therapy, or audiology, that elevate practice and leadership to the highest academic degree (Upvall & Ptachcinski, 2007). The *Position Statement on the Practice Doctorate in Nursing* from the American Association of Colleges of Nursing (AACN, 2004) affirms the fundamental need for DNP-prepared leaders, noting that "the knowledge required to provide leadership in the discipline of nursing is so complex and rapidly changing that additional or doctoral level education is needed" (p. 7) and that "practice-focused doctoral nursing programs prepare leaders for nursing practice" (p. 11). One of the *Essentials of Doctoral Education for Advanced Nursing Practice* (AACN, 2006, p. 10) is "Organizational and systems leadership for quality improvement and systems thinking." Specifically, DNP graduates should be prepared to:

1. Develop and evaluate care delivery approaches that meet the current and future needs of patient populations based on scientific findings in nursing and other clinical sciences, as well as organizational, political, and economic sciences.
2. Ensure accountability for the quality of health care and patient safety for populations with whom they work.
   a. Use advanced communication skills/processes to lead quality improvement and patient safety initiatives in healthcare systems.
   b. Employ principles of business, finance, economics, and health policy to develop and implement effective plans for practice-level and/or system-wide practice initiatives that will improve the quality of care delivery.

    c. Develop and/or monitor budgets for practice initiatives.

    d. Analyze the cost-effectiveness of practice initiatives accounting for risk and improvement of healthcare outcomes.

    e. Demonstrate sensitivity to diverse organizational cultures and populations, including patients and providers.

3. Develop and/or evaluate effective strategies for managing the ethical dilemmas inherent in patient care, the healthcare organization, and research (AACN, 2006, pp. 10–11).

Although the DNP has met some controversy within the discipline of nursing (see Chase & Pruitt, 2006; Dracup, Cronenwett, Meleis, & Benner, 2005; Joachim, 2008; Otterness, 2006; Webber, 2008), some leaders have observed that it has approached the "tipping point" (Gladwell, 2000), proclaiming that "the question facing the nursing community is no longer whether the practice doctorate is 'future or fringe'" (Marion et al., 2003) but rather how do we move forward together (O'Sullivan, et al., 2005). DNP programs continue to grow throughout the United States, the United Kingdom, Canada, and Australia (Acorn, Lamarch, & Edwards, 2009; Brown-Benedict, 2008; DeMarco, Pulcini, Haggerty, & Tang, 2009; Edwards, 2009; Ellis, 2006, 2007; Loomis, Willard, & Cohen, 2006; Sperhac & Clinton, 2008; Starck, Duffy, & Vogler, 1993; Stein, 2008; Wall, Novak, & Wilkerson, 2005). Graduates of DNP programs are beginning to fulfill the hope for a new more effective advanced practitioner and leader.

The complexity of healthcare systems, advances in technology, emphasis on evidence-based practice, information explosions in science, and a new world of ethical issues only amplify the need for new leadership grounded in expert clinical practice. It is the hope of the profession that the DNP-prepared leader will offer the highest level of practice expertise, "integrated with the ability to translate scientific knowledge into complex clinical interventions tailored to meet individual, family, and community health and illness needs" (Bellflower & Carter, 2006, p. 323). As a DNP-prepared leader, you will be expected to guide and inspire organizational systems, quality improvement, analytic evaluation, policy development and translation, and interdisciplinary collaboration to improve health care (Bellflower & Carter, 2006). Prepared at the highest level of practice, you will understand the broad perspective of resource management in a sociopolitical environment to influence policy decisions and "ultimately improve the standard of health care" (Yam, 2005, p. 564). There is good reason to hope that you will be able to invent systems of care yet unknown that will strengthen, correct, and transform healthcare systems as we know them today.

BRINGING THE PERSPECTIVE OF EXPERT CLINICIAN TO ENHANCE LEADERSHIP: ENVISIONING NEW ROLES

A decade ago, Starck et al. (1993) pointed out that "Nursing in the next century will reflect changes in the healthcare system, and although the profession has made great strides in preparing nurse researchers, the current system has a serious gap that must be addressed; that of preparing clinical leaders." Their statement remains true, and insightful clinicians are responding to the call. The professional background of the advanced clinician provides the unique opportunity for new eyes to examine the leadership tradition, including the vision of new roles for the leader and others. This book cannot tell you what new roles you will envision. It can only help you to prepare to invent and to lead in those roles. You must find the fearlessness and creativity to envision the role. If you reach deep into your own knowledge and find the courage to step out of old habits, you will design and fulfill the models that will work.

To become a transformational leader requires both theoretical or conceptual understanding and the real-world practice of leadership. Leadership is a discipline in itself, with a body of knowledge, theories, culture, and practice expertise. By learning from theories and principles of leadership, then applying vision and courage, you will become a citizen of the community of leaders who will solve the problems of the future.

One of your challenges as an advanced clinician and you become a leader at the organizational level will be to shift the perspective of care from the individual patient to that of entire populations of professionals, peers, patients, and other stakeholders. Savage (2003, p. 1) noted that "nursing leaders must shift focus from tactical to strategic, concentrating on the future state and the larger picture." The viewpoint of the expert clinician is critical to leadership for the future of health care, but it requires that nurses specifically "transition from the operational (doing) aspect of work to the strategic (reflective) element" (Savage, 2003, p. 2). Evidence is mounting that links the influence of transformational leaders to both improved nursing practice at the bedside, and positive patient outcomes in the aggregate (Gifford, Davies, Edwards, Griffin, & Lybanon, 2007; Wong & Cummings, 2007). There is a need for more research and practice results in this area, particularly aimed at developing effective leadership roles.

The expertise of the advanced clinician in the position of the organizational leader offers a treasure of perspective, professional and personal knowledge, and in-the-trenches experience that are frequently missing in health care today. For example, currently in settings where the chief executive officer is not a clinician, which is frequently the case, it is often the chief nursing officer who provides the insight, experience, and model for clinical leadership. Clinical expertise brings context, credibility, and a good dose of reality to a leadership position. So many areas of health care will benefit from the clinical leadership roles yet to be invented. Such roles are currently needed in areas of access to care, healthcare policy and reform. New leadership roles are needed in clinical areas of child health and risk reduction for chronic conditions, transitions of aging, palliative, and end-of-life care. They are needed in settings of acute care, community, such as new kinds of comprehensive preventive screening centers, immigrant health, internet health care, and others yet unimagined. In the environment of fast-paced complex systems, the bold and creative expert clinician will invent the new roles needed to lead care teams, patient groups, public interests, and organizations that may better manage the challenges, and solve the problems so vexing at the moment.

HERITAGE AND LEGACY: HISTORICAL PERSPECTIVES

The early history of leadership provides an interesting glimpse of the seeds of leader qualities and theories in practice today. The earliest examples of leadership likely include the code of Hammurabi, the wisdom of Confucius, the spiritual guidance of Moses, the philosophical influence of Socrates and Aristotle, and the cunning of Machiavelli. Although leadership obviously began in some form and called by some term from the beginning of civilization, the word *leadership* did not appear in the English dictionary until the 19th century (Davis & Cushing, 1999; *Leadership*, n.d.; Stogdill, 1974). The beginning of the industrial revolution marked a need for attention to leadership beyond political, military, or cultural/religious organizations toward effective business.

Early explorations of leadership followed the "great man theory" of historians attributed to Thomas Carlyle, who is credited with saying, "The history of the world is but the biography of great men" (Jézégou, n.d.). Carlyle perpetuated a view of leadership as possessed by heroes with influence apparently born to be leaders. Traditional history books are filled with stories of great political, social, or religious leaders. My own college history teacher referred to "history by the study of dead white men," and Stewart (2004, p. 10) referred to them as "heroic, larger than life," and "often on horseback."

The story of modern Western nursing begins with lesser noted but no less "great women," and traditionally starts with Florence Nightingale. Although not usually described from a purely leadership perspective, the inspiration and effectiveness of her leadership have been celebrated for over 150 years. Her work in Scutari designing safer healthcare environments and hospital structures, training nurses, and using epidemiologic data to improve health can only be described as "transformational." The list of transformational leaders in the history of nursing practice is daunting, including some who go relatively unrecognized today. It includes people like Mary Ann Bickerdyke, who cared for men of the Union army in the American War Between the States. Kalisch and Kalisch (1995, pp. 46–47) quoted her authoritative words in 1861 as she agreed to carry medical supplies, "I'll go to Cairo [Illinois], and I'll clean things up there. You don't have to worry about that, neither. Them generals and all ain't going to stop me" (Baker, 1952, p. 11). In the South, volunteer nurse Kate Cummings recorded the courageous efforts of women who cared for confederate troops, "We are going for the purpose of taking care of the sick and wounded of the army . . . for awhile I wavered about the propriety of it; but when I remembered the suffering I had witnessed, and the relief I had given, my mind was made up to go. . ." (Harwell, 1959, pp. 9, 169; Kalisch & Kalisch, 1995, p. 51). Other well-known charismatic leaders in nursing of the 19th century were Clara Barton, who founded the American Red Cross; Dorothea Dix, who championed advocacy for patients and prisoners, and ruled her staff nurses with an iron fist; and, perhaps, even Walt Whitman, the celebrated poet who was a volunteer nurse in the American Civil War.

Best known and revered models for the heritage of leadership in nursing include the handful of women in North America at the dawn of the 20th century who are credited with the vision of professional nursing: Isabel Hampton Robb, Mary Adelaide Nutting, Lavinia Lloyd Dock, and Lillian Wald. Robb led the nurse training school at Johns Hopkins in Baltimore. Her vision was for standardized education for nurses and nursing teachers. She recognized the need for qualified leadership:

We all recognize that the position of superintendent of nurses requires a woman of executive ability, education, tact, refinement, and keen perceptions . . . and a thorough all-round training in every practical detail of nursing as well as thorough courses in the theory of her work" (American Society of Superintendents of Training Schools for Nurses [ASSTSN], 1897–1900; Gosline, 2004; Reverby, 1985).

Nutting was Robb's student at Johns Hopkins, who was among the first visionaries to foresee academic nursing education, rather than apprentice nurse training solely in hospitals. She led efforts to develop the first university nursing programs at Teachers College Columbia University, and to secure funding for such programs (Gosline, 2004; Nutting, 1926; Marshall, 1972).

Dock was the character that every nurse wants to meet in the next life. She worked with Robb at Johns Hopkins when Nutting was a student. She firmly believed in self-governance for nurses, and called for them to unite and stand together to achieve professional status. She was among the founders of the Society for Superintendents of Nursing and an author of one of the first textbooks for nurses and a history of nursing. She encouraged nurses and all women to become educated, to engage in social issues, and to expand their views internationally (Lewenson, 1996). She was known as a "militant suffragist" and champion for a broad range of social reforms, always fighting valiantly for the rights of nurses for self-governance and for women's right to vote.

At the top of the list of heroes who modeled leadership in autonomous nursing practice is surely Lillian Wald, who founded the first independent public health nursing practice at Henry Street in New York. Wald dared to venture outside the hospital or private home to offer care. She not only devoted her life to caring for the poor people of the Henry Street tenements, but also was the first to offer clinical experience in public health to nursing students. She worked for the rights of immigrants, for women's right to vote, for ethnic minorities, and for the establishment of the Federal Children's Bureau. In1899, she shared her views:

> The one idea I wish above all to bring out is, that among the many opportunities for civic and altruistic work pressing on all sides, nurses having superior advantages in their practical training should not rest content with being only nurses, but should use their talents wherever possible in reform and civic movements. (ASSTSN, 1897–1900; Gosline, 2004; Reverby, 1985, p. 57)

Modern leadership for advanced practice, ultimately leading to the development of the DNP, must also recognize the vision, courage, and leadership of Loretta Ford and Henry Silver at the University of Colorado, who began the first nurse practitioner program in the United States in 1965. Early certificate programs did not award an academic degree. By the 1990s, advanced nursing practice had moved to the master's degree. Now, in the face of increasing complexity of health care, the trends among other healthcare disciplines toward the practice doctorate, and the urgent need for knowledge workers and wise leaders, the practice doctorate is becoming the required preparation for advanced practice. You are among the pioneer leaders to move health care forward to better serve those in need.

The other side of the history of nursing is its legacy of challenges of feminine roles, paternalism, and hesitancy to take up its full measure of autonomy and authority. Porter-O'Grady (2001, p. 65; Ashley, 1976, p. 158) both lamented and warned, "Nursing often comes to the table of the future a day late and a dollar short, trying to catch up to a world that has already passed by. Nursing history is rife with examples of poor timing and choices with regard to politics, licensure, practice, services, equity, education, and payment for services."

Nevertheless, today's healthcare leaders inherit courage, vision, and grit that must not be disregarded. A handful of valiant nursing leaders of the past left a foundation that cries for study of its meaning, and legacy for leadership today. They were visionary champions for causes that seem so essential to us today, but were only dreams at their time. They dared to think beyond the habits and traditions of the time. Lurking in the closets and archives of your own community are the stories of other exemplar leaders in nursing and health care. Who were they? What can we learn from them?

We have moved from the "great person" era to an age of information, with the explosion of knowledge of facts and complexity of systems. You were likely trained as a clinician to meet the challenges of simply keeping up with growing information. Futurists predict with hope that the next generation will be the age of wisdom. What will be needed next are vision and wisdom regarding how to best employ information, resources, and people to meet healthcare needs within complex systems. Leadership can be learned and practiced, and you are in the right time and place to do it. Critical clinical skills and judgment, amplified and enriched by thoughtful, wise decision making, and leadership are what is most needed now.

FOUNDATIONAL THEORIES OF LEADERSHIP

Although a theme of this text is transformational leadership, it is important to understand that the purpose, content, and principles of this book are not confined to the tenets of a specific transformational theory for leadership. To become a full citizen of the discipline, it is important that the transformational leader in health care understands the history, culture, and theoretical language of the science and practice of the discipline of leadership.

Although the attraction of any particular theory for leadership may wax or wane, some leadership principles are timeless. Any truly transformational leader will have a solid foundation of understanding in many theories and will employ and integrate aspects of a variety of theories most appropriate to leadership in practice. Current theories have been admirably reviewed (see Avolio, Walumbwa, & Weber, 2009). Nevertheless, like any leadership text worth its salt, here, several best known prominent leadership theories of the modern Western world are reviewed briefly.

The first principle among theories recognized today is that leaders be grounded in some set of ethics or values, that guide human behaviors and actions. No matter how brilliant the strategy or how productive the actions, if leaders do not carry the trust or best interests of those they represent, there is no true leadership. Yoder-Wise and Kowalski (2006, p. 62) outlined the following principles and their meanings for ethical leadership: respect for others, beneficence (promoting good), veracity (telling the truth), fidelity (keeping promises), nonmaleficence (doing no harm), justice (treating others fairly), and autonomy (having and promoting personal freedom and the right to choose). Such principles are stipulated among the theories reviewed here.

Traditional Management Theories and Methods

Traditional management theories were developed during the industrial revolution and reflected the factory environment of worker productivity. They moved away from the "great man" theories toward the idea that common people with skill and competence might gain power and a position of leadership (Clawson, 1999; Stone & Patterson, 2005). Theories included classic and scientific management theory. They emphasized the organization and formal processes of the organization rather than the characteristics or behaviors of the individual. Primary concepts include hierarchical lines of authority, with chain-of-command decision making, division of labor, and rules and regulations. Such theories were originated by early 20th century industrial thinkers, such as Max Weber, Frederick W. Taylor, F. W. Mooney, and Henri Fayol. Approaches focused on organization and processes. They included time-and-motion studies, mechanisms, and bureaucracy. Advantages of such theories were clear organizational boundaries and efficiency. Disadvantages included rigid rules, slow decision making, authoritarianism, and bureaucracy (Garrison et al., 2004). Ironically, an advantage of such theories is their setting the stage for management by objectives (Stone & Patterson, 2005). We may think we have passed the industrial age, but you might recognize some of the elements of traditional management theories in some organizations still today.

Environment and Worker Needs Theories

In the mid-20th century, management focus turned away from the organization and moved toward people within the organization. This was the time of the well-known Hawthorne studies that sought to enhance human productivity and pride in work accomplished. Leaders and thinkers of these new management theories were not industrialists, but psychologists, such as Elton Mayo (1953). Emphasis was on enhancing the human work environment to meet human needs and increase productivity. Maslow's (1954) Hierarchy of Needs became the trend, that once the worker's basic physiological, security, and social needs were met, productivity would be increased. Thus, leaders focused on meeting basic needs for satisfaction toward self-actualizing of workers. Herzberg's (1966) Motivation-Hygiene Theory furthered Maslow's ideas by proposing to meet workers' intrinsic and extrinsic needs.

Nevertheless, even with a new focus on people rather than organizations, both traditional industrial theories and behavioral theories promoted "linear thinking, compartmentalization, functional work, process orientation, clear and fixed job requirements, and predictable effects" (Capra, 1997; Cook, 2001; Wheatley, 1994).

Behavioral Theories

More recent behavioral theorists moved the focus from people, or even leaders themselves, to an emphasis on the concept of leadership. Thus, the ideas of leadership behaviors and styles emerged. Styles were considered people-based, task-based, or a combination. Such styles include authoritarian, democratic, and laissez-faire (Lewin, Lippitt, & White, 1939). Barnard (1938) proposed that organizations survived only to the degree that they were effective both in productivity and in considering the motives of the workers, both of which were dependent on the behavior of the leader to determine objectives, initiate action, and coordinate the efforts of workers.

One of the best known behavioral theories is Theory X-Theory Y (McGregor, 1960). A simplified description is the following. Theory X, or directive style, is characterized by the leader making decisions, giving directions, and expecting compliance. Worker productivity is related to incentives or inducements and punishments, often reduced to money and/or security. Theory Y, or participative style, seeks consensus, and involves others in decision making. Workers are directed toward quality and productivity and are rewarded for their own problem solving. Theory Z (Ouchi, 1981) built on Theory Y by expanding the notion of reward and concern for the group, and a focus on concentrating decision making at the level of the team or unit. Theory Z proposed the development of workgroups and quality circles to enhance the sense of employee engagement and productivity at the level of the work.

Blake and Mouton (1964; 1978) built further on theories X-Y-Z, and designed a managerial grid plotting five leadership styles based on the leader's concern for people or for production. The "impoverished style" indicates low concern for either, with "middle-of-the-road style" in the middle, "country club style" high on people concerns, "produce or perish style" high on goal accomplishment, and "team style" high on both people and production concerns.

Pitcher (1997) offered a unique list of leadership styles, based on her empirical analysis of managers and leaders. She proposed three types of leaders: artists, who are "imaginative, inspiring, visionary, entrepreneurial, intuitive, daring, and emotional"; craftsmen, who are "well-balanced, steady, reasonable, sensible, predictable, and trustworthy"; and technocrats, who are "cerebral, detail-oriented, fastidious, uncompromising, and hard headed." Pitcher asserted that although few leaders showed all styles, one or another may be preferred, depending on the situation.

Problems with behavior or style theories are related to the issue of context. For example, in the heat of a crisis such as pandemic influenza, which style is most effective? The artist or the craftsman? Produce-or-perish or middle-of-the-road? Theory X or Theory Y? Do the styles describe all aspects of the personality, character, motivation, or behavior of the leader? Do the behavioral styles account for all situations? Which, if any, style is uniquely applicable to leaders in health care?

Trait Theories

Current trait theories seem, in some respect, to return to the "great person" approach as they target the intellectual, emotional, physical, and personal characteristics of the leader. The difference is that trait theories propose that desirable characteristics of successful leaders may be learned, developed, and/or mentored. In reality, the theoretical contribution of trait approaches is less *theory*, associated with concepts and propositions, and more *lists* of universal and often common-sense characteristics, descriptions, or qualifications of effective leaders. Such characteristics include honesty, integrity, fairness, trustworthiness, energy, goal orientation, and communication skills. Stogdill (1948, 1974) is best known for first reviewing trait theories and pointing to the importance of situation or context. Gardner (1989) proposed a list of effective leadership attributes that appeared to endure across a variety of situations. The list included physical vitality and stamina, intelligence and action-oriented judgment, eagerness to accept responsibility, task competence, understanding of followers and their needs, skill in dealing with people, need for achievement, capacity to motivate people, courage and resolution, trustworthiness, decisiveness, self-confidence, assertiveness, and adaptability. Gardner's tasks of leadership are highly related to his list of leadership attributes and generally related to trait theory. The descriptions of the tasks reflect basic traits and characteristics developed in early life and enhanced by leadership education (Gardner, 1986a, 1986b, 1987a, 1987b). The tasks are the following: envisioning goals, affirming values, motivating, managing, achieving workable unity, explaining, serving as a symbol, representing the group, and renewing. Later, other theorists proposed the idea of clusters of traits for different situations (Wright, 1996).

One well-known and popular approach to leadership is Covey's (1989) seven habits, which is considered by some to be an extension of the servant leadership theory, to be discussed, but actually resembles a trait perspective in that it describes a list of characteristics, orientations, actions, or habits for success. Covey described habits as the intersection of knowledge, skill, and desire. Covey's common-sense habits include the following: (1) Be proactive, meaning to take goal-directed action rather than react to circumstances; (2) begin with the end in mind, or adopt a goal-oriented approach; (3) put first things first, or distinguish and accomplish the important rather than the urgent; (4) think win-win, or negotiate to mutual benefit; (5) seek first to understand, then to be understood, or to engage in communication where listening is the priority; (6) synergize, or engage in activities that amplify the most effective aspects of all leadership habits; and (7) sharpen the saw, or attend to personal maintenance and renewal. Covey (2004) later added an eighth habit, which is finding and expressing your voice in vision, discipline, passion, and conscience. Covey's perspective has always included an aspect of servant leadership or generativity. For example, part of the eighth habit is to cultivate positive influence to help others to find their own voice and realization of their best potential.

Another approach related to trait theory that has caught the attention of some leaders in health care is the work of George (2003) on "authentic leadership" (Goffee & Jones, 2000; Shirey, 2006; 2009), characterized by concepts or attributes of genuineness, trustworthiness, reliability, compassion, and believability.

Trait theories continue to be popular. Just pass by the book counter in any airport to find shelves full of business or leadership self-help books based on some list of qualities, behaviors, or habits marketed for success. The influence of the idea of successful leadership traits cannot be denied, but the science of predicting optimal traits under differing circumstances has still not matured. There are several inherent problems with trait theories. First, how do we know what is *the* comprehensive list for the perfect leader in all situations? What about the leader who has some traits but not others? Is it possible to teach or learn successful traits? Which traits are cultivated as behaviors or habits? Does the leader of a state public health department need the same traits as the chief nursing officer of a large hospital system? What is the evidence for the success of a particular list of traits or habits?

Situational/Contingency Theories

Situational theories grew largely as a reaction to trait theories, with the opposite premise that the characteristics of the situation, not the personal traits of the person, produced the leader. Theorists called for a repertoire of leadership traits or styles, and defined the appropriate style to specific types of situations. Building on the work of Lewin (1939), situational theory would propose that authoritarian leadership may be required in a time of crisis, a democratic style in situations for team or consensus building, and laissez-faire style in traditional single-purpose, well-established organizations. Thus, the leader would adjust behaviors according to circumstances of worker experience, maturity, and motivation. Less motivated workers would require a directive task focus, and more highly motivated workers would require a focus on support and relationships.

Contingency theory was a natural outgrowth of situational theory. Fiedler (1967) identified relationship-oriented and task-oriented styles, showing no favored *style*, but rather *situations* where one or the other style was most effective. He proposed that leadership effectiveness was an interaction between style and the extent to which the situation allowed the leader's influence. Factors of the situation included the nature and quality of the relationship between the leader and followers, the nature of the task or goal, and the formal and informal power of the leader (Fiedler, 1967, 1997; Fiedler & Garcia, 1987). The Fiedler contingency model is similar to the work of Blake and Mouton (1964), and on their managerial grid of five leadership styles discussed earlier.

Vroom and Yetton (1973) further built on the idea of describing leadership situations with a situational contingency theory. They developed a taxonomy of leadership situations used in a decision model connecting leadership styles to specific types of situations. Vroom is known for decision-making theory, and proposed that leaders allow followers to participate in decision making according to situational factors. Hersey and colleagues (Hersey & Blanchard, 1977; Hersey, Blanchard, & Johnson, 2008) added to such theories by a focus on describing both leader and follower characteristics. Their model identified four leadership styles and the associated situations where they were effective: (1) telling, or giving direction; (2) selling, or participatory coaching; (3) participating, or sharing decision making; and (4) delegating, or assigning responsibility for the task or goal achievement. Thus, the model explains both relationship and task behaviors.

Goleman's work on emotional intelligence (Goleman et al., 2002) is an example of theoretical thinking that bridges situational leadership style and transformational leadership ideas. Within the conceptual framework of emotional intelligence, Goleman and colleagues empirically identified six styles of leadership with the expectation that leaders might have instinct or could be taught to employ a particular style depending up on the particular situation or circumstance. The styles are visionary, coaching, affiliative, democratic, pacesetting, and commanding. According to principles of emotional intelligence and circumstance, leaders may choose the appropriate style. The visionary inspires by a focus on integrating individual values into long-term goals. The coaching leader helps others to find success in areas of individual responsibility within the enterprise. The affiliative leader creates a warm working atmosphere that focuses on emotional climate and on meeting the emotional needs of others. The democratic leader works for consensus and group decision making. The pacesetter sets ambitious goals and monitors progress on achievement, and the commanding leader issues autocratic instructions and expects compliance. Each of the styles is most appropriate under a particular set of circumstances. According to ideas of emotional intelligence, the leader must be sensitive to the appropriate style and circumstance, largely by empathic listening to self and others.

Situational/contingency theories represent valiant attempts to consider both the leader and the situation, but often, the situations examined were typical American middle-class male organizations with little regard for other situations or styles that considered gender, culture, political climate, or for specific types of organizations such as those of health care.

Constituent Interaction Theories

Several theories propose leadership as the guidance of human interactions or relationships. The idea is that work productivity and outcomes are improved in an environment of optimum human relationships.

Exchange theory focuses on the mutual interaction between leader and follower. Graen (1976) proposed that effective leaders work differently with different people and within different relationships. Concepts include "in group" and "out group" relationships, reflecting the quality of the leader-member relationship (Miner, 2007). Important aspects of the theory are the responsibility on the follower as well as the leader in the dyad and the systematic development of followers from the "out" to the "in" group.

The path-goal theory is based on the expectancy theory of motivation, similar to contingency theory. House (1971) described transactional leader behaviors of being achievement oriented, directive, participative, or supportive. He connected these behaviors in a path-goal model to various environmental and follower factors or situations. Rather than interaction of leadership style and situation, the path-goal theory suggests that leadership style responds to or matches follower motivation in a working relationship. Thus, the leader identifies and removes barriers, gives support and direction, secures resources, and acts to facilitate goal or task achievement of followers. Leaders focus on follower needs for affiliation and control by promoting clarity of expectations and supportive structure. The theory suggests that the leader influences the worker's perceptions of work and self-related goals, paths to attain the goals, and creates expectancies for goal attainment.

Transformational Theories

As noted at the beginning of this chapter, transformational theory, as originated by Burns (1978, 2003), argued a distinction between transactional and transformational leaders. Transactional leadership implies a transaction or exchange of actions by followers for rewards or punishments by the leader. Bass (1985) further refined the theory to diminish the idea of polar concepts between the two types of leadership, and instead on how the transformational leader employs and transforms the transactional needs of the organization. There is a current surge of interest in transformational theory, and many authors promote some aspects of it, although not always explicitly. Doyle and Smith (2009) proposed that the works of such authors and thinkers as Bennis (2009), Kouzes and Posner (2007), and Covey (1989), on leader as a catalyst for change, and Senge (1990) on leader as a strategic visionary, might be considered transformational theories.

Transformational leadership is increasingly the focus of empirical study among healthcare organizations. For example, one study examined the relationships among transformational leadership, knowledge management, and quality improvement initiatives among various departments in 370 hospitals in all 50 states. Results demonstrated that transformational leadership and quality management improve knowledge management. Researchers concluded that transformational leadership skills among healthcare executives promote effective knowledge management initiatives that enhance quality improvement programs. Furthermore, the integration of transformational leadership, knowledge management, and quality improvement was closely associated with organizational and patient outcomes, including patient safety (Gowen, Henagan, & McFadden, 2009). There is particular hope for transformational leadership paradigms to energize human resources, and optimize intellectual capital in healthcare organizations more than current "traditional hierarchical organizations that are team driven and mission oriented" (Schwartz & Tumblin, 2002, p. 1419). The idea of transformational theories sometimes refers to a group of several different approaches that focus on "positive constructs such as hope, resiliency, efficacy, optimism, happiness, and well-being as they apply to organizations" (Avolio et al., 2009, p. 423), rather than on traditional models, some of which focus on deficit reduction, or working on what is wrong with a leader.

Quantum Leadership

In the early 1990s, writers from a variety of disciplines began to apply principles of mathematics and physics to human environments and leadership. Wheatley (1994) was among the first to articulate the relationship of quantum theory to leadership. She proposed that periods of disequilibrium, disorganization, or chaos lead a natural course to new orders, that "order and change, autonomy and control were not the great opposites that we had thought them to be" (Wheatley, 1994, p. 2). Rather, constant change is a way of being, and embrace of change offers new ways to discover or maintain order. Leadership and organizations can thrive on the "paradox that disorder can be a source of order" (Garrison et al., 2004, p. 25).

Porter-O'Grady and associates (Porter-O'Grady, 1992; Porter-O'Grady & Malloch, 2007; Wilson & Porter-O'Grady, 1999) carried quantum theory one step further. They proposed that the traditional long-term vision of a leader is not sufficient or effective in a rapid-changing environment of chaos. Rather, they promoted the idea that leaders lead from a "template, a set of principles that elucidate the relationship" between work or productivity needs and "values guiding their activities" (Wilson & Porter-O'Grady, 2991, p. 26). They proposed four basic principles for leadership in a new age: partnership, accountability, equity, and ownership.

Servant Leadership

The concept of servant leadership is attributed to Robert Greenleaf (1977; Greenleaf, Spears, & Covey, 2002). Eloquent disciples of servant leadership include Senge (1990), Covey (2004), Jaworski (1998), and others. The major distinction of servant leadership is its expectation that the leader's "primary motivation is to serve and meet the needs of others" (Stone & Patterson, 2005, p. 12). Thus, the servant-leader does not direct followers but rather inspires, motivates, influences, and empowers. Based on the works of Greenleaf, the 10 characteristics of servant leadership are the following:

1. *Listener First*. The servant-leader listens intently and pays attention to the inner voice, [enabling] the leader to respond to the total expression of the other person.
2. *Empathy Through Framing Questions*. Servant-leaders assume good intentions of those who question. They act courageously by asking curious questions, to seek to understand others through questions, seek to enlighten themselves and others through the discovery that questions bring.
3. *Heal to Make Whole*. Servant-leaders willingly address broken spirits and emotional hurts.
4. *Awareness*. Such awareness includes self-awareness as well as choosing to view situations from a more integrated, holistic position.
5. *User of Persuasion*. Servant-leaders are effective at consensus building.
6. *Conceptualization*. Servant-leaders cultivate the ability to think beyond day-to-day reality and nurture other's capacity to work outside their usual frame of thinking.
7. *Foresight*. Servant-leaders show the ability to see the probable outcome or situation.

8. *Stewardship.* Stewardship is about holding something in trust for the greater good of society. Servant-leaders choose service over self-interest. They honor highly their accountability for outcomes without controlling.
9. *Commitment to the Growth of People.* Servant-leaders have a strong belief that people have intrinsic value beyond their employable skills.
10. *Cobuilder of Learning/Working Communities.* Servant-leaders seek to identify ways to build community. (Greenleaf Centre for Servant-Leadership Australia/New Zealand, n.d.)

Keith's "seven pillars of servant leadership" are described as key practices of leaders: to be a person of character, put people first, become a skilled communicator, be a compassionate collaborator, have foresight, be a systems thinker, and embrace moral authority (Sipe, 2009). Patterson (2003) further distilled the elements of servant leadership to "seven virtuous constructs:" agapao love, humility, altruism, vision, trust, empowerment, and service. At least one study has found that leaders in hospitals focus on intellectual rather than spiritual development, suggesting that servant leadership may be an area for development in future clinical leaders (Farrell, 2003). The popularity of the ideas of servant leadership has opened the arena for other more spiritual-focused theories that include concepts of forgiveness, kindness, and hope (Fry, 2003).

As a leader in health care, servant leadership has significant meaning. Never forget that after all the theories, structures, and processes, health care is about promoting health and caring for the suffering. Health care happens with patients and their families. As a leader, if you do not serve patients and families by your own direct care, you serve someone who does. All leadership is ultimately about serving those who promote health and care for others who suffer.

From an empirical and theoretical perspective, evidence for the effectiveness of transformational theories remains to be demonstrated. Such theories continue to secure a major place in contemporary literature on leadership. There seems to be a hunger in society for the positive hope and promise of the transformational leader. The discipline of nursing offers a welcome laboratory to test the promise of transformational leadership. Nursing practice is grounded in concepts of caring and altruism; it already attracts people motivated toward self-actualization, achievement, and helping; and it embraces tenets of holism (Jackson, Clements, Averill, & Zimbro, 2009). Such principles are highly consistent with those of transformational leadership.

Theories and Models in Nursing Leadership

The major theories discussed have been applied in all types of organizations, including healthcare systems. The current trend seems to be to integrate or promote concepts of transformational leadership. A few studies have examined transformational leadership specifically among nurses, but most of these studies are confined to nurse executives in hospital settings. Dunham-Taylor (2000) sampled 396 hospital nurse executives. Scores on transformational leadership were positively related to staff satisfaction and work group effectiveness. Leach (2005) also studied nurses in hospitals, examining the relationship between nurse executive leadership and nurse manager leadership, and between nurse executive leadership and organizational commitment among staff nurses. Management styles between nurse executives and nurse managers were highly related. Nurse executives who scored high as transformational leaders were more likely to promote an environment that fostered employee commitment. McDaniel and Wolfe (1992) examined the characteristics of transformational leadership among nurses in executive, midlevel, and staff positions, confirming transformational leadership scores among nurse executives, with a cascading effect to higher transactional leadership scores among staff nurses. Ohman (2000, p. 46) found critical care nurse managers to be highly transformational, "using inspiration, motivation, and vision to empower staff."

There is perhaps a need to discover or develop an approach to clinical leadership that is distinctive and uniquely effective for both care workers and care receivers in the healthcare environment. Millward and Bryan (2005) proposed the need for a practical interpretation of the concept of clinical leadership that involves relationships among healthcare professionals, organizations, and service users.

Cummings et al. (2008) reviewed research on leadership in nursing and identified four groups of studies: behaviors and practices of individual leaders, traits and characteristics of individual leaders, influences of context and practice settings, and leader participation in educational activities. They also noted relatively weak designs among the studies and a need for robust theory and research on the development of nursing leaders needed for the future. Jennings et al. (2007) also reviewed works on nursing leadership and management from the perspective of competencies, noting little distinction between nurse managers and nurse leaders. Cook (2001) explored clinical nursing leadership in the United Kingdom, the United States, and Australia, observing that "few writers attempt to describe the difference between nursing leadership and nursing management, with none defining clinical nursing leadership" (p. 39). Indeed, the predominant leadership style among nurses appears to be transactional. Jumaa (2008, p. 997) further poked at prevalent "myths" in the literature of leadership in nursing: "everyone can be a leader," "leaders deliver business (service) results," "people who get to the top are leaders," and that "leaders are great coaches" (see Goffee & Jones, 2000). She chided, in confirming the need for models in nursing leadership, that such myths need to become realities.

There is a growing number of leadership theories grounded specifically in nursing. Jooste (2004, p. 220) proposed an "Arch of Leadership" model, composed of five key dimensions: Clarity—Are workers clear of their tasks? Commitment—What do followers need from their leader? Self-image—Do followers know their own abilities, what they can and cannot accomplish? Price—What is the price they pay or receive for working hard? Behavior—Does the leadership style promote positive and effective behavior among followers?

Although Jooste discussed issues of past, present, and future leadership settings, the role of authority, power and influence in leadership, and the need for solutions in a future dimension, the actual model appears to be drawn from other traditional leadership theories, largely transactional in style, and with little specific distinction for clinical leadership.

One intriguing proposal is the "nursing leadership knowing" theory adapted from patterns of knowing in nursing (Jackson, et al., 2009). The authors attempted to apply their theoretical ideas to a variety of areas including history and pedagogy (see Averill & Clements, 2007; Clements & Averill, 2006). Borrowing from previous thinkers on ways of knowing for nursing (see Carper, 1978; Heath, 1998; Munhall, 1993; White, 1995), Jackson et al. (2009) listed well-known ways of knowing for nursing as ways of leadership knowing: empiric, aesthetic, personal, sociopolitical, ethical, and unknowing, for which they outlined descriptions and qualities, as well as examples. Their theory seems to resonate with nursing, but its actual application to clinical leadership remains to be demonstrated.

The challenge of the next generation is to create an empirical foundation of evidence for best practices in leadership in complex healthcare organizations. Such leadership needs to work for nursing practice but must invite interprofessional engagement in the bigger picture of health care. Perhaps, the initiative of the advanced clinician in the organizational leadership role will launch that discovery. It is especially important to note that there seems yet to be developed, discovered, or invented a working theory, empirically tested and specific to clinical leadership in complex healthcare systems.

INNOVATION AND CREATING A FUTURE

Obviously, there are many impressive theories to explain or guide leadership of people and organizations, but few have included environment or setting as much more than an artifact or a backdrop, implying that context may not be relevant. But you know, as a healthcare provider, that the context of health care is uniquely challenging and complex. The innovative leader is able to think in terms of multiprofessional caregivers, patients, community, and context from a systems perspective. He or she understands not only leadership theory but also theories of complexity and complex adaptive systems. The new transformational leader will design new environments and systems for care—some we have not dared to imagine. Perhaps, theories of the past will be revised or proven altogether irrelevant. The world is waiting for your creativity to care for those in need, and to inspire other leaders to come together in new ways of thinking and practice.

Transformational leaders of the future will see the world with a new vision, break old rules, discover or create new rules, and thrive in the paradoxes of complexity. Porter-O'Grady and Malloch (2007, p. 27) listed a few of the contradictions that inspire innovation: "Chaos and order, creativity and tension, conflict and peace, difference and similarity, complexity and simplicity." Think about these concepts. What do they mean for innovation? Innovation requires the space for creativity and the courage to be wrong. Mistakes teach as much as success. The truth is, there is often no right or wrong but change, diversity, and helping people come together to solve problems and help others.

Steven Johnson (2006) told the story of London's worst epidemic of cholera in the mid-1850s that persisted in the face of hundreds of years of conventional thinking that smells in the air caused disease. The idea was held by the most distinguished scientists and physicians at the time. Johnson called it the "sociology of error," when bad ideas stay around too long. What are those errors in our own world? When I was a young graduate nurse, "science" required that we treat stomach ulcers with round-the-clock alternate doses through a nasogastric tube of dairy cream and liquid antacid. We would not have believed that any ulcer might be treated or cured by an antibiotic. What other errors ask for correction by creative thinking and testing? What bad ideas do we practice in leadership? What new miracles do we need to invite?

Innovation requires the paradox of your willingness to learn all you can, bring your clinical experience, and then eagerly suspend previous learning and experience to welcome the new idea, to recognize a different point of view, to embrace chaos to winnow what must remain and what must change, and to set a new course.

REFERENCES

Acorn, S., Lamarche, K., & Edwards, M. (2009). Practice doctorates in nursing: Developing nursing leaders. *Nursing Leadership, 22*(2), 85–91.

American Association of Colleges of Nursing (AACN). (2004). *AACN position statement on the practice doctorate in nursing.* Washington, D.C.: AACN.

American Association of Colleges of Nursing (AACN). (2006). *The essentials of doctoral education for advanced nursing practice.* Washington, D.C.: AACN.

American Society of Superintendents of Training Schools for Nurses (ASSTSN). (1897–1900). Annual conventions 1893–1899: The American Society of Superintendents of Training Schools for Nurses. In S. Reverby (Ed.), *The history of American nursing.* New York: Garland Press.

Ashley, J. A. (1976). *Hospitals, paternalism, and the role of the nurse.* New York: Teachers College Press.

Averill, J. B., & Clements, P. T. (2007). Patterns of knowing as a foundation for action-sensitive pedagogy. *Qualitative Health Research, 17*(3), 386–399.

Avolio, B. J., Walumbwa, F. O., & Weber, T. J. (2009). Leadership: Current theories, research, and future directions. *Annual Review of Psychology, 60,* 421–449.

Baker, N. B. (1952). *Cyclone in Calico: The story of Mary Ann Bickerdyke.* Boston: Little, Brown, & Company.

Barnard, C. I. (1938). *The functions of the executive.* Cambridge, MA: Harvard University Press.

Bass, B. M. (1985). *Leadership and performance beyond expectations.* New York: Free Press.

Bass, B. M. (1990, Winter). From transactional to transformational leadership: Learning to share the vision. *Organizational dynamics,* 19–31.

Bass, B. M., Avolio, B. J., Jung, D. I., & Berson, Y. (2003). Predicting unit performance by assessing transformational and transactional leadership. *Journal of Applied Psychology, 88*(2), 207–218.

Bass, B. M., & Riggio, R. E. (2006). *Transformational leadership.* Mahwah, NJ: Lawrence Erlbaum.

Bellflower, B., & Carter, M. A. (2006). Primer on the practice doctorate for neonatal nurse practitioners. *Advances in Neonatal Care, 6*(6), 323–332.

Bennis, W. (1989). *On becoming a leader.* Reading, MA: Addison Wesley.

Bennis, W. (2009). *On becoming a leader* (rev. ed.). Reading, MA: Addison Wesley.

Blake, R., & Mouton, J. (1964). *The managerial grid: The key to leadership excellence.* Houston, TX: Gulf.

Blake, R., & Mouton, J. (1978). *The new managerial grid.* Houston, TX: Gulf.

Bolman, L. G., & Deal, T. F. (1991). *Reframing organizations: Artistry, choice, and leadership.* San Francisco: Jossey-Bass.

Bowles, A., & Bowles, N. B. (2000). A comparative study of transformational leadership in nursing development units and conventional clinical settings. *Journal of Nursing Management, 8,* 69–76.

Brown-Benedict, D. J. (2008). The doctor of nursing practice degree: Lessons from the history of the professional doctorate in other health disciplines. *Journal of Nursing Education, 47*(10), 448–457.

Burns, J. M. (1978). *Leadership.* New York: Harper & Row.

Burns, J. M. (2003). *Transforming leadership: The pursuit of happiness.* New York: Atlantic Monthly Press.

Business Dictionary. (2009a). Transformational leadership. Retrieved July 9, 2009, from http://www.businessdictionary.com/defintion/transformational-leadership.html

Business Dictionary. (2009b). Leadership. Retrieved July 20, 2009, from http://www.businessdictionary.com/definition/leadership.html

Capra, F. (1997). *The web of life: A new synthesis of mind and matter.* London: HarperCollins.

Carper, B. (1978). Fundamental patterns of knowing in nursing. *Advances in Nursing Science, 1*(1), 13–23.

Carryer, J., Gardner, G., Dunn, S., & Gardner, A. (2007). The core role of the nurse practitioner: Practice, professionalism, and clinical leadership. *Journal of Clinical Nursing, 16*(10), 1818–1825.

Chase, S. K., & Pruitt, R. H. (2006). The practice doctorate: Innovation or disruption? *Journal of Nursing Education, 45*(5), 155–157.

Clawson, J. G. (1999). *Level three leadership: Getting below the surface.* Upper Saddle River, NJ: Prentice-Hall.

Clements, P. T., & Averill, J. B. (2006). Finding patterns of knowing in the work of Florence Nightingale. *Nursing Outlook, 54*(5), 268–274.

Collins, J. (2001). *Good to great.* New York: HarperCollins.

Cook, M. J. (2001). The renaissance of clinical leadership. *International Nursing Review, 48*(1), 38–46.

Covey, S. R. (1989). *The seven habits of highly effective people.* New York: Simon & Schuster.

Covey, S. R. (2004). *The eighth habit: From effectiveness to greatness.* New York: Simon & Schuster.

Loomis, J. A., Willard, B., & Cohen, J. (2006). Difficult professional choices: Deciding between the PhD and the DNP in nursing. *Online Journal of Issues in Nursing, 12*(1), 6.

Marion, L., Viens, D., O'Sullivan, A. L., Crabtree, K., Fontana, S., & Price, M. M. (2003). The practice doctorate in nursing: Future or fringe? *Topics in Advanced Practice Nursing E-Journal, 3*(2).

Marriner-Tomey, A. (1993). *Transformational leadership in nursing.* St. Louis, MO: Mosby.

Marshall, H. (1972). *Mary Adelaide Nutting: Pioneer of modern nursing.* Baltimore: Johns Hopkins University Press.

Maslow, A. H. (1954). *Motivation and personality.* Upper Saddle River, NJ: Prentice-Hall.

Mayo, E. (1953). *The human problems of an industrialized civilization.* New York: Macmillan.

McDaniel, C., & Wolf, G. A. (1992). Transformational leadership in nursing service: A test of theory. *Journal of Nursing Administration, 22*(2), 60–65.

McGregor, D. (1960). *The human side of enterprise.* New York: McGraw Hill.

McKenna, H., Keeney, S., & Bradley, M. (2004). Nurse leadership within primary care: The perceptions of community nurses, GPs, policy makers, and members of the public. *Journal of Nursing Management, 12*(1), 69–76.

Millward, L. J., & Bryan, K. (2005). Clinical leadership in health care: A position statement. *International Journal of Health Care Quality Assurance Including Leadership in Health Services, 18*(2–3), xiii–xxv.

Miner, J. B. (2007). *Organizational behavior 4: From theory to practice.* Armouk, NY: M. E. Sharpe.

Molero, F., Cuadrado, I., Navas, M., & Morales, J. F. (2007). Relations and effects of transformational leadership: A comparative analysis with traditional leadership styles. *Spanish Journal of Psychology, 10*(2), 358–368.

Munhall, P. (1993). "Unknowing": Toward another pattern of knowing in nursing. *Nursing Outlook, 41*(3), 125–128.

Nutting, M. A. (1926). *A sound economic basis for schools of nursing and other addresses.* New York: G. P. Putnam's Sons.

Ohman, K. A. (2000). The transformational leadership of critical care nurse-managers. *Dimensions of Critical Care Nursing, 19*(1), 46–54.

O'Sullivan, A. L., Carter, M., Marion, L., Pohl, J. M., & Werner, K. E. (2005). Moving forward together: The practice doctorate in nursing. *Online Journal of Issues in Nursing, 20*(3).

Otterness, S. (2006). Is the burden worth the benefit of the doctorate of nursing (DNP) for NPs? Implications of doctorate in nursing practice—still many unresolved issues for nurse practitioners. *Nephrology Nursing Journal, 33*(6), 685–687.

Ouchi, W. G. (1981). *Theory Z: How American management can meet the Japanese challenge.* Reading, MA: Addison-Wesley.

Patterson, K. A. (2003). Servant leadership: A theoretical model. *Servant Leadership Research Roundtable Proceedings.* Virginia Beach, VA: School of Global Leadership & Entrepreneurship, Regent University.

Pitcher, P. (1997). *The drama of leadership.* New York: John Wiley & Sons.

Porter-O'Grady, T. (1992). Transformational leadership in an age of chaos. *Nursing Administration Quarterly, 17,* 17–24.

Porter-O'Grady, T. (2001). Beyond the walls: Nursing in the entrepreneurial world. *Nursing Administration Quarterly, 25*(2), 61–68.

Porter-O'Grady, T., & Malloch, K. (2007). *Quantum leadership: A resource for health care innovation* (2nd ed.). Boston: Jones & Bartlett.

Reverby, S. (1985). *The history of American nursing.* New York: Garland Press.

Savage, C. (2003, July/August). Nursing leadership: Oxymoron or powerful force? *AAACN Viewpoint,* 1–8.

Schwartz, R. W., & Tumblin, T. F. (2002). The power of servant leadership to transform health care organizations for the 21st-century economy. *Archives of Surgery, 137*(12), 1419–1427.

Senge, P. (1990). *The fifth discipline: The art and practice of the learning organization.* New York: Doubleday.

Shirey, M. R. (2006). Authentic leaders creating healthy work environments for nursing practice. *American Journal of Critical Care, 15,* 256–267.

Shirey, M. R. (2009). Authentic leadership, organizational culture, and healthy work environments. *Critical Care Nursing Quarterly, 32*(3), 189–198.

Sieloff, C. I. (1996). Nursing leadership for a new century. *Seminars for Nurse Managers, 4*(4), 236–233.

Sipe, J. W. (2009). *Seven pillars of servant leadership: Practicing the wisdom of leading by serving.* New York: Paulist Press.

Sperhac, A. M., & Clinton, P. (2008). Doctorate of nursing practice: Blueprint for excellence. *Journal of Pediatric Health Care, 22*(3), 146–151.

Starck, P. L., Duffy, M. E., & Vogler, R. (1993). Developing a nursing doctorate for the 21st century. *Journal of Professional Nursing, 9*(4), 212–219.

Stein, J. V. (2008). Becoming a doctor of nursing practice: My story. *Nursing Forum, 43*(1), 38–41.

Stewart, T. A. (2004, January). The leader's secret self. *Harvard Business Review, 82(1)*, 10.

Stichler, J. F. (2006). Skills and competencies for today's nurse executive. *AWHONN Lifelines: The Association of Women's Health, Obstetric and Neonatal Nurses, 10*(3), 255–257.

Stogdill, R. M. (1948). Personal factors associated with leadership: Survey of literature. *The Journal of Psychology, 25,* 35–71.

Stogdill, R. M. (1974). *Handbook of leadership: A survey of theory and leadership.* New York: Free Press.

Stone, A. G., & Patterson, K. (2005, August). *The history of leadership focus.* Paper presented at the Servant Leadership Research Roundtable, School of Leadership Studies, Regent University. Retrieved August 17, 2009, from http://www.regent.edu/acad/global/publications/sl_proceedings/2005/stone_history.pdf

Tracy, B. (2004). Transformational leadership. *Perfect Customer.* Retrieved June 23, 2009, from http://www.perfectcustomers.com/utility/printpage/indes.cfm?Objectl

Trofino, J. (1993). Transformational leadership: The catalyst for change. *International Nursing Review, 40,* 179–187.

Upvall, M. J., & Ptachcinski, R. J. (2007). The journey to the DNP program and beyond: What can we learn from pharmacy? *Journal of Professional Nursing, 23*(5), 316–321.

Vroom, V. H., & Yetton, P. W. (1973). *Leadership and decision-making.* Pittsburgh, PA: University of Pittsburgh Press.

Wall, B. M., Novak, J. C., & Wilkerson, S. A. (2005). Doctor of nursing practice program development: Reengineering health care. *Journal of Nursing Education, 44*(9), 396–403.

Webber, P. B. (2008). The doctor of nursing practice degree and research: Are we making an epistemological mistake? *Journal of Nursing Education, 47*(10), 466–472.

Wheatley, M. J. (1994). *Leadership and the new science: Learning about organization from an orderly universe.* San Francisco: Berrett-Koehler.

White, J. (1995). Patterns of knowing: Review, critique, and update. *Advances in Nursing Science, 17*(4), 73–86.

Wicks, W. W. (1997). *Shared values: A history of Kimberly-Clark.* Greenwich, CT: Greenwich Publishing Group.

Wilson, C. K., & Porter-O'Grady, T. (1999). *Leading the revolution in health care.* Gaithersburg, MD: Aspen.

Wong, C. A., & Cummings, G. G. (2007). The relationship between nursing leadership and patient outcomes: A systematic review. *Journal of Nursing Management, 15*(5), 508–521.

Wright, P. (1996). *Managerial leadership.* London: Routledge.

Yam, B. M. (2005). Professional doctorate and professional nursing practice. *Nursing Education Today, 25*(7), 564–572.

Yoder-Wise, P. S., & Kowalski, K. E. (2006). *Beyond leading and managing: Nursing administration for the future.* St. Louis, MO: Mosby Elsevier.

2

Characteristics of a Transformational Leader

> Leadership is an art—a performing art—and the instrument
> is the self. The mastery of the art of leadership comes from the
> mastery of the self.
>
> — *Jim Kouzes*

It seems that every book on leadership provides a list of characteristics or traits that "all leaders must have." As an aspiring or current leader, it can make you crazy. George, Sims, McLean, and Mayer (2007, p. 129) reported that in the past 50 years, over 1,000 studies have attempted to determine the most important characteristics of great leaders, without success. "Thank goodness," they responded, "If scholars had produced a cookie-cutter leadership style, individuals would be forever trying to imitate it. . . . No one can be authentic by trying to imitate someone else. You can learn from others' experiences, but there is no way you can be successful when you are trying to be like them."

Nevertheless, for the last 20 years, Kouzes and Posner (2007) have asked people to rate the seven top characteristics of leaders they admire. They consistently report the following adjectives in rank order: honest, forward looking, competent, inspiring, intelligent, fair minded, broad minded, supportive, straightforward, dependable, cooperative, determined, imaginative, ambitious, courageous, caring, mature, loyal, self-controlled, and independent. Academics never get tired of making lists.

Carroll (2005) proposed the following six most important attributes for nursing leaders: (1) personal integrity (ethical standards, trustworthiness, and credibility), (2) strategic vision and action orientation, (3) team-building and communication skills, (4) management and technical competencies, (5) people skills (empowering others, networking, valuing diversity, and working collaboratively), and (6) personal survival attributes (political sensitivity, self-direction, self-reliance, courage, and candor). Another nurse listed the following:

> . . . moral and ethical values, technical competence, knowledge and conceptual skill, a desire to be a leader, personality, and people skills. . . . Leaders must have in-depth knowledge in the field in which they lead, an ability for abstract thinking, a history of achieving results, ability to communicate, motivate, and delegate, an ability to cultivate talent in others, good judgment, and good character. Leaders are able to motivate others, use highly developed knowledge and technical skill, and lead change. Some are inspirational, or charismatic; all

27

need to be clear communicators who show commitment and compassion. A leader must be willing, trustworthy, and just. Moral leadership is critical; one must do good, in as honest and courageous a way as possible. Leadership means to be vulnerable, to take risks and to be willing to accept mistakes. (Jaffe-Ruiz, 2008, pp. 334–335)

Although Zaccaro (2007) wrote extensively to challenge trait-based perspectives of leadership, he still proposed his own list of "proximal" and "distal" clusters of attributes of a leader. Proximal characteristics, those most closely related to the environment, included expertise and tacit knowledge, problem-solving skills, and social-appraisal skills. Necessary, but more distal, attributes included motives and values, cognitive abilities, and personality.

Stichler (2006, p. 256) provided the following list of "personal attributes of successful nurse leaders": integrity, trustworthiness, fairness, honesty, emotional intelligence, passion, energy, intelligence, political sensitivity, self-direction, self-reliance, courage, candor, humility, and trust. What? Walking on water missed the list? It is far too easy to simply collect lists of the desirable traits of a leader. Perhaps, it is even tempting to measure yourself against each item on the list. The truth is that you are meeting challenges in the best way you can. If you do it in a deliberate manner by which you reflect on what you are doing, seek what information you need, listen to the perspective of others, and plan how will you do better next time, you will acquire what you need from each long list of traits. Who knows if the best characteristics of a leader are innate or learned? But we know they can be developed. You can learn from the stories and traits of other great leaders, and decide who you are as a leader.

Transformational leadership has been demonstrated to be positively associated with followers' commitment to improvement and change (Herold, Fedor, Caldwell, & Liu, 2008). There are a few characteristics of a transformational leader that do merit discussion. They include reflection and mission orientation, goal direction, presence and emotional intelligence, accountability and authenticity, vulnerability and fearlessness, creativity and innovation, building on strengths, and moral sensitivity.

REFLECTION AND PERSONAL MISSION

The idea of effective leadership has changed in the past 50 to 100 years, from the viewpoint of command and power toward the concepts of "confidence to empower others" (Jaffe-Ruiz, 2008, p. 335). To empower others, it is important to know yourself, to be willing to examine your actions in real time in order to understand others, to be able to take the perspective of others, and at the same time to set the cadence for the entire organization toward the desired future. Knowing one's self comes from deep personal reflection.

Among healthcare professionals, nurses are especially aware of the importance of reflective practice (Duffy, 2007; Manthey, 2001; Morgan, 2009). Just as important is the practice of reflective leadership (Horton-Deutsch & Sherwood, 2008). Reflective leaders are acutely aware of how they connect with others, where they are in the progress of their own and organizational goals, and how they are opening paths for clear communication and goal fulfillment (Oestreich, 2009). Reflective leadership requires a willingness to submit to assessment and analysis, both privately and publicly.

Related to the willingness to cultivate personal reflection is the willingness to be lonely, on occasion, as a leader. Stichler (2006, p. 257) warned, "The nurse executive must also be comfortable with 'aloneness' because great leaders must be comfortable being out in front of others, and standing alone and firmly on issues critical to the mission and vision." She pointed to Drucker's (1996, p. 9) statement that "great leaders have to walk alone sometimes." Such aloneness can facilitate reflection.

Make your time alone fulfilling and fruitful by personal reflection. Meditate, keep a diary, or simply find regular quiet space to allow the work energy to subside and the quiet ideas to wash over you like the sunshine. Reflection not only allows contemplation but also creates a space to invite perspective, to refresh the mind, and to enable sorting and refining ideas and decisions. Reeves (2002) suggested keeping a leadership journal to collect a series of snapshots of your daily life and progress as a leader. Ask the following questions: "What did I learn today? Whom did I nurture today? What difficult issues did I confront today? What is my most important challenge right now? What did I do today to make progress on my most important challenge?" One of my own mentors coined the daily questions for reflection of "What?" "So what?" and "Now what?" "What happened or what is happening?" "So what does it mean?" "Now what are my next steps?"

Qualitative researchers speak of participant observation as a method where a person has an active and significant role within a culture, context, or situation, but at the same time reflects upon the situation from an insider-outsider viewpoint. The participant observer may have intimate familiarity with the group, but brackets personal perspectives to engage in more distant reflection. Sometimes, it is helpful, especially as a leader, to engage in participant observation within your own work environment. Take mental and emotional notes as an anthropologist to "notice" signs, behaviors, and needs that you may have overlooked inside the daily work activities. Pretend you are foreign to the environment and reflect on situations with new eyes.

Atchison (2006) identified a human "X-factor," or synergy factor, that connects the attributes of success with four specific human "intangibles" evident in the successful leader: joy, pride, respect, and trust. These profoundly personal attributes are cultivated by commitment and deep personal reflection. They are emulated "through example as energy and synergy that is infectious and ignites passion in others to work toward the common vision" (Stichler, 2006, p. 257). Improved organizations result when such positive human attributes become embedded within the culture. Creating trust eases interpersonal tensions among workers, showing respect increases motivation, community pride is developed by providing meaningful challenges, and joy is unleashed by reducing barriers and providing positive experiences to increase satisfaction (Atchison, 2006). Thus, your daily reflection might include where you improved trust, how you promoted respect, where you feel pride, and what happened to instill joy.

From your reflection can also emerge your own personal sense of direction. It is helpful to formalize your direction and goals into a personal mission statement. A mission statement is a short, simple, and powerful reminder of who you are, what you do, and why you are doing what you are doing. It is a statement of your purpose. It reflects your reason for being. It defines what success is for you. It should be no more than two or three sentences, and may be reduced to a personal slogan, motto, or mantra, but it must "fit." It should align with your personal values and goals.

Medical educators analyzed 100 personal mission statements of medical students from 10 different schools across the United States. Amazingly, themes were similar among students across all schools. Themes included professional skills, such as listening and empathy, negative perceptions of training, and personal growth and development; personal qualities like wholeness, humility, and constancy; and scope of professional practice, such as physician relationships, healing, service, spirituality, and balance. Authors noted that the mission statements did not reflect existing institutional professionalism statements, but rather "dealt with fears, personal-professional balance, love, nonhierarchical relationships, self-care, healing, and awe" (Rabow, Wrubel, & Remen, 2009, p. 336). Their conclusion was that, perhaps, medical school curricula should adapt to the personal aspirations reflected by students. Likewise, when you articulate your personal mission statement as a healthcare leader, colleagues and the entire care environment will be drawn to evolve toward your mission statement. Such exercises are powerful to the individual, and the organization ultimately benefits.

Once you create your personal mission statement, you should be able to wear it comfortably, and it should live for you. Although you may change it along your way, it can be a kind of compass to remind you who you are and where you are going. When your mission statement is clear, it becomes easier to set and achieve goals toward its fulfillment. You can be more clear to know when you are off or on track toward success. Reflection and personal mission benefit the individual leader, but more than that, they provide the leader with a perspective that can become contagious within the organization. The steady confidence and sense of direction from the reflective leader give trust and assurance, and foster a sense of stability.

GOAL DIRECTION

Personal reflection and a personal mission statement open the mind-space to see what needs to be done to enable the development of specific and appropriate goals. One of the most critical characteristics of a successful leader is orientation toward goal setting. Studies have shown that the goal-focused leader actually enables conscientious workers to perform their own jobs more effectively, because they have a better understanding of how their jobs fit with organizational priorities. Cobert and Witt (2009) found that workers were actually more committed and effective in their assignments when they perceived that their leader set goals that included defining roles, responsibilities, and priorities.

The origin of goal-directed leadership is often credited to Peter Drucker (1954), who proposed "management by objectives." Major characteristics include (1) defined goals or objectives for the organization, (2) individual objectives by the leader and followers, (3) shared decision making, (4) setting a specific time frame for achievement of goals and objectives, and (5) shared evaluation of performance based on the objectives. Drucker (1992) later developed the well-known SMART technique for evaluating goals. Goals and objectives must be (1) specific, (2) measurable, (3) achievable, (4) realistic, and (5) time related.

Using Drucker's guide, goal setting is just as important for your own life and career as it is in the accomplishment of tasks of your current job. Part of your preparation as you achieve the highest credential for practice is to fulfill the promise of leadership in health care at the highest levels. That means an entirely new perspective on aspiring to the job, getting the job, and doing the job. Do not let false modesty or personal insecurity restrain you from aspiring, preparing, and planning for a leadership position at the highest level you desire, where you might make a transforming difference. Personal goal setting is the important first step.

There is an art to effective goal setting and achievement. Few things are more discouraging that to set a list of goals and not be able to achieve them. Begin with a few focused goals and commit to them. Focus on a few key issues, enjoy the satisfaction of fulfilling the goal, then move to the next. Help others to be realistic in their own goals as you move forward step by step toward your vision.

PRESENCE AND EMOTIONAL INTELLIGENCE

While goals mark the path to the future, presence ennobles the moment. Wheatley (2009, p. 81) noted, "All fear (and hope) arises from looking backward or forward. The present moment is the only place of clear seeing unclouded by hope or fear." Presence is one of the most underrated characteristics of an exceptional leader (Lubar & Halpern, 2004; Melander, 2006). The fundamental rule for leadership is to "show up." Wherever you are working, you must be present and accountable in the moment. Others can easily perceive if you are present where you are. They know if you are truly listening. Having presence helps others to feel that their time, energy, contributions, and feelings are valued. Presence builds trust and commitment. Presence accompanies authenticity, high emotional intelligence, and communication. Be there, without distraction, highly focused, and engaged. Make sure you connect. Practice how you might show confidence, energy, empathy, and credibility. One minute of presence is worth 1,000 minutes of distraction or preoccupation. Halpern and Lubar (2003) suggested four simple rules of presence: (1) Being present, not pretentious. Be there completely in the moment and with full attention. That means you put aside anything else going on in your mind. (2) Reaching out, not looking down. Build relationships through listening and empathy. (3) Being expressive, not impressive. Express yourself with confidence, using appropriate words, tone of voice, body language, and facial expression. (4) Being self-knowing, not self-absorbed. Accept yourself. Let your values, confidence, and authenticity precede you. Then get over yourself, let go, and *be* there.

Presence is not only a gift to others, it also is your own treasure. It centers you and frees you from the pull and baggage of the past, or from the urgent uncertainty of the future. It provides gifts of "clarity and resolve" (Wheatley, 2009, p. 81). It frees your mind to see the moment, to see the person, and, often, to see the next right action. It takes effort to stay in the moment, and effort is required to continually bring yourself back, but it is worth the practice.

There is a variety of ways to show presence in leadership. First is to make the intellectual, emotional, and social commitment to be there. Attend meetings. Even if you are not able to stay through the entire time, make sure that while you are there, your total attention is to what is going on within the meeting. Listen, exchange, ask questions, and engage. Wherever possible, when you are in person, be there without texting, telephone, or other technology between you and the moment. A second way to show presence is to "lead by walk-around." Take some time each day to casually walk around the organization, engaging with full attention along the way. It is amazing how many problems can be prevented or solved by simply walking around. Third, always remember that when you are present as the official leader, you carry an air of clout. You have no need to remind anyone by your demeanor or words that you are the leader. It is not about you—it is about listening and engaging, and being present in the moment of the other.

Related to presence is the use of what is now called emotional intelligence. Currently, there is growing interest in developing emotional intelligence in health care (Freshman & Rubino, 2002; Triola, 2007). Stewart (2004, p. 10) observed, "We've all known leaders with highly developed intellects but stunted emotions—and wonderfully, leaders who bond with others in profound ways." Perhaps, "part genetic predisposition, part life experience, and part old-fashioned training," emotional intelligence seems important to modern leadership (Clarke, 2004, p. 27). The concept of emotional intelligence was probably introduced by Salovey and Mayer (1990), who referred to monitoring of emotions in self and others, and to guiding interpersonal decisions and actions based on such perceptions. Goleman and associates (Goleman, 2006; Goleman, Boyatzis, & McKee, 2002) are credited with bringing the concept into mainstream business and leadership literature, and are now best known for the concept. They identified four domains of emotional intelligence that bridge with 18 competencies of leadership: self-awareness, self-management, social-awareness, and relationship management.

The first two domains are associated with personal competence and self-knowledge. These require being present in the self, listening to one's self with awareness of emotions, values, standards, and effects on others. Self-awareness includes accurate self-assessment, emotional self-awareness, and self-confidence. Self-management includes emotional self-control, transparency, adaptability, achievement, initiative, and optimism.

The last two domains refer to social competence that grows from empathic listening to others, and learning to resonate and understand other's emotions, thoughts, and actions. Social awareness includes empathy, awareness of the climate and culture of the environment, and service to others. Relationship management includes teaching, coaching, conflict management, collaboration, promoting teamwork, influencing, and inspiring.

Goleman et al. (2002) further outlined five steps for learning leadership skills, which, not surprisingly, focus on emotional intelligence and listening: Step 1 is to identify the "ideal self," or to discover personal core values and beliefs. It requires listening to the following questions that must be asked of the self: What is important to me? What is the image of the person I aspire to be? What is my passion? Step 2 is to identify the "real self" or how one appears to others. This requires honest feedback from others and empathic listening to their viewpoints, and the courage and authentic humility to confront the dissonance between the ideal self and the real self. Identification of strengths and gaps in the discrepancy provides insight and perspective to guide self-development. Step 3 is to create a plan that builds on strengths, and closes those gaps between the ideal and the real self. This exercise gives insight into the most important factors for improvement. Step 4 is to practice and experiment with purpose to focus on areas identified for change in the plan of Step 3. Finally, Step 5 is to develop trust and encourage others, providing support through the entire process as a learning experience.

Emotional intelligence is increasingly recognized as critical to healthcare leaders of the future. Such leaders bring tradition and expectations of analytical and creative business skills, but they must also possess some element of emotional intelligence to be able to inspire passion (Piper, 2005).

Thus, the value of emotional intelligence is largely unchallenged. However, we have yet to answer the following questions posed by Stewart (2004, p. 10): "Can emotional intelligence be learned? Can you have too much? How can a person compensate for weakness in emotional intelligence?" Such questions need to be answered by the next generation of healthcare leaders.

ACCOUNTABILITY AND AUTHENTICITY

For the expert clinician making the transition to organizational leader, it is sometimes difficult to transform thinking about accountability and responsibility. It requires a shift in considering accountability from a personal issue or task to be accomplished, to a team or organizational perspective while still retaining personal accountability. An example is the fine art of delegation. Transferring the responsibility for a task, process, or outcomes while retaining ultimate accountability requires faith, skill, and practice. Although referring specifically to basic and direct nursing care, the National Council of State Boards of Nursing (2009) outlined steps of successful delegation that may be appropriately applied to any level of leadership: (1) identify the task to be done, (2) select the most capable person to do the task, (3) use clear communication of the goals and purpose of the task, (4) establish an appropriate time frame, (5) monitor the progress of the job, (6) provide guidance, and (7) assess the performance and accomplishment (Greenberg, 2008).

Regardless of the point of service, the accountable leader understands and takes full responsibility for the organization at all levels. The leader never has a day or even an hour "off"; the leader is always on duty as keeper of accountability of the organization to its constituents.

That does not mean that the leader carries the burden of responsibility for all the attitudes and actions of the organization. Porter-O'Grady and Malloch (2007, p. 322) reminded that, "Accountability is more than the background against which everyday decisions are made. In fact, the way in which accountability is created, negotiated, communicated, and evaluated lies at the heart of an organization's operations." Accountability among all workers is closely related to initiative in that it implies taking ownership of the vision, the mission, and the work of the organization. The concept of accountability does not only appear when something goes wrong and someone needs to be blamed. Porter-O'Grady and Malloch (p. 323) pointed to the following definition of accountability by Connors, Smith, and Hickman (1994):

> It is the process of seeing it, owning, it, solving, and doing it. It requires a level of ownership that includes making, keeping, and proactively answering for personal commitments. It is a perspective that embraces both current and future efforts, rather than reactive and historical explanations.

Thus, obviously, the challenge of the leader is to promote personal accountability among all members of the team. That is no small effort, but it is helped by the example of a leader who is willing to take responsibility for failures as well as successes, who is able to acknowledge missteps, and who extends compassion to all workers. Stewart (2004, p. 10) described the "truly healthy leader" as "intense, passionate, and responsible—the kind of leader we want to have, the kind of leader we want to be." To create a climate of accountability in an organization, an authentic leader is required.

The concept of authentic leadership is relatively new in healthcare literature. (Buell, 2008; Kerfoot, 2006; Shirey, 2006a; Triola, 2007). The term seems simple enough. To be authentic is to be real, to possess sincerity, honesty, and integrity (Goffee & Jones, 2005). Among the most accepted, but least researched, is the trait of integrity. Storr (2004) noted that leader integrity improves organizational effectiveness, although the documented consequences of the full scope of power and influence of the leader with integrity remain largely unknown. Bolman and Deal (2001) cautioned in our rediscovery of the mystery and magic of charisma that we not miss integrity. They quoted Warren Buffet, who reported that he looked for three characteristics of new leaders: "integrity, intelligence, and energy. Hire someone without the first, and the other two will kill you" (Reynolds, 1998, p. 37).

Integrity is one of those few qualities that come from deep within and is likely the most important quality of authenticity. It is the beginning of wisdom. The currently highly sought charisma of the transformational leader is tinny and dross if not grounded in the soul of a person with integrity. Your most important responsibility as a leader is trust. "Having trust signifies that, 'I will do what I say; I will act to the best of my ability.' Simple things can build trust: responding to people in a timely manner and dealing with their concerns, big or small" (Kibort, 2005, p. 55). Show trust, gain trust, and honor trust as your prized possession.

Most sources on authentic leadership go back to Cashman (1998) and George (2003), who described the authentic leader as one who is genuine, trustworthy, reliable, and believable. Others have defined authentic leaders as transparent in their behaviors, and "those individuals who are deeply aware of how they think and behave and are perceived by others as being aware of their own and others' values and moral perspective, knowledge, and strengths, aware of the context in which they operate, and who are confident, hopeful, optimistic, resilient, and high on moral character" (Avolio, Gardner, Walumbwa, & Luthans, 2004, p. 804). George outlined five key characteristics of the authentic leader: (1) the ability to understand his or her own purpose, (2) adherence to solid values, (3) the capacity to lead with the heart, (4) the establishment of enduring relationships, and (5) the practice of self-discipline. Thus, the authentic leader is true to personal core values (Shirey, 2006a). Authentic leadership has been further defined as "a pattern of transparent and ethical leader behavior that encourages openness in sharing information needed to make decisions while accepting follower's inputs" (Avolio, Walumbwa, & Weber, 2009). Shirey (2006a) reviewed works on authentic leadership in nursing to find very little specific research in the area.

George, Gergen, and Sims (2007) found from their study of business leaders that authentic leaders emerge by understanding their life stories and by learning from their own experiences. They are aware of their strengths and weaknesses. They are humble and courageous to listen to feedback, and they use formal and informal networks to seek such feedback. Self-awareness is the first step toward authentic leadership. You must come to know yourself enough to know not only what you are about, but also how you are seen by others. Next, it is critical to recognize and live according to a set of core values. On good days, it is easy to list your values, but they do not become your own—they do not become the foundation of your leadership—until they are tested, until you are put in a position to sacrifice, defend, or act on your core moral principles, and lead from the heart.

You can only lead from the heart when you are firmly grounded to a foundation of ethical/moral values that includes the self-discipline to stick to the job. That allows you to develop compassion. By listening and sharing life stories, you develop shared meaning with those with whom you work. Then you can let passion light the way, developing important enduring relationships, and building effective teams to fulfill the goals of the organization. To be authentic is to consistently be true to your word, to "walk the walk," to consistently match words with actions (Goffee & Jones, 2005), and to be resilient. When times are bad, authentic leaders do not work from fear, but from their own inner compass of what is right and what is best, which comes from genuine interest and engagement with others (George, Gergen, et al., 2007). From a context of leader authenticity, others are empowered to lead, enhancing the effectiveness of the entire enterprise.

Furthermore, you can only lead with the heart when your own heart is congruent with your own actions, and with the mission of the organization you lead. Thomas Stewart (2004, p. 10), editor of *Harvard Business Review* warned, "A leader gets into trouble when there's dissonance between the inside and the outside—what today we'd call a 'disconnect.'"

Michael Dell, of *Dell Computers,* reported (Stewart & O'Brien, 2005, p. 106):

> The worst thing you can do as a leader at Dell is to be in denial—to try to convince people that a problem's not there or play charades. A manager is far better off coming forward and saying, "Hey, things aren't working, here's what we think is wrong, here's what we're going to do about it." Or even, "Hey I need some help. Will you help me?" That manager won't have a problem. The manager who covers up and says it's really not as bad as it looks—he'll have a big problem.

Because they are grounded to a value system, authentic leaders are able to endure. Although some studies have shown that narcissistic or opportunistic people have a propensity to emerge into positions of leadership (Brunell et al., 2008; Rooke & Torbert, 2005), their durability has not been demonstrated. George, Gergen, et al. (2007, p. 130) noted, "It may be possible to produce short-term outcomes without being authentic, but authentic leadership drives long-term results."

VULNERABILITY, RISK TAKING, AND FEARLESSNESS

Authentic leaders are able to share their own vulnerability. Vulnerability, risk taking, and fearlessness are highly related. The leader who is willing to become vulnerable must also be wise enough to weigh options and take appropriate risks for improvement, and must be fearless to both expose vulnerability and reach out to risk.

Traditionally, *vulnerability* is not a term to describe the fearless leader because it is often associated with weakness. But transformational leaders must cultivate a type of vulnerability that allows a measure of humility that opens them to take the risks involved in promoting change and transforming others. To be vulnerable is to admit to uncertainty, to realize that you do not know everything, but are willing to learn and to be open to growth.

Porter-O'Grady and Malloch (2007, pp. 170–180) described six stages to a "cycle of vulnerability." The first stage is to become vulnerable, which is to recognize and value uncertainty. People naturally seek certainty, but current healthcare settings are increasingly dynamic, chaotic, self-evolving, and unpredictable. The willingness to acknowledge vulnerability allows you to let go of long-standing viewpoints, and opens your mind for new ways of thinking. The second stage is to "choose to take risks that challenge the status quo." Complex healthcare environments require leaders who will reach out to new ideas and take the risk to use them. This does not mean impulsive actions, but rather risk taking from a perspective of evidence, experience, and evolving new models of thinking and practice. The third stage of Porter-O'Grady and Malloch is to "stretch organizational capacity by stimulating the latent potential of employees." Once you have exposed your truth of vulnerability and shared your embrace of uncertainty, they propose that the best next step is to immediately put out new ideas and to involve others in all aspects of stretching the capacity of the entire organization to change, adapt, produce, and serve in new and more effective ways. The fourth stage is to "live the new capacity." Put on the new roles and ways of functioning and try them for fit. Expect the unexpected as you integrate new ideas and processes, coach others, and "lead the way to a state of mutual trust" (p. 177). The fifth stage is to evaluate outcomes, and the final stage is to "cherish the resulting new knowledge." On the face of these, the steps seem idealistic, but Porter-O'Grady and Malloch provide a model to practice vulnerability that leads to shared accountability and trust toward change and, most important, opens the arena for new thinking.

Related to vulnerability is humility. Traditional leadership development programs will not advise you to be humble. Rather, you will be coached to "toot your own horn," "build on your strengths," and "show confidence." Humility is not the simple antithesis of these. It is much deeper. Humility is modesty, without pretense, or genuinely not believing you are superior to others (Martinuzzi, 2007). It includes being courteous, gracious, and respectful. Marcum (2009, p. 249) described the "epistemically virtuous clinician" as possessing the "responsibilitist intellectual virtues of curiosity, courage, honesty, and humility" as the best prepared leader in the current crisis of quality of care.

In the research for his classic work, *Good to Great*, Jim Collins (2001) noticed a unique characteristic among what he termed the highest, "Level 5," or "great" leaders. That quality was "extreme personal humility with intense professional will." "They were self-effacing individuals who displayed the fierce resolve to do whatever needed to be done to make the company great...[They] channel their ego needs away from themselves and into the larger goal of building a great company" (p. 21). Level 5 leaders were "modest and willful, humble and fearless" (p. 22). Such leaders exhibited "compelling modesty" combined with an unwavering commitment to the work of the organization. Collins (2005) described one such leader who explained simply, "I never stopped trying to become qualified for the job."

The quality of humility is illusive to teach or learn. Of course, the minute you focus on your own humility is when you lose any that you might have had. There are a few things you can do to "practice" humility: (1) Swallow your pride when indicated; be gracious; just stop talking and allow another to have attention. (2) Cultivate saying "You are right." (3) Reflect on your own moments of "preaching." Does your propensity to correct others actually meet the needs of others or yourself? (4) See the honest input and critique of others, and listen (Martinuzzi, 2007).

Such humility seems counter-intuitive to the image of the transformational, charismatic, visionary leader. Collins' research (2001, 2005), however, showed that the leader, indeed the great leaders, need not be bigger than life. Indeed, the most visionary and effective leader looks away from self, toward the organization, and looks forward to success for the next generation.

Visionary leadership is a highly personal and courageous act. You must act with fearlessness and courage to pursue your vision. The very word *courage* comes from the French word for "heart." Courage may take many forms in leadership. It may be reaching to be first, to be different, to speak the truth, to listen, to act, and even to fail (Segil, 2003, p. 38). Wheatley (2008a, p. 2) distinguished between courage and fearlessness, "Courage emerges in the moment, without time for thought. . . . Someone jumps into an ice lake to save a child, or speaks up at a meeting, or puts themselves in danger to help another." Fearlessness reflects wisdom. We "bravely encounter our fear. We turn toward it, we become curious about it, its causes, its dimensions. We keep moving closer, until we're in relationship with it. And then, fear changes. Most often, it disappears" (Wheatley, 2008a, p. 2) and we are fearless. Fearlessness is sometimes quiet, and other times is demonstrated in charisma or the ability to stir the hearts of others. Furthermore, when you are fearlessly charismatic as a leader, the values of your followers are more likely to align with yours (Brown & Treviño, 2009), and followers are more likely to take initiative to respond (Boerner & Dütschke, 2008).

How do you know if you are fearless? Segil (2003, p. 38) made the following suggestions: You are fearless if you speak up and tell the truth even when "others don't want to hear it." You are fearless if you encourage debate and diversity, if you listen, and if you take risks and accept the possibility of failure. Segil (p. 40) also pointed out that fearlessness is not "recklessness." Fearlessness requires thought, assessment, planning, analysis of evidence, method, and deliberate planned risk taking. It requires trust in yourself and in others, and it will engender trust in you and inspire courage in others. Segil (p. 42) further suggested the following steps to develop fearlessness in yourself and others: Identify what makes you fearful and how it is expressed. Describe the worst thing that could happen as a result of your action and face it. Focus on potential positive outcomes. Make a commitment to try at least one new opportunity regularly. Review risks that you have taken and identify what made them successful. Identify what happens to others when they fail. Change it from asking "What went wrong?" to "What did you learn?" Reward learning rather than punishing failure. Fearlessness and courage result from sharing of power and providing a consistent, sustained model in your own behavior. The courage to embrace your own vulnerability will support you as you practice truly being a fearless leader.

To be fearless is also to face your reality, to recognize what you can do and what is not possible. Wheatley (2008b, p. 15) warned against deluding yourself that you can "through your own act of will, be more powerful than you are." In the face of criticism, fearlessness is to stand firm in what you know is right, in your deepest held values and beliefs, and in what is right for those for whom you are responsible.

INSPIRED CREATIVITY AND INNOVATION

A chief executive officer announced, "The most critical competencies in a leader, and the least susceptible to measurement, are creativity and vision" (Orsino, 2003, p. 34). Others proclaimed, "A company's most important asset . . . is creative capital" (Florida & Goodnight, 2005, p. 124). Complex problems that pervade current healthcare systems are laden with such enmeshed issues of tradition, habits, and special interests that they seem to cry for some new breath of creativity. Some authors suggest that creativity is critical for competitiveness, and the very survival of any business organization (George & Zhou, 2002; Gong, Huang, & Farh, 2009; Oldham & Cummings, 1996; Zhou, 1998). Gong et al. (2009) demonstrated that employee creativity is positively related to job performance, that transformational leadership is a significant predictor of employee creativity, and that relationships among creativity, job performance, and transformational leadership are mediated by employee creativity self-efficacy.

Maxwell (1998) retold the story of Henry Ford, who began as one of America's most creative innovators with the Ford Motor Company. His dream was to produce an affordable high-quality automobile. He fulfilled his dream with the Model T and changed not only American life, but also American manufacturing paradigms. But the dark side of his story is that once he produced the Model T, he resisted any innovation to improve it. For nearly 20 years, there was only one Ford design, as Ford himself resisted creativity, innovation, or inspiration from any of his subordinates. His automobile, which began as the prototype with over 50% of the American market, eventually fell well below its competitors, and his company steadily lost money, not to recover until a new leader was at the helm.

Azzam (2009) pointed out that creativity and critical thinking are sometimes perceived as opposed. Perhaps, it is because we often think of creativity as free and brainstorming, while critical thinking is more concrete and systematic. The truth is that the creative process may begin with a whimsical new idea, but eventually will systematically solve a problem. Genuine creativity must be applied to critical thinking about the problem. Disciplined creative thinking is especially important today in the face of such complex issues facing health care. To lead to effective outcomes, creative thinking must be taught, encouraged, disciplined, and practiced. Our traditional ways of thinking about problems and processes emanate from the industrial culture. Innovation has produced our current informational culture, but the future demands creativity to move toward a culture of wisdom. Part of innovation is "the ability to foresee disruptive events" (Kibort, 2004, p. 12). Loss of creative thinking is a risk with our current focus on standardized educational practices and measures, standardized care protocols, and rule-driven practice. Creativity likely needs to begin in the educational preparation of clinicians and leaders. Traditional approaches to content mastery and packaged protocols cannot continue to endure.

Azzam (2009, p. 25) further noted, "Too often now we are systematically alienating people from their own talents. . . . It is a fundamental human truth that people perform better when they're in touch with things that inspire them." Indeed, inspiration begets inspiration, and creative ideas are born in a culture that fosters creativity. Thus, "Most original thinking comes through collaboration and through the stimulation of other people's ideas." Thus, if we approached the healthcare setting as an arena for diverse interdisciplinary exchange of ideas, building on each other's successes, think what might be accomplished.

While it is true that creative people invent new ideas that pioneer new products and processes, it is a challenge for a leader to nurture an environment of innovation. Such a culture is necessarily often unstructured, complex, and chaotic. At the same time, in health care, leaders must be the guardians of efficiency, quality, and productivity. Florida and Goodnight (2005) outlined principles for leaders to support creativity in the face of the challenges of reality. First, remove distractions from employees and promote intellectual engagement to encourage them to do their best work. Second, require managers to be responsible for creativity and engage them in such processes. Finally, engage customers, clients, and the community as creative partners.

It is not enough simply for a leader to be innovative by nature. Special knowledge and skills are required to integrate new ideas throughout an organization. Shirey (2006b) described a five-stage process of diffusing an innovation. Diffusion is a well-worn communication and education theory that explains the process by which a new idea, policy, or practice is communicated and applied over time among members of an organization or a social system (Rogers, 2003).

The five-stage process to diffuse innovations begins with *knowledge* as members of the organization become aware of the idea, new evidence, or new policy. In this stage, selective exposure refers to the propensity of some to respond or not respond to communication and information regarding the new idea. Selective perception is the behavior of people to accept or reject the idea based on their existing beliefs or attitudes, and selective retention refers to the degree to which the new idea or policy is sustained. The role of the leader in this stage is to communicate the innovation and to describe how and why it works.

The second stage is *persuasion*. In this stage, the leader's charge is to influence positive responses to the innovation by demonstrating its merits and benefits, and the personal or professional individual benefits of the new plan. It is in the third stage of *decision* that the leader should have marshaled support to make the decision to adopt the innovation. Informal opinion leaders are especially important during this stage. It may be wholesale change, a pilot test, a restricted timed implementation, or other creative ways to implement. The fourth stage is *implementation*, which can be fraught with issues of support, resources, resistance to change, troubleshooting, operational issues, and other technical problems related to making the change. Finally, at the fifth stage is *confirmation*, where the leader must reinforce, reverse, or change the manner of implementation (Shirey, 2006b). Obviously, in today's complex healthcare organizations, the diffusion process often must take place almost overnight. Leaders and organizations that are nimble in the diffusion process and flexible in applications and evaluations seem more likely to succeed and sustain employee innovation and satisfaction.

It is truly hard to imagine a creative person whom you would want to follow who did not have a sense of humor. In such a sometimes grim business as health care, humor can save the sanity of all concerned (Hawley, 2009). Lighten up. Take your business seriously but yourself lightly. Find wit and warmth where you can and share them.

BUILDING ON STRENGTHS

Wit and humor are needed to endure the unfortunate power of negative feedback that is pervasive in our culture. Perhaps, because the American healthcare system is problem based, our approach to leadership is focused on highlighting problems, criticism, and negative feedback. I suspect in your own last evaluation at work, the category of "areas that need improvement" attracted the most interest of both your supervisor and yourself. We are socialized to fix, repair, and treat. It is deeply ingrained throughout our paradigm of caring for the sick. Examples include our general focus on disease rather than prevention or wellness, or a look at the very language of our charting systems (problem, chief complaint, and normal findings are considered "negative" while pathology is considered "positive"). Of course, in health care, we treat diseases, we care for the suffering, and we deal with people with problems. But must our approach to leadership always be problem based? A new era of strength-based leadership is emerging. Well known for the more positive paradigm of appreciative inquiry, Cooperrider and Whitney (2005, p. 3) asked,

> Could it be that we . . . have reached the end of problem solving as a mode of inquiry capable of inspiring, mobilizing, and sustaining significant human system change? What would happen to our change practices if we began all our work with the positive presumption that organizations, as centers of human relatedness, are alive with infinite constructive capacity?

In his classic work, Collins (2001) proposed that building on personal strengths promotes advancement through five levels of leadership: (1) highly capable individual, (2) contributing team member, (3) competent manager, (4) effective leader, to (5) executive. The healthcare system of the future needs executives who know their strengths and build on them, who recognize the strengths of others, and who develop effective approaches that heal others. Unfortunately, it is sometimes easier to identify your personal weaknesses than to know your strengths and build on them.

Building on Strengths to Prepare for the Role

Once you make the decision to lead, take advantage of the myriad of opportunities to build on your strengths to prepare or renew for a leadership role. Join and participate in major professional organizations. Take advantage of opportunities to be near other admired leaders. Watch how they function. Seek out mentors. Mentors come in a variety of types. An immediate supervisor may be helpful to share information and opportunities from the inside of your organization. A national leader may be a model. Find mentors outside your discipline to clue into the thinking and wisdom of leaders outside the cover of your cultural umbrella. In addition to peers in similar positions at other organizations, among my most admired mentors have been a law professor, a development executive, a corporate chief executive officer, and an informed stay-at-home wise woman. Connect with people who are not only models of effective leadership, but also who have your personal best interests at heart. You will be surprised at how many people are anxious to share and help. Good leaders love to be generative. Some help with navigating through systems, some help you personally to know how you are doing, and some treasured mentors are sages who support you through your lifetime.

The process of securing a position of leadership is different than simply getting a job. It often begins with participation in an executive leadership development activity. Several programs for executive leadership development provide excellent retreat-like training experiences aimed at general executive positions, specific healthcare leadership preparation, or even leadership development targeted to women in particular. Among the best known are the Johnson & Johnson Wharton Fellows Program at the University of Pennsylvania (see http://www.executivefellows.net), the Robert Wood Johnson Foundation Executive Nurse Fellows Program (see http://futurehealth.ucsf.edu/Program/rwj), the Harvard Management Development Program (see http://www.gse.harvard.edu/ppe/highered/index.html), and Higher Education Resource Services in Denver, at Bryn Mawr College, and at Wellesley College (see http://www.hersnet.org/Institutes.asp). There are many other fine programs and opportunities across the country, some perhaps within your own organization. Such programs are helpful to use as a kind of rite of passage for leadership, in that they bring you to the threshold of officially taking the role of leadership. They help you to identify your own personality and personal characteristics for leadership by formal testing and/or by peer and professional consultation. They also provide opportunities to meet and network with others with goals and experiences similar to your own, and other leaders from a variety of disciplines, and of course, a major benefit is partaking of the actual teaching of the programs. Participation can help you to hone your life goals, reframe your way of thinking about yourself as a leader, and be life changing.

The formal process to secure a major leadership position is described as "the search." It often begins with a search consultant or headhunter whose work is to match the candidate with the position. When you are ready to launch into a new adventure in leadership, become acquainted with such professionals who can help you fulfill your professional goals and secure the right position. Listen to them. Ask questions about expectations, demeanor, and how best to present yourself for the position you seek.

The best way to assure "good luck" in securing the role you would like to have is to prepare. Be ready for opportunities. Work on your own physical, emotional, and social health. Learn what your own strengths are and play to them.

Roberts et al. (2005) outlined a process called the Reflected Best Self exercise. The first step of the exercise is to ask for feedback from a selected group of respondents. Send an e-mail message to about a dozen people who know you. They may include a family member, peer or subordinate colleagues of past and present, and any others who know you. Ask them to describe your strengths, and to provide specific examples of "how you used those strengths in ways that were meaningful to them" (p. 77). Next, identify patterns and themes among the responses. Does anything surprise you? Third, compose your own "self-portrait," a description of yourself that reflects your strengths shown in the themes of the responses. Finally, redesign your job or how you do it according to your strengths. Make a plan that supports your own growth. Emphasize those traits described in your e-mail responses, and translate the themes into improved job performance. This is not an exercise to stroke your ego. It should help you to identify areas of which you may not have been aware, to validate what you may already know, and to provide a positive foundation that can inspire you to do better.

Building on Strengths in the Role: Appreciative Inquiry

How nurses rise to leadership is an interesting study in itself. You have been educated and socialized to be the clinical leader, the expert clinician. Many or most nursing leadership degree programs focus on the development of midlevel managers. You may know why you chose to pursue your own path to leadership, and you probably did it independently of a specific program or career advisement. We know too little of paths to high-level leadership among expert clinicians in nursing. Bondas (2006) identified what she called the Path of Ideals, the Path of Change, the Career Path, and the Temporary Path. The study was done among Finnish nurses and has universal applications. The Path of Ideals is characterized by a "personal drive" and the conscious choice to become a leader. Leaders who chose this path reported an inner knowledge, enthusiasm, and dream of creating and making things better. Nurses choosing the Career Path identified themselves as informal leaders, and sought ways to move upward to satisfy interests and ambitions that included more power in decision making, more control over working hours, and more freedom within the organization. The Path of Chance included nurses who more passively were discovered by others, moved into leadership by decisions of others, and continued a kind of laissez-faire attitude toward being a leader. The Temporary Path describes the trajectory of nurses who began by circumstance when an opportunity opened, then returned, or planned to return, to a subordinate position. Such trajectories seem unique to nursing leadership.

Once you are in a position of leadership, your job becomes to build not only on your own strengths, but also on those of others and of the entire organization. The period of transition into a leadership role offers unique opportunities and challenges that may offer a short window for response. You may have a comfortable period to ease into identifying the lay of the land, but most likely you will be expected to hit the ground running. You may follow a poor leader or era of difficulties in the organization, but sometimes, just as challenging is to follow a beloved leader with a legacy of success. The organization may be in transition of processes or firmly planted on a tradition and heritage that has worked for ages. In any case, you are best served by identifying your strengths specifically as they relate to the challenges and opportunities as you see them. Try to carve some time for assessment and reflection. Organize your time and resources to learn everything you can about the organization, quickly build a leadership team drawing from values of the organization, create effective alliances within the organization, and secure some early success to assure trust and perceptions of you as a leader (Watkins, 2009).

Appreciative inquiry is an approach that is especially helpful to build success from the beginning. It is based on the idea that organizations function and change according to how they inquire or evaluate themselves. Those who focus on problems will continue to find more problems, but organizations that appreciate themselves or search for strengths will continue to find more of what is good or positive. Cooperrider and Whitney (2005) proposed that to "appreciate" means to value or recognize the best in people, processes, or organizations, while "inquiry" is to ask, explore, search, or discover. Hammond (1998, pp. 6–7) asserted the following:

> The traditional approach to change is to look for the problem, do a diagnosis, and find a solution. The primary focus is on what is wrong or broken; since we look for problems, we find them. By paying attention to problems, we emphasize and amplify them. . . . Appreciative inquiry suggests that we look for what works in an organization. . . . The [process] results in a series of statements that describe where the organization wants to be, based on the high moments of where they have been. Because the statements are grounded in real experience and history, people know how to repeat their success.

The "appreciative executive" is a "scholar, colleague, and sculptor of conversation who seeks to give new voice to the *mystery*, not mastery, and *wonder*, not problems, of organizational life" (Keefe & Pesut, 2004, p. 103; Srivastva, Fry, & Cooperrider, 1999, p. 33). Thus, the leader who employs appreciative inquiry asks questions, then listens; welcomes and encourages creativity; and distinguishes between problems to be solved and "aspirations" to be fulfilled (Keefe & Pesut, 2004, p. 103). Such a leader helps the organization to make its vision reality.

The model of appreciative inquiry includes a cycle of four concepts, the four "Ds:" discovery, dream, design, and delivery. Discovery includes inquiry into the "positive core" based on the assumption that within any organization, something is working well. The discovery task is to align strengths for a competitive advantage and to identify and share best practices, to appreciate "what is." The dream task is to imagine and envision "what might be" with a strategic view. The design task is to articulate the values of the organization and to state the principles and propositions of the best future of the organization, determining "what should be." The delivery task is to act on the dream, to live the vision, and to sustain the plan, creating "what will be" (Cooperrider & Srivastva, 1987; Cooperrider & Whitney, 2005, p. 30; Keefe & Pesut, 2004, p. 104; Whitney & Schau, 1998).

Appreciative inquiry has been used to support nursing leadership in academic settings to promote transformation for dealing with the complex issues of technology advancement and blurred boundaries of practice (Moody, Horton-Deutsch, & Pesut, 2007). As a leader, you may draw from specific models, such as appreciative inquiry, or you may design your own. Regardless of your formal approach, even if you continue a problem-based model, at some point, you must recognize and build on the strengths of individuals and the organization. Strength-based approaches help you to articulate personal and organizational values, to enliven the vision, and to bring strategic planning into reality.

Besides inviting a general sense of uplift and satisfaction, appreciative leadership can be most effective to creating professional partnerships (Sherwood, 2006). Opening the discussion with inquiry into the strengths and areas of positive interdependence begins a strong foundation for collaboration. It provides a means to enhance communication, cultural awareness, and sensitivity (Havens, Wood, & Leeman, 2006).

MORAL SENSITIVITY AND REASONING

Moral sensitivity and reasoning are about recognizing values, and the influence of personal and organizational values on both the leadership and productivity of the organization. The idea of values-based leadership has emerged in importance in the past decade. A value is defined as a "principle or quality intrinsically valuable or desirable," or an enduring belief in a principle or mode of conduct that is socially preferable (Graber & Kilpatrick, 2008, p. 180). Successful organizations are those whose system values are aligned with the values of the individuals within the organization and within the community in which they reside. Particularly in the United States, there is sometimes a natural tension between values that rank collectivist or community welfare above that of the individual and more individualistic values (Graber & Kilpatrick, 2008). This is among the core issues in current political discussions regarding healthcare reform.

Health care is a value-laden enterprise. Nevertheless, there are differences among the personal values of those involved in health care. For example, several studies have demonstrated that the values of empathy and altruism decline as medical students advance in their programs (Hojat et al., 2004; Newton et al., 2000). On the other hand, nursing students score higher on altruism, while management students score highest on authority and advancement (Thorpe & Loo, 2003). Such differences may have important implications in the healthcare setting where physicians, nurses, and administrators pursue distinct personal and professional interests, while working together to create the social environment of the workplace (Graber & Kilpatrick, 2008).

Secretan (1999, 2009) asserted that personal and organizational values must align in regard to destiny, cause, and calling. Defining destiny addresses the question, "Why are we here?" Cause is defined by response to the questions "How will we be?" and "What will we stand for?" The sense of calling is affirmed by the question, "How will we use our gifts and talents to serve?" Secretan further promoted the following principles or values, called the CASTLE model, as essential to the successful organization: courage, authenticity, service, truthfulness, love, and effectiveness. One study in Canada examined the relationship between scores on moral reasoning and either transformational or transactional leadership styles. Leaders who scored highest on transformational leadership also scored highest on moral reasoning, while there was no relationship between moral reasoning and transactional leadership behaviors (Turner, Barling, Epitropaki, Butcher, & Milner, 2002).

Transformational leaders build trust and model ethical values. They lead by ethics and morals, but are not moralistic.

> They increase the awareness of what is right, good, important, and beautiful, when they help to elevate followers' needs for achievement and self-actualization, when they foster in followers higher moral maturity, and when they move followers to go beyond their self-interests for the good of their group, organization, or society. (Homrig, 2001, p. 6)

Moral reasoning and ethical values provide the foundation for the successful transformational leader.

MEN AND WOMEN: ARE THERE DIFFERENCES IN LEADERSHIP?

Among the early of studies of leadership styles at the dawn of the 20th century, lists of preferred leadership traits included masculinity. Indeed, some authors have pointed out that common understandings of the concept of leadership continue to lack critique from a feminist perspective (Ford, 2005). Furthermore, subsequent explorations of transformational leadership attributed many of its characteristics to the male gender. However, a recent meta-analysis of 45 studies of transformational, transactional, and laissez-faire leadership styles found women leaders to exhibit more transformational attributes. Men were found to be more likely transactional or laissez-faire leaders (Eagly, Johannesen-Schmidt, & van Engen, 2003). Ford (2005) asserted that there is a need throughout the healthcare industry for increased awareness of gender in leadership, and the adoption of more culturally sensitive and locally based approaches that account for personal experience, identity, and power relations that allow for the entire range of masculine and feminine leadership styles and behaviors. There will always be differences.

Currently, women are more likely to move in and out of employment across their lives (Hewlett & Luce, 2005). In ranked order, the top five reasons women leave the workforce are (1) for family time, (2) to earn a degree or other training, (3) because work was not satisfying, (4) to relocate residence, and (5) to change careers. Whereas the rank order of the top five reasons men leave the workforce are (1) to change careers, (2) to earn a degree or other training, (3) because work was not satisfying, (4) loss of interest in the field, and (5) for family time. Because of the broad range of losses both to companies and to individuals when a person leaves the workforce, and because of the difficulties of reentry, several organizations have begun special initiatives to retain workers, especially women leaders (Hewlett & Luce, 2005). Women also continue to carry the greater portion of parenting and household responsibilities. Indeed, 92% of women employed outside the home still manage all household tasks (Barsh, Cranston, & Craske, 2008).

Some biobehavioral research of the last decade has demonstrated other distinct differences between men and women, such as brain activity. Women are more likely to think in integrated matrices, moving more "gracefully from intellect to intuition and from linear to nonlinear thought" than men do (Maraldo, 2008, p. 252), and are thus more facile at multitasking, while men tend to be more focused and linear. Thus, women may be generally suited to become transformational leaders in current and future environments of chaos and complexity. Furthermore, women in healthcare or nursing leadership are likely to exhibit the same characteristics of personal integrity, ethical standards, trustworthiness, and credibility as do women leaders in other disciplines (Carroll, 2005).

Although many more women than men enter healthcare professions, relatively few women reach the highest leadership positions. The McKinsey Leadership Project was an initiative to uncover what drives and sustains successful women leaders (Barsh et al., 2008, p. 35). From the project emerged a model of "five broad and interrelated dimensions" that likely pertain to men as well as women:

(1) meaning, or finding your strengths and putting them to work in the service of an inspiring purpose; (2) managing energy, or knowing where your energy comes from, where it goes, and what you can do to manage it; (3) positive framing, or adopting a more constructive way to view your world, expand your horizons, and gain the resilience to move ahead even when bad things happen; (4) connecting, or identifying who can help you grow, building stronger relationships, and increasing your sense of belonging; and (5) engaging, or finding your voice, becoming self-reliant and confident by accepting opportunities and the inherent risks they bring, and collaborating with others.

In reality, whether man or woman, no leader has all the characteristics needed to do the whole job of leadership, regardless of the position. Ancona, Malone, Orlikowski, and Senge (2007, p. 92) suggested that we "end the myth of the complete leader." Instead, with confidence and humility, recognizing personal strengths and challenges, the leader must engage the talents and perspectives of others. Indeed, more than a decade ago, Bolman and Deal (1992) demonstrated little or no support for stereotypical expectations of differences between men and women as leaders. They found that, generally, men and women in comparable positions were more alike than different. The larger issue was that women were less likely to be represented at the highest levels of leadership. Ancona et al. suggested that the following four capabilities are critical and can be shared regardless of gender: (1) sensemaking, which is understanding and interpreting the environment, its culture, and complexities; (2) relating, or trusting and engaging others; (3) visioning, or developing and sharing a compelling image of the future; and (4) inventing, or finding new approaches for mission accomplishment and "to bring the vision to life."

Furthermore, there is no single, magic formula, gender, style, or list of traits for effective transformational leadership. One nurse leader voiced concern that our current focus on personality and charisma substitute for skills (Christmas, 2009). Collins (2001) warned that leading by charisma alone is dangerous, that a strong self-focused personality may insulate a leader from the truth. We have all had at least one starched, old-school, autocratic leader under whom we thrived by his or her sheer organization and commitment—just as we have grown from the warm, dynamic, shared-vision leader who inspired us. Which leader will you be? What are your best characteristics? What will be your legacy?

REFERENCES

Ancona, D., Malone, T. W., Orlikowski, W. J., & Senge, P. M. (2007). In praise of the incomplete leader. *Harvard Business Review, 85*(2), 91–100, 156.

Atchison, T. (2006). *Leadership's deeper dimensions: Building blocks to superior performance.* Chicago: Health Administration Press.

Avolio, B. J., Gardner, W. L., Walumbwa, F. O., & Luthans, F. (2004). Unlocking the mask: A look at the process by which authentic leaders impact follower attitudes and behaviors. *Leadership Quarterly, 15,* 801–823.

Avolio, B. J., Walumbwa, F. O., & Weber, T. J. (2009). Leadership: Current theories, research, and future directions. *Annual Review of Psychology, 60,* 421–449.

Azzam, A. M. (2009, September). Why creativity now? A conversation with Sir Ken Robinson. *Educational Leadership, 67*(1), 22–26.

Barsh, J., Cranston, S., & Craske, R. A. (2008). Centered leadership: How talented women thrive. *McKinsey Quarterly, 4,* 35–36.

Boerner, S., & Dütschke, E. (2008). The impact of charismatic leadership on followers' initiative-oriented behavior: A study in German hospitals. *Health Care Management Review, 33*(4), 3323–3340.

Bolman, L. G., & Deal, T. E. (1992). Leading and managing: Effects of context, culture, and gender. *Educational Administration Quarterly, 28*(3), 314–329.

Bolman, L. G., & Deal, T. E. (2001). *Leading with soul: An uncommon journey of spirit.* San Francisco: Jossey-Bass.

Bondas, T. (2006). Paths to nursing leadership. *Journal of Nursing Management, 14,* 332–339.

Brown, M. E., & Trevi o, L. K. (2009). Leader-follower values congruence: Are socialized charismatic leaders better able to achieve it? *Journal of Applied Psychology, 94*(2), 478–490.

Brunell, A. B., Gentry, W. A., Campbell, W. K., Hoffman, B. J., Kuhnert, K. W., & Demarree, K. G. (2008). Leader emergence: The case of the narcissistic leader. *Personality & Social Psychology Bulletin, 34*(12), 1663–1676.

Buell, J. M. (2008). What it takes to be an authentic and transparent leader: Living the organization's mission, vision, and values. *Healthcare Executive, 23*(6), 20–24.

Carroll, T. L. (2005). Leadership skills and attributes of women and nurse executives. *Nursing Administration Quarterly, 29*(2), 146–153.

Cashman, K. (1998). Five touchstones of authentic leadership. *Management Review, 87,* 58–60.

Christmas, K. (2009). 2009: The year of positive leadership. *Nursing Econimic$, 27*(2), 128–133.

Clarke, S. (2004, January). Leading by feel. *Harvard Business Review, 82*(1), 27.

Cobert, A. E., & Witt, L. A. (2009). The role of goal-focused leadership in enabling the expression of conscientiousness. *Journal of Applied Psychology, 94*(3), 790–796.

Collins, J. (2001). *Good to great.* New York: Harper Business.

Collins, J. (2005, July–August). Level 5 leadership: The triumph of humility and fierce resolve. *Harvard Business Review,* 136–146. [Original: Collins, J. (2001). Level 5 leadership: The triumph of humility and fierce resolve. *Harvard Business Review, 79*(1), 66–76, 175].

Connors, R. T., Smith, T., & Hickman, E. (1994). *The Oz principle: Getting results through individual and organizational accountability.* Englewood Cliffs, NJ: Prentice Hall.

Cooperrider, D. L., & Srivastva, S. (1987). Appreciative inquiry in organizational life. In R. Woodman & W. Pasmore (Eds.), *Research on Organizational Change and Development* (Vol. 1, pp. 129–169). Stamford, CT: JAI Press.

Cooperrider, D. L., & Whitney, D. (2005). *Appreciative inquiry: A positive revolution in change.* San Francisco: Berrett-Koehler.

Drucker, P. (1954). *The practice of management.* New York: HarperCollins.

Drucker, P. (1992, September–October). The new society of organizations. *Harvard Business Review, 70*(5), 95–105.

Drucker, P. (1996). *The leader of the future.* San Francisco: Jossey-Bass.

Duffy, A. (2007). A concept analysis of reflective practice: Determining its value to nurses. *British Journal of Nursing, 16*(22), 1400–1407.

Eagly, A. H., Johannesen-Schmidt, M. C., & van Engen, M. L. (2003). Transformational, transactional, and laissez-faire leadership styles: A meta-analysis comparing women and men. *Psychology Bulletin, 129*(4), 569–591.

Florida, R., & Goodnight, J. (2005, July–August). Managing for creativity. *Harvard Business Review, 83*(7), 124–131, 193.

Ford, J. (2005). Examining leadership through critical feminist readings. *Journal of Health Organization Management, 19*(3), 236–251.

Freshman, B., & Rubino, L. (2002). Emotional intelligence: A core competency for health care administrators. *Health Care Management, 20*(4), 1–9.

George, B. (2003). *Authentic leadership: Rediscovering the secrets to creating lasting value.* San Francisco:
Jossey-Bass.

George, B., Gergen, D., & Sims, P. (2007). *True north: Discover your authentic leadership.* San Francisco:
Jossey-Bass.

George, B., Sims, P., McLean, A. N., & Mayer, D. (2007). Discovering your authentic leadership. *Harvard
Business Review, 85*(2), 132–138, 157.

George, J. M., & Zhou, J. (2002). Understanding when bad moods foster creativity and good ones don't:
The role of context and clarity of feelings. *Journal of Applied Psychology, 87,* 687–697.

Goffee, R., & Jones, G. (2005). Managing authenticity: The paradox of great leadership. *Harvard Business
Review, 83*(12), 86–94, 153.

Goleman, D. (2006). *Emotional intelligence: Why it can matter more than IQ.* New York: Bantum.

Goleman, D., Boyatzis, R., & McKee, A. (2002). *Primal leadership.* Boston: Harvard Business School
Press.

Gong, Y., Huang, J., & Farh, J. (2009). Employee learning orientation, transformational leadership, and
employee creativity: The mediating role of employee creative self-efficacy. *Academy of Management
Journal, 52*(4), 765–778.

Graber, D. R., & Kilpatrick, A. O. (2008, Fall). Establishing values-based leadership and value systems in
healthcare organizations. *Journal of Health & Human Services Administration, 31*(2), 179–197.

Greenberg, M. J. (2008). Delegation. In H. R. Feldman, M. Jaffe-Ruiz, M. L. McClure, M. J. Greenberg, &
T. D. Smith (Eds.), *Nursing leadership: A concise encyclopedia* (pp. 159–161). New York: Springer.

Halpern, B. L., & Lubar, K. (2003). *Leadership presence: Dramatic techniques to reach out, motivate, and inspire.* New York: Gotham.

Hammond, S. A. (1998). *The thin book of appreciative inquiry.* 2nd Ed. Plano, TX: Thin Book Publishing.

Havens, D. S., Wood, S. O., & Leeman, J. (2006). Improving nursing practice and patient care: Building
capacity with appreciative inquiry. *Journal of Nursing Administration, 36*(10), 463–470.

Hawley, G. (2009). Humor can have a place in healthcare leadership. *Oncology Nurses Society Connections, 24*(7), 4.

Herold, D. M., Fedor, D. B., Caldwell, S., & Liu, Y. (2008). The effects of transformational and change
leadership on employees' commitment to a change: A multilevel study. *Journal of Applied Psychology, 93*(2), 346–357.

Hewlett, S. A., & Luce, C. B. (2005, March). Off-ramps and on-ramps: Keeping talented women on the
road to success. *Harvard Business Review, 83*(3), 43–54.

Hojat, M., Mangione, S., Nasca, T., Rattner, S., Erdmann, J., Gonnella, J., et al. (2004). An empirical study
of the decline in empathy in medical school. *Medical Education, 38*(9), 934–941.

Homrig, M. A. (2001). *Transformational leadership.* Retrieved July 8, 2009, from http://www.au.af.mil/
au/awc/leadership/documents/homrig.htm

Horton-Deutsch, S., & Sherwood, G. (2008). Reflection: An educational strategy to develop emotionally-
competent nurse leaders. *Journal of Nursing Management, 16*(8), 946–954.

Jaffe-Ruiz, M. (2008). Leadership traits. In H. R. Feldman, M. Jaffe-Ruiz, M. L. McClure, M. J. Greenberg, & T. D. Smith (Eds.), *Nursing leadership: A concise encyclopedia* (pp. 334–336). New York:
Springer.

Keefe, M. R., & Pesut, D. (2004). Appreciative inquiry and leadership transitions. *Journal of professional
Nursing, 20*(2), 103–109.

Kerfoot, K. (2006). Authentic leadership. *Medical Surgical Nursing, 15*(5), 319–320.

Kibort, P. M. (2004, July–August). The written word: Literature and leadership. *Physician Executive,
30*(4), 10–13.

Kibort, P. M. (2005, November–December). I drank the Kool-Aid—And learned 24 key management
lessons. *Physician Executive, 31*(6), 52–55.

Kouzes, J. M., & Posner, B. Z. (2007). *The leadership challenge* (4th ed.). San Francisco: Jossey-Bass.

Lubar, K., & Halpern, B. L. (2004). *Leadership presence.* New York: Gotham.

Manthey, M. (2001). Reflective practice. *Creative Nursing, 7*(2), 3–4.

Maraldo, P. (2008). Gender and leadership. In H. R. Feldman, M. Jaffe-Ruiz, M. L. McClure, M. J.
Greenberg, & T. D. Smith (Eds.), *Nursing leadership: A concise encyclopedia* (pp. 251–254). New York:
Springer.

Marcum, J. A. (2009). The epistemically virtuous clinician. *Theory & Medical Bioethics, 30*(3), 249–265.

Martinuzzi, B. (2007). Humility: The most beautiful word in the English language. *MindTools.* Retrieved October 3, 2009, from http://www.mindtools.com/pages/article/newLDR_69.htm

Maxwell, J. C. (1998). *The 21 irrefutable laws of leadership: Follow them and people will follow you.* Nashville, TN: Thomas Nelson.

Melander, R. (2006). *A generous presence: Spiritual leadership and the art of coaching.* Herndon, VA: The Alban Institute.

Moody, R. C., Horton-Deutsch, S., & Pesut, D. J. (2007). Appreciative inquiry for leading in complex systems: Supporting the transformation of academic nursing culture. *Journal of Nursing Education, 46*(7), 319–324.

Morgan, G. (2009). Reflective practice and self-awareness. *Perspectives in Public Health, 129*(4), 161–162.

National Council of State Boards of Nursing (NCSBN). (2009). Retrieved August 26, 2009, from http://www.ncsbn.org

Newton, B., Savidge, M., Barber, L., Cleveland, E., Clardy, J., Beeman, G., et al. (2000). Differences in medical students' empathy. *Academic Medicine, 75*(12), 1215.

Oestreich, D. (2009). *What is reflective leadership?* Retrieved September 20, 2009, from http://www.unfoldingleadership.com/blog/?p=171

Oldham, G. R., & Cummings, A. (1996). Employee creativity: Personal and contextual factors at work. *Academy of Management Journal, 39*, 607–634.

Orsino, P. S. (2003). Leadership demands creativity and vision: Can they be taught? *Healthcare Papers, 4*(1), 34–36, 88–90.

Piper, L. E. (2005). Passion in today's health care leaders. *Health Care Management, 24*(1), 44–47.

Porter-O'Grady, T., & Malloch, K. (2007). *Quantum leadership: A resource for health care innovation* (2nd ed.). Sudbury, MA: Jones & Bartlett.

Rabow, M. W., Wrubel, J., & Remen, R. N. (2009). Promise of professionalism: Personal mission statements among a national cohort of medical students. *Annals of Family Medicine, 7*(4), 336–342.

Reeves, D. (2002). *The learning leader: How to focus school improvement for better results.* San Francisco: Jossey-Bass.

Reynolds, S. (1998). *Thoughts from Chairman Buffett: Thirty years of unconventional wisdom from the sage of Omaha.* New York: HarperBusiness.

Roberts, L. M., Spreitzer, G., Dutton, J., Quinn, R., Heaphy, E., & Barker, B. (2005, January). How to play to your strengths. *Harvard Business Review, 83*(1), 75–80.

Rogers, E. M. (2003). *Diffusion of innovations* (5th ed.). New York: Free Press.

Rooke, D., & Torbert, W. R. (2005). Seven transformations of leadership. *Harvard Business Review, 83*(4), 66–76, 133.

Salovey, P., & Mayer, J. D. (1990). Emotional intelligence. *Imagination, Cognition, & Personality, 9*(3), 185–211.

Secretan, L. (1999). *Inspirational leadership: Destiny, cause, and calling.* Caledon, Ontario, Canada: The Secretan Center.

Secretan, L. (2009). *The Secretan center.* Retrieved September 7, 2009. from http://www.secretan.com

Segil, L. (2003, Winter). Leading fearlessly. *Leader to Leader, 2003*(28), 38–43.

Sherwood, G. (2006). Appreciative leadership: Building customer-driven partnerships. *Journal of Nursing Administration, 36*(12), 551–557.

Shirey, M. R. (2006a). Authentic leaders creating healthy work environments for nursing practice. *American Journal of Critical Care, 15*(3), 256–267.

Shirey, M. R. (2006b). Evidence-based practice: How nurse leaders can facilitate innovation. *Nursing Administration Quarterly, 30*(3), 252–265.

Srivastva, S., Fry, R., & Cooperrider, D. (1999). The call for executive appreciation. In S. Srivastva & D. Cooperrider (Eds.), *Appreciative management and leadership: The power of positive though and action in organizations* (rev. ed., pp. 1–35). Euclid, OH: Williams Custom Publishing.

Stewart, T. A. (2004, January). The leader's secret self. *Harvard Business Review, 82*(1), 10.

Stewart, T. A., & O'Brien, L. (2005, March). Execution without excuses. *Harvard Business Review, 83*(3), 102–111.

Stichler, J. F. (2006). Skills and competencies for today's nurse executive. *AWHONN Lifelines: The Association of Women's Health, Obstetric and Neonatal Nurses, 10*(3), 155–157.

Storr, L. (2004). Leading with integrity: A qualitative research study. *Journal of Health Organization Management, 18*(6), 415–434.

Thorpe, K., & Loo, R. (2003). The values profiles of nursing undergraduate students: Implications for education and professional development. *Journal of Nursing Education, 42*(2), 83–90.

Triola, N. (2007). Authentic leadership begins with emotional intelligence. *American Association of Critical Care Nurses (AACN) Advances in Critical Care, 18*(3), 244–247.

Turner, N., Barling, J., Epitropaki, O., Butcher, V., & Milner, C. (2002). Transformational leadership and moral reasoning. *Journal of Applied Psychology, 87*(2), 304–311.

Watkins, M. D. (2009, January). Picking the right transition strategy. *Harvard Business Review, 87*(1), 46–53, 114.

Wheatley, M. (2008a). *Can I be fearless?* Retrieved October 5, 2009, from http://www.margaretwheatley.com/writing.html

Wheatley, M. (2008b, August). Fearlessness: The last organizational change strategy. *Business Executive,* 14–15.

Wheatley, M. (2009, March). The place beyond fear and hope. *Shambhala Sun,* 79–83.

Whitney, D., & Schau, C. (1998, Spring). Appreciative inquiry: An innovative process for organizational change. *Employment Relations Today,* 11–21, 25(1),.

Zaccaro, S. J. (2007). Trait-based perspectives of leadership. *American Psychologist, 62*(1), 6–16.

Zhou, J. (1998). Feedback valence, feedback style, task autonomy, and achievement orientation: Interactive effects on creative performance. *Journal of Applied Psychology, 83,* 261–276.

Cultivating the Habits of a Transformational Leader

> While many people believe that transforming organizations . . .
> is the most difficult, the truth is that transforming ourselves is
> the hardest job. And if we transform ourselves, we transform our world.
>
> — *Dag Hammarskjold*

Stephen Covey has devoted a career to convince us that there are seven or eight habits of a successful leader (see Covey, 1989, 2004). Hamric, Spross, and Hanson (2009, p. 254) reviewed current leadership models and concluded that only three habits are most important to the transformational leader in clinical practice: (1) empowerment of colleagues/followers, (2) engagement of stakeholders within and outside nursing in the change process, and (3) provision of individual and system support during change initiatives. But we all know there are many more essential habits for the effective transformational leader. Consequential leadership requires the cultivation of a lifetime of habits that build others and strengthen self.

LEADERSHIP COMPETENCIES: HABITS FOR PERFORMANCE

There is growing agreement on the need for better leadership in health care but little consensus or evidence regarding which specific areas of knowledge, skills, attitudes, habits, or competencies are best suited to the leaders of the next century (Baker, 2003) or how they are best acquired. Thus, it seems that every leadership guru creates a list. We have lists of competencies from experts and expert panels, from authorities in business and health care, from government agencies, from the Institute of Medicine, and from every practice discipline.

Much of the literature on leadership in health care actually refers to specific management skills with a focus on performance. And performance is usually defined by competencies. Although the idea of *competency* carries an intuitive, implied definition, there is little agreement on a generally accepted operational definition. There are numerous examples of competency lists for healthcare managers and many definitions of the concept. One author mused, "Definitions and terminology surrounding the concept of competency are replete with imprecise and inconsistent meanings, resulting in a certain level

51

of bewilderment among those seeking to identify the concept" (Shewchuk, O'Connor, & Fine, 2005, p. 33). A commonly accepted definition of competency is the following: "a cluster of related knowledge, skills, and attitudes that: 1) affect a major part of one's job, role, or responsibility, 2) correlate with performance on the job, 3) can be measured against well accepted standards, and 4) can be improved by training and development" (Lucia & Lepsinger, 1994; Shewchuk et al., 2005, p. 33). Five underlying characteristics of competencies are motives, traits, self-concept, knowledge, and skills that optimize job performance (Shewchuck et al., 2005; Spencer & Spencer, 1993).

Competency models originate from private and public sector business and industry as well as academe, each one with its own list of dimensions. The dimensions usually include items related to productivity, personal characteristics, and personnel relationships. Such models have now found their way into healthcare organizations.

Many of the competency models rely on some sort of 360-degree evaluation model, which refers to regular, formal, and direct leader feedback related to performance on specific goals based on stated organizational values. This model begins with self-evaluation and then integrates formal evaluation from superiors, peers, and subordinates. The critiques are reviewed with an immediate supervisor, and a plan for improvement is developed. It is commonly used in business and increasingly incorporated into healthcare environments (Burkhart, Solari-Twadell, & Haas, 2008).

As in the business literature, it seems that every healthcare author has a list of the most important, or core, competencies for the healthcare manager. Many come from the personal experience and thoughts of the author, with little reliable empirical data to adequately distinguish, predict, or even to teach the most important competencies. Some are derived from Delphi or card-sort studies that boil large lists down to palatable collections (Hudak, Brooke, & Finstuen, 2000; Shewchuk, O'Connor, & Fine, 2006). One such study sought the most important competencies for physicians to become healthcare leaders. Results indicated that most highly ranked were interpersonal, communication skills, professional ethics, and social responsibility. Other desired competencies were influencing peers to adopt new approaches in medicine and administrative responsibility in a healthcare organization (McKenna, Gartland, & Pugno, 2004).

There is increasing interest in the empirical discovery and measurement of competencies for successful leaders. Guo and Anderson (2005, 2009) promoted a paradigm that identified four essential dimensions: conceptual, participation, interpersonal, and leadership. They subsequently identified the following core competencies: healthcare system and environment competencies, organization competencies, and interpersonal competencies (Guo, 2009). Stoller (2008) outlined six more specific key leadership competency domains: (1) technical skills and knowledge (operational, financial, information systems, human resources, and strategic planning), (2) industry knowledge (clinical processes, regulation, and healthcare trends, (3) problem-solving skills, (4) emotional intelligence, (5) communication, and (6) commitment to lifelong learning. Another list includes planning, organizing, leading, and controlling (Anderson & Pulich, 2002). Still, another cluster includes teamwork, negotiation, interpersonal skills, communication, vision, customer service, and business operations (Finstuen & Mangelsdorff, 2006). And yet another model outlines 52 competencies in four domains of technical skills (operations, finance, information resources, human resources, and strategic planning/external affairs), industry knowledge (clinical process and healthcare institutions), analytic and conceptual reasoning, and interpersonal and emotional intelligence (Robbins, Bradley, & Spicer, 2001). Intuitively, the list seems to be comprehensive and useful. Each of the competencies has been defined theoretically and operationally. Nevertheless, it is daunting to the aspiring leader, who might ask, "Where do I begin?"

One group of competencies that has been extensively researched originates from the National Center for Healthcare Leadership in Chicago, IL. The Health Leadership Competency Model was developed from extensive academic and clinical study. The model comprises three domains of transformation, execution, and people. Under each domain is a list of the following competencies:

1. *Transformation competencies*: achievement orientation, analytical thinking, community orientation, financial skills, information seeking, innovative thinking, and strategic orientation.
2. *Execution competencies*: accountability, change leadership, collaboration, communication skills, impact and influence, information technology management, initiative, organizational awareness, performance measurement, process management/organizational design, project management.
3. *People competencies*: human resources management, interpersonal understanding, professionalism, relationship building, self-confidence, self-development, talent development, team leadership (Calhoun et al., 2004, 2008).

Most daunting is the Healthcare Leadership Alliance Competency Directory (Evans, 2005; Healthcare Leadership Alliance, 2007; Stefl, 2008), which lists 300 competences under the five domains of leadership, communications and relationship management, professionalism, business knowledge and skills, and knowledge of the healthcare environment. If leadership performance could be learned from a dictionary, this would be the one of choice. It is a large classification system of knowledge and skill areas searchable by an elaborate system of key words. Sponsored by the American College of Healthcare Executives, the American College of Physician Executives, the American Organization of Nurse Executives, the Healthcare Financial Management Association, the Healthcare Information and Management Systems Society, and the Medical Group Management Association, it provides an impressive inventory of leadership concepts "to ensure that future healthcare leaders have the training and expertise they need to continue meeting the challenges of managing the nation's healthcare organizations" (Healthcare Leadership Alliance, 2007, p. 3). Unfortunately, it does not provide mentorship, role models, personal experience, or inspiration for the soul of the aspiring leader.

Each new list or model announces something like, "The model of leadership competencies presented . . . [here] will become an essential tool for organizations in their pursuit of leaders to implement and drive successful change. This leadership competency model . . . will ensure that essential steps of change are followed and provide organizations with a blueprint for success" (Hall, 2004). If nothing, current experts appear to be confident in their competency paradigms.

Not to be outdone by healthcare managers, nursing leaders also have their own lists of competencies. These include competencies specific to areas of practice, such as professionalism, network and team building, communication, problem solving and prioritizing, vision, awareness of nurse subordinates, and knowledge of policies and procedures of the unit and larger organization (Grossman, 2007). Most lists developed by nurses are not uniquely distinct from those of the management disciplines. A study using focus groups of nurses produced the following "essential nursing leadership competencies": skills in listening and conflict resolution; the ability to communicate a vision, motivate, and inspire; and "technological adroitness, fiscal dexterity, and the courage to be proactive during rapid change" (Eddy et al., 2009, p. 1). Stichler (2006, pp. 256–257) asserted that creating and fostering a vision were most important, followed by 15 positive personal attributes, leadership skills that "ignite passion in others and influence them to make things happen," clinical knowledge and skills, and business competencies. Sherman, Bishop, Eggenberger, and Karden (2007) developed a competency model from a list of six competency categories. The categories were systems thinking, personal mastery, financial management, human resource management, interpersonal effectiveness, and caring.

Huston (2008, p. 906) outlined eight "essential" leadership competencies for the nurse leader of 2020: (1) a global perspective of healthcare and professional nursing issues, (2) technology skills that facilitate mobility and portability of relationships, interactions, and operational processes, (3) expert decision-making skills rooted in empirical science, (4) the ability to create organization cultures that permeate quality health care and patient/worker safety, (5) understanding and appropriately intervening in political processes, (6) collaborative and team-building skills, (7) the ability to balance authenticity and performance expectations, and (8) being able to envision and proactively adapt to a healthcare system characterized by rapid change and chaos. Whew! The list is as daunting as the healthcare system itself.

The challenge to discover or develop the right list of competencies is exceeded only by the problem of how to measure competencies among leaders. But, not to despair, a growing collection of models has been designed to assess skill sets and performance (see Griffith, Warden, Neighbors, & Shim, 2002; Henning & Cohen, 2008; Philpot, Devitt, Parr, & Nixon, 2002; Robbins et al., 2001). In addition, specific healthcare agencies and settings often outline specific mechanisms to track or measure competencies within the organization. Jennings, Scalzi, Rodgers, and Keane (2007) noted increasing ambiguity between leadership and management competencies and urged not only effective identification of requisite competencies, but also alignment of educational programs to better prepare leaders on the selected competencies.

The current emphasis on competencies and competency measurement appears to be in direct response to economic and social pressures of healthcare organizations for performance as well as the fact that "rapid change in the organization, financing, and provision of healthcare services . . . demand greater efficiencies and better clinical and organizational performance" (Shewchuk et al., 2005, p. 33). With the proliferation of competency-based leadership evaluation that targets efficiencies and safety, caution seems prudent regarding the potential return to traditional mechanistic, industrial efficiency models of providing health care. Furthermore, Shewchuk et al. (2005, p. 33) quoted Zemke's (1982) observation:

> Competency, competencies, competency models and competency-based training are all Humpty Dumpty words meaning only what the definer wants them to mean. The problem comes not from malice [or] stupidity . . . but instead from some basic procedural and philosophical differences among those racing to define the concept and to set the model for the way the rest of us will use competencies.

Despite our tongue-in-cheek journey through the world of competencies, still, it may be helpful to know those specific competencies where nurse leaders might focus. Some say that there is a need for greater business acumen (Kleinman, 2003); others promote the need for more "caring competencies" (O'Connor, 2008). The Center for Nursing Leadership (1996) outlined nine dimensions of leadership that reflect unique caring competencies: holding the truth, intellectual and emotional self, discovery of potential, quest for the adventure towards knowing, diversity as a vehicle to wholeness, appreciation of ambiguity, knowing something of life, holding multiple perspectives without judgment, and keeping commitments to one's self. Again, there is little evidence of empirical testing. Some models from nursing include specific characteristics of transformational leadership, but most fall short of identifying clinical applications, and many borrow from models in business and healthcare management.

Competencies are necessary, of course, to provide a framework to document and assure performance, especially in areas of productivity, accuracy, and efficiency, but it is difficult to inspire workers or even endear clients or patients with catalogs of expectations. Without vision, competencies are only chore lists for managers. Porter-O'Grady and Malloch (2007, p. 421) reminded that "Leadership is not simply as set of skills [and competencies], but a whole discipline." Wear (2008, p. 625) warned that while competencies are important, turning every measure of practice into a competency "is an ill-advised leap that transforms a complex educational [clinical, and leadership] mission into a bottom-line venture." It is important that we broaden the focus to include "ongoing reflective processes and humility that mark the lifelong development of skilled, empathic" clinicians and leaders (Wear, 2008, p. 625).

As you consider new roles or simply a new perspective for existing clinical leadership role with advanced preparation at the highest level of clinical practice, it would be most unfortunate if you were to reinvent the entire concept of competency. Think about what is most needed. Search the evidence for the empirical foundation and then ask: What habits and skills must the next generation of leaders possess? Is healthcare leadership only about skills? What are common assumptions and expectations? What needs might be uniquely met by a leader rooted in a clinical focus? Who and where are the leaders?

VISION: PERSPECTIVE AND CRITICAL ANALYSIS

Vision is probably one of the most discussed and commonly accepted attributes of leaders. Vision is their habit. Visionary leaders do not stop at simply holding workers accountable to competencies. They make it their habit to look up and beyond, foreseeing next steps and future challenges, opportunities, and accountabilities. Their own vision enlivens formal vision statements and integrates the meaning of the statements into their very beings. Vision releases forces to attract commitment and energize people, to create meaning in the lives of others, to establish standards of excellence, and to bridge the present and the future (Nanus, 1992). If you have no vision of where you are going, why should anyone follow you? Followers expect leaders to know where they are going and to strike the path toward a vision. Kouzes and Posner (2007) are credited with the well-known statement, "There's nothing more demoralizing than a leader who can't clearly articulate why we're doing what we're doing." By the same token, to spare themselves their own personal demoralizing sense of daily drudgery and burden, visionary leaders take the larger perspective, beyond day-to-day tasks and operations.

What is vision and how do you cultivate the habit of sustaining your vision? Vision is the image of the future you want to create. It is your picture of what is possible. Vision requires a dream and a perspective that set a direction that others want to follow. Heathfield (2009) proposed the following fundamental requirements for vision to actually make a difference: The vision must clearly set a direction and purpose for the entire organization. It must inspire a commitment, loyalty, caring, and genuine interest in personal involvement in the enterprise. The vision should reflect the unique culture, values, beliefs, strengths, and the direction of the organization. It must "fit." The vision always promotes the feeling among followers that they are part of something greater than themselves, that their daily work is more than operational, but part of some greater future. Such a vision challenges others to stretch, to reach, and to produce beyond their own expectations.

The leader who sets such a vision will have the larger perspective not only of the official vision statement or strategic plan but also beyond. Nevertheless, the effective visionary leader does not only see the big picture of the vision, but also is able to sensitively support others in the daily work of all members of the organization. To the perceptive leader, the vision is more than a rallying cheer. It represents a substantive direction for action and achievement. The vision is only one aspect of a strategic plan for action, but it is the vital life force of that plan. Inspiring leaders have the courage and the drive to dream. In times of near despair, confusion, chaos, or even routine and boredom, we need dreams. As a leader, you must believe in your dream; you must believe that it can happen. Kouzes and Posner (2007, p. 17) observed:

> Every organization, every social movement, begins with a dream. The dream of vision is the force that invents the future . . . . Leaders gaze across the horizon of time, imagining the attractive opportunities that are in store . . . . They envision exciting and ennobling possibilities. Leaders have a desire to make something happen, to change the way things are, to create something that no one else has ever created before.

One of my most visionary students reminded me of the story of Ferdinand de Lesseps, a French diplomat assigned to areas of the Mediterranean and the Middle East. His dream was a passage from the Mediterranean to the Red Sea, eliminating the long sea journey around Africa. He was not an engineer, but a diplomat and leader with a vision who used his influence to build the Suez Canal. Not satisfied with one dream, he then went to work to begin the Panama Canal. Deterred by a significant difference in geography, he did not live to see its completion—but his dream was eventually fulfilled by subsequent leaders who shared his vision (W. M. Scott, personal communication, September 13, 2009; BBC, 2009).

Dreams that actually become fulfilled are shared among members of a critical mass. A leader must have followers. Solitary vision that is not shared is only daydreaming. Transformational leaders must be vigilant that they do not follow their own light so far in the distance that followers are left in the dark. Shared dreams "fit," and they grow in the hearts of those committed to the organization. Stichler (2006, pp. 255–256) reminded:

> The nurse leader is responsible for creating a vision for the organization and clearly articulating that vision to others. The vision must be so compelling that others can feel passionately enough about it to direct their efforts toward achieving the vision. The vision must be viewed as being for the "common good," and the [leader] must foster that sense of common commitment so that others are willing to follow on the quest toward the vision . . .
>
> Along with the vision, the [leader] is responsible for defining the philosophy of care and translating that philosophy with others into care delivery models . . . . [The leader] directs the

care delivery process and accomplishes the mission and goals of the organization through others in a manner that empowers nurses and other professional providers to achieve autonomy in their practice.

A vision statement is a helpful way to articulate the dream. The most effective vision statements are short (two to three sentences), reflect the values of the organization, and reflect a picture of what the organization is about to become. It is a helpful exercise to engage people in creating a vision statement. When brainstorming to develop the vision statement, be bold to use metaphor, poetry, images, stories, and emotion. People need to truly experience the image. As the leader, you guide them through the adventure and to the place you see ahead. Vividly describe it, discuss it, and encourage all to share their view of it. Then articulate it in a clear, succinct statement—one that is so clear that the only response is, "Yes! That's who we are. That's what we want to be. That's where we are going!"

A shared vision gives perspective. It allows everyone to look up from many lists of competencies and the daily grind that hovers over nearly every organization at some time or another. As a leader with a vision in your heart, you are the guardian of perspective. You are able to critically appraise what is important and what simply appears to be urgent at the time. You help people to cut through the daily lists of "stuff" that must be done to see what really might be done for the better future. Sometimes, it is just a moment of reflective reminder; sometimes, it is a change of schedule or procedure; sometimes, it is a different use of language. Language is important in the vision statement, particularly. It must be beautiful in that it clearly reflects the image of where you are going, the picture of the desired future.

The leader who believes and constantly carries the vision is able to critically analyze decisions, solve problems, and effectively predict next steps. The vision is not about you, your career goals, or your personal desires. It is about the organization as a living organism, as a community, perhaps even as a family. You are the steward of the vision of the organization. For your vision to be authentic, you must love the place, the people, and the work you are doing. One of the best bits of wisdom of my career was shared by a nurse manager at a children's hospital where I worked as a young graduate nurse. She said, "If you don't love it here, please don't stay." Stichler (2006, p. 257) counseled that "The new executive must have a love for people because [he/] she must trust them to do the work to accomplish the mission and vision. That trust empowers others to be autonomous, accountable for their own actions and fulfilled with a sense of accomplishment." There are so many opportunities for service in health care that you do not need to work anyplace or do anything as a leader that you do not love. You must love the vision, the place, and the work (Bryant, 2009; Secretan, 2006).

Because the vision is integrated into your being as the leader, many plans and decisions will seem to automatically flow in the direction of the vision. Opportunities will appear, or you will suddenly see opportunities in a new way to allow you to move toward the vision. The vision becomes your habit. It will not be easy, but a clear vision allows purposeful critical analysis and helps to winnow away issues that cloud direction. It allows you to better trust your decisions because you know where you are going, and your actions are more likely to be trusted because you have the creditability of a clear direction. Critical analysis becomes easier, almost second nature, because you have set your own benchmark. You know where you are going.

TAKING AN ORGANIZATIONAL AND SYSTEMS PERSPECTIVE

Developing and nurturing vision will prepare you to sustain an organizational or systems perspective. It helps you to see the whole. As an expert clinician, you have the education and the experience to care for the whole person, usually as one person or family at a time. Reframing that point of care to an entire system is the task, and must become the habit, of the transformational leader.

It is often a challenge for clinicians who are accustomed to focus on the care of individual patients to acquire the larger organization and systems perspective, like learning a new language or culture. To take the perspective of the entire organization or system requires a different way of thinking. It includes an emphasis on how people and processes are related, how they work, and how they are connected. Kibort (2005, p. 52) offered the following analogy: "As with pathophysiology, you can't just treat symptoms—there are processes and feedback loops out there that need to be understood . . . . While physicians understand this in their clinical work, we seem to forget this . . . . Too often, we want to cure management symptoms, and not look at the systems and processes. " Unlike thinking of a procedure or problem in a one step-at-a-time linear fashion, organization or systems thinking considers multiple ideas, activities, and people connecting in a matrix of processes. Many dimensions are at play at the same time.

Systems thinking is the only hope to solve some of the most entangled problems. In Johnson's (2009) *Ghost Map*, he told the story of the unlikely pair of an entrepreneurial physician and a minister who creatively thought across boundaries, viewed the world from what Johnson (2009) called "the long zoom," or from the microscopic to the whole geographic landscape and back again, and proved that radical change for the good was possible. They are credited with saving millions of lives in the worst cholera epidemic in 19th century London when they traced the cause to a single water pump handle in the city. They bucked conventional thinking of bad air and crowding to show that contaminated water was the cause of the illness before the germ theory was even discovered.

Cipriano (2008, p. 6) explained why systems thinking is critical for leaders in current healthcare settings:

> A systems thinker sees how the parts of an organization interact and how effectively people are working together. This new way of thinking permits us to see things we didn't see before. Expanded thinking allows us to recognize and imagine ways of solving problems by grasping entire processes and systems. Such thinking also reinforces the idea that the whole is greater than the sum of its parts.

Systems thinking is not simply moving the focus from the individual patient to the unit, organization, or even the institution. It requires an ability to begin with the big picture and to live in the world of an entire system. Most scientists and clinicians have been socialized according to a Descartian reductionist approach to deductively see the parts of the whole. Systems thinking is based on the opposite idea that the parts are best understood, and problems are best solved, as they relate to the whole system.

Most clinicians and healthcare leaders are familiar with traditional systems theory with its concepts of environment, feedback, inputs, and outputs (von Bertalanffy, 1968). It has become part of the very language of health care. Although it provides a foundation for thinking, systems thinking in the complex healthcare environment is of a higher order of consideration than simple systems theory. A system is a dynamic and complex whole. Porter-O'Grady and Malloch (2007, pp. 47–48) explained the difference between elements of the institution and the system as a whole, that within institutions, most of the operational work is compartmentalized and organized vertically and distal from the administrators. They describe institutions as "unilateral, nonaligned, driven by self-interest, focused on structure . . . , and highly competitive," whereas systems are "multifocal," show "strong alignment of stakeholders," "focus on relatedness, and are outcomes driven." Furthermore, "Leaders must operate out of an understanding that each element of a system is a microcosm of the system. To lead any one element, a leader must direct his or her vision from the whole to the part, rather than the reverse" (Porter-O'Grady & Malloch, 2007, p. 54).

The leader who is a systems thinker understands that systems are about relationships, matrices of connections, community, and culture. It is often a fine dance to lead both the individual at the point of service, who is focused on getting a discrete job done, and the larger system of connections and relationships related to the health, thriving, and future of the organization or constituency of organizations. It is also a bit of an act of faith to understand that complex social systems self-organize within a context of chaos. Systems thinking is not for the faint hearted.

There are multiple advantages to systems considerations. Systems thinking facilitates the analysis of structures, patterns, and cycles rather than a series of isolated events. From this viewpoint, problem solving becomes more systematic, and the solution to one problem affects the solution to another within the system. The leader may think in terms of "leverage points" or positive change in one element of the system that subsequently improves another part (McNamara, 2009). Not only does systems problem solving show immediate or subsequent synergistic effects, but often, the positive effects are also long-term rather than short lived.

Drucker (2004, p. 59) further promoted eight practices that distinguished effective executives and enhance systems thinking. Such leaders see the big picture and take action from the perspective of entire systems. Drucker's adapted list is the following: (1) They ask, "What needs to be done?" (2) They ask, "What is right for the enterprise?" (3) They develop action plans. (4) They take responsibility for decisions. (5) They take responsibility for communicating. (6) They are focused on opportunities rather than problems. (7) They run productive meetings. And (8) They think and say "we" rather than "I."

USING EVIDENCE TO MAKE A DIFFERENCE

Particularly from a systems perspective, use of evidence in health care is no longer an option (Porter-O'Grady & Malloch, 2008). It must become the habit of leaders and clinicians. If use of evidence, or empirical research data, is truly to make a difference, it must be embraced at all levels, from point of contact to the broadest systems perspective. Furthermore, evidence must be implemented and evaluated from the perspective of all aspects of leader, clinician, and patient experiences. The effects or outcomes of evidence cannot be evaluated from any sole viewpoint. Evidence must be integrated and synthesized into the practice experience, into the patient response, into the entire caregiving or healing event. "Evidence of making a difference is . . . evidence of collaboration, integration, and systemization of all the related contribution" (Porter-O'Grady & Malloch, 2007, p. 54).

According to Melnyk and Fineout-Overholt:

Evidence-based practice is the conscientious use of current best evidence in making decisions about patient care (Sackett, Straus, Richardson, Rosenberg, & Haynes, 2000). It is the problem-solving approach to clinical practice that integrates:

- A systematic search for and critical appraisal of the most relevant evidence to answer a burning clinical question
- One's own clinical expertise
- Patient preferences and values (2005, p. 6)

The current sweeping movement toward evidence-based practice has been largely promoted by academics and targeted to clinicians in direct patient care. Nurse leaders have long been accustomed to the challenges of promoting research utilization within healthcare organizations. Current care settings are often laden with practices of habit, tradition, and routine. Nevertheless, Porter-O'Grady and Malloch (2008, pp. 185–186) warned against joining "the evidence-based practice fad," that the current surge toward use of evidence should "not exclude other nonquantitative sources of evidence," and cautioned not to oversimplify clinical nursing knowledge. It is important as we embrace evidence-based practice that we not lose, but rather empirically document, other significant ways of knowing and practice such as clinical intuition, attention to individual differences, the art of practice based on clinical expertise, and professional autonomy (Tracy, Dantas, & Upshur, 2003). Indeed, Råholm (2009, p. 168) "challenged the wisdom of basing the practice of leadership on a narrow, reductionistic understanding" of evidence and defended the meaning of context in the definition of evidence.

Although the development, discovery, and use of evidence for clinical practice continue to mount, there is a continuing need to close the gap between evidence and practice (Hay et al., 2008). In most clinical settings, truly integrated evidence-based practice is still not second nature. Indeed, Shirey (2006a) cited data that suggest that 85% of current practice is not based on scientific evidence. Thus, only about 15% of nurses consistently practice within an evidence utilization paradigm, while we have other data showing that patient outcomes are improved by 28% when evidence-based practice is in place (Melnyk, 2005; Shirey, 2006a).

There is a movement underfoot to emphasize the role of the nurse manager and leader in executing the appropriate use of evidence into practice. Unfortunately, we have little evidence on how this is best accomplished. Gifford, Davies, Edwards, Griffin, and Lybanon (2007) reviewed the literature on what may constitute effective nursing leadership in leading the charge toward evidence-based practice. They found the following leadership activities that influenced nurses' use of research: managerial support, policy revisions, and auditing. They also found that, often, organizational practice structures impose barriers to both leaders and nurses to access, promotion, and ultimate use of evidence. They concluded that "both facilitative and regulatory" measures for leaders are necessary and proposed research that links leadership to promote evidence-based practice and relates it to patient outcomes. DeSmedt, Buyl, and Nyssen (2006) found that implementation of evidence-based practice is best facilitated by clear communication, provision of summaries of evidence, easily understood protocols, and Web-based databases accessible within the work environment in addition to leaders themselves who practice more with evidence and less from sheer personal experience. It is the role of the leader to remove barriers and provide resources for clinicians to access the best research evidence. Such practice often represents a change of culture and total integration of use of evidence in clinical communications (Hannes et al., 2005).

It continues to be largely the responsibility of the leader to break the path, to facilitate the culture for evidence-based practice to be comprehensive throughout all systems. Use of evidence must simply become a way of doing and being in clinical practice. Indeed, leadership and operational structures must align to "place clinical practice at the center of the organization's purpose and build the structures and processes necessary to support it" (Goad, 2002; Porter-O'Grady & Malloch, 2008, p. 177). The entire organizational culture, especially its leadership, must support the ongoing practice of evidence-based decision making, actions, and evaluation of outcomes. Holloway, Nesbit, Bordley, and Noyes (2004) and Quinlan (2006) pointed out that although the literature may offer methods to teach evidence-based practice, traditional teaching methods for integrating evidence-based practice do not lead to sustained, integrated change. This can be done only by setting standards, clearly outlining role expectations, and supporting practices that use and promote the wise use of evidence. Leaders must incorporate the language and concepts of evidence-based practice into the organizational mission and strategic plans, establish clear performance expectations related to the use of evidence, integrate the work of evidence-based practice into the governance structures of the system, and recognize and reward performance and outcomes based on the use of evidence (Titler, Cullen, & Ardery, 2002). The transformational leader coaches and promotes collaboration among clinicians, patients, and researchers to create a "professional culture and transformed environment of care in which decisions are made on the basis of best evidence, patient preferences and needs, and expert clinical judgment" (Worral, 2006, p. 339).

Thus, it is well established that evidence-based practice will not thrive without leadership support (Berwick, 2003; Carr & Schott, 2002; Everett & Titler, 2006; Shirey, 2006a; Stetler, 2003). Leaders must provide access to evidence, authority to change practice, an environment of collaboration, and policies that support evidence-based practice (Everett & Titler, 2006; Thomson O'Brien et al., 2002; Titler, 2004).

With all of our attention to the trend of the past decade toward evidence-based practice, although we have become more careful to seek and use research for aspects of patient care, we have largely neglected the need to generate and use evidence specifically related to leadership practices. We have a growing body of clinical guidelines used internationally (Hutchinson, McIntosh, Anderson, Gilbert, & Field, 2003; Mäkelä & Kunnamo, 2001), but we do not have an empirically tested database for best practices in leadership. Vance and Larson (2002) reviewed nearly 20 years of research on leadership outcomes in health care. Of 6,628 articles, only 4% was data based, and 41% was purely descriptive of the demographic characteristics or traits of leaders. Thus, we know little about either what actually works for leaders or what or how to teach effective leadership (Welton, 2004). We are just beginning to document and promote models for evidence-based decision making in leadership (Nicklin & Stipich, 2005). Porter-O'Grady and Malloch (2008, p. 182) warned, "There is not a long-term, time-tested script upon which leaders can depend. They are writing a new script as they travel, which is always the conditional circumstance of a new reality. Leaders must now be inventive, stretching the limits of experience with the efforts of knowledge creation, generation, application, and evaluation." The next generation of transformational leaders must pick up the task of discovering and utilizing best evidence for successful leadership.

USING POWER EFFECTIVELY

Leadership, authority, and power are often confused. *Leadership* may be formal or informal and is always characterized by the ability to influence others toward the attainment of some task or goal. We have already described transformational leadership as value driven and grounded from an ethical foundation. It includes the personal qualities and behaviors of the leader. *Authority* is a formal designated or organizationally endowed ability, accountability, or right to act and make decisions. *Power* is the ability to exert influence, but may or may not be rooted in an ethical value system. It may also be formal or informal. Gardner is said to have defined power as "the basic energy needed to initiate and sustain action or . . . the capacity to translate intention into reality and sustain it" (National Defense University [NDU], n.d., p. 2). Positional power "confers the ability to influence decisions about who gets what resources, what goals are pursued, what philosophy the organization adopts, what actions are taken, who succeeds and who fails" (NDU, n.d., p. 4). The source and use of power by world leaders has been a fascination throughout the centuries (Greene, 1998).

Power is key to leadership. It is its underlying energy. To become an effective leader, you must become comfortable with power. It takes many forms. There is power of position, power of personality, power in presence or of charisma, power of informal authority, and power by relationships with others of greater power. Power is the ability to move others, to move causes forward, and to extend both energy and assurance or confidence. No matter what the external source of authority, power is eventually ineffective if some sense of personal power does not burn from within. It emanates from conviction, drive, and confidence in self; a greater self; and the direction of the organization.

The use of power can be subtle and positive or cunning and ruthless. History has long shown that seeking or using power for its own sake or for personal satisfaction reflects an unfortunate level of professional immaturity that undermines ethics and effectiveness and can do damage in the long run to the organization.

To lead with power, you must build a power base. The power base is both a process and a structure of connecting to personal attributes, skills, organizations, and people to contribute to the creation and control of strategic goals, direction, and resources. A power base is built by engaging in communication, information, and personal networks; reaching out to influential others for mentorship; acquiring your own reputation as powerful; and reflecting the influence and reputation of your own organization (NDU, n.d.).

Pfeffer (1992) outlined the following attributes of a leader to acquire and sustain a strategic power base:

High energy and physical endurance, including the ability and motivation to personally contribute long and sometimes grueling hours to the work of the organization.

Directing energy to focus on clear strategic objectives, with attention to logistic details embedded with the objectives.

Successfully reading the behavior of others to understand key players, including the ability to assess willingness and resistance to following the leader's direction.

Adaptability and flexibility to redirect energy, abandon a course of action that is not working, and manage emotional responses to such situations.

Motivation to confront conflict, the willingness to face difficult issues, and the ability to challenge difficult people to execute a successful strategic decision.

Subordinating the personal ego to the collective good of the organization, exercising discipline, restraint, and humility.

Authentic, transforming power emanates from values and principles. Such principles carry their own form of power to be expanded by the person who carries them forward. Principle-based power is not self-aggrandizement or self-advancement. Indeed, the more one empowers others, the more power is generated.

Power is not control; indeed, it is often enhanced by letting go of control. In new paradigms of self-organization and transformational leadership, power is generated from sharing, it is enhanced by a shared vision, and it becomes the amplified energy for change when understood and used as the secret treasure of the leader who shares it strategically with the organization. It may seem paradoxical, but power is not to be "seized" but given (Bolman & Deal, 2001, p. 112). Giving the gift of power actually expands the power of the giver. When people feel like power is taken from them, they engage in actions to "hoard" power: "sabotage, passive resistance, withdrawal," or outright rebellion. But a sense of having power frees energy and promotes a sense of self-efficacy, positive influence, commitment, and more willingness to give. Conflict is reduced and influence becomes more positive and shared. This all sounds so reasonable and easy. It is not easy. But it is worth the effort to cultivate skills in sharing power and influence.

THINKING AS AN ENTREPRENEUR

Appropriate use of power releases freedom to innovate and tap into your entrepreneurial leanings. Preparation as a healthcare professional is not rooted in entrepreneurial thinking. Entrepreneurship is largely absent in American professional clinical curricula. Indeed, a review of entrepreneurial activities of nurses and other healthcare workers revealed that most of the studies have been done in Scandinavia and the United Kingdom (Austin, Luker, & Roland, 2006; Exton, 2008; Mackintosh, 2006; Sankelo & Akerblad, 2008, in press; Traynor et al., 2008; Whitehead, 2003). I remember when a creative, nonconformist nurse asked me while we were at work years ago, "Do you ever think of your entrepreneurial self?" I did not have a clue what she was talking about. I have often wondered what happened to her. I always imagined that she started her own care business or consulting firm. I have always assumed that entrepreneurs either had patrons to support their inventive habits or put their family fortunes at risks on whimsical new business ideas. I was wrong. Entrepreneurial habits are ways of thinking, creating, and solving problems.

Never have there been more opportunities for entrepreneurial thinking in health care. The American system cries for innovative answers to difficult complex problems. It may be a new kind of independent practice; it may be a consultation service to solve unique sticky problems (Shirey, 2006b; Tumolo, 2006); it may be a new kind of business relationship between the practitioner and the agency. But we need more independent, creative approaches to solve problems.

You can be a system employee and still be an entrepreneur. Synonyms for entrepreneur include adventurer, promoter, producer, explorer, hero, opportunist, voyager, and risk taker. Our healthcare systems need entrepreneurial thinkers. We need someone willing to risk a new idea, to provide evidence for its value, to take the responsibility for its implementation and evaluation, and to nurture teams to risk innovative practices for positive outcomes. An entrepreneurial thinker resists habits of "stuck" thinking and forms new habits of looking at old problems in new ways. If such approaches are done within the system effectively, the entrepreneur may become even more valued by the system. When you see a problem, before lamenting the problem, reflect on the problem, let it simmer, then brainstorm at least three ways to solve the problem. Search the evidence on the problem. Think some more. Create a plan to address the problem, marshal the team to commit, implement the new idea, then test the outcomes. The process is as old and familiar as practice, but it is the reframing of the problems and ideas for solutions that cry for some adventure.

Given the pioneering roots of professional nursing, in general, and of advanced practice nursing, in particular, it is ironic that the entrepreneurial spirit seems so foreign to current daily practice. Lillian Wald dared to envision, champion, and create public health nursing. Following the loss of her own two children and the heartache of observing the lack of health care in rural America, Mary Breckinridge did not hesitate to nearly single-handedly bring the independent practice of nurse-midwifery to the United States. And Loretta Ford legitimized the primary care practice of public health nurses by establishing the first nurse practitioner program. Why, then, is entrepreneurial nursing not evident in the everyday practice of every nurse leader today? Several authors have pointed out that worldwide, although expertise among nurses is increasingly recognized, traditional organizational bureaucratic and hierarchical mechanisms, ingrained cultures, and ambivalence and ambiguity among practitioners in shaping "new" identities and practices continue to restrain entrepreneurial activities that might improve health care (Aranda & Jones, 2008; Austin, Luker, & Roland, 2006; Exton, 2008).

Entrepreneurial habits need to be fed. Ideas are not born of nothing. They come from watching, listening, and reading widely. Begin today with the habit of reading within and outside the healthcare literature. Read business magazines and newspapers. Notice how chiefs of other industries are solving problems. Drucker (2004, p. 59) chided, "Ask what needs to be done. Note that the question is not, 'What do I want to do?' Asking what has to be done, and taking the question seriously, is crucial for managerial success. Failure to ask this question will render even the ablest executive ineffectual." Is there a policy that must be changed? What is your idea to change it? Are you willing to give the time and commitment to see it through (Traynor et al., 2008; Whitehead, 2003)?

Once you are committed to a new idea, passion alone is not enough for success. Nurses are generally not prepared to face the challenges of an entrepreneurial practice. You must commit to become an expert in securing resources and relationships to help with legal issues, financial management, marketing strategies, payment plans, defining your role and niche, time management (Caffrey, 2005), and outcomes measurement. It takes courage and the willingness to risk, but the world needs more nurses willing to break new paths in healthcare leadership in entrepreneurial ways.

CARING FOR OTHERS: WHAT SERVANT LEADERSHIP REALLY MEANS

Unlike some entrepreneurs in the general marketplace who creatively feed self-interest, effective entrepreneurial leaders in health care foster some aspect of altruism. At the root of healthcare leadership is caring for and about others. No industry is more appropriate for servant leadership.

"Leadership is giving. Leadership is an ethic, a gift of oneself to a common cause, a higher calling" (Bolman & Deal, 2001, p. 106). The unique power and prerogative of a leader is the freedom to share yourself, your style, your values, and your influence for a better future. Bolman and Deal (2001, p. 106) reminded:

> The essence of leadership is not giving things or even providing visions. It is offering oneself and one's spirit. Material gifts are not unimportant. We need both bread and roses. Soul and spirit are no substitute for wages and working conditions. But . . . the most important thing about a gift is the spirit behind it . . . . The gifts of authorship, love, power, and significance work only when they are freely given and freely received. Leaders cannot give what they do not have . . . . When they try, they breed disappointment and cynicism. When their gifts are genuine and the spirit is right, their giving transforms an organization from a mere place of work to a shared way of life.

The concept of servant leadership was introduced by Robert Greenleaf in the 1970s (1977, 1998) and has been further developed by Spears (1995). Servant leadership releases powerful energy and proposes skills that are particularly effective in healthcare disciplines where some degree of altruism is at the heart. It resonates in special ways within the discipline of nursing (Howatson-Jones, 2004; Swearingen & Liberman, 2004). It encourages the professional growth of the leader and clinician and promotes positive health outcomes. It facilitates collaboration, teamwork, shared decision making, values, and ethical behavior (Barbuto & Wheeler, 2007; Neill & Saunders, 2008).

Eleven characteristics of servant leadership include having a sense of calling, listening, empathy, healing, awareness, persuasion, conceptualization, foresight, stewardship, growth, and building community.

Peter Senge (1990, 2006) suggested the following five elements of the servant-leader: (1) personal mastery, or "continually clarifying and deepening personal vision . . . focusing energies, developing patience, and seeing reality objectively" (1990, p. 7); (2) mental models, or deep assumptions, generalizations, or images "that influence how we understand the world and how we take action" (1990, p. 8); (3) building shared vision, or sharing the image we create of the future; (4) team learning, or fundamental learning as a team unit rather than as individuals; and (5) systems thinking.

Some people are natural servant-leaders. You know who they are in your own life. But more important, one can learn to become a servant-leader. It begins with commitment and practice to lifelong personal and professional learning. Personal mastery is the first step. It means to commit to continual engagement in redefining and clarifying your own personal mission. It means that you cultivate exquisite self-knowledge and personal growth, that you set personal goals related more to the advancement of others than to self-aggrandizement, and that you take time for reflection and feeding your inner self. You come to see your work with a sense of calling.

To be aware of mental models means that you are sensitive to your own personal biases, viewpoints, history, and style and that you strive to use your best self to promote the effective work of others to achieve organizational goals. You examine your own thinking and strive to create a clear vision that you can valiantly communicate and defend. You cultivate exquisite sensitivity in listening, awareness, and empathy. You approach your work and relationships from a perspective of healing.

The shared vision is the common and persuasive image of the future. As the leader, you conceptualize and facilitate that picture with foresight and empower others to share the dream and focus energies to make the changes and do the work to achieve shared goals.

Team learning reflects your ability to suspend your personal assumptions and pace in order to bring the team together to listen to each other and to work in synchrony or harmony. It means that your focus is on the needs and strengths of the team and that you create ways to develop the team to foster collaboration and effectiveness. You lead the team with a sense of stewardship and interest in the growth of its members and help them to build a community together. Systems thinking allows you to see the whole as a synergistic concept rather than simply as parts put together. It allows you to see the influence of your own actions and the work of the team on the entire system.

Secretan (2009a) identified the following five "shifts" in servant leadership: from self to other, from things to people, from breakthrough to "kaizen" (celebration of doing things differently rather than simply doing things better), from weakness to strength, and from competition and fear to love. He reminded leaders to ask how we use our gifts to serve. He further outlined six values or principles for "higher ground" leadership:

1. *Courage*: Being brave enough to reach beyond the boundaries created by our existing, often deeply held, limitations, fears, and belief. Initiating change in our lives—of any kind—happens only when we are courageous enough to take the necessary action . . .
2. *Authenticity*: Committing oneself to show up and be fully present in all aspects of life, removing the mask and becoming a real, vulnerable, and intimate human being, a person without self-absorption who is genuine and emotionally and spiritually connected to others . . .
3. *Service*: Focusing on the needs of others by listening to them, identifying their needs, and meeting them. Being inspiring, rather than following a self-focused, competitive, fear-based approach . . .
4. *Truthfulness*: Listening openly to the truth of others and refusing to compromise integrity or to deny universal truths—even when avoiding the truth might, on the face of it, especially in testing times, seem easier . . .
5. *Love*: Embracing the underlying oneness with others and life. Relating to, and inspiring, others and touching their hearts in ways that add to who you both are as persons . . .
6. *Effectiveness*: Being capable of, and successful in, achieving the physical, material, intellectual, emotional, and spiritual goals we set in life . . . (Secretan, 2009b).

When a leader adopts the transformational stance, along with transforming the organization is a tacit promise to transform others. This is an unspoken covenant to guard the integrity, respect, and good works of others. This is done in a myriad of ways. Create traditions replete with ceremonies and rituals that provide a sense of community, belonging, and the image that significant things are happening and that the people involved are important. Celebrate successes and rejoice in the achievements of others. Find ways to distinguish good work and reward it. Create an environment with high standards to which people are drawn with assurance that their work is appreciated. Servant leadership is based on the assumption that the people are more important than the task and that authentic service to people gets the task done.

CARING FOR SELF

The first rule of servant leadership is self-mastery, and the first rule to have authentic or credible influence on the lives of others is to attend to one's own sense of being. The idea of work-life balance is a myth, so the priority must be on balancing energy. Manage personal resources to find what restores you and put some part of that restoration into each day (Barsh, Cranston, & Craske, 2008). Positions of leadership are often described as lonely. In positions of leadership, you have few lateral peers with whom you exchange on a daily basis. You are required to make difficult decisions that are sometimes unpalatable to others. You must keep confidences that should you disclose might explain and defend your actions and positions that may be misunderstood by some. Others may speak pejoratively about you, but you are restrained from saying anything about others. You generously announce the accomplishments of others but may not even mention your own latest award. These factors and others can create a sometimes lonely existence.

Finally, Kibort (2005, p. 54) warned, "Get used to no thank-you's." It is an old adage that as a leader, if you are doing what you should, someone will be unhappy. I remember I had worked for a year to develop a plan that provided significant resources for some of my workers to acquire advanced education. I imagined that it would be among the greatest gifts in their lives. When it became a reality, I was amazed at the paucity of thanks—and treasured the few expressions that came. As a leader, you will work behind the scenes to advance the interests and careers of people who may well hold you in least regard, who may be unaware of their benefactor, but you will find fulfilment in your generative role as a leader. Eventually, I learned that much of the satisfaction from your accomplishments as a leader must come from a maturity that you may not have even known you have. It comes from within your vision and authentic caring for what you do and the people you serve. As you care for others, you must find a way to care for yourself that preserves your own energy and facilitates positive influence on others.

The physical and emotional effects of stress are so well-known. If only knowledge were required to ameliorate its effects, we would all be in a continual state of serenity. Thus, you do not need to know more about stress and its effects. You know your stressors and their effects. You know what they are in your own life: knot-in-the-stomach anxiety, overeating, overworking, or whatever it is for you. But what do you do to reduce the effects of stress in your life? What works for you? Cryer, McCraty, and Childre (2003) proposed five steps for leaders to reduce the negative effects of stress: (1) Recognize and disengage, meaning to recognize the stomach knot and impose on yourself a "time out." Isolate and put aside the source of stress for a moment as if you are moving on to the next e-mail message. In an instant, switch mental gears. (2) Breathe through your heart. After recognizing and suspending the source of stress, shift your attention and focus like a laser to a familiar symbol, such as a specific part of your body. For example, consciously focus on your own heart, physically and emotionally, and breathe deeply. (3) Invoke a positive feeling. Turn your mind to an image in your life that only brings joy: the laughter of your child, "the smell of pine," new snow—whatever it is for you. (4) Ask yourself, "Is there a better alternative?" Take an objective view of the problem and consider another possible way to address it. (5) Note the change in perspective. Take the time to notice what it feels like to feel better. Is your head clearer? Are you more generous? Are you willing to try it again?

One warning for the transformational leader is that "paradoxically, the energy that gets people going can also cause them to give up" (*Transformational Leadership*, 2009). One of the most attractive and effective characteristics of transformational leaders is their energy and enthusiasm, but if not tempered in reality and sensitivity, these can wear out the followers.

That dark side of highly energetic transformational leadership can ambush even the best leader or organization. If the leader does not tend to the care of self and others, or to the details of reality, the temptation for vision, passion, confidence, and enthusiasm to carry the day, without the balance of ruthless adherence to the reality of the details, will send success tumbling like a falling star. It is especially helpful for leaders to surround themselves with reality checkers, confidants, and transactional managers to blow the bugle when the leader may be marching so far ahead of the followers that he or she loses them or if he or she is about to charge over the edge of a cliff. Part of caring for yourself as a leader is to be sure you have some support staff who care for you, who can protect both the organization and you against yourself when you and/or the organization need it. Also, remember that transformational leaders see the big picture. Thus, every organization also needs someone to follow the details, add the figures, and count the beans.

Furthermore, truly invested leadership takes all the energy of your being all the time. You are always in charge and can carry the burden of being the responsible one all the time, which can become physically and emotionally exhausting and depersonalizing soon, you have forgotten who you are and where you were going. It is rightly called burnout because your sense of self is burned away from the flames of your flurried frenzy to be all to everyone. Only by finding and sustaining a spiritual center can you reclaim yourself.

Identify what people, situations, or activities are toxic to your personal, emotional, social, and professional health and avoid them wherever possible. When you cannot avoid, reframe an image and acquire a role that allows you to be sensitive, but does not allow them to eat inside you. Find what feeds you, then find ways to integrate that treasure into your life. Is it a hobby? Is it beautiful music? Do you need to go fishing? Skiing? Shopping? Take a nap? Find time that is yours and hold it inviolate. If you travel professionally, take an extra day to go to a concert, a museum, an art gallery, or to a ballgame. Find ways to see the personal joy in your work. Invite beauty, energy, and love, and they will be returned to you.

FINDING THE SPIRITUAL CENTER

It is possible that the most important thing you do as a leader is to come to know yourself as a spiritual being. Your only consistent travel companion in this journey of life, work, and leadership is the self. As noted earlier, leadership at any level can be lonely at times, so one must find fulfillment and fascination with the company of the self. Furthermore, the person who is well acquainted with his or her whole self is able to build on personal strengths, acknowledge and improve on areas of personal weakness, and move beyond the self to lead, lift, and guide others to better service.

Finding the spiritual center is about finding meaning. Barsh et al., (2008, p. 35) reminded that meaning "provides energy and inspires passion. Without meaning, work is a slog between weekends. With meaning, any job can become a calling." A central finding of the landmark study of spirituality in the workplace by Mitroff and Denton (1999) was that people do not want to fragment or compartmentalize their lives to exclude meaning or spirituality from their work. Their second major finding was that few organizations provide successful models to integrate spirituality.

"Spirituality is a universal human phenomenon" (Allen & Marshall, in press). Spiritual care to patients is a growing area of concern in health care. Indeed, the Joint Commission (2009) now requires health systems to address spiritual care. Attention to spirituality is associated with improved physical, psychological, and social health outcomes (Burkhart et al., 2008, p. 33). Spirituality "is the inclination to commune with a higher power beyond self, to find meaning within oneself, or to connect with something transcendent or metaphysical that is central to being spiritual. It is internal to the person . . . giving hope, promoting interconnectedness, and provides a sense of well-being" (Allen & Marshall, in press; Lubkin & Larsen, 2006). It implies a sense of transcendence, and it requires the time and space for personal reflection. It invites us to explore the deepest dimension of our uniqueness and potential for altruism as human beings (Wolf, 2004). It invites us to explore why we entered health care. It promotes a focus on values and a sense of community. It has been observed to help those within the organization to discover the human elements of the mission of the organization, break down silos that separate people, promote a balance of work and personal activities, uncover a perspective of health care from transactional to relational, and promote personal and leadership development (Wolf, 2004, p. 25). Spirituality may or may not be associated with religion and is not synonymous with religiosity (Burkhart & Solari-Twadell, 2001). It is about sensitivity to the soul.

Thomas Moore (1992; 1994) called the soul that vast expanse, that universe of all of who we are. He explained, "Soul is not a thing, but a quality or a dimension of experiencing life and ourselves. It has to do with depth, value, relatedness, heart, and personal substance," rather than an object of religious belief (p. 5). Get to know yourself, like yourself, and become interested in that person who is you. Moore (1992) reminded that "care of the soul begins with observance of how the soul manifests itself and how it operates," that "we can't care for the soul unless we are familiar with its ways." Finding your spiritual center helps you to be honest, to embrace who you are, and to accept others. It empowers you to observe and reflect, to learn from, and to honor what you learn about yourself. It creates a confidence in authenticity and absolute honesty.

There is a variety of ways by which you gain insight into the soul and who you are. Take this little test to discover who you are. Ask yourself, "What do others believe about you that you don't think is true?" Is there some prickly inconsistency that you would like to smooth? Is your leadership person a role you assume like a comfortable professional wardrobe, or is it a role of which you tire and long for relief? Ask yourself the next question, "What is your fatal flaw? Is there something that others don't know about you that you don't like and would like to change? Are you working on it? Is there someone who can help?" Next question, "What is your benign flaw? What is acceptable to others, but you would like to change?" Be cautioned not to look for errors and mistakes as points of self-condemnation, but instead value them, feel them, bring them into your presence. Talk to yourself about them as if those faults, habits, or mistakes were errant charges over which you can correct with gentleness. Mistakes and solutions, wounds and healing, regrets, and renewal of purpose are all part of the journey of finding the spiritual center as a leader.

Still, another indirect and nonthreatening way to discover yourself is to tell someone a fairy tale. You choose the story, and tell it with all the detailed narrative you can embellish. Then ask, "Which character am I?" "Why did I choose this particular story?" "What do I learn about myself?" Are you Little Red Riding Hood, always trying to serve and afraid of the wolf? Or are you Jack-in-the-Beanstalk, climbing great heights to face the giants to save the village below? What do you learn about yourself? How can such self-knowledge lend confidence, compassion, and new energy to your leadership?

On the way to fulfilling leadership, work to acquire your own repertoire of helpful habits to feed the spirit. The first is to find an enduring faith, faith in some greater power than self: in God, in a higher power, in a positive energy, or in a greater self—some faith that allows you to release custody of the lingering problems at the end of the day to a greater meta-physical influence that allows rest and renewal so you can face them in the morning. The second habit of the spiritually centered leader is to love. Love here means to have meaning-ful, supportive relationships; to associate with nurturing people; and to avoid destructive, toxic people. Evidence is abundant on the value of social support in nearly every aspect of human life, including leading. Bolman and Deal reminded that every organization can be a bit like a family, either caring or dysfunctional (and perhaps a some of both). To move toward a caring organization "begins with knowing—it requires listening, understanding, and accepting. It progresses through a deepening sense of appreciation, respect, and ulti-mately, love. Love is a willingness to reach out" (Bolman & Deal, 2001, p. 108).

Another aspect of leadership love is altruism. When one nurtures the sense of giving or charity, somehow, the spirit of leadership is enlivened, and the leader assumes a position of strength, confidence, and humanity.

To sustain the spiritual self in leadership requires a concerted attention to the physical self. Enormous energy is required of leaders in health care that requires moderation in diet, activity, personal maintenance, and sleep. Positive health habits not only sustain the leader but also set a standard and model for colleagues and even patients. Other positive habits include embracing beauty and aesthetics, humor, and congruency. Specific spiri-tual practices also include meditating, music, journeying to or designating sacred places, and prayer (Bolman & Deal, 2001; Porter-O'Grady & Malloch, 2007).

Because it seems so personal, inviting spirituality into the leadership and work envi-ronment requires courage. Those who do it, however, note that it is worthwhile and con-ducive to creating an environment of respect, ethics, values, and integrity (Wolf, 2004). Furthermore, leaders who promote spiritual exploration among workers and patients must be authentic. You must inspire and model your best self. When you find your spiri-tual center, you will be amazed at your abilities to positively influence others. They will be drawn to you. You will enable your positional authority or power to become influence.

HAVING INFLUENCE

"Influence is more important than authority" (Sullivan, 2004, p. 3). Making the decision to become influential is the first and most important criterion to actually have influence. You must first decide to have influence.

Securing the Position

Once you decide that you want to make a difference, that you want to have influence as a leader in health care, you may decide that it is time to aspire to the next step in an official leadership position. The first step to become influential is "to assess the way you present yourself" (Sullivan, 2004, p. 8). Especially as a first impression, never underestimate the power of the image that you portray on your influence and success. Image will not sustain leadership effectiveness in the absence of other substantive knowledge and skills, but it can open or close doors, attract or deny whether you are taken seriously, and amplify or diminish the energy you must bring to exert and sustain your personal position of influence or leadership.

Career coaches Martin and Bloom (2003) outlined principles to avoid derailment and to facilitate success at the outset of your career in leadership. First is personal presentation. Whether you like it or not, people evaluate your abilities within the first 8 to 30 seconds of the first meeting (Martin & Bloom, 2003). First impressions are important. People expect to see an open, interesting, positive, and hardworking general attitude. Walk tall, smile generously, make eye contact, and give a firm handshake. Dress appropriately. The old adage to dress for the position to which you aspire instead of the one you currently hold is true. When interviewing, and even after you secure the position, set the standard for dress and appearance. To be well groomed, neat, and clean goes without saying. Martin and Bloom (2003, p. 21) referred to a professional leader who advised, "Dress so that dress is not an issue" (C. Pederson, personal communication to Martin, October, 2000). For interviews, standards for men include neutral colors of navy, gray, and black jacket; conservative shirt color; and an interesting but not flamboyant tie. Women generally find less forgiveness in dress than men. Attention to detail is critical. Avoid anything that calls attention away from you as a leader and instead directs eyes and comments toward your appearance. That means to avoid too many accessories, strange hair colors, bright nail polish, too-short skirts, clunky shoes, or barefoot flip flops. Martin and Bloom shared their own experience that they have rarely observed women candidates ascend to the highest levels of executive positions who wore pantsuits to first interviews, but be assured that you must be true to yourself and to your own style. Make sure the fit is right for you. Nevertheless, at the same time, part of your skill as a leader is sensitivity to the culture where you aspire to a position of leadership.

Making the Difference

Once you secure the job, Patterson and associates (Patterson, 2009; Patterson, Grenny, Maxfield, McMillan, & Switzler, 2008) asserted that to solve problems, "It all comes down to human influence." They outlined eight principles to have positive influence. The first principle is to "change the way you change minds." As a leader, you must decide for yourself and be willing to help others believe that a change of outlook, action, or behavior can be done and will be worth the effort. The authors suggested creating personal experiences rather than just trying to persuade. In other words, help others to experience the change. Use field trips to other organizations where the values or environments you want to emulate exist. For example, make friends with colleagues at your competing organizations and secure invitations to send workers to actually observe the competition at work. The second principle is to "find vital behaviors," meaning to be informed by the evidence regarding what works to make the difference. Especially in health care, we are sometimes lured by current trends in thinking and practice. Instead of following the usual modes, the influential leader studies the evidence inside and out of the usual practices to discover what really works. The third principle is to "make the undesirable desirable." Sometimes, basic requirements to get the job done are "noxious, painful, boring, or simply less desirable than other tasks." Find ways to make such tasks palatable. Perhaps, that means to change the task itself, to reframe it, or to see that it is clearly tied to some reward or desirable outcomes.

Patterson's fourth principle is to "surpass your limits." Do what it takes and help others to surpass the expected. This usually means to acquire superior abilities by practice. In the bestselling book *Outliers: The Story of Success*, Malcolm Gladwell (2008) explained the "ten-thousand-hour rule," that behind every great achiever is 10,000 hours devoted to practice, practice, and practice. You cannot expect yourself or others to surpass your limits without committed practice to your art and skill. As a leader, you set the example and use your influence to encourage others to devote the time and energy needed to be the best.

To "harness peer pressure" is Patterson's fifth principle of influence. To influence others, it is important to identify respected opinion leaders within your organization. Invite them as mentors or peers and involve them into the change processes. The sixth principle is to "find strength in numbers," or to surround yourself with positive and supportive peers who share your goals. Avoid or reduce the effects of toxic individuals and find ways to mutually support people who nurture each other and stand for the principles of the organization.

Patterson suggested that leaders "design rewards and demand accountability," as principle number seven. Reward positive, innovative, and healthy behaviors. Measure progress and reward success. Make sure that rewards are meaningful to the individual. It may not always be money, but perhaps time, flexible work hours, or just a show of simple appreciation. The eighth principle is to "change the environment." Look at the work physical, social, and intellectual environment with new eyes. What needs to happen to influence others for success? In addition, Patterson (2009) suggested to encourage honesty and candid feedback; give clear signals; manage fairness in worker input, being sure to include those most distant; and continually review processes. The effective employment of emotional intelligence is a powerful tool for positive influence.

GENERATIVITY: PREPARING THE NEXT GENERATION

The transformational leader in health care has an eye on and a heart for the next generation of leaders. Leadership development, coaching, and mentoring are integrated into the very life of the transformational leader. That is the only hope of society for a better future. That is how you leave a living legacy. As the number of experienced managers and leaders in health care continues to diminish at the same time the demand for competent and visionary leaders increases, entire organizations are now beginning to integrate leadership development into the everyday life of clinical practice (Spallina, 2002). Unfortunately too many disciplines in professional health care have histories of a kind of professional hazing (as in "if I did it, so should you"), including long hours with assigned shift work; sink-or-swim approaches to practice; see-one, teach-one, do-one; or "probie" approaches to learning. Such traditions simply will not work in the new competitive environment that must focus on quality improvement, patient outcomes, cost containment, and professional recruitment and retention. A study in Belgium attempted to identify the impact of a specific clinical leadership development program on the clinical nursing leader, the nursing team, and the caregiving process. Although the study uncovered insights related to the leader's progress toward a transformational style and its effects on nursing staff, effects on care processes were more challenging (Dierckx de Casterlé, Willemse, Verschueren, & Milisen, 2008). Another exploration in England demonstrated the value of structured planning and programs in professional development and coaching for future leaders (Alleyne & Jumaa, 2007). There is certainly room for more study in this area.

Drucker (2000) proposed four ways to motivate and develop future leaders: (1) know people's strengths, (2) place them where they can make the greatest contributions, (3) treat them as associates, and (4) expose them to challenges. Wells and Hijna (2009) proposed five key elements to develop new talent for leadership in health care: (1) identification of leader competencies, (2) effective job design, (3) a strong focus on leadership recruitment, development, and retention, (4) leadership training and development throughout all levels of the organization, and (5) ongoing leadership assessment and performance management. Of course, this is common-sense jargon, but how do we do it in a way that inspires the dreams and hopes of new leadership?

One way to inspire the next generation for leadership is to tell your own story. Some research has demonstrated that storytelling, especially directly related to the aspiring leader, is effective in developing managers with high potential for success (Ready, 2002). Stories need to be related to the context of current situations and at the level understood by the potential leader. Effective stories are told by respected role models. Share the passion and drama of your experiences, how you failed and learned from the failure, what your successes were, and how you learned to survive. And listen to the stories of aspiring leaders. What is their context and where are they going? How can you help them get there?

Stichler (2006, p. 256) advised that the leader "must consider a logical succession plan in developing tomorrow's nurse leaders and demonstrate competencies and skills as a mentor, coach, role model, and preceptor. The [leader] teaches by example and fosters continual growth" and extends increasing responsibilities to those to assume future leadership. One nurse leader suggested specific steps to approach succession management as a professional obligation, calling it a "migration risk assessment" (Ponti, 2009). First, assess potential attrition and emerging leaders within the organization, establish core competencies for leadership positions, and develop individual plans while identifying critical success factors for upcoming leaders. Then prioritize, coach, and mentor aspiring leaders.

Many healthcare organizations recognize the need to develop future leadership and provide formal programs. The National Center for Healthcare Leadership offers a comprehensive lifelong, competency-based, and assessment-oriented leadership development program. Its focus is on leadership competencies, team effectiveness, organization climate, strategic human resource systems, governance alignment, cultural diversity practices, and organizational performance (Davidson, Griffith, Sinioris, & Carreon, 2005).

The transformational leader with a constant eye on developing others for leadership is investing in the future. Generativity is a characteristic of leaders with passion for what they do, a vision for a better future, and a genuine interest in helping others to grow. By enabling the next generation, you extend a living legacy of your own efforts, you enliven our own experiences, and you contribute to a positive human investment in making the world a better place.

REFERENCES

Allen, D., & Marshall, E. S. (in press). Spirituality as a coping resource for African-American parents. *MCN: American Journal of Maternal Child Nursing.*

Alleyne, J., & Jumaa, M. Q. (2007). Building the capacity for evidence-based clinical nursing leadership: The role of executive co-coaching and group clinical supervision for quality patient services. *Journal of Nursing Management, 15*(2), 230–243.

Anderson, P., & Pulich, M. (2002). Managerial competencies necessary in today's dynamic health care environment. *Health Care Management, 21*(2), 1–11.

Aranda, K., & Jones, A. (2008). Exploring new advanced practice roles in community nursing: A critique. *Nursing Inquiry, 15*(1), 3–10.

Austin, L., Luker, K., Roland, M. (2006). Clinical nurse specialists as entrepreneurs: Constrained or liberated. *Journal of Clinical Nursing, 15*(12), 1540–1549.

Baker, G. R. (2003). Identifying and assessing competencies: A strategy to improve healthcare leadership. *Healthcare Papers, 4*(1), 49–58.

Barbuto, J. E., & Wheeler, D. W. (2007). Becoming a servant leader: Do you have what it takes? In *NebGuide.* Lincoln, NB: University of Nebraska-Lincoln Extension. Retrieved April 15, 2010 from http://www.ianrpubs.unl.edu/epublic/live/g1481/build/g1481.pdf

Barsh, J., Cranston, S., & Craske, R. A. (2008, September). Centered leadership: How talented women thrive. *The McKinsey Quarterly Online Business Journal.* Retrieved April 15, 2010 from http://www.bnet.com/2403-13058_23-243562.html?tag=content;col1.

BBC. (2009). Ferdinand de Lesseps (1805–1894). *Historic figures.* Retrieved September 20, 2009, from http://www.bbc.co.uk/history/historic_figures/lesseps_ferdinand_de.shtml

Berwick, D. M. (2003). Disseminating innovations in health care. *Journal of the American Medical Association, 289*(15), 1969–1975.

Bolman, L. G., & Deal, T. E. (1991). *Reframing organizations: Artistry, choice, and leadership.* San Francisco: Jossey-Bass.

Burkhart, L., & Solari-Twadell, P. A. (2001). Differentiating spirituality and religiousness through a review of the nursing literature. *Nursing Diagnosis, 12,* 45–54.

Burkhart, L., Solari-Twadell, P. A., & Haas, S. (2008). Addressing spiritual leadership: An organizational model. *Journal of Nursing Administration, 38*(1), 33–39.

Bryant, J. H. (2009). *Love leadership: The new way to lead in a fear-based world.* San Francisco: Jossey-Bass.

Caffrey, R. A. (2005). Independent community care gerontological nursing: Becoming an entrepreneur. *Journal of Gerontological Nursing, 31*(8), 12–17.

Calhoun, J. G., Dollett, L., Sinioris, M. E., Wainio, J. A., Butler, P. W., Griffith, J. R., et al. (2008). Development of an interprofessional competency model for healthcare leadership. *Journal of Healthcare Management, 53*(6), 375–389.

Calhoun, J. G., Vincent, E. T., Baker, G. R., Butler, P. W., Sinioris, M. E., & Chen, S. L. (2004). Competency identification and modeling in healthcare leadership. *Journal of Health Administration Education, 21*(4), 419–440.

Carr, C. A., & Schott, A. (2002). Differences in evidence-based care in midwifery practice and education. *Journal of Nursing Scholarship, 34*(2), 153–158.

Center for Nursing Leadership (CNL). (1996). *Dimensions of leadership.* Retrieved August 13, 2009, from http://www.cnl.org/ways_of_leading.htm.

Cipriano, P. F. (2008). Improving health care with systems thinking. *American Nurse Today, 3*(9), 6.

Covey, S. R. (1989). *The seven habits of highly effective people.* New York: Simon & Schuster.

Covey, S. R. (2004). *The eighth habit: From effectiveness to greatness.* New York: Simon & Schuster.

Cryer, B., McCraty, R., & Childre, D. (2003, July). Pull the plug on stress. *Harvard Business Review, 81*(7), 102–107.

Davidson, P. L., Griffith, J. R., Sinioris, M., & Carreon, D. (2005). Evidence-based leadership development for improving organizational performance. *Joint Commission Journal on Quality and Patient Safety.* Retrieved April 15, 2010 from http://www.ph.ucla.edu/hs/HS422_Davidson_Griffith_article_W06.pdf

DeSmedt, A., Buyl, R., & Nyssen, M. (2006). Evidence-based practice in primary health care. *Student Health & Technology Information, 124,* 651–656.

Dierckx de Casterlé, B., Willemse, A., Verschueren, M., & Millisen, K. (2008). Impact of clinical leadership development on the clinical leader, nursing team, and care-giving process: A case study. *Journal of Nursing Management, 16*(6), 753–763.

Drucker, P. (2000). Managing knowledge means managing oneself. *Leader to Leader, 16.* Retrieved October 6, 2009, from http://www.leadertoleader.org/knowledgecenter/journal.aspx?Article

Drucker, P. (2004, June). What makes an effective executive. *Harvard Business Review, 82*(6), 58–63.

Eddy, L. L., Doutrich, D., Higgs, Z. R., Spuck, J., Olson, M., & Weinberg, S. (2009). Relevant nursing leadership: An evidence-based programmatic response. *International Journal of Nursing Education Scholarship, 6*(1 Art. 22), 1–17.

Evans, M. (2005). Textbook executive: The skills and knowledge that all healthcare execs need to master can now be found in one big directory. *Modern Healthcare, 35*(37), 6–16.

Everett, L. Q., & Titler, M. G. (2006). Making EBP part of clinical practice: The Iowa model. In R. F. Levin & H. R. Feldman (Eds.), *Teaching evidence-based practice in nursing* (pp. 295–324). New York: Springer.

Exton, R. (2008). The entrepreneur: A new breed of health service leader? *Journal of Health Organization Management, 22*(3), 208–222.

Finstuen, K., & Mangelsdorff, A. D. (2006). Executive competencies in healthcare administration: Preceptors of the Army-Baylor University graduate program. *Journal of Health Administration Education, 23*(2), 199–215.

Gifford, W., Davies, B., Edwards, N., Griffin, P., & Lybanon, V. (2007). Managerial leadership for nurses' use of research evidence: An integrative review of the literature. *Worldviews on Evidence Based Nursing, 4*(3), 126–145.

Gladwell, M. (2008). *Outliers: The story of success.* New York: Little, Brown, & Company.

Goad, T. W. (2002). *Information literacy and workplace performance.* Westport, CT: Quorum Books.

Greene, R. (1998). *The 48 laws of power.* New York: Viking.

Greenleaf, R. K. (1977). *Servant leadership: A journey into the nature of legitimate power and greatness.* New York: Paulist Press.

Greenleaf, R. K. (1998). *Power of servant leadership.* San Francisco: Bennett-Koehler.

Griffith, J. R., Warden, G. L., Neighbors, K., & Shim, B. (2002). A new approach to assessing skill needs of senior managers. *Journal of Health Administration Education, 20*(1), 75–98.

Grossman, S. (2007). Assisting critical care nurses in acquiring leadership skills: Development of a leadership and management competency checklist. *Dimensions of Critical Care Nursing, 26*(2), 57–65.

Guo, K. L. (2009). Core competencies of the entrepreneurial leader in health care organizations. *Health Care Management, 28*(1), 19–29.

Guo, K. L., & Anderson, D. (2005). The new health care paradigm: Roles and competencies of leaders in the service line management. *International Journal of Health Care Quality Assurance Including Leadership in Health Services, 18*(6–7), suppl. xii-xx.

Hall, L. (2004). A palette of desired leadership competencies: Painting the picture for successful regionalization. *Healthcare Management Forum, 17*(3), 18–22.

Hamric, A. B., Spross, J. A., & Hanson, C. M. (2009). *Advanced practice nursing: An integrative approach* (4th ed.). St. Louis, MO: Saunders Elsevier.

Hannes, K., Keys, M., Vermeire, E., Aertgeerts, B., Buntinx, F., & Depoorter, A. M. (2005). Implementing evidence-based medicine in general practice: A focus group based study. *BMC Family Practice, 9*(6), 6–37.

Hay, M. C., Weisner, T. S., Subramanian, S., Duan, N., Niedzinski, E. J., & Kravitz, R. L. (2008). Harnessing experience: Exploring the gap between evidence-based medicine and clinical practice. *Journal of Evaluation in Clinical Practice, 14*(5), 707–713.

Healthcare Leadership Alliance (HLA). (2007). *HLA competency directory user's guide.* Retrieved August 13, 2009, from http://www.healthcareleadershipalliance.org/directory.htm

Heathfield, S. M. (2009). *Leadership vision: Leadership success secrets.* Retrieved July 20, 2009, from http://humanresources.about.com/od/leadership/a/leader_vision.htm

Henning, S. E., & Cohen, F. L. (2008). The competency continuum: Expanding the case manager's skill sets and capabilities. *Professional Case Management, 13*(3), 149–150.

Holloway, R., Nesbit, K., Bordley, D., & Noyes, K. (2004). Teaching and evaluating first and second year medical student's practice of evidence based medicine. *Medical Education, 38*(8), 869–878.

Howatson-Jones, I. (2004). The servant leader. *Nursing Management, 11*(3), 20–24.

Hudak, R. P., Brooke, P. P., Jr., & Finstuen, K. (2000). Identifying management competencies for health care executives: Review of a series of Delphi studies. *Journal of Health Administration Education, 18*(2), 213–243.

Huston, C. (2008). Preparing nurse leaders for 2020. *Journal of Nursing Management, 16,* 905–911.

Hutchinson, A., McIntosh, A., Anderson, J., Gilbert, C., & Field, R. (2003). Developing primary care review criteria from evidence-based guidelines: Coronary heart disease as a model. *British Journal of General Practice, 53*(494), 690–696.

Jennings, B. M., Scalzi, C. C., Rodgers, J. D., 3rd, & Keane, A. (2007). Differentiating nursing leadership and management competencies. *Nursing Outlook, 55*(4), 169–175.

Johnson, S. (2006). *The ghost map: The story of London's most terrifying epidemic—and how it changed science, cities, and the modern world.* New York: Riverhead.

Johnson, S. (2009, September). *The ghost map.* Paper presented to the American Association for the History of Nursing, St. Paul, MN.

Joint Commission on Accreditation of Healthcare Organizations (JCAHO). (2009). *Accreditation programs.* Retrieved September 20, 2009, from http://www.jointcommission.org/AccreditationPrograms/Hospitals/

Kibort, P. M. (2005, November–December). I drank the Kool-Aid—And learned 24 key management lessons. *Physician Executive, 31*(6), 52–55.

Kleinman, C. S. (2003). Leadership roles, competencies, and education: How prepared are our nurse managers? *Journal of Nursing Administration, 33*(9), 451–455.

Kouzes, J. M., & Posner, B. Z. (2007). *The leadership challenge* (4th ed.). San Francisco: Jossey-Bass.

Lubkin, I. M., & Larsen, P. D. (2006). *Chronic illness: Impact interventions* (6th ed.). Sudbury, MA: Jones & Bartlett.

Lucia, A. D., & Lepsinger, R. (1999). *The art and science of competency models: Pinpointing critical success factors in organizations.* San Francisco: Jossey-Bass.

Mackintosh, M. (2006). Transporting critically ill patients: New opportunities for nurses. *Nursing Standard, 20*(36), 46–48.

Mäkelä, M., & Kunnamo, L. (2001). Implementing evidence in Finnish primary care: Use of electronic guidelines in daily practice. *Scandinavian Journal of Primary Health Care, 19*(4), 214–217.

Martin, N. A., & Bloom, J. L. (2003). *Career aspirations and expeditions: Advancing your career in higher education administration.* Champaign, IL: Stipes.

McKenna, M. K., Gartland, M. P., & Pugno, P. A. (2004). Development of physician leadership competencies: perceptions of physician leaders, physician educators and medical students. *Journal of Healthcare Administration Education, 21*(3), 343–354.

McNamara, C. (2009). *Field guide to consulting and organizational development.* Minneapolis, MN: Authenticity Consulting.

Melnyk, B. M. (2005, November). *Leading a change to evidence-based practice through collaborative partnerships.* Paper presented at the 38th Biennial Meeting of Sigma Theta Tau International, Indianapolis, IN.

Melnyk, B. M., & Fineout-Overholt, E. (2005). *Evidence-based practice in nursing and healthcare.* Philadelphia: Lippincott Williams & Wilkins.

Mitroff, I. I., & Denton, E. A. (1999). *A spiritual audit of corporate America: A hard look at spirituality, religion, and values in the workplace.* San Francisco: Jossey-Bass.

Moore, T. (1992). *Care of the soul: A guide for cultivating depth and sacredness in everyday life.* New York: HarperCollins.

Moore, T. (1994). *Soul mates: Honoring the mysteries of love and relationship.* New York: HarperCollins.

Nanus, B. (1992). *Visionary leadership.* San Francisco: Jossey-Bass.

National Defense University (NDU). (n. d.). Leveraging power and politics. *Strategic leadership and decision making.* Retrieved September 15, 2009, from http://www.au.af.mil/au/awc/awcgate/ndu/strat-ldr-dm/pt4ch17.html

Neill, M. W., & Saunders, N. S. (2008). Servant leadership: Enhancing quality of care and staff satisfaction. *Journal of Nursing Administration, 38*(9), 395–400.

Nicklin, W., & Stipich, N. (2005). Enhancing skills for evidence-based healthcare leadership: The executive training for research application (EXTRA) program. *Nursing Leadership, 18*(3), 35–44.

O'Connor, M. (2008). The dimensions of leadership: A foundation for caring competency. *Nursing Administration Quarterly, 21*(1), 21–16.

Patterson, K. (2009). 10 tips from Kerry Patterson. *Lifetips.* Retrieved September 15, 2009, from http://www.lifetips.comexpert-guru/6189-kerry-patterson.html

Patterson, K., Grenny, J., Maxfield, D., McMillan, R., & Switzler, A. (2008). *Influencer: The power to change anything.* New York: McGraw-Hill.

Pfeffer, J. (1992). *Managing with power: Power and influence in organizations.* Boston: Harvard Business School Press.

Philpot, A., Devitt, R., Parr, J., & Nixon, B. (2002). Leadership competency models: Roadmaps to success. *Hospital Quarterly, 6*(1), 42–45.

Ponti, M. A. (2009). Transition from leadership development to succession management. *Nursing Administration Quarterly, 33*(2), 125–141.

Porter-O'Grady, T., & Malloch, K. (2007). *Quantum leadership: A resource for health care innovation* (2nd ed.). Sudbury, MA: Jones & Bartlett.

Porter-O'Grady, T., & Malloch, K. (2008). Beyond myth and magic: The future of evidence-based leadership. *Nursing Administration Quarterly, 32*(3), 176–187.

Quinlan, P. (2006). Teaching evidence-based practice in a hospital setting: Bringing it to the bedside. In R. F. Levin & H. R. Feldman (Eds.), *Teaching evidence-based practice in nursing* (pp. 279–293). New York: Springer.

Råholm, M. B. (2009). Evidence and leadership. *Nursing Administration Quarterly, 33*(2), 168–173.

Ready, D. A. (2002, Summer). How storytelling builds next-generation leaders. *MIT Sloan Management Review, 43*(4), 63–69.

Robbins, C. J., Bradley, F. H., & Spicer, M. (2001). Developing leadership in healthcare administration: A competency assessment tool. *Journal of Healthcare Management, 46*(3), 188–202.

Sackett, D. L., Straus, S. E., Richardson, W. S., Rosenberg, W., & Haynes, R. B. (2000). *Evidence-based medicine: How to practice and teach EBM.* London: Churchill Livingstone.

Sankelo, M., & Akerblad, L. (2008). Nurse entrepreneurs' attitudes to management, their adaptation of the manager's role, and managerial assertiveness. *Journal of Nursing Management, 16*(7), 829–836.

Sankelo, M., & Akerblad, L. (2009). Nurse entrepreneurs' well-being at work and associated factors. *Journal of Clinical Nursing, 18*(22), 3190–3199.

Secretan, L. (2006). *One: The art and practice of the conscious leader.* Caledon, Ontario, Canada: The Secretan Center.

Secretan, L. (2009a). *The Secretan center.* Retrieved September 7, 2009, from http://www.secretan.com.

Secretan, L. (2009b). *The higher ground leadership challenge.* Retrieved September 7, 2009, from http://www.secretan.comaboutus_hgl_challenge_castle.php

Senge, P. (1990). *The fifth discipline: The art and practice of the learning organization.* New York: Doubleday.

Senge, P. (2006). *The fifth discipline: The art and practice of the learning organization* (rev. ed.). New York: Doubleday.

Sherman, R. O., Bishop, M., Eggenberger, T., & Karden, R. (2007). Development of a leadership competency model. *Journal of Nursing Administration, 37*(2), 85–94.

Shewchuk, R. M., O'Connor, S. J., & Fine, D. J. (2005). Building an understanding of the competencies needing for health administration practice. *Journal of Healthcare Management, 50*(1), 32–47.

Shewchuk, R. M., O'Connor, S. J., & Fine, D. J. (2006). Bridging the gap: Academic and practitioner perspectives to identify early career competencies needed in healthcare management. *Journal of Health Administration Education, 23*(4), 367–392.

Shirey, M. R. (2006a). Evidence-based practice: How nurse leaders can facilitate innovation. *Nursing Administration Quarterly, 30*(3), 252–265.

Shirey, M. R. (2006b). Building authentic leadership and enhancing entrepreneurial performance. *Clinical Nurse Specialist, 20*(6), 280–282.

Spallina, J. M. (2002). Clinical program leadership: Skill requirements for contemporary leaders. *Journal of Oncology Management, 11*(3), 24–26.

Spears, L. C. (1995). *Reflections on leadership: How Robert K. Greenleaf's servant leadership influenced today's top management thinkers.* New York: Wiley.

Spencer, L. M., & Spencer, S. M. (1993). *Competence at work: Models for superior performance.* New York: John Wiley & Sons.

Stefl, M. E. (2008). Common competencies for all healthcare managers: The Healthcare Leadership Alliance model. *Journal of Healthcare Management, 53*(6), 360–373.

Stetler, C. B. (2003). Role of the organization in translating research into evidence-based practice. *Outcomes Management, 7*(3), 97–105.

Stichler, J. F. (2006). Skills and competencies for today's nurse executive. *AWHONN Lifelines: The Association of Women's Health, Obstetric and Neonatal Nurses, 10*(3), 255–257.

Stoller, J. K. (2008). Developing physician-leaders: Key competencies and available programs. *Journal of Health Administration Education, 25*(4), 307–328.

Sullivan, E. J. (2004). *Becoming influential: A guide for nurses.* Upper Saddle River, NJ: Pearson/Prentice Hall.

Swearingen, S., & Liberman, A. (2004). Nursing leadership: Serving those who serve others. *Health Care Manager, 23*(2), 100–109.

Thomson O'Brien, M. A., Oxman, A. D., Haynes, R. B., Davis, D. A., Freemantle, N., & Harvey, E. L. (2002). Local opinion leaders: Effects on professional practice and health care outcomes (Cochrane review). *Cochrane Library* (2).

Titler, M. G. (2004). Methods in translation science. *Worldviews on Evidence-Based Nursing, 1*, 38–48.

Titler, M. G., Cullen, L., & Ardery, G. (2002). Evidence-based practice: An administrative perspective. *Reflections of Nursing Leadership, 28*(2), 26–27.

Tracy, C. S., Dantas, G. C., & Upshur, R. E. (2003). Evidence-based medicine in primary care: Qualitative study of family physicians. *BMC Family Practice, 9*(4), 6.

Transformational Leadership. (2009). Retrieved June 18, 2009, from http://changingminds.org/disciplines/leadership/styles/transformation

Traynor, M., Drennan, V., Goodman, C., Mark, A., Davis, K., Peacock, R., et al. (2008). "Nurse entrepreneurs": A case of government rhetoric? *Journal of Health Services Research & Policy, 13*(1), 13–18.

Tumolo, J. (2006). Thinking outside the box: How nontraditional practice is paying off for some NP entrepreneurs. *Advanced Nurse Practitioner, 14*(4), 37–39, 40.

Vance, D., & Larson, E. (2002). Leadership research in business and health care. *Journal of Nursing Scholarship, 34*(2), 165–171.

von Bertalanffy, L. (1968). *General systems theory.* New York: Braziller.

Wear, D. (2008). On outcomes and humility. *Academic Medicine, 83*(7), 625–626.

Wells, W., & Hijna, W. (2009). Developing leadership talent in healthcare organizations. *Healthcare Financial Management, 63*(1), 66–69.

Welton, W. E. (2004). Managing today's complex healthcare business enterprise: Reflections on distinctive requirements of healthcare management education. *Journal of Health Administration Education, 21*(4), 391–418.

Whitehead, K. (2003). The health-promoting nurse s a health policy career expert and entrepreneur. *Nurse Educator Today, 23*(8), 584–592.

Wolf, E. J. (2004, March/April). Spiritual leadership: A new model. *Healthcare Executive, 19*(2), 23–25.

Worral, P. S. (2006). Traveling posters: Communicating on the frontlines. In R. F. Levin & H. R. Feldman (Eds.), *Teaching evidence-based practice in nursing* (pp. 337–346). New York: Springer.

Zemke, R. (1982). Job competencies: Can they help you design better training? *Training, 19*(5), 28–31.

4

Understanding Contexts for Transformational Leadership

> The significant problems we face cannot be solved at the same
> level of thinking we were at when we created them.
>
> — *Albert Einstein*

There are few more important qualities to acquire as a transformational leader than the ability to understand and function effectively within the realities of the context and environment in which you work. Stichler (2006, p. 255, emphasis added) reminded:

> Today's [leader] is more challenged than ever to manage multiple, competing priorities in organizations with ever-diminishing financial and human resources. Accountability for ensuring positive patient outcomes, productivity goals, financial targets, retention quotas, customer and provider satisfaction goals, and other performance metrics demand that the contemporary [leader] possess and demonstrate well-developed leadership skills and organizational management competencies . . . [and] *excel in developing a culture and work environment that fosters professional models of care*, evidence-based practice, interdisciplinary and collaborative practice, professional autonomy and, quality nursing leadership.

National and international calls continue to go forward for healthcare system reform. Such calls are grounded in current ongoing uncertainty, mandates for change, and cries for transformation (Hamrick, Spross, & Hanson, 2009). The new jargon is all too familiar: chaos, quantum leadership, complexity, change, aggregates, and populations. What do these mean for the next generation of leaders?

They all refer to context. In the past, context of care was simple. It referred to *settings*, like hospital, clinic, or home—all with fairly simple linear and hierarchical models for care of the sick. Context as mere setting did not matter so much then to the role of leader. Now, and for the foreseeable future, context is everything. Not only is any single setting more complicated than in the past, but also, the very nature of context itself is more complex. Context is the circumstance of your work. It refers to the multifaceted climate, background, domain, and terrain of service. It is more than setting or environment, although it includes those. It comprises all systemic, physical, social, emotional, professional, informal, and formal aspects of service. Context of care for leadership has become as challenging as any aspect of leadership itself.

Beyond physical, social, or professional context, the context of our very thinking is challenged. The easy things have been done. All problems are more complex. Our old ways of thinking will not bring us to solutions. We must have the courage to think in new ways.

CHAOS, QUANTA, AND COMPLEXITY IN HEALTHCARE SYSTEMS

Nearly every discussion of current issues and contexts in health care begins with mention of chaos, quantum theory, or complexity. Complexity has become the introduction, the theoretical explanation, and the metaphor for the current and future state of health care. Consequently, chaos theory and complex adaptive systems are discussed in so many situations that they have become the catch phrases of the industry, with little general agreement on definitions and even less precision of application. Indeed, Paley (2007) critically pointed to references on complex systems in healthcare literature in every area from dentistry to holistic philosophy. Paley (2007, p. 234) further chastised writers in health care literature for misuse and error in what he called "the over-hasty adoption of complexity ideas" as "essentially just one more intellectual fad" (McKelvey, 1999; Stacey, Griffin, & Shaw, 2000). It is true that it has become fashionable to make "expansive claims" and "grand gestures" (Paley, 2007, pp. 233, 240) regarding chaos, complexity, and health care. Nevertheless, the perspective continues to prevail, and it is hard to argue that chaos and complexity have no real influence. Thus, it is helpful for any leader to have a basic awareness of such approaches to thinking about and practicing in a new world of health care.

Space is not adequate in this text to provide the quick-and-easy comprehensive discourse in chaos and complexity theory often desired by the emerging leader. The concepts cross a wide range of disciplines in their meanings and applications. Many of the ideas are abstract and perhaps even poetic. They have been applied to areas as divergent as biology and art. Nevertheless, the complexity of the very concepts and theories of complexity should not intimidate you as a leader. These are areas that should be studied from a range of authors and perspectives. Further, application of such theories to your daily practice as a leader can be daunting. Precisely because they are often discussed in areas far distant from health care provides an excellent opportunity for learning and practice for innovation in thinking and leading.

Chaos, Quanta, and Complexity Theory

Chaos theory arose in the 1960s from biology and physics. Meteorologist Lorenz discovered that chaotic systems in weather forecasting appeared to be random, but actually eventually emerged as patterns. In other words, underlying natural phenomena that appear disordered, confused, or chaotic are actually processes of emerging order.

Quantum theory comes from the discipline of physics as a set of principles that describe reality at the most fundamental level of the atom. The word *quantum* refers to a discrete unit (or "amount," as the word actually means) assigned to certain physical quantities, "such as the energy of an atom at rest" or discrete "energy packets" of waves

(Quantum Mechanics, 2009). In a most simplified sense, the idea of quantum refers to a kind of fluidity of the particles of reality such that the state or velocity of the particles, or fundamental units, cannot be determined with certainty (Capra, 1982, 1996). Thus, the movement and relationships among the units are more significant than the individual nature of any particular particle. Capra (1982, p. 81) mused "As we penetrate into matter, nature does not show us any isolated basic building blocks, but rather appears as a complicated web or relations between various parts of a unified whole." Thus, quantum theory provides a metaphor for the integrated complex relationships among the numerous and varied elements of health care, as opposed to a focus on either the characteristics of any single element or the hierarchical linear building of individual parts. Quantum theory requires us to let go of traditional notions of *building blocks* of systems and instead to adopt a perspective of ever-changing fluid integration of units as parts of a whole. Such a change of paradigm requires a new courageous leadership.

When I think of this change of perspective, I am reminded of how I was taught algebra. Back in the 1960s and 1970s, my school used the then innovative approach of programmed learning. Students were put out to learn independently. We were secluded into individual study carrels, or small desks surrounded on three sides by walls. Our only companion in that isolated cell was a thick book that contained one principle or problem per page, with instructions to complete page 1, which led to page 2, and so on. Learning was assumed to be built one principle at a time—one page at a time—block by block, until we learned the entire body of basic algebra. Guess what. It did not work! Few students today would tolerate such an isolated way of learning. Even algebra is not a linear, step-by-step body of knowledge. Furthermore, even as concrete as our learning needs were, we did not retain concepts learned only one page at a time without exposure to some human to describe relationships, some conceptual network in which to capture and integrate the new knowledge and skills, but most of all without some context. Even to learn something as discrete as algebra requires an understanding of basic principles as they relate to a larger web of relationships among other elements of mathematics. Although study carrels may still be found lurking in libraries and schools, they are now most often computer stations where students learn by access to a variety of interrelated modes and methods.

Porter-O'Grady and Malloch (2007, p. 2) referred to "quantum leadership" as "leading in a fluid world" where "linear thinking will be replaced by relational and whole systems thinking . . . structure is about wholes, not parts . . . the value of work is a function of the outcome, not the process . . . new rules will apply . . . [and] the context [of] leadership . . . will change" (pp. 13–18). They further proposed that quantum theory has changed our view of organizations and of life itself to reveal the following quantum characteristics: "multifocal . . . nonlinear structures, focus on relatedness, multi-systems scientific processes, center-out decision making, complexity-based models of design, and value-driven action" (p. 20).

Complexity science is related to chaos theory and quantum perspectives. Complexity science is applicable in biology, physics, mathematics, economics, sociology, management, and the healthcare disciplines. It examines the "behavior and dynamics of systems which are composed of many interacting elements" and searches "the principles and processes that explain how order and change emerge in these systems" (Lindberg, 2009, p. 3). Complexity science applies to living systems, examining the "unpredictable, disorderly, nonlinear, and uncontrollable ways that living systems actually behave" (Burns, 2001; Zimmerman, Lindberg, & Plsek, 1998). According to chaos theory, complex systems are integrated and support "emergence through novel behavior" (Pesut, 2008c, p. 123).

Complexity science focuses on the interacting elements of systems, seeking to identify principles and processes that explain how order emerges from change within the systems. Change is desirable and a natural way of being. Interacting elements of chaos may appear to be without order but actually occur in patterns, although not predictable in traditional ways of thinking. Key principles are diversity, emergence, self-organization, embeddedness, distributed control, the coexistence of order and disorder, nonlinearity, and inability to predict in traditional ways of thinking (Lindberg, 2009). Self-organization is the inclination of the organization to generate new patterns and structures, and order emerges from such patterns of relationships (Stroebel et al., 2005). According to complexity science, small changes can make enormous impact; thus, the poetic "butterfly effect" was coined, that the fluttering of the butterfly's wings on one side of the world may set off a tornado on the other side (Gleick, 1987; Lorenz, 1993).

Theory of Complex Adaptive Systems

The theory of complex adaptive systems, as one aspect of complexity science, adds a dimension called "the edge of chaos, which lies between stability and chaos and where creativity thrives" (Penprase & Norris, 2005, p. 128). Burns (2001, p. 475) described this edge as the area where "there is not enough stability to have repetition or predictability; but not enough instability to create anarchy." Although complex adaptive systems appear to be unpredictable, order is inherent and emerges in change and within complexity.

Cilliers (1998, pp. 3–5) and Holden (2005, p. 654) outlined the specific characteristics of a complex adaptive system: many elements that interact in a dynamic way exchanging information; rich, nonlinear interactions with a limited range; open systems with enhancing or detracting feedback loops; continual change and constant flow of energy where there is no equilibrium; embedding in a context of history, where no single element can control or comprehend the whole and "systems are embedded within other systems" and continue to coevolve (Plsek & Greenhalgh, 2001, p. 626). Complexity is the result of patterns of interactions.

A complex adaptive system is an "open, dynamic and flexible network that is considered complex due to its composition of numerous interconnected, semi-autonomous competing and collaborating members" (Indianapolis Discovery Network for Dementia, n.d.). It is "a collection of individual agents with freedom to act in ways that are not always totally predictable, and whose actions are interconnected so that one agent's actions change the context for other agents" (Plsek & Greenhalgh, 2001, p. 625). It can be seen as a large network of agents and interactions. The behavior and nature of the entire system emerge from the interaction among the agents.

Many professionals refer to various aspects of health care as complex adaptive systems (Miller, Crabtree, McDaniel, & Stange, 1998), although the term *healthcare system* has a variety of meanings itself. It may refer to the entire health care industry, including structures, processes, and personnel, or it may refer to a single organization or system within an organization. Some may argue that although health care is complicated, it may not be the best example of a complex adaptive system. A complex adaptive system is characterized by flexibility and patterns of emerging change as opposed to predetermined change based on hierarchical or central control. Any clinician can enumerate a long list of areas in health care that persist in the linear, hierarchical paradigm. Nevertheless, quanta, chaos, and complexity offer models to frame the issues in the current realities of health care toward a hopeful transformation to a better future. Indeed, some of the current problems of health care may relate to the challenging transition from traditional thinking to a complexity perspective.

There are several key characteristics of complex systems. The first is emergence, or the idea that behaviors, patterns, and order emerge as a result of nonlinear patterns of relationships and interactions among the elements or units of the organization. Second, relationships are short range, or interchanged from within a unit or near neighbors in a matrix of networks within the larger whole. The units, or parts, cannot contain, determine, or control the whole. Relationships are nonlinear, seldom cause-and-effect, and contain feedback loops. Feedback may be damping (negative) or amplifying (positive), and a small stimulus may have a large powerful effect or none at all. Because complex systems are open, energy and information constantly cross boundaries and create constant change (Seel, 2008; Stroebel et al., 2005). Coevolution is a "process of mutual transformation" for both smaller units and the larger organizational environment (Stroebel et al., 2005).

The "fitness landscape" is how an organization fits within an independent/dependent interaction with other agents, units, or organizations. Penprase and Norris (2005, p. 128) explained within the complexity of a hospital environment:

> As one unit makes changes, other nursing units are positively or negatively affected depending upon how each unit elects to adapt to that change. Because change cannot occur without its effects rippling into other competing areas or units, both competition and coevoluation work together, as characterized by dynamic equilibrium and causing continuous changes in outcomes (Seel, 2008). Thus, each nursing unit is dependent on another nursing unit as each hospital is dependent on the actions of other hospitals and must adapt to change caused by internal and external factors in order to survive.

Such interactions among various groups of people or units form feedback loops that move the organization toward its fitness landscape. It is important to understand that such feedback loops are not conceptualized in the same way as feedback loops of traditional systems or leadership theories, where such loops serve to support homeostasis. Rather, feedback loops in complexity theory support communication within the larger organization, feeding new information and creative thinking throughout the organization (Penprase & Norris, 2005). Think of them as webs of informal communication networks interconnected across and within all levels of the organization.

Another important concept is "attractors." Attractors are values, ideas, activities, issues, plans, or other entities to which individuals or groups are naturally drawn. Attractors serve to "stabilize" or provide order from the evolving networks and guide or govern behavior. They serve as an institutional memory and place of information processing. Attractors may be stable or unstable, hidden or overt (Kaufman, 1995; Penprase & Norris, 2005; Walls & McDaniel, 1999).

The very language of complexity theories can be intimidating: chaos, unpredictability, and change as desirable. Such ideas set fear inside traditional clinicians and leaders accustomed to predictable and controlled systems where change initiatives are based on top-down implementation of prescribed protocols or "best practices." For example, one nurse leader framed alarm about hospital errors in a context of complexity theory as she warned, "Because health care is a . . . complex adaptive system, it's more prone to accidents. . . . By definition, a complex system has interacting components that work in both expected and unexpected ways. If one component fails, all downstream components may fail . . . we can't predict how each component will respond. . . . In our healthcare system, humans contribute to this element of unpredictability, creating the possibility of error or innovation" (Cipriano, 2008, p. 6). The very image of "downstream" reflects linear, unidirectional thinking. Leaders of the next generation will embrace complexity and promote positive emergence. Complexity and chaos viewpoints promote the opportunity for integrated independent autonomy and action to prevent (rather than cause) error onsite in real time. Complexity models may also promote accountability for more effective error prevention. We must move beyond the idea that complexity promotes error. Inherent in the challenges of complexity are opportunities for creativity and power to make critical immediate decisions and actions that change lives for the better. But it requires personal integrity, accountability, commitment, and creative leadership.

The concepts and images of complex adaptive systems may inspire or confuse the leader dealing with real life-and-death issues on a daily basis. Specific application can be challenging. Penprase and Norris (2005) provided a specific example of the application of complex adaptive systems theory to nursing leadership.

A vice president for nursing was frustrated at attempts to implement a new community outreach program:

> She became frustrated with her staff's lack of ability to move the nursing department forward to adopt a community outreach program that was needed within their hospital system. In response, she disbanded previous committees that had been formed to develop and implement strategies for the new community outreach program and instead implemented a complex adaptive system framework for institutional change. She promoted her vision of what she hoped for the new community outreach program, stressing its importance to the community and the hospital. In doing so, she gave the staff three basic and simple rules to follow: any nurse could take up to a half-day a week to undertake a community health interaction that she cared about; nothing could be done that was illegal; and nurses could take funds needed to support the initiative from the nursing department's outreach budget. Within a short time, 27 projects had been initiated, some more successful than others, but all that helped create a very successful community outreach program. Through a clear vision, [a few simple rules and guidelines] . . . and the freedom to spontaneously regroup into similar interests, results were quickly obtained. (Penprase & Norris, 2005, p. 131)

Margaret Wheatley (2007) summarized what she called "the real world" from a complexity perspective:

> It is a world of interconnected networks, where slight disturbances in one part of the system create major impacts far from where they originate. In this highly sensitive system, the most minute actions can blow up into massive disruptions and chaos. But it is also a world that seeks order. When chaos erupts, it not only disintegrates the current structure, it also creates the conditions for a new order to emerge. Change always involves a dark descent into meaninglessness where everything falls apart. Yet if this

period of dissolution is used to create new meaning, then chaos gives way to the emergence of new order.

This is a world that knows how to organize itself without command and control or charisma.

Such perspectives provide images for leadership that border on the poetic. They offer an invitation for the most adventurous and courageous actions to lead others into the next century of health care where systems truly offer hope and healing.

Chaos, Quanta, and Complexity as Metaphors for Health Care

It is important to distinguish between complexity theories that may explain a variety of life phenomena and the growing reality that health care itself is complex and complicated. Regardless of the purist cautions on the misuse of the science of complexity to describe health care, it serves as a useful model. It provides leaders with a new viewpoint and strategy to lead in such times of real chaos, complexity, and change. It provides an alternate metaphorical lens to the industrial perspective of the "well-oiled machine" with replaceable parts and predictable behaviors based on financial incentives, regulation, and rigid specific protocols.

Nevertheless, the wise leader is not the proselyte of a singular trend, style, or neo-philosophy. Although proponents of complexity theory set up industrial, mechanistic models for target practice, there may well be some places where the machine-like linear phenomena are effective. Burns (2001) cautioned that wise leaders recognize and distinguish when chaos works, as in creating innovative ideas, and when mechanism works, as in emergency medical procedures or other highly technical, necessary, and linear or prescribed tasks. Effective leaders must alternate mechanistic leadership activities with quantum moves. Nevertheless, Burns reminded, "attempting to predict, direct, and control the chaotic healthcare environment is futile" (2001, p. 476). One of the major challenges of our time is that mechanical mental models are so prevalent and institutional cultures so ingrained that it is difficult for leaders to manage in any other ways. Healthcare organizations, in particular, are built on a strong traditional foundation of defined roles and lines of authority, planning, predicting, and forecasting. Evolving self-organization can be a foreign, frightening proposition. When organizations are not able to adapt to complexity, attempts at change and growth are thwarted (Morgan, 2001). Leadership requires wisdom and balance.

Lindberg, Herzog, Merry, and Goldstein (1998) cautioned that institutions do not need to adopt wholesale, grand-scale chaos and complexity, but might create specific areas for exploration and self-organization. Even Paley (2007, p. 240) suggested, in contrast to "overambitious metaphors" in healthcare literature, to employ complexity "piecemeal," using small, modest steps.

The role of the leader is to create a vision, "decipher trends," support confidence in change, and help the unit or organization to sustain its identity, purpose, and focus (Penprase & Norris, 2005, p. 131). Knowledge of theory and principles as well as planning is important, "but beyond that our best strategy is to get out of the way and let the system seek its own level" (Marion, 1999, p. 267; Penprase & Norris, 2005). In complexity theory, the need for knowledge is less about gaining information and more about building a platform for more learning. (Stroebel et al., 2005). We are reminded that "nurse leaders need to anticipate and invite surprise rather than to fear it." We need to learn to live with unpredictability (Penprase & Norris, 2005, p. 131). It is the leader's role to "pay more attention to the quality of the relationships among agents than to the quality of the individual agents . . . and be sensitive to the fact that relationships are non-linear and dynamic, and therefore, often result in high levels of surprise and un- certainty." Leaders shift from a focus on a series of single events or processes toward a sensitivity to "patterns, interrelated processes, and relationships" (Stroebel et al., 2005, pp. 439–440).

The effective leader need not be the expert on complexity theory but rather must iden- tify what works to navigate the complex terrain of health care. The effective leader bal- ances vision with pragmatism; a well-informed sensitivity and courage help. Benson (2005, p. 6) suggested that the "undetected flap of multiple butterfly wings within hun- dreds of processes and sub-processes has the capacity to either adversely or positively affect quality, safety, and satisfaction." She advised to watch for the butterfly wings and the "attractors," such as values, behaviors, or other entities or forces that create margins or boundaries from which patterns may emerge. Wheatley (1999) called them pivotal events, process steps, or people. Sometimes, beginning in simple small ways is best for groups of people to self-organize to identify a new approach, to solve a mystery, or to discover the solution to a long-term problem. With an expanded repertoire of thinking, watch for opportunities for effective application of complexity perspectives. Changing to a new outlook simply for the sake of change is ultimately not helpful.

DEALING WITH CONTINUAL CHANGE

Living and Working in Change

An understanding of complexity theory can provide a foundation for learning how to deal with change. Regardless of the theoretical perspective, continual change is a real- ity of life. Well-known leadership scholar John Kotter is thought to have said, "While management is about coping with complexity, leadership is about coping with change" (Hill, 2003, p. 5). Ellis (2003) observed that change is accelerating. Bolman and Deal (1991) warned that change is about survival. It is a necessary way of life for any group, organi- zation, or leader to succeed in contexts of uncertainty and complexity. Effective change affects the culture, structure, and processes in an organization. Change can be planned or unplanned, tactical or strategic, evolutionary or revolutionary.

Modern human societies have developed across several distinct ages. The transitions, or change, between each era have been marked with turmoil. Between each age is a mix of thrill and concern, excitement and fear, energy and resistance, prophets and doom- sayers. And there is always some chaos. Likely, there was strife as villages were born as farming communities moving from a hunter-gatherer age to the agricultural age. Harder still were the disruption of family life and the eruption of whole new diseases, public health issues, and new economic paradigms when society moved from the farm to the industrial age. We learned how to live and love the industrial age with its rules, its linear thinking, and its focus on efficiency and production. We also became comfortable as a society with hierarchical leadership and regulation of our lives. There were few sources for answers or information: the person in charge, an expert sage, or a book in a library. There were few choices of products and, usually, no choices for public services. We were simply happy to have dependable public services. We are now in the midst of transition from the industrial age to the information/technology age. All the rules have changed. Whatever was familiar is foreign. Sources of information are vast and highly accessible and the range of choices has exploded. Consider how many choices and forms there are for a telephone, for example. Just over a decade ago, who would have thought you might listen to music, access e-mail, or even watch a movie on your telephone! We have more avenues for more information than any individual can accommodate.

Drucker (2000, p. 8) predicted:

> In a few hundred years, when the history of our time is written from a long-term perspective, it is likely that the most important event historians will see is not technology, not the internet, not e-commerce. It is an unprecedented change in the human condition. For the first time— literally—substantial and rapidly growing numbers of people have choices. For the first time, they will have to manage themselves. And society is totally unprepared for it.

Never have so many had access to so much. We are well into an information age. But it will not be the last call for change. Will the next era be one of wisdom?

Porter-O'Grady and Malloch (2007, p. 9) described a universal cycle of transformation in the transitional period of chaos, driven by sociopolitical, economic, and technical forces toward our adaptation from the industrial age to the age of technology. They pointed to "universal dynamics of transformation": loss, chaos, new work, new rules, new scripts. We are beginning to recognize that at the moment we become comfortable, another age will emerge.

Supporting Others in Change

Recent fiscal realities have brought unforeseen change to nursing employment, practice, and leadership. Like other major industries, hospitals and some other healthcare facilities have engaged in restructuring to manage costs. For the first time in recent memory, positions in nursing have decreased in abundance. One study in Canada demonstrated that hospital restructuring imposed significant negative physical and emotional health effects on nurses. The same study also showed effects related to nursing leadership styles. Nurses who worked for "resonant," or emotionally intelligent, leaders reported positive health and opportunities to provide quality patient care, whereas nurses who worked for "dissonant" leaders reported greater negative effects of hospital restructuring. The study launched a theory that resonant leaders "invest energy into collaborative relationships with nurses, thereby positively influencing health and well-being, and, ultimately, outcomes for patients" (Cummings, 2006, p. 321). Thus, the leader who supports workers through change makes all the difference for quality patient care and worker satisfaction.

Remember when you invite others to engage in change, a light heart helps. Engage in fulfilling, fun, and meaningful activities toward the goals of change. Acknowledge the dragons and monsters and other scary unknowns lurking out there in change. Provide resources and support to colleagues. Identify what they—and you—are willing to do. Sort what may be kept and what must go, and be sure that all workers are aligned for the change (Duck, 2001). Ensure some protection from "change fatigue" that can result from continuing, "relentless" change where workers have little input or can lose trust (Reineck, 2007, p. 388).

Leading Change

Change means to transform or to become something different. Some may argue a distinction between managing change, called "more science than art," and leading change as "more art than science" (Bruhn, 2004, p. 132; MacPhee, 2007). Bruhn (2004) described managing change as efforts to maintain stability and contain the effects of unwanted or unexpected change. But to lead change is to generate and mobilize resources toward innovation and improvement. Change is described in terms of first-order and second-order change. First-order change is an adjustment within an existing structure, doing more or less of something, and is reversible. Second-order change, on the other hand, is transformational. It requires new ways of perceiving and doing things, new learning, and is irreversible. The rules are different in second-order change. Such change requires new learning and creates a new story (National Academy for Academic Leadership, 2009; Pesut, 2008a). Pesut (2008a) further explained that problem-oriented change looks at what is wrong or why and how are we limited by the problem. Whereas an appreciative approach directs change toward identifying what is good, what is already working, what is desired, and what resources exist to achieve the desired result. Planned change often emerges from review of the meaning and relevancy of the organizational mission statement, from facing new systems or technology, from recognition of the need for new ways of decision making, practice, and policies.

Change agents lead and support others in change by creating environments that promote desired change. They use their power to support and influence others toward change. Effective leaders are change agents. Change agents must be:

> Trustworthy, reliable, honest, competent, and credible. . . . They must possess persuasion, negotiation, and effective listening skills. . . . [They] embody leadership through demonstration of a strong work ethic supported by enthusiasm and respect for individual differences. They have the ability to think conceptually and organize thoughts logically as well as the skill to plan and execute activities and plans. They have good judgment and strong communication skills and are able to coach and facilitate others. . . . [Change management requires] visioning, planning, implementing, reviewing, and learning. (Pesut, 2008b, pp. 103–104)

The success of follower engagement in implementing change is highly related to the style and support of the leader. One study confirmed that transformational leadership was more strongly related to follower's commitment to change than even to change-specific management practices, especially when the change had specific personal implications (Herold, Fedor, Caldwell, & Liu, 2008). In environments of change, effective leaders are early adapters of innovation. They are able to see change as opportunities to learn and improve. They are optimistic and adaptable (Rogers, 1995). MacPhee (2007, p. 406) observed that "Change is more effective when it is framed as a pulling strategy; pulling people or attracting them toward promising possibilities rather than pushing or pressuring to move away from negative conditions" (Eisenbach, Watson, & Rajinandini, 1999).

"The illiterate of the 21st century will not be those who cannot read and write, but those who cannot learn, unlearn, and relearn" is the well-known message attributed to Alvin Toffler. Wheatley (Boyce, 2008, p. 104; Wheatley & Frieze, n.d.) further declared that effective "change never happens as a result of top-down, preconceived strategic plans. . . . Change begins as local actions spring up simultaneously in many different areas." We have learned that "the world doesn't change one person at a time. It changes as networks of relationships form among people who discover they have a common cause and vision of what's possible. . . . Community is the answer." Thus, the traditional notion of building or gathering a critical mass is less important than building networks. Then as local networks multiply and become communities of practice, new systems emerge and change happens. Leaders do not hand down mandates for change. Instead, they wisely identify needs or directions on the horizon and they support, encourage, and feed local inclinations and movements toward change.

Nevertheless, leaders in health care are often required by administrative mandate to implement change. Important steps to encourage and promote local commitment to change include creating a vision, expanding the target audience and broadening the power base to assure maximum engagement, keeping open communication with all areas of the organization, creating a sense of urgency, and managing the processes for successful change. The leader must be committed, have the power and resources to make it happen, and "clearly support the change through everyday behaviors, communication, and execution management" (National Defense University, n.d.).

Several experts recommend specific tools to lead change. MacPhee (2007) reminded to first return to your vision and mission statement. Begin by including all involved in the change to review the mission and examine personal values related to the mission and the organization. Next, renew confidence and trust by pre-planning and team building. Identify critical success factors and draw from your strategic planning to renew a SWOT analysis (strengths, weaknesses, opportunities, and threats). Identify the individual styles and needs of stakeholders and team members. Invest in team building and psychological preparation. Develop a specific plan for the change project including transition monitoring. Finally, celebrate the success of the change implementation. Of course, all of these steps are based on the assumption that the change is manageable in an appropriate time period for planning. Often, in today's world, change happens much more quickly. Still, the wise leader will review the steps and be nimble in integrating and monitoring team response and activities.

Powerful principles of leading change are reflected in Kotter's (1995, p. 61) well-known eight steps for organizational transformation:

1. Establish a sense of urgency.
2. Form a powerful guiding coalition.
3. Create a vision.
4. Communicate the vision.
5. Empower others to act on that vision.
6. Plan for and create short-term wins.
7. Consolidate improvements and produce more change.
8. Institutionalize new approaches.

Change can happen through power, by empowering others to engage and contribute to the change. It can happen through reason by appealing to logic and rationale or by education and re-education to provide knowledge and skills. Change also happens by altering structures and processes. Behavioral approaches are used to change work by developing new communication or collaboration patterns (Reineck, 2007). The leader must identify which approach is the most appropriate. For example, if workers already *know* information or skills, but feel powerless to make decisions, then development of education or training programs will not produce desired changes. Rather, workers may need more independence, autonomy, and accountability in decision making.

Change is a journey taken together with those with whom you work. Each change process is unique. And it is important to remember that even as nimble as your organization may be, change usually takes longer than you expect.

The effective leader is well aware that not all organizations are necessarily ready for or even need immediate transformation at any given moment. Sometimes, resistance to change can be so strong as to defeat even the most charismatic leader. Even if it is your perception that immediate change is needed, particularly in a new role, take some time for assessment—be the chief listening officer for awhile. Sometimes, no action is better than the full court press, at least for assessment. A sensitive systems thinker, especially in a new position, may be well advised to take time to simply watch. It is often wise to watch and wait.

Change and Reflective Adaptation

The process of reflective adaptation is a helpful method to conceptualize and facilitate local change. Although complexity and emergent change may be attractive and exciting for the new transformational leader, some planning, strategy, and a place for reflection must accompany such change initiatives. Five guiding principles support a successful, reflective adaptation processes:

1. Vision, mission, and shared values are fundamental in guiding ongoing change processes in a complex adaptive system.
2. Creating time and space for learning and reflection is necessary for complex adaptive system to adapt to and plan change.
3. Tension and discomfort are essential and normal during complex adaptive systems change.
4. Improvement teams should include a variety of system's agents with different perspectives of the system and its environment.
5. System change requires supportive leadership that is actively involved in the change process, ensuring full participation from all members and protecting time for reflection. (Indianapolis Discovery Network for Dementia, n.d.; Stroebel et al., 2005)

Using the reflective adaptive process, the leader models "reflection-action" cycles and encourages team members to reflect on change and learning. The leader guides the team to strengthen relationships and improve self-organization processes, provides images of adapting processes rather than a sole focus on outcomes, and facilitates the team in creating new "stories" or different ways to perceive, understand, and work in new conceptual environments (Stroebel et al., 2005, p. 442). The sensitive leader, even in the midst of chaos, plans, reflects, and allows the group involved in change to plan, practice change, and reflect on learning from the experience.

Change as a Personal Challenge for the Leader

Most leadership texts address change as something that leaders are not only involved in but also encourage and manage. Few experts acknowledge the challenge of living with continual change for leaders themselves. Change can invoke feelings of incompetence, loss of power, or loss of confidence. It can create confusion, alter the clarity and stability of roles and relationships, and provoke feelings of loss (National Defense University, n.d.). Wheatley (2009, p. 81) described a state of "groundlessness," when nothing seems to be working. She reminded, "Groundlessness is a frightening place . . . , at least at first, but as the old culture turns to mush, we would feel stronger if we stopped searching for ground, if we sought only to locate ourselves in the present and do our work from *here*."

It is important to manage your own time and stress. Identify a confidant who will support you through the challenges of your work. That person can help you to recognize the effects of your own nature on others during the change process. Stand strong to your own values and maintain the image of your change model firm in your mind, recognizing that your image likely will not be exactly what eventually evolves. Resist the temptation to either overcontrol or "do the work yourself." Allow others to put their own mark on the initiative while you ensure that the change activities support the mission of the organization. Identify and share early successes. Remember that you are changing processes or products, not people or personalities. Build on strengths where you can. Build in accountabilities. Identify opportunities for learning for everyone and celebrate accomplishments along the way.

Facing the uncertainty of change is a personal challenge, particularly if you are in charge of the lives and work of others. Realities in health care sometimes bring mandates for change and the requirement for you as a leader to move it forward. Although the temptation may be to resist or stall, often, the best way to find a sense of power or security is to simply step forward and engage yourself and others in change processes. Porter-O'Grady (2003, p. 59) proposed that "the greatest tragedy . . . is the nurse's failure to engage the demand for change in clinical practice at the right time thereby leaving nurses to simply react to these demands too long after their emergence." Clinical leaders must develop a sense of timing and a willingness to engage in the rhythm of change processes. It requires anticipation, responsiveness, nimble action, and the willingness to lead others into a new reality. You can become the model of change for others and, thereby, can communicate the invitation and urgency for transformation.

One of the most critical, and least discussed, aspects of change leadership is the fundamental principle of trust. Such trust is earned only by consistent ethical behavior and clearly defined values. Regardless of our rhetoric on embracing complexity and relishing change as a way of life, usually, change is difficult for people to accept. Subordinates often fear that change will "happen" to them, and there is sometimes an uneasy expectation that change will threaten control, autonomy, habit, or comfort. The wise leader will be honest and transparent. He or she loves the truth, the work, and colleagues above personal delight in innovation. Furthermore, the successful leader will remember that "*truth* is more important during periods of change and uncertainty than good news" (Rogerson, n.d.). Such a leader will always consider perceptions and the dynamics of human relationships when launching change. Real change will happen only when each individual makes the decision to implement the change. If people trust you as the leader, and you share a clear direction and vision and extends meaningful opportunity for input and contribution into the change planning and processes, followers will help to define the most effective path to change and improve quality as a matter of their own personal integrity and commitment to the mission of the organization and the work.

THE LARGER WORLD OF PRACTICE: DRAWING FROM ALL OF THE EXPERTS

Effective change does not happen within the purview of a solitary leader. In the position of leader, you have the freedom and opportunity to network with experts from all disciplines. The world of leadership in healthcare practice is wide. The effective leader learns the language, reads the literature, and becomes interested and informed about the inside view of a vast variety of disciplines, both within and outside health care.

Referring to the words of Nohria, Joyce, and Roverson (2003), Kibort (2004, p. 12) advised, "Build and maintain a fast, flexible flat organization. Trim every possible vestige of unnecessary bureaucracy . . . rules and regulations and outdated formalities." Successful organizations owe their success to the "dedication and inventiveness" of their people. At the end of the day, our progress and success depend on each other—each other as peers, colleagues, subordinates, and strangers. We are all explorers in the new world of the future. We must develop our own areas of expertise, respect the expertise of others, and acknowledge where we must come together when none of us has the answer. Wheatley reflected (2006):

> The more I contemplate these times, when we truly are giving birth to a new world view, the more I realize that our culture has to take this journey through chaos. The old ways are dissolving, and the new is only beginning to show itself. . . . We need to realize that no single person . . . has the answer. . . . We need to realize that we must inquire together to find the new. We need to turn to one another as our best hope for inventing and discovering the worlds we are seeking . . . in this voyage to a new world, you and I have to make it up as we go along, not because we lack skills or expertise, but because this is the nature of reality . . .
>
> The answer is, together. We need each other differently now. We cannot hide behind any old boundaries or hold onto the belief that we can make it on our own. We need each other to test our ideas, to share what we're learning, to help us see in new ways, to listen to our stories. We need each other to forgive us when we fail, to trust us with their dreams, to offer their hope when we've lost our own. . . . After all is said and done, we have the gift of each other. We have each other's curiosity, wisdom, and courage.

In the context of complex adaptive systems, do not confine your thinking to working only with people you know inside the organization or even by the usual professional networking. Furthermore, do not be limited to collaboration only with healthcare professionals. One of the delights of being a leader is the ability to invite collegiality with a broad range of professional friends. It is amazing how people respond when you simply introduce yourself and ask them to help. In this age of Web sites and e-mail, when you admire the work of an expert, do not be afraid to send off a note or make a call. Be prepared, respectful and gracious, and specific in your need.

Think about including experts in business, politics, anthropology, geography, languages, and even the arts as you build your personal style and repertoire to lead the next generation. Read the works of other disciplines, including those of current great minds. Think about how their thoughts might contribute to your work. Imagine how your world might expand and how others will benefit from your renaissance approach to healthcare leadership. Among the most inspiring mentors in my own experiences in healthcare leadership have been a lawyer, a development officer, a musician, and a professor of Italian.

Drucker (2000) also suggested volunteering in a nonprofit organization where you have responsibility, see results, and learn the organizational values. There, you discover your strengths and skills, and you develop relationships that become treasures to your own organization and to your development as a person and leader.

There is a growing global movement toward convening communities of practice. Wheatley (2007) pointed to such communities as sources of emergence, or large-scale change toward important solutions and innovations in a variety of disciplines. The idea of a community of practice is thought to have originated with cognitive anthropologists Jean Lave and Etienne Wenger (Lave & Wenger, 1991) and has developed throughout a variety of disciplines and settings (Wenger, 1998, 2006; Wenger, McDermott, & Snyder, 2002; Wenger & Snyder, 2000). Communities of practice are self-organized in an emergent method by groups of people in similar endeavors in a process of collective learning. They are not support groups, social groups, or professional organizations, but networks of people with similar commitment, competence, and practice in a specific domain. Note that domain may not be the same as professional discipline. Indeed, the domain of interest may cross disciplines. They share ideas, resources, skills, information, and stories related to the specific shared area. In health care, they may provide a foundation for practice-based evidence (McDonald, 2007). Other examples may include as educators working on similar issues, engineers trying to solve similar problems, or new healthcare managers sharing best practices. As these separate local networks grow, they become a "system of influence" and can exert a powerful influence toward cultural shifts toward positive change (Wheatley, 2007). The fundamental unit of successful organizations is its human relationships.

When you draw from a broad range of disciplines and communities, you create generative relationships (Rowe & Hogarth, 2005) that release energy, create ideas, and support change. When there is productive sharing of ideas, problems, responsibility for decisions, and a variety of viewpoints, your work becomes more fulfilling and productive. It generates goodwill, positive change, worker satisfaction, and a generative foundation for the next generation of leaders. Soon, you will be surprised how others will be drawn to your leadership and your organization. They will want to be part of your team.

THE LARGER WORLD OF LEADERSHIP: WORKING WITH AGGREGATES AND PATIENT POPULATIONS

Along with increasing complexity and professional social networks, among the growing contexts for health care, is population-based care. Population-based care, or care of aggregates and populations, crosses a vast array of disciplines in health and social sciences, with a focus toward optimum well-being and health care for all (Weinstein, Hermalin, & Soto, 2001). Our language, processes, and models of care are moving away from traditional categories of medical diagnosis and body systems of the individual toward population-based models and ways of thinking about health care. The increasing complexity of care managed by healthcare providers requires attention to patient aggregates.

An aggregate or patient population is simply a collection of people within some discrete unit which may be defined by a number of distinguishing factors such as demographics, geography, interest, illness experience, or many others. Sometimes, the terms *population health, public health, community health,* and *population-focused* (or *population-based*) *health care* are used interchangeably (Radzyminski, 2007). They can be distinguished by their overall goals. The goal of population health is to "maximize the health of the population," with a management view toward health promotion, disease prevention, and emphasis on risk reduction related to the mental, behavioral, and social factors of health. The goal of public health is generally considered to be organized governmental or community efforts to promote and improve health among its citizens. Public health management also includes health promotion, risk reduction, and disease prevention, focusing on public safety and environmental issues. Community health includes health care for individuals in a context of families or other social groups at the community level. Thus, community health management includes health promotion and disease prevention among specific social groups who share common interests or characteristics within a community (Radzyminski, 2007, p. 42).

Rising costs and renewed emphasis on quality and outcome measurement have forced expansion of the paradigm of individual episodic patient care encounters to care along the entire spectrum of patients within a defined population. Such attention must now include all aspects of care: prevention, treatment, and chronic disease management. Healthcare leaders, specifically advanced practice nurses, must be able to lead the management of patients at the individual, organization, and population care level. This is a challenge for healthcare providers, especially physicians and nurse practitioners who have been prepared to diagnosis and treat conditions in individual patients. Advanced practice professionals have a history of pride in their distinction to provide direct patient care. However, such a focus on primary care often does not address population-based care any further than by applying the results of aggregate patient data to individual patients. Furthermore, population-based care has not been adequately defined or articulated into the practices of many individual primary care providers (Dalzell, 2998). That is the challenge for clinical leaders of the future.

According to the Association of American Medical Colleges (1999, p. 130), a population health perspective "encompasses the ability to assess the health needs of a specific population; implement and evaluate interventions to improve the health of that population; and provide care for individual patients in the context of the culture, health status, and health needs of the populations of which that patient is a member." Population-focused health is influenced by physical, social cultural, and economic environmental factors. Leadership in population-focused health care requires the ability to conceptualize and analyze health and care from the larger community, or "macro" perspective, that includes environment, behavior, social attitudes and lifestyle, and values along with policy issues all linked with health (DeSouza, Williams & Meyerson, 2003; Radzyminski, 2007). The *Healthy People 2010* campaign (U.S. Department of Health & Human Services, 2007) and other sources of clinical guidelines also provide definitions, data, and other information from a population-based perspective to guide care for aggregates.

A focus on population health includes aspects of behavior, lifestyle, culture, environment, and society. It also includes the following:

Health care based on assessment of relationships derived from the population's (a) genetic predisposition; (b) behaviors . . . and lifestyle; and (c) societal and environmental factors. . . . Healthcare activities based on an assessment of the ecosystem and its subsystems [including] the healthcare system. . . . Healthcare activities based on assessment of the population's (1) knowledge, attitudes, beliefs, values, and perceptions that facilitate or hinder motivation for change; (2) rewards or feedback following the adoption of a health behavior; and (3) skills, resources, or barriers that help or hinder desired behavioral or environmental changes (Green & Kreuter, 2005; Radzyminski, 2007, p. 39).

As nurses and other providers continue to recognize and serve aggregate populations, there will be shifts from resource-based to population-based planning and evaluation. Furthermore, some leaders have proposed the development of new specialists in health lifestyle and behavioral health to include the role of environment and societal factors that influence health (Radzyminski, 2007).

Even the primary care provider may take a perspective of care of aggregates by providing population-focused care: "When caring for a population, you should measure outcomes for all your patients with the targeted condition, not just those who come to your office. This is largely what differentiates population-based care from traditional, individual-centered care" (Rivo, 1998).

Radzyminski (2007, pp. 41–42) provided a specific hypothetical example of population-based care in contrast to "population-focused" individual primary care:

Clinical Nurse Specialists (CNS) or Nurse Practitioners (NP) in pediatric nursing typically include infants and children as their specialty population for which they deliver expert care services. This does not mean that they deliver care based on the population health framework. Take, for example, the common childhood problem of otitis media. . . . If the nurse examines the infant, diagnoses otitis media, prescribes treatment (usually under protocol), provides discharge instructions, and arranges for follow-up, the nurse is operating in the advanced practice nursing model. . . . If the nurse uses his or her experience with all other patients in this population and takes into consideration the cost and the efficacy of one antibiotic over another, success rates of therapies, availability of services for the family . . . and so on, then the nurse can be said to be providing population-focused care. For the nurse to work in the population health model, the antibiotic treatment for the disease would be a secondary care provision. The primary goal would be to investigate why the children [in the *community*] contract the disease, why children continue to contract the disease in spite of treatment options, and what contributes to the large number of children who contract that disease, often repeatedly, year after year. Perhaps, in this example, the nurse would identify the mode of infant feeding as being associated with the high incidence of otitis media. . . . The nurse would have to investigate the culture, beliefs, values . . . not only of the parents of the infants but also of the whole community in which they live. . . . The population health nurse would then approach the problem of otitis media by implementing health care strategies that change infant feeding practices. . . . As nurses providing population-focused care continue to treat infants with otitis media with the best available therapy, population health nurse experts will work to . . . support healthy infant feeding practices, develop programs aimed at addressing the cultural components involved in infant feeding practices, and so on.

Obviously, effective patient care must focus on the care of both individuals and aggregates in the broadest sense. The transformational leader must be able to balance, vision, and navigate across both arenas. He or she must direct individual care within the framework and vision of care for entire communities.

To lead effectively in health care for aggregates and populations requires a different model than those that focus on traditional primary or acute care. One well-worn approach is the Precede-Proceed model by Green and Kreuter (2005). This model emerged from health education and epidemiology. It promotes the idea of predisposing, enabling, and reinforcing factors of human behavior, demographic factors, beliefs, attitudes, values, knowledge and perceptions, skills, resources, barriers, risk conditions, and environment as they contribute to disease prevention, health promotion, risk reduction, and optimum well-being. It allows for interventions at the individual and population level.

The focus on health care for aggregates and populations will continue to grow. Thus, leadership in this arena is critical, especially for practitioners who are accustomed to the traditional model of individual care. As the aggregate focus becomes more effective, the movement will continue to benefit individual patients as well as populations. Some have called the aggregate focus "denominator medicine" (Halpern & Boulter, 2000). The denominators (or populations) represent groups with similar demographics, or with similar disease conditions, with the numerator being the individual within the group. Such a model allows data tracking for screening, treatment, or other factors toward goals to identify quality metrics, patterns of utilization of services, or other outcomes.

Population-based care promotes a community perspective. It is complementary to individual care. It promotes the development of effective protocols and sharing of best practices. At the same time, it invites ethical considerations to meet the needs of underserved populations as well as attention to idiosyncratic needs of individual patients and families. More important from a leadership perspective, population-based practice calls for planning, teamwork, interdisciplinary collaboration, and creative transformational leadership.

Context of care will continue to be a critical factor in healthcare leadership. Chaos, complexity, and change will continue to be predominant themes of context. Healthcare practice will expand its focus on aggregates and patient populations. Context is more than setting or backdrop for practice. It is the very circumstance of service that surrounds the work of the leader.

REFERENCES

Association of American Medical Colleges (AAMC). (1999). Contemporary issues in medical informatics and population health: Report II of the Medical School Objectives Project. *Academic Medicine, 74,* 130–141.

Benson, H. (2005). Chaos and complexity: Applications for healthcare quality and patient care. *Journal of Healthcare Quality, 27*(5), 4–10.

Bolman, L. G., & Deal, T. E. (1991). *Reframing organizations: Artistry, choice, and leadership.* San Francisco: Jossey-Bass.

Boyce, B. (2008, September). Complexity, chaos, collapse, community, creativity, compassion: Why we need new ways of thinking. *Shambhala Sun,* 41–47, 104–105.

Bruhn, J. G. (2004). Leaders who create change and those who manage it: How leaders limit success. *Health Care Management, 23*(2), 132–140.

Burns, J. P. (2001). Complexity science and leadership in healthcare. *Journal of Nursing Administration, 31*(10), 474–482.

Capra, F. (1982). *The turning point.* Toronto, Ontario, Canada: Bantam.

Capra, F. (1996). *The web of life.* New York: Anchor.

Cilliers, P. (1998). *Complexity and postmodernism: Understanding complex systems.* London: Routledge.

Cipriano, P. F. (2008). Improving health care with systems thinking. *American Nurse Today, 3*(9), 6.

Cummings, G. G. (2006). Hospital restructuring and nursing leadership: A journey from research question to research program. *Nursing Administration Quarterly, 30*(4), 321–329.

Dalzell, M. D. (1998, September). Just what the devil is population-based care? *Managed Care Magazine.* Retrieved October 6, 2009, from http://www.managedcaremag.com/archives/9809/9809.population.shtml

DeSouza, R. M., Williams, J., & Meyerson, F. (2003). *Critical links: Population, health, and the environment.* Washington, D.C.: Population Reference Bureau.

Drucker, P. F. (2000). Managing knowledge means managing oneself. *Leader to Leader, 16,* 8–10.

Duck, J. D. (2001). *The change monster: The human forces that fuel or foil corporate transformation and change.* New York: Crown.

Eisenbach, R., Watson, K., & Rajinandini, P. (1999). Transformational leadership in the context of organizational change. *Journal of Organizational Change, 12*(2), 80–89.

Ellis, D. (2003). *The acceleration of innovations.* Retrieved January 2, 2010, from http://hfd.dmc.org/upload/docs/acceleration.pdf

Gleick, J. (1987). *Chaos: Making a new science.* New York: Penguin.

Green, L., & Kreuter, M. (2005). *Health promotion planning: An educational and ecological approach.* Mountain View, CA: Mayfield.

Halpern, R., & Boulter, P. (2000, November). Population-based health care: Definitions and applications. *Tufts Managed Care Institute,* 1–5.

Hamrick, A. B., Spross, J. A., & Hanson, C. M. (2009). *Advanced practice nursing: An integrative approach.* St. Louis, MO: Saunders Elsevier.

Herold D. M., Fedor D. B., Caldwell S., & Liu, Y. (2008). The effects of transformational and change leadership on employees' commitment to a change: A multilevel study. *Journal of Applied Psychology, 93*(2), 346–357.

Hill, F. W. (2003, 10 October). *Leadership: A personal journey.* Speech given to the Sixth Annual Conference of the Harvard Business School African-American Association, Boston, MA.

Holden, L. M. (2005). Complex adaptive systems: Concept analysis. *Journal of Advanced Nursing, 52*(6), 651–657.

Indianapolis Discovery Network for Dementia (IDND). (n. d.). *What is a complex adaptive system?* Retrieved October 5, 2009, from http://www.indydiscoverynetwork.com/cas.html

Kaufman, S. (1995). *At home in the universe.* New York: Oxford University Press.

Kibort, P. M. (2004). The written word: Literature and leadership. *Physician Executive, 30*(4), 10–13.

Kotter, J. P. (1995, March–April). Leading change: Why transformational efforts fail. *Harvard Business Review, 73*(2), 59–67.

Lave, J., & Wenger, E. (1991). *Situated learning: Legitimate peripheral participation.* Cambridge, UK: Cambridge University Press.Lindberg, C. (2009, July). *Complexity science basics: A (very) brief introduction.* Retrieved August 25, 2009, from http://www.plexusinstitute.org/ideas/show_elibrary.cfm?id=1217

Lindberg, C., Herzog, A., Merry, M., & Goldstein, J. (1998). Health care applications of complexity science: Life at the edge of chaos. *Physician Executive, 24*(1), 6–20.

Lorenz, E. N. (1993). *The essence of chaos.* Seattle, WA: University of Washington Press.

MacPhee, M. (2007). Strategies and tools for managing change. *Journal of Nursing Administration, 37*(9), 405–413.

Marion, R. (1999). *The edge of organization: Chaos and complexity theories of formal social systems.* London: Sage.

McDonald, P. W. (2007). From evidence-based practice making to practice-based evidence making. *Health Promotion Practice, 8*(2), 140–144.

McKelvey, B. (1999). Complexity theory in organization science: Seizing the promise or becoming a fad? *Emergence, 1,* 3–32.

Miller, W. L., Crabtree, B. F., McDaniel, R., & Stange, K. C. (1998). Understanding change in primary care practice using complexity theory. *Journal of Family Practice, 46*(5), 369–376.

Morgan, G. (2001). *Images of organization.* Retrieved October 5, 2009, from http://plexusinstitute.com/edgeplace

National Academy for Academic Leadership (NAAL). (2009). *Leadership and institutional change.* Retrieved August 25, 2009, from http://www.thenationalacademy.org/ready/change.html

National Defense University (NDU). (n. d.) *Strategic leadership and decision making: Vision and the management of change.* Retrieved December 17, 1009, from http://www.au.af.mil/au/awc/awcgate/ndu/strat-ldr-dm/pt4ch19.html

Nohria, N., Joyce, W., & Roverson, G. (2003, July). What really works. *Harvard Business Review, 81*(7), 42–52.

Paley, J. (2007). Complex adaptive systems and nursing. *Nursing Inquiry, 14*(3), 233–242.

Penprase, B., & Norris, D. (2005). What nurse leaders should know about complex adaptive systems theory. *Nursing Leadership Forum, 9*(3), 127–132.

Pesut, D. J. (2008a). Change. In H. R. Feldman, M. Jaffe-Ruiz, AM. L. McClure, M. J. Greenberg, & T. D. Smith (Eds.), *Nursing leadership: A concise encyclopedia* (pp. 100–102). New York: Springer.

Pesut, D. J. (2008b). Change agents and change agent strategies. In H. R. Feldman, M. Jaffe-Ruiz, AM. L. McClure, M. J. Greenberg, & T. D. Smith (Eds.), *Nursing leadership: A concise encyclopedia* (pp. 103–105). New York: Springer.

Pesut, D. J. (2008c). Complex adaptive systems (chaos theory). In H. R. Feldman, M. Jaffe-Ruiz, AM. L. McClure, M. J. Greenberg, & T. D. Smith (Eds.), *Nursing leadership: A concise encyclopedia* (pp. 123–124). New York: Springer.

Plsek, P. E., & Greenhalgh, T. (2001). Complexity science: The challenge of complexity in health care. *British Medical Journal, 323,* 625–628.

Porter-O'Grady, T. (2003). Of hubris and hope: Transforming nursing for a new age. *Nursing Economic$, 21*(2), 59–64.

Porter-O'Grady, T., & Malloch, K. (2007). *Quantum leadership: A resource for health care innovation* (2nd ed.). Sudbury, MA: Jones & Bartlett.

Porter-O'Grady, T., & Malloch, K. (2008). Beyond myth and magic: The future of evidence-based leadership. *Nursing Administration Quarterly, 32*(3), 176–187.

Quantum Mechanics (2009). Retrieved October 5, 2009, from http://en.wikipedia.org/wiki/Quantum_mechanics

Radzyminski, S. (2007). The concept of population health within the nursing profession. *Journal of Professional Nursing, 23*(1), 37–46.

Reineck, C. (2007). Models of change. *Journal of Nursing Administration, 37*(9), 388–391.

Rivo, M. (1998). It's time to start practicing population-based health care. *Family Practice Management, 5*(6). Retrieved January 1, 2010, from http://www.aafp.org/fpm/980600/popbased.html

Rogers, E. (1995). *Diffusion of innovations* (4th ed.). New York: Free Press.

Rogerson, L. (n. d.). *Twelve principles for managing change.* Retrieved September 16, 2009, from http://www.lynco.com/12prin.html

Rowe, A., & Hogarth, A. (2005). Use of complex adaptive systems metaphor to achieve professional and organizational change. *Journal of Advanced Nursing, 51*(4), 396–405.

Seel, R. (2008). *Complexity & OD: An introduction.* Retrieved January 1, 2010, from http://www.new-paradigm.co.uk/complex-od.htm

Stacey, R. D., Griffin, D., & Shaw, P. (2000). *Complexity and management: Fad or radical challenge to systems thinking?* London: Routledge.

Stichler, J. F. (2006). Skills and competencies for today's nurse executive. *AWHONN Lifelines: The Association of Women's Health, Obstetric and Neonatal Nurses, 10*(3), 255–257.

Stroebel, C. K., McDaniel, R. R., Jr., Crabtree, B. F., Miller, W. L., Nutting, P. A., & Stange, K. C. (2005). How complexity science can inform a reflective process for improvement in primary care practices. *Joint Commission Journal on Quality & Patient Safety, 31*(8), 438–446.

U.S. Department of Health & Human Services (USDHHS). (2007). Healthy *People 2010.* Retrieved October 6, 2009, from http://www.healthpeople.gov

Walls, M., & McDaniel, R. (1999). Mergers and acquisitions in professional organizations: A complex adaptive systems approach. *Seminars for Nurse Managers, 7*(3), 117–124.

Weinstein, M., Hermalin, A., & Soto, M. (2001). *Population health and aging: Strengthening the dialogue between epidemiology and demography.* New York: New York Academy of Sciences.

Wenger, E. (1998). *Communities of practice: Learning, meaning, and identity.* Cambridge, England: Cambridge University Press.

Wenger, E. (2006). *Communities of practice: A brief introduction.* Retrieved January 31, 2010, from http://www.ewenger.com/theory/index.htm

Wenger, E., McDermott, R., & Snyder, W. (2002). *Cultivating communities of practice: A guide to managing knowledge.* Cambridge, MA: Harvard Business School Press.

Wenger, E., & Snyder, W. (2000, January–February). Communities of practice: The organizational frontier. *Harvard Business Review, 78*(1), 139–145.

Wheatley, M. (1999). *Leadership and the new science: Discovering order in a chaotic world.* San Francisco: Berrett-Koehler.

Wheatley, M. (2006). *Journeying to a new world.* Retrieved October 6, 2009, from http://www.margaretwheatley.com/articles.journeying.html

Wheatley, M. (2007, Spring). How large-scale change really happens: Working with emergence. *The School Administrator.* Retrieved October 7, 2009, from http://www.margaretwheatley.com/articles/largescalechange.html

Wheatley, M. (2009, March). The place beyond fear and hope. *Shambhala Sun,* 79–83.

Wheatley, M., & Frieze, D. (n. d.). *Using emergence to take social innovation to scale.* Provo, UT: The Berkana Institute.

Zimmerman, B., Lindberg, C., Plsek, P. (1998). *Edgeware: Insights from complexity science for health care leaders.* Irving, TX: Voluntary Hospitals of America.

5

Leading Among Leaders

Never doubt that a small group of thoughtful, committed citizens can change the world. Indeed, it is the only thing that ever has.

— Margaret Mead

As you advance in clinical preparation, formal education, and leadership development, you become more than an expert clinician. You become a citizen of the larger discipline of healthcare leadership and a leader among leaders. Assume your role as leader. Take up the banner of your citizenship among leaders. The world awaits your ideas, skills, and the unique contribution you will make. You claim membership among thoughtful, committed people who can make a difference. Doors open, opportunities appear for you to make transformational change in ways you could not imagine before you entered the society of leaders. The challenges are too complex to be overcome by a sole creative person, or even by representatives of a single discipline. Transformational change happens only by the collaborative choreography of groups and teams of leaders. You must prepare to be a leader among leaders.

There are others who struggle with similar issues and who may share your concerns but who have different perspectives, complementary skills, and new ideas that amplify your abilities. We have so much to learn from leaders in other disciplines to transform our vision of practice to improve lives. Just as this work focuses on the talents and skills for leadership among nurses, the need for effective leadership in health care is recognized and promoted among a variety of professions, each with ideas, advice, and rationale for why each discipline is best poised to be the leaders of the future (see Falcone & Satiani, 2008; Schwartz & Pogge, 2000). For example, some have proclaimed that "most physicians possess the traits essential for leadership" (Falcone & Satiani, 2008, p. 187). Others claim that this is the time for nurses to take the helm as the leaders to transform health care. Still others propose that the best leadership can come only from a business model. The truth is that we are working together. Success in the next century can come only from a community of leaders to understand the values, theories, and approaches of each other to finally invent the true interprofessional leadership. You will be a leader among those leaders.

FORMAL AND INFORMAL NETWORKS

The commonly assumed context of leadership is the formal organization, with divisions, departments, positions, job descriptions, and tasks. Entry and advancement are by credential, qualification, merit, or seniority. Leaders and other workers are employees with designated positions, and the higher the position, the greater is the presumed authority to lead. Every such organization also has an informal context within its formal structure. The informal structure is an extension of the social structures that develop within the formal context. It includes individuals with personal qualifications, goals, and motivations, as well as the spontaneous emergence of groups and organizations with their own activities and goals. Leaders often emerge from the informal context by virtue of charisma, personal qualities, and the ability to influence others. Formal leaders are wise to be sensitive and supportive of informal leadership contexts, to recognize and emulate influence and interest in others, to care for individuals and their goals and means of communication. Attention to and engagement in informal contexts outside the organization are also critical to the effective leader.

Wheatley (2008, p. 1) declared, "A leader is anyone willing to help, anyone who sees something that needs to change and takes the first steps to influence that situation." When we worry about where have all the leaders gone, often we need only to look inside the situation at the most local level. In a context of complex adaptive systems, or simply within any community, people are willing to notice, risk, help, and lead. Indeed, many great movements of the world can be attributed to one person noticing a need, persistently working on the problem, enlisting the help of others, and not giving up. That is precisely how Lillian Wald founded public health nursing, how Loretta Ford invented nurse practitioners, and how you will make a difference. It is not easy, but it does work: One person picks up the cause and wears his or her heart out; others take note and join; and thus a movement is formed and changes the world. But it is not only the individual who makes the difference. The individual provides the leadership, but the difference is made with a local network, then a community or perhaps a community of practice, then communities become systems of influence (Wheatley & Frieze, n.d.).

Wheatley and Frieze (n.d.) described the power of networks as the most effective way of organizing for change. They pointed out that networks are formed only by living systems, are born of self-organization, and have always existed but are just now observed through a new lens. They self-organize where individuals of a species "recognize their interdependence and organize in ways that support the diversity and viability of all." Consider migrating birds in flight, citizens for ecological sustainability, surgeons working on a new technique, or nurse leaders dealing with practice design. All are networks that make a difference from the synergy of the natural confluence of talented individuals. Wheatley and Frieze further pointed out that networks provide the conditions for and become the first step toward emergence, "which is how life changes."

One specific and important collaboration model in health care is the academic and clinical partnership (American Association of Colleges of Nursing, 1999). Although such partnerships are often discussed, there is a broad range of types and degrees of success (see Campbell, Prater, Schwartz, & Ridenour, 2001; Horns et al., 2007; McConnell, Lekan, Hebert, & Leatherwood, 2007; Stanley, Hoiting, Burton, Harris, & Normal, 2007; Wotton & Gonad, 2004). They may include innovative initiatives such as dedicated teaching units (Edgecombe, Wotton, Gonda, & Mason, 1999; Moscato, Miller, Logsdon, Weinberg, & Chorpenning, 2007), goals of expanding educational enrollment capacity (Murray, 2007), improving clinical education (Bartz & Dean-Baar, 2003; Mulready-Shick, Kafel, Banister, & Mylott, 2009), or clinical staff recruitment (Pontre et al., 2005).

MacPhee (2009) proposed a logic model for such partnerships. The model outlined inputs that include partnership champions, compatible philosophies of partners, a shared vision, key stakeholder commitment, formalized agreements, shared goals and accountabilities, and dedicated time and resources. Activities include open, ongoing communications; shared decision making; and shared professional development. Outputs include shared and/or compatible action and strategic planning, and outcomes include productive short-term, action-plan, or tactical goals and successful completion of long-term strategic goals.

Successful academic-clinical partnerships bring together key stakeholders, create a common vision to enhance the mission and culture of each organization, and commit to effective collaborative communication and shared decision making. This requires uncommon mutual leadership and exemplary collaboration and shared vision among staff, students, and all other constituents. In addition, it requires sustained human and fiscal resources from each partner and commitment to track outcomes that support the work of both the clinical and academic endeavors.

In the long run, results and outcomes become secondary to effective personal relationships. Indeed, some research has demonstrated that people with strong social and professional networks and mentors "enjoy more promotions, higher pay, and greater career satisfaction" (Barsh, Cranston, & Craske, 2008, p. 35).

Among the most effective and emerging informal network structures is the community of practice discussed in the last chapter. Such self-organized communities are networks of people who come together because of shared interest in a specific domain. Often, such communities form through distance media. They share stories, resources, skills, and information to solve a problem, enhance information, share experience, collaborate, and map knowledge in the domain. A community of practice may reflect interdisciplinary practitioners, government groups, educational groups, and members of social groups. They may be formalized or informal (Wenger, 1998, 2006).

Seldom discussed in the context of networking is the cost to enter and sustain networks. Sometimes efforts at networking are random and haphazard on the assumption of the more the merrier, and the more involvement per individual, the better. Engagement in networks takes time and energy in communication, meetings, and other personal contributions and can sometimes actually detract from performance or quality. Cross, Liedtka, and Weiss (2005) cautioned that rather than assuming that more collaboration is always better, leaders are best advised to take a strategic outlook and determine specific goals from networking, what patterns and levels of connectivity would best meet the goals, and develop initiatives that secure effective networks.

The formal concept of networking probably emerged 30 to 40 years ago. New technologies and perspectives on emergent creation of communities will change the traditional view of networking. Tomorrow's leader will have a whole new world of choices, relationships, and new means to sustain networking across discipline, culture, and geography. It will require new ways of thinking and connecting and will change leadership as we know it.

INTERPROFESSIONAL COLLABORATION

Interprofessional collaboration is a growing formal concept, practice, and mandate among leaders prepared at the highest levels of clinical practice. It has been most commonly defined, applied, and discussed in Canada, the United Kingdom, and South Africa (see D'Amour, Ferrada-Videla, Rodriguez, & Beaulieu, 2005; Stacey, Légaré, Pouliot, Kry-woruchko, & Dunn, in press; Zwarenstein, Goldman, & Reeves, 2009). Although calls for interprofessional approaches to solve the many crises of American health care are heard above the sound of nearly every other cry, reaction has been slow. Numerous national organizations and commissions have officially mandated interdisciplinary collaboration as one of the primary hopes for improved health care of the future. The Pew Health Professions Commission (1998) noted that interdisciplinary modes of care draw on the best practice and instincts of all health care experts, and the Institute of Medicine (Greiner & Knebel, 2003) recently called for interdisciplinary health professional education and practice. Richardson, Haber, and Fulmer (2008) pointed out the efforts of several other major organizations toward encouraging interprofessional collaboration. Among them are the American Nurses Association Social Policy Statement (American Nurses Association, 2003) and the Geriatric Interdisciplinary Team Training by the John A. Hartford Foundation (Fulmer et al., 2005). Richardson and colleagues further reminded that nearly every major professional document on preparation, practice, and research includes some element of interdisciplinary collaboration. Health care has become far too complex to depend on any single organization to rely on its own dedicated employees without collaboration either across the organization or across disciplines (Weiss & Hughes, 2005).

Most professionals, particularly those in health care, are educated and socialized into discipline-specific bodies of knowledge and practice built on strong discipline-specific theories and frameworks. They are licensed and regulated into rigid professional jurisdictions. It is an impressive challenge for such highly trained professionals to move out of the comfort and habit of their disciplines to work together. Such work requires sensitivity to other theoretical foundations and ways of knowing and thinking. It requires learning new language and skills. Interprofessional collaboration requires applying a major change in professional logic, adopting new paradigms, and working in new social environments (D'Amour et al., 2005).

D'Amour and coworkers (2005) reviewed concepts and theoretical frameworks among empirical reports of interprofessional collaboration. Such collaboration was described as a dynamic, interactive, and evolving process. Process steps might include negotiation and compromise in decision making or shared planning and intervention, transcending professional or disciplinary boundaries. They identified five major over arching concepts of collaboration, partnership, interdependency, power, and team. They found the following concepts most often mentioned in definitions of collaboration: sharing, partnership, interdependency, and power. Furthermore, they identified several uses of the concept of sharing as a construct of collaboration, including shared responsibilities, decision making, healthcare philosophy, values, data, and planning and intervention.

Partnership was characterized by a collegial relationship that is authentic and constructive, open, and honest and noted by awareness of and value of the contributions and perspectives of others, common goals, and specific outcomes. Interdependency implies mutual dependence. The concept of power was conceived as shared and as symmetrical in power relationships and characterized by empowerment of all parties. D'Amour et al., (2005) also identified a variety of terms in the context of team environments. Terms included *multidisciplinary*, *interdisciplinary*, and *transdisciplinary*, all rarely defined clearly and often used interchangeably in the literature. Challenges to successful interprofessional collaboration include poor communication (Daly, 2004), lack of knowledge of other professional roles, minimal understanding of when and to whom to refer specific patient problems, the need for training in successful team function, and the need for evidence of improved patient outcomes (Moaveni, Nasmith, & Oandasan, 2008).

Increasingly, preparation of nurses for advanced leadership in health care is recognized, and nurse leaders are given broader ranges of stewardship and control, including areas beyond nursing practice (Arnold et al., 2006), but that is not enough. Porter-O'Grady and Malloch (2008, p. 177) suggested that "What is needed is less emphasis on individual role specificity or clarity and more emphasis on role complement and contribution to patient outcomes." Although each discipline must be able to distinguish the specific scope of its contribution to patient care, the authors pointed out that nevertheless, "the contemporary truth is that the complexities of clinical service spread the locus of control broadly among a number of critical decision makers making no one person the permanent 'captain of the ship'" (Porter-O'Grady & Malloch, 2008, p. 178). They called for an "innovative and brave leader" who "creates an organizational wilderness where the various constituencies meet together to reacquaint themselves with each other and reconfigure both their conversations and relationships in a way that challenges their history and redefines their future" (Anderson, 2001; Porter-O'Grady & Malloch, 2008, p. 279).

Few can argue that interprofessional collaboration in health care would best be facilitated at the foundation of educational preparation of the various professions. Although there are some valiant attempts, actual formalized, integrated collaboration is not widespread. Thibault (2010) outlined the following barriers to generalized interprofessional education:

1. *Cultural:* Strongly held value systems of each profession.
2. *Structural:* Different schedules and locations (in educational preparation).
3. *Faculty:* Not comfortable and not rewarded (for interprofessional collaborative endeavors).
4. *Temporal:* Establishing the ideal developmental times for (interprofessional) interaction. (For example, are first-year medical students and first-year nursing students in parallel developmental times in their preparation?)
5. *Non-core*: Elective experiences at off-hours. (Many groups who have tried interprofessional collaboration in education provided such opportunities only as elective experiences requiring additional time beyond the requisite program.)
6. *Nonsustaining*: Series of "cameos." (Most programs have been short-term demonstration projects dependent on limited or temporary resources.)
7. *Lack of leadership from the top*: Usually driven by passion of one or two faculty members.
8. *Asymmetry*: [Have not been] equally supported by all participating professions.

Despite the barriers to interprofessional preparation, there are some hopeful initiatives to support such collaboration between medicine and nursing (Macy, 2010), for example. Furthermore, many doctor of nursing practice (DNP) programs promote interprofessional collaboration as a core component of preparation. Such programs offer promise for a brighter future of collaboration in the daily work of health care among a variety of professions.

Effective collaboration not only is personally and professionally satisfying to those involved, but also contributes to a unified approach to patients and clients, facilitates faster internal decision making, reduces cost through shared resources, and promotes innovation (Weiss & Hughes, 2005). Successful partnerships are particularly enriching to the leaders involved, who are able to work with new friends, new perspectives, and new supporters outside the daily work environment. We are just beginning to understand the real-world value of interprofessional collaboration on actual patient outcomes (Zwarenstein et al., 2009). It will be the responsibility of leaders of the future to develop working models for collaboration and shared decision making (Stacey et al., in press) and demonstrate the effects of such partnerships and collaboration on actual health care outcomes (Davoli & Fine, 2004; Zwarenstein et al., 2008). As you enter a new leadership role, regardless of the setting, efforts to connect and secure collaborative projects with leaders outside your organization are likely to produce lasting professional friends and colleagues, creative contributions, and renewed energy and insights. Such personal benefits spill into effective service to patients and to the community.

COMMUNICATION, CONFLICT, AND DECISION MAKING

Communicating, dealing with conflict, and making decisions are skills discussed in every leadership class and described in every leadership book. Thus, of course, they will be addressed here.. Theories on these issues abound across business management and healthcare leadership. But do not be fooled; no teacher, no guru, no book has the answers. They will have great advice, helpful insights from experts, and abundant evidence from research, but they will not be able to tell you exactly what will work best for you, for your style, or in your situation. Nevertheless, the topics are so important that they cannot be avoided. Throughout your career, you will learn your own lessons about communication, how to handle conflict, and how to make better decisions, so you must share your own learning along the way. Here you will learn what has worked for others.

Communication

Human communication is among the few things absolutely essential to life. Human beings must connect: physically, emotionally, intellectually, and spiritually. It is as necessary as breathing, but much more complex (Yoder-Wise & Kowalski, 2006). We all know that there is the message sender and the message receiver, but myriads of factors affect the actual communication. Between two people, each brings filters that include attitude, assumptions, intentions, beliefs, emotional state, physical conditions, history, culture, and experience. All affect the nature or the quality of the communication.

Verbal and written communication are deal makers and breakers for the aspiring leader. It makes all the difference in how you present yourself. You are the package that people will notice before they take your message.

Key to effective communication is self-knowledge and sensitivity to others. The well-known Johari Window (Oestreich, 2009; Yen, 1999) helps to illustrate interpersonal processes, and facilitate personal reflection on skills in interpersonal relationships. It includes four rooms or panes (think of window panes). The first is called the "open arena," which includes what others know about me and what I know about myself. The second is called "blind" or the "blind spot," or "what others know about me, but what I do not know about myself." The third pane is the "hidden" or "façade," or what others do not know about me, but what I know about myself. And finally, the last pane is the "unknown," or what others do not know about me and what I do not know about myself. All rooms affect my communication. The panes of the window help to understand nuances and complexities of human communication (Table 5.1).

Whether we realize it or not, communication in some form is reflected in every room of your life. We communicate in speech, writing, actions, body language, and even in silence. Effective communication begins with an awareness of your own style, of how others respond to you. For example, just considering speech communication, others respond to your tone, volume, word choices, ethnic or regional accent, expressions—and that does not even account for your body language or facial expressions. As you aspire leadership at the highest levels, it is most important to examine your own speaking style. Do you overuse jargon, do you use colloquial phrases, do you have an accent that makes people strain to understand you? Is your style either too informal or pedantic? Is your voice gentle, soft, harsh, or intimidating? Are you comfortable expressing yourself?

Among the most effective tools for successful communication is active listening. Indeed, listening is often more important and effective than speaking. Often problems are solved simply by listening. Successful listening simply requires that people feel "heard." In today's world of handheld distractions, it is a treasured gift to give full focused attention and listen to another human being. Active listening is especially important. Yoder-Wise and Kowalski (2006) outlined the characteristics of active listening. They noted that the purpose is to assure the speaker that he or she has been heard, that the intensity of tone or emotion is heard and understood, and that it is safe to continue. As an active listener, paraphrase both the content and the tone of the message and reflect them back to the speaker in a genuine, empathetic manner. Sometimes, it is simply helpful to reflect the person's own words, but you must be truly interested. If you are just practicing a technique, it will not be helpful and will come off as near mockery.

After listening, speaking is the most important signature of your leadership style. One of the most common means of communication for leaders is the "meeting." When I moved from a faculty position to an administrative role, the first, biggest, and most distressing shock was the sheer number of meetings. Then I began to note the length of the meetings. I found that if you set a meeting for 2 hours, it will take 2 hours and 5 minutes. Furthermore, if you set a meeting for 1 hour, it will take 1 hour and 5 minutes. The tradition was for our meetings to be scheduled on 2-hour blocks. I found that every meeting of every group, committee, and task force required the full 2 hours and 5 minutes. I changed the meeting schedule to 1½ hours. Guess what? The work still got done and we cut 2½ hours off each meeting day.

Now, that is not to say that the work might have been done in 1-hour or 15-minute meetings. But not knowing the threshold of time needed, we simply filled the time space allotted. It is important to hold face-to-face meetings in many situations, and it is often preferred. But think about the purpose of the meeting and what is to be accomplished. Communication must be clear, must be fair, and must facilitate the views of all. It must

TABLE 5.1 *The Johari Window*

Open	Blind
What everyone knows about me	What others know about me that I don't know
Hidden	Unknown
What I know about myself that others don't know	What no one knows about me

be worth the enormous number of person-hours, which is the cost that any meeting exacts. Think about not only your agenda but also the agenda on the mind of every member of the group. Meetings should be for group process or for very important messages from the leader that can only be delivered personally. Meetings are also important to promote esprit de corps and a sense of belonging. After the meeting, other means of communication, such as e-mail, should be used appropriately to facilitate the results of the meeting. Sometimes the entire "meeting" can be held by e-mail.

Communication specialist Sue (2001) outlined the following 10 simple steps that must be addressed every time you make any presentation to a group: (1) Know your purpose. Ask both yourself and your audience why you are there. Do your homework. One tip is to send e-mails to 8 or 10 people in the group before the meeting and ask them about their issues, desires, and challenges. (2) Know what you want to happen from the gathering. What do you want and what do they want? (3) Make sure your opening is powerful. Capture attention and create interest. You might begin with some startling attention-getting information specifically about your topic. (4) State your case and support it with evidence, facts, and examples. (5) Re-engage your audience every 6 to 8 minutes. Tell a relevant story, share a surprising statistic, have the group do something, but keep them with you. (6) Use visual information, but only if it is powerful. Do not have your PowerPoint *be* your presentation. Remember, it is only a blue screen with a few words. *You* must convey the message. (7) Use notes, but never memorize or read your presentation. (8) Set the rules early for how questions and answers will be handled. Is this an open discussion? Is it an information session to be peppered with questions? Or do you want to dump your whole spiel then entertain questions? (9) Rehearse what you are going to say at least four times without interruption, especially when the information is a surprise or bad news. Make an outline, keep it to only the number of points you can remember (for me, that is only three to five items), and know them. (10) Check the environment. Be sure you have set the stage on as many environmental factors as possible. Arrange the room, the chairs, the temperature, the clutter, the equipment, water, and food. Take away distractions and remove all barriers to your message. I am amazed how many times when, as the leader, I am also the one to clear the clutter and arrange the chairs, but it is always worth it!

After listening and speaking, written communication is your most important tool as a leader. Leaders are required to write every day. First, you must decide which form of written communication is most appropriate for the situation: e-mail, formal memo, letter, or public announcement? Even before that decision, you must decide to be a good writer. That means you must practice. Get help. Nothing will deflate your leadership balloon more quickly than poor writing. Consult models and collect "templates" to consult (I said "consult" not "copy") for things like letters of recommendation, executive summaries, proposals, or other documents that you write regularly. Then decide the purpose of your writing. Do you need to persuade, get information, clarify, motivate, solve a problem, make a recommendation, or defuse a crisis? Regardless of what you write, *always* make an outline. I even make an outline for a thank-you note. It helps to clarify your purpose and gives a structure for your message.

Even after you have become an expert in all aspects of communication, some challenge will erupt that tests all of your best skills. It helps in those times to step aside from yourself and examine your communication skills. You may need to edit your style. Take care not to be drawn into a style that is unbecoming or ineffective.

Wheatley (2005) lamented that in current hard times, organizations are reverting "backward" to a style of "command and control" communication. Perhaps it is a natural tendency for organizations, and the humans inside them, to pull in during times of reduced resources, stress, chaos, and uncertainty. Decisions become more centralized and more hierarchical, and more rules and regulations appear. Wheatley rhetorically asked, "Where have all these policies, procedures, protocols, laws, and regulations come from? And why do we keep creating more, even as we suffer from the terrible consequences of over-control?" As leaders try to get control or exert power for performance and productivity, the opposite actually happens. Workers who would normally take initiative to contribute ideas and willingly take responsibility also pull back and become discouraged, and morale drops. Then the effects compound on leaders, who lose spirit and power. And communication suffers. Wheatley cautioned, "When leaders take back power, when they act as heroes and saviors, they end up exhausted, overwhelmed, and deeply stressed. It is simply not possible to solve single-handedly the organization's problems." If we can trust self-managed teams, share the challenges, and engage the entire system into action during hard times, it is highly more likely that more ideas, more solutions, and more effective outcomes will result. Such outcomes always require successful communication.

No matter how well prepared the leader, how earnest the followers, and how successful the organization appears, it seems inevitable in the complexities of the healthcare environment that at some moment, things will go bad. Whether it is an unconscionable error, an economic crash, a disappointing employee, or a painful lawsuit, one day, suddenly, the leader will wish that she or he had aspired to be anything but to be "in charge." Such situations may include any of the following: when you must deliver a negative performance review; when you must confront unfair treatment, deception, breaches of confidentiality, or lack of commitment; when you must deal with a person who is abusive, needy, or irresponsible; when you must deliver bad news or share the results of a difficult decision; when you must say "no"; or when you must surmount enormous barriers to effective communication. And you wonder, "How will I survive this?" It may be a painfully public issue or one that is born in a quiet, hurting heart. Its source may be a circumstance or a person. If it is a matter that will or has become public, a notable banking leader gives the following advice for communication:

1. Get the bad news out as quickly as possible. Only then can you get out of the bunker and begin to move forward.
2. If you have been found guilty in the court of public opinion, you must apologize—publicly. Lawyers, financial specialists, and other "experts" may tell you that you are legally, technically, and practically in the right. It does not matter.
3. Make sure that employees are attuned to what is going on. If there is bad news, let them hear it from you before they read it in the newspapers.
4. Wherever possible, do not forget to have some fun. If you are outgunned or in a position of disadvantage, do not be afraid to do the unexpected or the outrageous, because what have you got to lose? (Hill, 2004, pp. 8–9)

Dealing With Conflict

If conflict leaves you faint hearted and ready to run away, remember that throughout history, many great leaders were born or made by conflict. Indeed, the first leadership theories were rooted in conflict. Even today, many leadership courses still require some readings from *The Art of War*, the oldest known military text from the third century B.C. Think of the great social and political leaders in world history: Elizabeth I, Abraham Lincoln, Harriet Tubman, Winston Churchill, Indira Gandhi, or Nelson Mandela. They were able leaders when they entered the fray, but they emerged to greatness from the crisis of conflict.

All human dynamics carry the potential for conflict. In any work situation, conflict is inevitable. Porter-O'Grady (2004, p. 181) pointed out that normal processes of human communication are "deeply embedded" with all the elements essential to conflict. Issues of stress and power create tension (Vivar, 2006). Furthermore, to recognize the diversity and fundamental differences in personal experience, viewpoints, and values among human beings is to acknowledge conflict to be a normal characteristic of human interaction. Conflict is a human experience. It is fundamentally about differences (Bar-Siman-Tov, 2004; Porter-O'Grady, 2004). Indeed, some have said that all human interaction is based on conflict (Porter-O'Grady, 2004; Tessier, Chaudron, & Muller, 2002).

Especially in complex environments with a highly diverse workforce and laden with high-risk situations, conflict happens. Nursing and healthcare organizations can be particularly vulnerable. A decade ago, nurse managers reported that they spent 20% of their time dealing with conflict management (McElhaney, 1996). Given the complexity and stresses of today, it is likely to be much higher. Conflict cannot be eliminated, particularly within health care, with its vast range of stressors and diversity of disciplines and professions. A professional mediator observed why the healthcare environment is particularly fraught with potential for conflict:

> The healthcare professional's typical day involves a frenetic race to coordinate resources, provide care, perform procedures, gather data, integrate information, respond to emergencies, solve problems, and interact with diverse groups of people. Regardless of the role of the professional. . . , as a group healthcare professionals face more conflict and greater complexity than any other profession. Despite the challenges of balancing competing interests, philosophies, training backgrounds, the endless question for adequate resources, and the emotional quality of the work that they do, very few healthcare professionals have had the opportunity to learn the skills and processes necessary for negotiating their environments. There is little formal training available to them in this area and role models for collaboration and good negotiation are far and few between. As a result, the clinical environment is one of competition, quick fixes, hot tempers, avoidance tactics and at times, hopelessness. . . . (Gerardi, 2010)

Furthermore, conflict is inherent in healthcare organizations where "disagreements sparked by differences in perspective, competencies, access to information, and strategic focus" are pervasive (Weiss & Hughes, 2005, p. 93).

Porter-O'Grady (2004) also argued that a significant factor in conflict is ambiguity. Lack of clarity from leadership contributes to misunderstanding and conflict responses. Such ambiguity may be reflected in incorrect information, inadequate information, different levels of understanding among individuals who then act on their own perceptions, information overload that strains tolerance, or frequent changes in direction that create confusion. The increasing complexity of clinical decision making and range of people making clinical decisions for any particular patient can also create misunderstanding and conflict based on information and practice issues of ambiguity.

Nevertheless, an environment of conflict is counterproductive to healing, which, in the heat of the battle of the day, is too often forgotten as the goal of health care. Indeed, conflict increases the cost of health care in many unbecoming ways (Forte, 1997). A positive, healthy professional care environment makes a difference in reducing error, improving safety, alleviating stress, and generally enhancing the patient and caregiver experience (Doucette, 2008).

Conflict nearly always carries three key characteristics: difference of opinion, high stakes, and intense emotion (Patterson, Grenny, McMillan, Switzler, & Covey, 2002). Conflict may occur among individual workers or between individuals and representatives of the organization. Although conflict is particularly common in healthcare environments among clinical professionals, few such practitioners have formal training in managing conflict (Vivar, 2006).

Thus, fundamental to the role of a leader is the understanding, embrace, and ability to deal effectively with conflict. Weiss and Hughes (2005, pp. 93–94) argued that "clashes between parties are the crucibles in which creative solutions are developed and wise trade-offs among competing objectives are made." But it is more than an "unnecessary nuisance" and can be seen as a resource for learning and insight. Thus, it is in the leader's best interest for the organization not to eliminate conflict but to embrace it and "institutionalize mechanisms for managing it." Unfortunately, neither the clinical nor the leadership training of most healthcare professionals prepares them for the realities of conflict management and resolution.

Managing conflict is among the finest arts. Done well, it requires an extraordinary maturity and skill. But it can be learned by the sensitive student. There are a few basic general principles. First, as a leader, it is important to bracket your own emotional responses. Draw upon your highest levels of emotional intelligence, which can help you to frame conflict situations as opportunities for learning. High levels of emotional intelligence have been associated with positive collaborative approaches and staff satisfaction with conflict management (Morrison, 2008).

The effective leader deals with conflict with sensitivity and wisdom. Stand back, stand firm, reflect the perspectives of both sides, and approach the situation as a compassionate mediator or therapist. Remember, you are the leader, not the parent or the referee. Examine your own thoughts and feelings. If it is helpful, share them with a trusted person outside the conflict to assure that your thinking is rational. Plan your response to the people involved in the conflict carefully and fairly. Do not respond to ambushes except to listen. Then listen carefully and responsively, reflecting the viewpoint of the parties in your best Rogerian style. As the leader, you set the time, place, and agenda for any official meeting to facilitate resolution. Remain calm as an arbitrator or counselor. Reflect and interpret to each other the viewpoints of the conflicting parties. Ask questions, and listen again. Separate fact from opinion, including your own, while considering the perspective of all parties involved. Separate people from problems in your own mind. It is rare that a person is simply "being difficult," although frustration may interpret it that way. Hang on to the goal of preserving human respect and working relationships.

Sometimes wise interpretation of each other's viewpoints to conflicting parties is enough. If not, take time to plan your response, record it in writing, hold parties accountable, follow up, consult internal or outside experts as appropriate, and be firm but gentle where possible. Promote compromise and/or collaboration. Help to facilitate others out of damaging entrenched positions by constructing graceful ways out of those corners that acrimony sometimes backs a person into. Sometimes you must resort to reassignment or other means to simply separate the parties. Whatever the approach, emphasize the strengths of each person, allow face-saving positive responses, and do not respond to grudges.

When you need to face a critical issue, you may take time for planning and reflection, but do not allow such contemplation to deteriorate into denial, avoidance, or stalling. Notice when and where it is safe to open the conversation, then continue to sustain that safety by willingness to take the perspective of the other and contrast what you do want or expect with what you do not want or expect regarding the specific behavior of the person (Patterson et al., 2002).

Occasionally, conflicts may elevate beyond your resolution as the local leader. If the issue is particularly complex or hazardous, the employment of a mediator may be helpful to avoid full-blown litigation, which is costly to organizational and human resources. Once conflicting parties engage attorneys, the rules change and you are required to work only through your own counsel.

Novice leaders soon learn that part of the mantle of their stewardship as leaders is the burden of carrying confidential knowledge of conflicts, misbehaviors, and mischief of some workers in the organization. Some of the mischief can be directed toward the leader. Hall talk can generate against the leader from grudges that may actually have little to do with you as an individual but are directed toward you as the leader. Others can talk, but you must often carry the burden of confidentiality and simply bear it gracefully.

Disruptive Clinician Behavior

Unique to many healthcare settings, especially hospitals, is conflict due to disruptive clinician behavior. Disruptive behavior among clinicians impose a heavy cost on worker morale, nurse retention, and patient safety (Benner, 2007; Rosenstein & O'Daniel, 2005, 2008a, 2008b; Saxton, Hines, & Enriquez, 2009; Veltman, 2007). The problem has become so severe in many hospitals that the Joint Commission has imposed special compliance criteria, setting standards to define and manage disruptive behavior (Grenny, 2009; Leiker, 2009). Ironically, some physicians have expressed concern regarding "encroachment on physician rights" by such standards (Leiker, 2009, p. 333).

Gerardi (2010) pointed out:

> In a competitive environment where mistakes can be lethal, it is difficult for health care professionals to be open to the fact that their idea or answer could be wrong. There is a need to be right so as not to hurt the patient. This trait carries over into conflict situations where everyone has the right answer to the problem and has difficulty hearing conflicting solutions. On a broader level, with varied levels of training, there is a built in tendency to believe that you know more than someone else because of specialty training, certification, more experience or position within the organization.

Although studies have demonstrated disruptive behavior among a variety of healthcare professionals, including nurses (Bigony, et al., 2009; Rosenstein & O'Daniel, 2005, 2008a; Veltman, 2007), the abundant evidence of disruptive behavior attributed to physicians uniquely predominates. Such behavior in medicine and health care is uniquely more rampant than in any other professional discipline, industry, or workplace (Benner, 2007; Rosenstein & O'Daniel, 2008b; Saxton et al., 2009; Walrath, Dang, & Nyberg, in press). It is well known that most physicians hold a special position in many healthcare settings because of the history and tradition of their economic power and social status, their unique relationship to the setting, and their distinctive relationship with the patient. Porter-O'Grady (2004, p. 184) pointed out:

> In most cases, the physician is a free agent, more often a guest, to the regular operating dynamics of the organization. The physician usually enters the organization to perform specific functions, completes those functions, and exits the organization to undertake work and activities related to his or her own practice. The employed physician has a stronger and more direct relationship to the organization, yet, even in this set of circumstances, the employed physician reflects a superordinate and separate role in the organization. Either because of the short-term nature of the interaction of most physicians' roles or the status of the role of the physician in the organization, there exists an opportunity for accelerating conflict.

As a growing number of physicians assume administrative roles in healthcare settings (Falcone & Satiani, 2008; Schwartz & Pogge, 2000), interdisciplinary communication, leader-to-leader collaboration, and appropriate interventions become more critical than ever (Grenny, 2009; Vazirani, Hays, Shapiro, & Cowan, 2005). One study demonstrated that more than 75% of physicians and nurses reported condescending, insulting, or rude behavior among clinicians, but the more alarming finding was that 20% of health professionals reported having seen actual harm to patients as a result of such behavior, with associated reluctance to confront or report such behavior. Thus, a "culture of silence" puts patient safety at risk (Grenny, 2009).

Conflict from physicians is most often from two sources. The first source is role, with associated issues related to patient care performance, function, or process. In these cases, the leader must facilitate resolution at the point of service, with care to include all key stakeholders. This requires supportive empathetic listening without taking over the problem, risking appropriate parties from the opportunity for sustained resolution. The second source of physician conflict is often deeper and requires greater leader tenacity toward resolution. That is identity conflict, which often involves perceptions of individuals or groups related to their role and relationship to the system. Such conflicts often involve how physicians and nurses view their roles, scopes of practice, and authority over clinical activities. Although such conflicts must be approached at the local, individual level (Porter-O'Grady, 2004; Rothman, 1997), obviously such conflict is a broad-based issue that requires ongoing dialogue and collaboration across disciplines. One intervention found to improve daily communication, collaboration, and understanding among physicians and nurses is the simple formal addition of a nurse practitioner to each inpatient medical team (Vazirani et al., 2005). Although this is thorny, we cannot shrink from positive resolution of such profound professional conflicts.

Beyond case-by-case real-world conflict resolution, the wise leader provides staff training and education in dealing with conflict. Because the topic is so conspicuously absent or underplayed in the educational programs preparing health professionals, it becomes your responsibility as the leader to raise awareness and educate colleagues. This can be done proactively through grand rounds, continuing education programs, invited experts, staff meetings, retreats, and other programs. It is topically at least as important as any clinical update. Role playing and training across disciplines may be especially helpful.

Health professionals are trained to solve problems. They are experts at assessing problems; developing plans, strategies, and tactics; securing resources; and curing the disease. Put colleagues to work to identify and address problems related to interpersonal conflict in a nonthreatening, collaborative setting and process. Model openness to alternative solutions to resolve complex problems. Encourage creativity beyond a new policy, guideline, or program. Provide an environment of trust and support. And adding a healthy dose of humor will not hurt.

A key aim is to provide a clear process for people to resolve issues independently without damage to relationships or organizational morale. Without a dependable structured process, conflicting individuals can get mired not only in the end result, but also in how to approach a solution. Furthermore, a systematic approach may prevent less optimal "split-the-difference" or deadlocked outcomes and promote goodwill. A clearly outlined process that is well integrated into daily work expectations, and not as an ad hoc personnel appeals process, is most effective (Weiss & Hughes, 2005, p. 94).

Providing workable mechanisms and fostering openness, support, goodwill, and encouragement of thoughtful reflection to solve problems across the entire interpersonal environment and across all hierarchical levels of leadership are challenging but worth the effort. Successful conflict resolution can result in improved therapeutic environments, strengthened human relationships, innovation in processes, shared meaning, and new stories.

Is There Such a Thing as Positive Conflict?

Business professor Michael Roberto (2005) wrote a book called *Why Great Leaders Don't Take Yes for an Answer*. His premise in the book is intriguing: that lack of conflict, good conflict that is, is a sign of an unhealthy organization. He suggests, "If people smile, nod, and say 'yes'. . . maybe it's time to start [an] argument" (Lagace, 2005). In other words, in healthy work environments, sparring, disagreeing, and even constructive conflict release creative energy, invite consensus, and promote effective decisions. Remember the story of Rasputin? He was the strange mystic healer and charlatan who won influence over the Tsar Nicholas II and the Romanov family. He held the entire royal family in his power by telling them what he wanted them to know and what they wanted to hear. Obviously, the life and story of Rasputin and the Romanovs are much more complicated, Rasputin has become the symbol for the person who nefariously only says "yes" and isolates the leader to his or her doom. Beware of the Rasputins during your leadership role. Beware of a "culture of yes," where people tell you only what they think you want to hear, or where people who disagree sit quietly in meetings, saying nothing, then undermine leadership and decisions in the hallways. Or they sit quietly, saying nothing, then simply passively resist progress or change efforts. Roberto reminded leaders that it can be difficult and uncomfortable for workers to express dissent. He warned that leaders should not wait for disagreement but seek it out, search for people willing to say "no," that passive leadership creates barriers to honest dialogue and debate. Indeed, those who are the least likely to express disagreement may be the very ones to whom you should be listening! Think about it. Knowing who disagrees with a decision and why that person disagrees may actually help you to make a different decision, to implement a decision in a more effective way, to clarify your rationale, or to invite change to a better way. On the other hand, a culture of too much "no," where workers have all power to veto or resist every decision, can stifle progress.

Roberto also described a "culture of maybe," where leaders and followers become mired in analysis, resist ambiguity, and continue to gather information, striving for the certainty of just the right answer. Such an environment can immobilize a leader and an entire organization. A bit of constructive conflict in such a situation can move toward a decision. Remember, when you make a decision that did not work, you can always make another one!

Also remember, however, that it is constructive conflict you seek—that is the art of it: how to make conflict constructive. Constructive conflict that fosters critical thinking, active engagement, vigorous debate, and commitment can enhance the quality of decisions while building consensus. It must be task oriented rather than emotion based. It helps to establish ground rules for civil dialogue, clarify roles, recognize differences in cognitive and communication styles, and build mutual respect. The process must be fair to promote ultimate commitment to decisions. Constructive conflict will not result in everyone getting the outcomes that they want. And feelings may still be hurt and relationships be wounded. The leader must attend to these immediately.

To promote fair, open processes of constructive conflict, Roberto (Lagace, 2005, p. 3) warned leaders to consider the following "rules of engagement." For people to believe that the process is fair, they must:

1. Have ample opportunity to express their views and to discuss how and why they disagree with other group members.
2. Feel that the decision-making process has been transparent, that is, that deliberations have been relatively free of secretive, behind-the-scenes maneuvering.
3. Believe that the leader listened carefully to them and considered their views thoughtfully and seriously before making a decision.
4. Perceive that they had a genuine opportunity to influence the leader's final decision.
5. Have a clear understanding of the rationale for the final decision.

Leaders strive for consensus. It is reassuring for both leaders and followers to know that they are working together. Consensus is not blind. It is earned after vigorous, healthy dialogue. Consensus is generally much better than majority vote that automatically comes with the dissenting opinion after the decision is made. Consensus represents a generally high level of commitment to the course of action, a buy-in to the process, and shared understanding of the direction of the work.

Decision Making

Decision making is one of the most studied topics in the social sciences, yet we continue to wonder how good decisions get made. Campbell, Whitehead, and Finkelstein (2009) studied faulty decisions made by otherwise capable leaders from a neuroscience perspective. They explained that when faced with a situation calling for a decision, we make assumptions and take a perspective based on previous experiences, judgments, and emotional patterns. Thus, we may think we understand a pattern based on past history or emotional experience, but we do not really understand the new situation. They identified three "red-flag conditions" of distorted patterns or "emotional tagging." First was inappropriate self-interest or conflict of interest that can bias judgment and decisions even unintentionally. The second tag is distorted attachments to people, places, or things. An example would be the reluctance of a leader to cut a program in which he or she had been directly involved. The third red flag is misleading memories that take our thinking in an inappropriate direction, where we might overlook or overvalue some important factor in a situation. To counteract such potential flaws, involve another person in the decision. Look to add a fresh mind, a different experience. Invite debate and challenge. Another approach is to institute governance safeguards, such as a process of ratification of decisions.

On the other hand, Hayashi (2001) pointed out the value of instinct and the intuitive skills of wise leaders to make critical decisions. We have all known leaders whose experience, native wisdom, and emotional sensitivity contribute to sound decisions. Some emotional context and business instinct is essential, especially at the highest levels of leadership. Nevertheless, Hayashi recommended to use self-checking and feedback. He warned, "Don't fall in love with your decisions. Everything's fluid. You have to constantly, subtly make and adjust your decisions" (Hayashi, 2001, p. 65).

Ken Chenault, chief executive officer of American Express, noted that the most difficult decisions are made by the leader when things are going well. He noted that, "In crisis, it is easier to get people to see the reasons why they should make changes" (Feinberg, 2005, p. 8).

In strategic decision making, the stakes are high, there may be novelty or ambiguity, or the decision represents substantial change or commitment of financial or human resources. Thankfully, most leaders make relatively few life-or-death strategic decisions, but it *is* the leader who does make the strategic decisions. Many routine, daily tactical decisions can be delegated. Further, leadership does not end with making the decision, however difficult that may be. After the decision is made, the leader must mobilize people and resources; sustain motivation of the entire organization; and navigate the sometimes troubled waters of disagreements, doubters, resisters, and those who simply do not know how to respond.

Regardless of the strategic or tactical value of a decision, the wise leader is always painfully aware of impact on real people's daily lives. Regardless of the organization, people are the greatest asset to be treasured and highly regarded.

Wise decision making does not grow from leadership style or personality, but instead style should be adapted to circumstance. Ken Chenault explained, "In some situations you have to be highly directive, because people are looking for clear direction from the leader. You always want to understand different perspectives, but in certain situations, you cannot manage by consensus. However, in being directive, you want to make sure that you're taking time to consider the consequences of your actions. Even in a crisis, you want to demonstrate to people that you understand what they're going through. You need to be empathetic and compassionate, but you must remain decisive, because the objective is to navigate the choppy waters and get people through it" (Feinberg, 2005, p. 9).

Remember, the easy things have been done. And the easy decisions are made before they come to you as the leader. You get the difficult decisions. That is your job as the leader. Know your personality preferences and style. Learn to bracket your personal viewpoints. Learn to consult counsel and cultivate network of sages and mentors. Educate yourself on the issues. Try on the alternatives. Rehearse the potential outcomes. Then be brave. Trust your wisest instinct. Plan, decide, then move forward!

DEALING WITH FEAR AND FAILURE

Fear and *failure* are terms not usually found in the table of contents of a leadership text. To teach leadership is usually to motivate, to paint the best and most hopeful picture, to instill fearlessness, and to draw on the assumption that you will not fail. But as an expert clinician, you have spent nearly a lifetime carrying the burden that if you make a mistake, someone could be damaged; someone could die. The nursing cap went away, but that fear of making a mistake stayed inside each of us. It is not an occupational legend; it is reality that errors in clinical practice can be grave, as we have recently been reminded by the Institute of Medicine (1999).

Know this for certain, that no leader who has accomplished anything has not had periods of fear or some major failure. Wheatley (2009, p. 81) assured that a "wild ride between hope and fear is unavoidable. Fear is the necessary consequence of feeling hopeful again." Hope and fear are born in the heart together. Wheatley continued, "Hope never enters a room without fear at its side. If I hope to accomplish something, I'm also afraid I'll fail. You can't have one without the other." Likewise, to be fearful is to hope that you will not fear. Wheatley further explained:

> Hope is what propels us into action. . . . We create a clear vision for the future we want, then we set a strategy, make a plan, and get to work. We focus strategically on doing only those things that have a high probability of success. As long as we "keep hope alive" and work hard, our endeavors *will* create the world we want. How could we do our work if we had no hope that we'd succeed?
>
> Motivated by hope, but then confronted by failure, we become depressed and demoralized. . . . At such a time, we learn the price of hope. Rather than inspiring and motivating us, hope has become a burden made heavy by its companion, fear of failing.

Wheatley (2009, p. 81) then admonished to replace fear and hope with the willingness to be insecure, to be vulnerable, to exchange "certainty for curiosity, fear for generosity." Be willing to treat plans and innovations as "experiments," to become less engaged in hope and fear and more willing to be engaged in discovery. Wheatley (p. 82) reminded that if we would remember that "we *are* hope, it becomes much easier to stop being blinded or seduced by hopeful prospects."

Every leader has met moments of failure. Do not ever think otherwise. I remember when I could feel the ground sink beneath my feet. Wheatley (2009, p. 81) described it as a state of "groundlessness:" "Systems and ideas that seemed reliable and solid dissolve. . . . People who asked for our trust betray or abandon us. Strategies that worked suddenly don't. Groundlessness is a frightening place. . . but. . . we would feel stronger if we stopped searching for ground. . . ." In my own experience of a perceived failure, I confessed to a friend and colleague that I could recall the very moment "my core confidence cracked." It was a breathless, life-changing jolt for me to believe I had failed. She responded simply, "We all have cracks in our core confidence." She was right. I had lived a professional life of one success upon another. I now know that every leader who has risked a better way has some healing wounds inside. As you mature as a leader, you find other leaders willing to share their own episodes of failure. No truly successful leader has not known some defeat. They are often our best teachers. Do not allow fear or failure to rob you of curiosity and the willingness to risk.

MOTIVATION AND MARKETING: TELLING THE STORY

Motivation is so much more than providing incentive for productivity. It is about inspiring and giving hope to colleagues and followers within the organization. And marketing is so much more than selling. It is also about inspiring and giving hope to colleagues and the public outside the organization. Although not usually considered together, the concepts of motivation and marketing are related.

Life today at best is unsteady and unpredictable. Complexity abounds not only in the workplace. It is the context of our daily lives. Wheatley (2009, p. 79) reflected, "Life these days is a roller coaster ride between hope and fear, oscillating wildly between what's possible and what is. Like all roller coasters, this one is both exhilarating and terrifying, often simultaneously. We are fully engaged in being part of the solution, and then we plunge into despair at the enormity of the challenges and the fear that our efforts will fail." Wheatley reflects the concerns of so many us, leaders, followers, patients, everyone. To motivate others is to listen to their fears and to show the way to hope. It is to tell stories: to listen and to share.

Motivation: What It Is and What It Is Not

For years, motivation experts have argued over whether intrinsic or extrinsic motivators are most effective. Remember McGregor's (1960) Theory X and Theory Y from your early lessons on management. Under Theory X at its extreme, workers are not predisposed to work, so the manager's job is to make them work. Workers are not responsible, so they need bosses, rules, and guidance. They are not interested in performance, productivity, or quality but are motivated by extrinsic incentives such as money, benefits, and time off. Under Theory Y, work is natural and self-fulfilling. Workers are self-directed, so the manager simply has to create the environment and provide the resources for workers to do the job, which they will do with responsibility and with pride in performance, productivity, and quality. Extrinsic motivators, such as money, benefits, and time off, are appreciated but are not the most important factors in worker satisfaction.

Motivation is larger than a polar paradigm between external and internal rewards. The truth is that everyone responds to both extrinsic and intrinsic sources of motivation. Extrinsic factors include things like power, money, and status, and intrinsic factors include finding meaning, growing, and learning. We all respond to both. Reviewing another traditional motivation theory, Hertzberg (1968) proposed that rather than a dichotomy, such factors are on a continuum of satisfiers-dissatisfiers or motivation-hygiene factors. Thus, satisfiers, or motivation factors, include encouragement and opportunities to create or develop new skills, and dissatisfiers, or hygiene factors, include compensation, benefits, and job security. Finally, the well-known theory of Maslow would frame motivation as two levels of survival and achievement. Survival would include basic needs like safety and compensation. With basic needs satisfied, workers are motivated by higher needs of achievement, emotional fulfillment, and personal growth (Yoder-Wise & Kowalski, 2006).

Intrinsic or internal motivation is personal passion. Behind it is energy to engage in the work, to set and pursue personal and organizational goals, to overcome obstacles, and to press forward. External incentives, such as money or status, are secondary to the satisfaction of engagement and achievement (Goleman, 1998; Porter-O'Grady & Malloch, 2007). The transformational leader in a healthy organization "operates on the principle that human beings, by their very nature, are internally motivated." Thus, the assumption is that people who are valued, encouraged, supported, and provided with the environment and resources to succeed will take initiative and perform creatively and effectively. From such groups will emerge collective wisdom, creativity, and some degree of self-governance. Such organizations move away from hierarchical structures with "chains of command encompassing many levels of superiors and subordinates." Thus, motivation moves from a focus on productivity to one of fruitfulness and personal fulfillment (Johnson, 2000; Porter-O'Grady & Malloch, 2007, pp. 260–261, 389).

Motivation is a powerful internal and external force that influences behavior. Motivation is not manipulative or coercive. Nurse leaders Yoder-Wise and Kowalski (2006, p. 135) introduced the following ideas of Kim (1996) to understand motivation in leadership:

1. Motivation is a force, positive or negative, that creates action.
2. Understanding the underlying motive that leads to taking action is the key to motivating people, including ourselves.
3. Every motive for taking action comes from a need and a desire to satisfy it.
4. Motives come in many forms and change throughout life.
5. Motives can change rapidly, even during a specific activity.

Wise leaders stay in touch with the people with whom they work. There is no magic theory, strategy, or practice for motivation that works universally every time. Motivation requires authentic passion about the work, genuine interest in the workers, and vigilance to human needs for encouragement, support, autonomy, and meaning.

Marketing: Telling Your Story

When you are doing something great from which others might learn or benefit, do not assume that your good work will be automatically valued and recognized. Indeed, unless you tell your story in an effective manner, it may be barely noticed. Regardless of your initiative, build relationships with others who may help you tell your story. Think about including the public relations or public communications officer of your organization, if one exists, or invite a local journalist to be part of your team. Invite key policymakers, such as local or state public officials, who might influence resources to translate your work to the larger community. And do not forget to go beyond traditional means of communication to using social media tools like Twitter, Facebook, and blogging to tell your story.

Understanding Marketing: From Clinician to Storyteller

What is marketing anyway? Is it creating a slick, beautiful brochure? Is it a catchy tag line? A great Web site? How do you promote your place, your idea, your work? How do you engage an entire population toward your endeavor? You simply find a way to tell your story. Long before words were written, they were told. We sat together and told stories about life, crops, death, and miracles. Many of the stories were so powerful that they became legends. Whole cultures formed around some of the stories. Marketing is the concept in modern business and industry that is telling the story, trying to promote, sell, influence, make someone believe, or invite someone to come. It may be reflected in Internet Web sites, newspapers, radios, television, brochures, posters, or social receptions, but it is all fundamentally about telling your story. Ultimately, you want others to share your story in their conversations, chat rooms, and texting. Image is always important, but most important to any story is the mission of the organization. Your story must be central to your mission.

Marking in a healthcare system is complex because there are so many possible audiences, or targets, for the marketing plan. It may be to recruit clinicians or other employees, to enhance the reputation of the institution with professionals or the community, to attract professional affiliations, to improve patient satisfaction, or to build other aspects of the business. Thus, any organization has many stories to tell, and many ways to tell any story.

Although healthcare leaders are key contributors to a marketing plan, it nearly always requires professionals in marketing or communication as a business to make it happen. The leader provides insights into the story, speaks for the mission of the organization, and knows the needs of the audience or community. The professional helps to frame the story.

We speak of telling the story, but it is also important to understand the language of marketing professionals. Traditionally market professionals refer to "The Four P's of Marketing": product, price, place, and promotion. *Product* may refer to an actual item or to services. A goal of marketing is to secure customer loyalty to the product. *Price* is cost to the customer. In health care, price gets complicated because it relates to service charges (which are not the same as cost), to employer costs for health insurance coverage, to other third-party costs to pay for services, and to provider costs to provide services, and all relate to cost for the patient. Thus, the audience for marketing also becomes complicated. *Place* in health care most often refers to access, location, and comfort of services. Focus on place in marketing might include the accessibility of a community clinic or the design of a patient room in a hospital. Finally, *promotion* refers to the communication plan for the marketing approach to tell the story of product, price, and/or place (Yoder-Wise & Kowalski, 2006).

Also key in marketing is the target population or the audience. *Segmentation* refers to a subgroup or "marketing segment" of the target audience for enhancement of the marketing approach. For example, adolescents might be a segment for a program on women's health and birth control. Obviously, the marketing approach would be different for an adolescent segment than for a community of elderly women. *Targets* further delineate the segment.

Leaders also need to understand concepts of *market share* and *market potential*. The market share of any organization is its estimated base of service of the total market. Market potential represents areas where the organization might grow to increase its market share. Today's healthcare organizations also keep an eye on the *competition's potential* of some other organization or competing interest to match or exceed the product, price, or place. Finally, leaders must understand the concept of *customer equity*, which is the "total asset value of the relationships which an organization has with its customers" (Blattberg & Deighton, 1996, p. 136). Blattberg and Deighton (1996) asserted that marketing is like a good conversation that begins a process to draw customers into progressively more satisfying relationships with the organization, thus building a kind of social equity. Waite (2002) further described three kinds of equity: First is *value* equity, which is a customer sense of special value in the company. In health care, that means we ask the question, "What is the value added, or the additional service, or other element of the four Ps that our organization offers?" The second kind of equity is *brand* equity, or recognition and attraction to a trusted name. Finally, *relationship* equity is the sense of personal relationship with the organization that brings the customer back. Thus, the image and mission of any healthcare organization are important for a successful marketing plan. Among the best kept secrets in healthcare marketing are the insights into customer desires and sources of satisfaction that you may offer as an expert clinician. As you advance in leadership roles, your clinical background that has connected you with real patients will be invaluable in marketing discussions of your organization. Your stories are grounded in authentic clinical experience. Indeed, one of my most perceptive DNP students brought my attention to a market professional's proposals to market nurse leaders as key contributors to the image of health care.

Heinrichs (2009) described the changing face of nursing, the increasing acceptance of nurse practitioners, and the future of the DNP. He offered specific suggestions for marketing approaches to invite the public to see the nurse beyond the culture of subservient roles and gender-specific stereotypes without losing the positive attributes that endear nurses to the public trust. The mission was to portray the nurse as a healer educated at the highest level. He asserted that appropriate marketing might follow the success of nurses expanding their scope of practice and influence to become recognized and valued players in healthcare reform. He proposed that such a marketing approach would saturate the markets with positive images of nurses in such advanced roles. Nurse leaders have a unique and valuable story to tell.

Ultimately as a leader, you must know the story of your organization so well that you are able and eager to tell it at any moment with passion. Purposely prepare a story moment. Prepare your "elevator moment," a 30-second version of your story. When someone asks what you do, you have already chosen the story and set each word as a jewel in a setting to share your clear and compelling message. Prepare your 5-minute moment for any opportunity when you are called to a podium or around a table to introduce yourself. Then take advantage of opportunities to be in the right meetings where you will be invited to tell your story, then stand up prepared and share. Do not confuse the 30-second moment with the longer one. Never overstay your welcome with your message. And above all, remember that your story is not about you, it is about the great organization that you have the opportunity to lead.

Storytelling as Communication

Although successful marketing is about telling a compelling story and stories are effective motivators (Pinkerton, 2006), storytelling in the larger sense is growing in importance in the social sciences, business (Denning, 2004), and the healthcare industry. It is especially powerful from the voice of a leader. Telling a compelling story helps you to convey ideas, vision, values, and images. Sandelowski (1991) noted the immense power in the ability of the narrative to inform, educate, and to enlighten. Stories impart wisdom and teach from experience. Leaders who tell persuasive stories draw others each to his or her own stories and thus draw people together. Every clinician's past has a closet full of stories. Reflect on your own stories. Begin to collect them from the corners of your memory. Practice telling them in a compelling manner with a sense of plot, characters, and mystery or humor. Tell your story and listen to the story of others. Find messages and meaning from them and share them. Help your colleagues develop and build the story of your organization. A compelling organizational story builds loyalty, pride in work, and a sense of community that can improve results. Stories shape the care culture (Smeltzer & Vlasses, 2004). Is your organizational story about healing? About profit? About people? About community? Is there a hero? Is there a villain? Several nursing leaders have proposed the following guidelines for creating stories (Kaye & Jacobson, 1999; Yoder-Wise & Kowalski, 2006, p. 182):

1. Look for themes that reflect your message, such as values, priorities, interests, or experiences.
2. Look for consequences reflected in the cause and effect of choices that generate meaning.
3. Look for lessons. What can be learned from the story?
4. Look for what worked. Success strategies are often found within the narrative of a good story.
5. Look for vulnerability. Some of the best stories are about mistakes, failures, and distractions or derailments that happen along the way.
6. Look for humor. The power of humor cannot be overestimated, and it is often most palatable and appreciated in a story. Laughter is medicine to hardworking, stressed workers.
7. Build for future experiences. A story can plant an image in the mind that can provide advice in some future situation.
8. Explore other resources. Identify and share stories from media, classic literature, movies, or other media.

Finally, I have not met a nurse who did not have a story of becoming and being a nurse. What is yours? What can you and others learn from your story? How does your story help you to become an effective leader? Your story can be transforming. How will you tell it?

REFERENCES

American Association of Colleges of Nursing. (1999). Education and practice collaboration: Mandate for quality education, practice, and research for health care reform. *Journal of Professional Nursing, 13*, 129–133.

American Nurses Association. (2003). *Nursing's social policy statement.* Washington, D.C.: ANA.

Anderson, W. T. (2001). *All connected now: Life in the first global civilization.* Los Angeles: Westview Press.

Arnold, L., Drenkard, K., Ela, S., Goedken, J., Hamilton, C., Harris, C., et al. (2006). Strategic positioning for nursing excellence in health systems: Insights from chief nursing executives. *Nursing Administration Quarterly, 30*(1), 11–20.

Barsh, J., Cranston, S., & Craske, R. A. (2008). Centered leadership: How talented women thrive. *McKinsey Quarterly,* (4), 35–36.

Bar-Siman-Tov, Y. (2004). *From conflict resolution to reconciliation.* New York: Oxford University Press.

Bartz, C., & Dean-Baar, S. (2003). Reshaping clinical nursing education: An academic-service partnership. *Journal of Professional Nursing, 19*(4), 216–222.

Benner, A. B. (2007). Physician and nurse relationships: A key to patient safety. *Journal of the Kentucky Medical Association, 105*(4), 165–169.

Bigony, L., Lipke, T. G., Lundberg, A., McGraw, C. A., Pagac, G. L., & Rogers, A. (2009). Lateral violence in the perioperative setting. *Association of Operating Room Nurses Journal, 89*(4), 688–696, 697–700.

Blattberg, R. C., & Deighton, J. (1996). Manage marketing by the customer equity test. *Harvard Business Review, 74*(4), 136–144.

Campbell, A., Whitehead, J., & Finkelstein, S. (2009). Why good leaders make bad decisions. *Harvard Business Review, 878*(2), 60–66, 100.

Campbell, S. L., Prater, M., Schwartz, C., & Ridenour, N. (2001). Building an empowering academic and practice partnership model. *Nursing Administration Quarterly, 26*, 129–133.

Cross, R., Liedtka, J., & Weiss, L. (2005, March). A practical guide to social networks. *Harvard Business Review,* 124–132.

Daly, G. (2004). Understanding the barriers to multiprofessional collaboration. *Nursing Times, 100*(9), 78.

D'Amour, D., Ferrada-Videla, M., Rodriguez, L. S. M., & Beaulieu, M. (2005). The conceptual basis for interprofessional collaboration: Core concepts and theoretical frameworks. *Journal of Interprofessional Care, Suppl. 1,* 116–131.

Davoli, G. W., & Fine, L. J. (2004). Stacking the deck for success in interprofessional collaboration. *Health Promotion Practice, 5*(3), 266–270.

Denning, S. (2004). Telling tales. *Harvard Business Review, 82*(5), 122–129, 152.

Doucette, J. N. (2008). Conflict management for nurse leaders. In H. R. Feldman, M. Jaffe-Ruiz, M. L. McClure, M. J. Greenberg, & T. D. Smith (Eds.), *Nursing leadership: A concise encyclopedia* (pp. 125–128). New York: Springer.

Edgecombe, K., Wotton, K., Gonda, J., & Mason, P. (1999). Dedicated education units: 1. A new concept for clinical teaching and learning. *Contemporary Nurse, 8*(4), 166–171.

Falcone, R. E., & Satiani, B. (2008). Physician as hospital chief executive officer. *Vascular & Endovascular Surgery, 42*(1), 88–94.

Feinberg, P. (2005, Fall). Q and Anderson: Kenneth Chenault on leadership. *Assets: UCLA Anderson School of Management,* 8–9.

Forte, P. S. (1997). The high costs of conflict. *Nursing Economics, 15,* 119–123.

Fulmer, T., Hyer, K., Flaherty, E., Mezey, M., Whitelaw, N., Jacobs, M. O., et al. (2005). Geriatric interdisciplinary team training program: Evaluation results. *Journal of Aging & Health, 17*(4), 443–470.

Gerardi, D. (2010). *Conflict management training for health care professionals.* Retrieved January 3, 2010, from http://www.mediate.com/articles/gerardi4.cfm

Goleman, D. (1998). *Working with emotional intelligence.* New York: Bantam.

Greiner, A., & Knebel, E. (Eds.). (2003). *Health professions education: A bridge to quality.* Washington, DC: Institute of Medicine, National Academies Press.

Grenny, J. (2009). Crucial conversations: The most potent force for eliminating disruptive behavior. *Critical Care Nursing Quarterly, 32*(1), 58–61.

Hayashi, A. M. (2001, February). When to trust your gut. *Harvard Business Review,* 59–65.

Heinrichs, J. (2009, October). Re-brand nurse. *Southwest Airlines Spirit,* 44–50.

Hertzberg, F. (1968). One more time: How do you motivate employees? *Harvard Business Review, 46,* 53–62.

Hill, F. W. (2004, February/March). Leadership: A personal journey. *Executive Speeches,* 5–9. Retrieved April 20, 2010 from http://tppserver.mit.edu/esd801/readings/journey.pdf

Horns, P. N., Czaplijski, T. J., Engelke, M. K., Marshburn, K., McAuliffe, M., & Baker, S. (2007). Leading through collaboration: A regional academic/service partnership that works. *Nursing Outlook, 55,* 74–78.

Institute of Medicine. (1999). *To err is human: Building a safer health care system.* Washington, DC: National Academy Press.

Johnson, C. B. (2000). When working harder is not smarter. *The Inner Edge, 3*(2), 18–21.

Kaye, B., & Jacobson, B. (1999, March). True tales and tall tales: The power of organizational storytelling. *Training & Development,* 362–371.

Kim, S. H. (1996). *1001 ways to motivate yourself and others.* Hartford, CT: Turtle Press.

Lagace, M. (2005, 6 June). Don't listen to "yes." *Harvard Business School Working Knowledge.* Retrieved January 3, 2010, from http://hbswk.hbs.edu/cgi-bin/print?id=4833

Leiker, M. (2009). Sentinel events, disruptive behavior, and medical staff codes of conduct. *Wisconsin Medical Journal, 108*(6), 333–334.

MacPhee, M. (2009). Developing a practice-academic partnership logic model. *Nursing Outlook, 57*(3), 143–147.

Macy, J. (2010). *The Josiah Macy, Jr. Foundation.* Retrieved January 31, 2010, from http://www.josiahmacyfoundation.org/

McConnell, E. S., Lekan, D., Herbert, C., & Leatherwood, L. (2007). Academic-practice partnerships to promote evidence-based practice in long-term care: Oral hygiene care practices as an exemplar. *Nursing Outlook, 55*(2), 95–105.

McElhaney, R. (1996). Conflict management in nursing administration. *Nursing Management, 24,* 65–66.

McGregor, D. M. (1960). *The human side of enterprise.* New York: Harper & Row.

Moaveni, A., Nasmith, L., & Oandasan, I. (2008). Building best practice in faculty development for interprofessional collaboration in primary care. *Journal of Interprofessional Care, 22,* 80–82.

Morrison, J. (2008). The relationship between emotional intelligence competencies and preferred conflict-handling styles. *Journal of Nursing Management, 16*(8), 974–983.

Moscato, S. R., Miller, J., Logsdon, K., Weinberg, S., & Chorpenning, L. (2007). Dedicated education unit: An innovative clinical partner education model. *Nursing Outlook, 55*(1), 31–37.

Mulready-Shick, J., Kafel, K. W., Banister, G., & Mylott, L. (2009). Enhancing quality and safety competency development at the unit level: An initial evaluation of student learning and clinical teaching on dedicated education units. *Journal of Nursing Education, 48*(12), 716–719.

Murray, T. A. (2007). Expanding educational capacity through an innovative practice-education partnership. *Journal of Nursing Education, 46,* 330–333.

Oestreich, D. (2009). *What is reflective leadership?* Retrieved September 20, 2009, from http://www.unfoldingleadership.com/blog/?p=171

Patterson, K., Grenny, J., McMillan, R., Switzler, A., & Covey, S. R. (2002). *Crucial conversations.* New York: McGraw-Hill.

Pew Health Professions Commission. (1998). *Recreating health professional practice for a new century: The fourth report of the Pew Health Professions Commission.* Retrieved August 28, 2009, from http://www.futurehealth.ucsf.edu/pdf.files/rept4.pdf

Pinkerton, S. (2006). Stories as motivators. *Nursing Economic$, 24*(3), 166–167.

Pontre, P. R., Hayes, C., Coakley, A., Stanghellini, E., Gross, A., Perryman, S., et al. (2005). Partnering with schools of nursing: An effective recruitment strategy. *Oncology Nursing Forum, 32*(5), 901–903.

Porter-O'Grady, T. (2004). Embracing conflict: Building a healthy community. *Health Care Management Review, 29*(3), 181–187.

Porter-O'Grady, T., & Malloch, K. (2007). *Quantum leadership: A resource for health care innovation* (2nd ed). Sudbury, MA: Jones & Bartlett.

Porter-O'Grady, T., & Malloch, K. (2008). Beyond myth and magic: The future of evidence-based leadership. *Nursing Administration Quarterly, 32*(3), 176–187.

Richardson, H., Haber, J., & Fulmer, T. (2008). Interdisciplinary leadership in nursing. In H. R. Feldman, M. Jaffe-Ruiz, M. L. McClure, M. J. Greenberg, & T. D. Smith (Eds.), *Nursing leadership: A concise encyclopedia* (pp. 310–314). New York: Springer.

Roberto, M. (2005). *Why great leaders don't take yes for an answer.* Upper Saddle River, NJ: Pearson.

Rosenstein, A. H., & O'Daniel, M. (2005). Disruptive behavior and clinical outcomes: Perceptions of nurses and physicians. *American Journal of Nursing 105*(1), 54–65.

Rosenstein, A. H., & O'Daniel, M. (2008a). A survey of the impact of disruptive behaviors and communication defects on patient safety. *Joint Commission Journal on Quality and Patient Safety, 34*(8), 464–471.

Rosenstein, A. H., & O'Daniel, M. (2008b). Invited article: Managing disruptive physician behavior: Impact on staff relationships and patient care. *Neurology, 70*(17), 1564–1570.

Rothman, J. (1997). *Resolving identity-based conflicts in nations, organizations, and communities.* San Francisco: Jossey-Bass.

Sandelowski, M. (1991). Telling stories: Narrative approaches in qualitative research. *Journal of Nursing Scholarship, 23,* 161–166.

Saxton, R., Hines, T., & Enriquez, M. (2009). The negative impact of nurse-physician disruptive behavior on patient safety: A review of the literature. *Journal of Patient Safety, 5*(3), 180–183.

Schwartz, R. W., & Pogge, C. (2000). Physician leadership: Essential skills in a changing environment. *American Journal of Surgery, 180*(3), 187–192.

Smeltzer, C. H., & Vlasses, F. (2004). Storytelling: A tool for leadership to shape culture: Listen to nurses' stories. *Journal of Nursing Care Quality, 19*(1), 74–75.

Stacey, D., Légaré, F., Pouliot, S., Kryworuchko, J., & Dunn, S. (in press). Shared decision making models to inform an interprofessional perspective on decision making: A theory analysis. *Patient Education & Counseling.*

Stanley, J. M., Hoiting, T., Burton, D., Harris, J., & Normal, L. (2007). Implementing innovation through education-practice partnerships. *Nursing Outlook, 55,* 67–73.

Sue, M. P. (2001). *Sparkle when you speak: 10 presentation tips for communicating results.* Retrieved January 14, 2010, from http://www.managerwise.com/article/phtml?id=69

Tessier, C., Chaudron, L., & Muller, H. (2002). *Conflicting agents: Conflict management in multi-agent systems.* New York: Kluwer Academic.

Thibault, G. E. (2010, January). *Interprofessional healthcare education and teamwork: Making it happen.* Paper presented at the meetings of the American Association of Colleges of Nursing Doctoral Education Conference, Captiva Island, FL.

Vazirani, S., Hayes, R. D., Shapiro, M. F., & Cowan, M. (2005). Effect of a multidisciplinary intervention on communication and collaboration among physicians and nurses. *American Journal of Critical Care, 14*(1), 71–77.

Veltman, L. L. (2007). Disruptive behavior in obstetrics: A hidden threat to patient safety. *American Journal of Obstetrics & Gynecology, 196*(6), 587.e1–587.e5.

Vivar, C. G. (2006). Putting conflict management into practice: A nursing case study. *Journal of Nursing Management, 14*(3), 201–205.

Waite, T. J. (2002, February). Stick to the core—or go for more? *Harvard Business Review, 80*(2), 31–41.

Walrath, J. M., Dang, D., & Nyberg, D. (in press). Hospital RNs' experiences with disruptive behavior: A qualitative study. *Journal of Nursing Care Quality.*

Weiss, J., & Hughes, J. (2005, March). What collaboration? Accept—and actively manage—conflict. *Harvard Business Review,* 93–101.

Wenger, E. (1998). *Communities of practice: Learning, meaning, and identity.* Cambridge, UK: Cambridge University Press.

Wenger, E. (2006). *Communities of practice: A brief introduction.* Retrieved January 31, 2010, from http://www.ewenger.com/theory/index.htm

Wheatley, M. (2005). *How is your leadership changing?* Retrieved October 6, 2009, from http://www.margaretwheatley.com/articles/howisyourleadership.html

Wheatley, M. (2008). *What is our role in creating change?* Retrieved October 6, 2009, from http://www.margaretwheatley.com/writing.html

Wheatley, M. (2009, March). The place beyond fear and hope. *Shambhala Sun,* 79–83.

Wheatley, M., & Frieze, D. (n.d.). *Using emergence to take social innovation to scale.* Provo, UT: The Berkana Institute.

Wotton, K., & Gonad, J. (2004). Clinician and student evaluation of a collaborative clinical teaching model. *Nurse Education & Practice, 4*(2), 120–127.

Yen, D. H. (1999). *Johari window.* Retrieved September 20, 2009, from http://www.noogenesis.com/game_theory/johari/johari_window.html

Yoder-Wise, P. S., & Kowalski, K. E. (2006). *Beyond leading and managing: Nursing administration for the future.* Philadelphia: Mosby Elsevier.

Zwarenstein, M., Goldman, J., & Reeves, S. (2009). Interprofessional collaboration: Effects of practice-based interventions on professional practice and healthcare outcomes. *Cochrane Database Systematic Reviews, 8*(3), CD000072.

Zwarenstein, M., Reeves, S., Barr, H., Hammick, M., Koppel, I., & Atkins, J. (2008). Interprofessional education: Effects of professional practice and health care outcomes. *Cochrane Database of Systematic Reviews,* (1), CD002213.

Current Challenges in Health Care: The Role of the Leader

> I long to accomplish a great and noble task, but it is my chief duty to accomplish humble tasks as though they were great and noble. The world is moved along, not only by the mighty shoves of its heroes, but also by the aggregate of the tiny pushes of each honest worker.
>
> — *Helen Keller*

Current challenges for healthcare leaders are enormous. They affect patients, families, communities, clinicians, and leaders. Each of the specific challenges briefly described in this chapter merits a book-length discussion of its own. Each brings its own ironic tangled burden of potential despair and promise of hope. And there are many important concerns beyond those described here that pertain to particular populations and care systems. The purpose of this chapter is not to analyze each of these challenges in depth, but rather to briefly explore some of the issues you will face as you launch from expert clinician to transformational leader. These challenges provoke pronouncements and recommendations of official panels of major organizations, appear as topics of professional white papers, provide fodder for curriculum change in health professions education, perplex researchers and clinicians, and vex leaders in every academic and clinical setting. They are your inheritance as the next generation of leaders. You will struggle with them; you will make progress to alleviate some of them in some small way; and others you may totally eradicate. You will be one of a band of committed professionals facing these challenges while the world hopes you find ways to overcome them.

ELIMINATING HEALTH DISPARITIES: REACHING THE UNDERSERVED

The well-worn definition of health is "the state of complete physical, mental, and social well being and not merely the absence of disease" (World Health Organization [WHO], 2000a). The vast unjust differences in health status and outcomes among various population groups have come to be referred to as health disparities. Conditions in health care are not equal across populations. Members of racial or cultural minorities are generally "sicker and more likely than whites to die of numerous diseases" (Brewington, 2009). Ten percent of White Americans report fair or poor health, compared with 17% of Hispanic and 16% of Black Americans. Disparity reflects not only differences in actual health status but also differences in access to healthcare services, experiences across systems, and in the health care workforce itself.

The United States is among the most diverse countries in the world. Alexander (2008, p. 154) reminded that 25% of the American population is African American, Hispanic, Native American, or Asian/Pacific Islander. By the year 2050, minority populations will represent nearly half the country's population (Alliance for Health Reform [AHR], 2006). Smedley and Stith (2002) noted, "The diversity of the American population is one of the nation's greatest assets; one of its greatest challenges is reducing the profound disparity in health status of American's racial and ethnic minorities."

The unfortunate fact is that general quality of health care is inferior for racial and ethnic minority groups compared with nonminorities, and too few Americans are unaware of the problem (AHR, 2006). Disparities exist in the prevalence of specific clinical conditions, particularly chronic diseases such as diabetes, asthma, hypertension, and heart disease. Differences persist not only in the prevalence of diseases but also in access to care, actual experiences in healthcare systems, and outcomes of care (American Academy of Nursing, 2008; Agency for Healthcare Research & Quality, 2004; Institute of Medicine [IOM], 2003). In the United States, Black men are twice as likely to have prostate cancer as White men, Hispanics are twice as likely to have diabetes than Whites, Vietnamese-American women are five times more likely to have cervical cancer than White women (Brewington, 2009), and Black women are less likely than White women to survive breast cancer. All minorities are less likely to receive screening or treatment procedures than their White counterparts (Agency for Healthcare Research & Quality, 2000; Lee, 2006). States with the greatest racial diversity, also show greatest disparities in cancer deaths, immunization rates, infant mortality, income disparity, and insurance coverage. Such differences pervade all areas of our healthcare systems (Sack, 2008). Even when insurance coverage is available, minorities often receive lower quality of care (AHR, 2006). Such disparities affect quality and length of life and diminish all of us as a society. Eliminating health disparities is one of the greatest current challenges for leaders in health care.

The diversity of Americans is much broader than racial. It includes factors of geography, culture, economics, and the very nature of the healthcare workforce and systems. As interest in outcomes of healthcare practice has increased, we have become more enlightened about serving specific groups or populations. As we have focused more on outcomes of care, we have become more sensitive to disparities in care among various population groups and more aware of underserved populations. Generally, underserved populations are described as "groups whose demographic, geographic, or economic characteristics impede or prevent their access to health services" (Weitz, 2000). The list of underserved populations in our society goes far beyond racial and ethnic minorities. The list is far too long. It includes the poor, the children, the elderly, cultural groups, and others. Leaders in health care are challenged to define and serve underserved populations. For example, questions include, "What demographic variables are of particular concern?" "How do we define geographic barriers?" (Weitz, 2000), and "How do we overcome the barriers?"

Beyond the ethical or moral implications of disparities in health, cost to American society of racial health disparities is over $75 billion per year. In order to eliminate disparities in health care, future leaders will be required to think and act creatively. The traditional systems and approaches are simply not reaching significant members of our communities. New approaches to coverage, such as statewide or national programs and interprofessional partnerships, as well as new approaches to access, such as school-based and community healthcare centers, need to be explored and fortified to become more effective. Health disparities are too easy to overlook as leaders and clinicians work with nearsighted diligence to meet the daily demands of their work. Part of the problem is the dearth of minority representation among healthcare providers (AHR, 2006; Sullivan Commission, 2004). It requires a step back for perspective and sustained commitment to measurement of outcomes at the individual and aggregate level. It requires leaders to come together across professions and settings to examine disparities and create new ways that work.

IMPROVING HEALTH LITERACY

The need for improved health literacy is a common problem among minorities and the underserved. It is among the silent challenges to healthcare quality that are gaining increasing attention. Inadequate health literacy affects patients and families. It pervades all aspects of health care and is becoming an increasingly important issue for leaders. Health literacy is generally recognized as the ability to obtain, process, understand, and use basic health information to make appropriate healthcare decisions (Committee on Health Literacy for the Council on Scientific Affairs, 1999). Over 90 million people in the United States lack adequate health literacy to make decisions for their own health promotion and maintenance (Committee on Health Literacy of the IOM, 2004; National Center for Education Statistics, 2006). Recent Surgeon General of the United States Richard Carmona (2006, p. 803) referred to the "poor state of health literacy in America" as a "crisis," and the Institute of Medicine (IOM) has identified health literacy as one of the most important cross-disciplinary issues in health care. It is the currency for understanding and navigating the health care system (Berry, Seiders, & Wilder, 2003; Parker, Baker, Williams, & Nurss, 1999). Poor health literacy contributes to misunderstanding or lack of health care information, including instructions, guidelines, and prescription drug labels. It compromises optimum management of chronic illness and is generally associated with poor or adverse health outcomes, including inadequate use of preventive services and increased incidence of chronic illness (DeWalt, Berkman, Sheridan, Lohr, & Pignon, 2004; Pignone, DeWalt, Sheridan, Berkman, & Lohr, 2005).

Culture, language differences, and socioeconomic status are highly interactive and associated with low health literacy. Implications are especially critical in areas of perceptions of health; risk reduction; screening; and treatment choices, compliance, and follow-up (see Davis et al., 2001; Donelle, Arocha, & Hoffman-Goetz, 2008; Friedman & Hoffman-Goetz, 2008). Indeed, health literacy has been called the "newest vital sign" (Weiss et al., 2005). Although research has begun to identify the relationship of poor health literacy with some adverse health outcomes, little research has addressed health literacy among specific populations such as the elderly or even young people as they begin to make lifelong healthcare decisions (Matzke, Machtmes, & Marshall, 2007; Matzke, Marshall, Melton, & Chopak-Foss, 2009). Health literacy appears to be a confounding factor in regard to health disparities and inadequate health care among rural and underserved populations. It certainly has not been adequately addressed as an issue in healthcare leadership.

As leaders attempt to meet current challenges to provide effective service, health literacy needs to be considered in all aspects of care. Furthermore, the goal for leaders may be better set at promoting health *fluency*. If literacy refers to the basic ability to understand

and process information, certainly, the goal for better health would be skilled fluency, ease, and effectiveness in using healthcare information. This is an issue for all settings including acute care, primary care, and community health. Practice models and patient care interventions are of little value if full use of healthcare information is not available to all patients. Poor health literacy is too often unnoticed but is a critical issue for leaders who guide and inspire clinicians. Indeed, failure to improve health literacy among those we serve may be considered a risk to patient safety.

BEYOND PATIENT SAFETY TO PRACTICE EXCELLENCE

It finally happened. The forces we warned about—increasing system complexity, higher costs, greater technology, decreased nurse staffing, increasing age and battle fatigue among nurses, and decreasing public trust in healthcare institutions—all came together and drew nurses into the crisis. Nurses had enjoyed continued public regard as patient advocates and remained largely invisible in the conflicts for power among healthcare administrators, physicians, and insurers. But quietly, one fall morning in the year 2000, the headline of *The Chicago Tribune* ambushed and brought nurses into the war: "Nursing Mistakes Kill, Injure Thousands" (Berens, 2000). Later that month, 1,500 nurses went on strike in Washington, D.C., citing workplace issues placing patient safety at risk. To our patients, we are now part of the problem; we are part of a health care system in crisis and a system that has been deemed unsafe.

Over a decade later, behind the headlines, overwhelming issues continue to threaten the nursing workforce: staffing cuts, mandatory overtime, and use of unlicensed personnel to perform nursing care, all at the cost of patient safety. Meanwhile, the IOM (2000, 2001, 2004) gave public notice that heralded the current avalanche of efforts toward assuring patient safety. The IOM announced that health care should be safe, effective, patient centered, timely, efficient, and equitable.

Safety is the most basic and essential expectation of effective health care. It is simply to "minimize risk of harm to patients and providers through both system effectiveness and individual performance" (Cronenwett, 2010; Cronenwett et al., 2007, p. 122). Reason demands that it be the right of anyone receiving care.

Despite a flurry of efforts, and more than a decade after the IOM report heralded the warning, safety issues continue to plague our work. Nearly 200,000 people continue to die from preventable medical injury each year, there is still no mandatory national reporting system for medical errors, and universal access to hospital safety information is not available (Crowley & Nalder, 2009). We have a long road ahead to make our healthcare environments safe. Especially in hospitals, the prevailing historical tradition sometimes imposes barriers that challenge efforts to change.

Gerardi (2010) observed:

As a result of the need to be right, there is a difficulty managing situations where it appears that the wrong choice was made or a system design flaw led to a bad outcome for the patient. Many conflicts in health care flare up around adverse outcomes or near misses with a patient's care. The quick jump to diagnosis usually results in a search for whom to blame for the bad outcome. The blame environment exacerbates the conflict by creating secrecy and shame. . . . Organizationally, hospitals and health care organizations must . . . find a way to reflect on how to improve their processes rather than foster a punitive environment that adds fuel to conflicts or drives them underground until the next adverse event occurs.

Cipriano (2008, p. 6) confirmed that attention to patient safety requires systems thinking. She asserted that, first, we must remove individual fear from the system, changing the question from "Who did this and what did the person do wrong?" to "What is the flaw in the system or process that provided the opportunity for error?" Thus, "eliminating fear and blame encourages people to report mistakes and allows creativity to flourish" to reduce errors and improve safety. She explained this in the context of the complex adaptive system of health care:

> By definition, a complex system has interacting components that work in both expected and unexpected ways. . . . In our healthcare system, humans contribute this element of unpredictability, creating [either] the possibility of error or innovation.

Conditions are changing. Nurses are quickly taking the lead to launch initiatives that improve patient safety. For example, the Quality and Safety Education for Nurses consortium, sponsored by the Robert Wood Johnson Foundation (Cronenwett, 2010; Cronenwett et al., 2007), has begun a major national effort to prepare health professionals, especially nurses, to lead in shaping professional identity among students and practitioners to commit to continuous improvement of quality care and patient safety. The project has begun to articulate specific knowledge, skills, and attitudes needed to promote patient care quality and safety. Specific goals, or competencies, of the project include patient-centered care; teamwork and collaboration; evidence-based practice; commitment to quality improvement, including use of data to monitor outcomes of care processes; safety; and informatics, or use of "technology to communicate, manage knowledge, mitigate error, and support decision-making" (Cronenwett, 2010).

Borrowing from other high-risk industries such as airlines, healthcare facilities are moving away from scrutinizing and condemning individual actions to emphasizing how to build safety into the entire complex system. It requires a change of assumptions, interprofessional collaboration, new views of policy, and universal transparency. Indeed, an expanded body of knowledge and a new realm of research on systems and patient safety are quickly emerging.

One model is a major hospital that set out to reduce error and improve safety in the performance of "hand-offs," or transfers of patients from one unit to another. From the perspective of appreciative inquiry, leaders opened discussions with all nurses to identify their ideal situation, to describe what was working, and to invent better mechanisms to improve safety. It worked. They were able to sustain positive change and integrate new plans into new ways of thinking and performing (Plexus, 2007).

Another key aspect of safety that has recently come to the forefront for nursing leadership is that of employee and nurse safety. Rogers (1997) outlined five areas of risks or hazards for nurses and other healthcare workers: biological/infectious disease risks, chemical hazards, environmental hazards, physical risks, and psychological risks. The American Nurses Association has launched several initiatives to raise professional, social, and policy consciousness about health, safety, and quality for nurses and healthcare leaders (De Castro, 2004; Herrin, Jones, Krepper, Sherman, & Reineck, 2006). The raising of consciousness to patient safety also provokes improved conditions for provider safety. These are key issues for leaders.

Much of the recent discussion on quality of health care has considered patient safety as if it were equivalent to quality. Safety is the minimum that any patient or provider has the right to expect. Safety should be the result of basic competence, and not the most to be expected from the highest level of excellence. This issue relates to Quinn's (2005, p. 75) question, "What separates the episodes of excellence from those of mere competence?"

Leaders in health care at this very moment, especially those who most closely oversee patient care, are diligently searching for ways to assure the safety of patients. We are doing research, creating plans, impaneling experts, and funding programs focused specifically on safety—but let us remember that safety is only the beginning. Safety reflects mere competence—safety is only doing no harm. Safety is simply not hurting or killing somebody. When will safety become second nature, the rightful outcome of every patient, family, and provider experience? When will safety be the everyday stipulation and reality of our work, and when will the focus of our practice move beyond safety to excellence? Your charge as a leader is to help to create the answers to these questions.

We must ask ourselves why major national panels must take official positions on patient safety, and we flutter to spend time and resources to design new models for safety. Think of it: *safety*—among the most basic needs. In other words, we are still trying to simply do no harm. Huge resources are now devoted to designing systems to prevent us from giving the wrong medication or the wrong dose to the wrong patient. We are developing programs with targets to avoid needless deaths in our system—a *health*care system, a system in which people enter unaware and with every right to expect that there is no possibility that they will be harmed or killed by the system. When can we move from safety to excellence and healing? The answer must come from the next generation of leaders.

QUALITY IMPROVEMENT AND CUSTOMIZED CARE: THE CURRENCY OF CUSTOMERS AND CLIENTS

Safety and quality may be the most common areas of discussion and action in health care today. They are critical to individual patient care and for the very survival of healthcare systems. The momentum of attention of the public and professionals began after a series of alarming reports from the IOM (2000, 2001, 2006) that exposed a variety of unfortunate realities of the American healthcare system regarding medical errors and other unacceptable conditions. Indeed, the American healthcare system was ranked 37th in the world by the World Health Organization (2000b) at its last rating.

Continuous quality improvement is the official jargon for creating an institutional culture that examines processes and systems of care to assure quality of care. Unfortunately, all too often, the focus on measuring quality stops at safety, or the absence of harm, rather than on elevation of standards beyond safety to excellence. Increased public scrutiny has pushed efforts toward improved quality throughout various types of healthcare systems (Advisory Board, 2004; Arnold et al., 2006). Arnold et al., (2006, p. 215) noted that chief nursing executives now spend the majority of their time on issues of quality, compliance, and patient safety requirements: "As regulatory requirements become increasingly intense and consumer expectations heighten, quality and compliance-related pressures mount." They pointed out that it is not unusual in large systems to see entire new structures created specifically for assurance and monitoring of quality. Indeed, quality ranked highest for chief nursing executives in a study of priorities and challenges among nurse leaders in hospitals (Arnold et al., 2006).

Kurtzman and Jennings (2008; Beecher, 2001) pointed to health policy analysts who found a lack of leadership in quality initiatives. Nursing leaders have begun to fill that leadership gap to make quality one of the most important current issues in all health care situations.

Brooks (2008) outlined a number of official databases or standards directed specifically at quality for nursing practice. These include the National Database for Nursing Quality Indicators, the Veterans Administration Outcomes Database, the National Voluntary Consensus Standards for Nursing Sensitive Care from the Joint Commission on Accreditation of Healthcare Organizations, and the standards of Transforming Care at the Bedside from the Institute for Healthcare Improvement (IHI) and Robert Wood Johnson Foundation. Much of the focus among these efforts is on hospital care, but similar issues of quality pervade health care throughout our communities.

The National Quality Forum ([NQF] 2004) outlined 15 "nursing-sensitive" measures now generally used in acute care institutions as indicators of quality. The measures are divided into three areas of patient-centered outcome measures, nursing-centered intervention measures, and system-centered measures. Patient-centered measures include failure to rescue (or death among surgical inpatients with treatable serious complications), pressure ulcer prevalence, patient falls prevalence, falls with injury, restraint prevalence, urinary catheter–associated urinary tract infections, central line catheter–associated infections, and ventilator-associated pneumonias. Nursing-centered measures include counseling patients with acute myocardial infarction, heart failure, or pneumonia regarding smoking cessation. System-centered measures include skill mix among registered nurses, practical nurses, and unlicensed personnel; nursing care hours per patient day; measures of nurse involvement in system governance and professional relationships; and voluntary turnover of nurse employees. Obviously, the list reflects important measures for patient survival, but if a stranger from another planet with superior health care visited our system, would that stranger find these measures as minimum for safety or as measures of excellence in healing? We are moving in the right direction with the focus toward improvement of care, and such efforts are making a difference in nursing performance and patient outcomes. But again, the challenge of leaders of the next level is to move performance to higher levels of excellence and healing.

There are several mechanisms by which leaders may engage the organization in pursuit and evaluation of quality. One common way for leaders to confirm, measure, or monitor quality is benchmarking. Benchmarking is a method of comparing aspects of performance with similar organizations. It is usually done to provide information for strategic planning or to improve the processes, productivity, and quality of services. It allows you to make a professional comparison of the quality of your own setting with that of others anywhere in the world (Hollingsworth, 2008). Indeed, engagement in benchmarking activities in itself is a step toward improvement of quality. There is a difference between benchmarking and adopting industry standards or regulatory guidelines. Benchmarking is a voluntary, thoughtful, and selective activity of identifying peer organizations or organizations to which you aspire to emulate on a specific process or outcome. You are then able to set specific goals related to the benchmark findings. The following are some of the steps outlined by Hollingsworth (2008, p. 70) for successful benchmarking:

1. Identify benchmarking partners or.
2. Determine what constitutes the benchmark calculation or data source.
3. Gather information from peer sources.
4. Compare actual data to benchmark data.
5. Identify variances and calculate gaps in performance.
6. Identify ideas for improvement, set goals, and develop and implement an action plan.
7. Measure results and compare with the benchmark.

Benchmarking is most commonly done in hospitals and educational settings, but the principles apply to other settings like primary care or public health.

Magnet designation is another mark of quality. It has been recognized for 25 years as a "hallmark of excellence" for quality and professional nursing in hospitals (Wolf, Triolo, & Ponte, 2008). Sponsored by the American Nurses Credentialing Center of the American Nurses Association, Magnet status recognizes four major areas:

1. The management, philosophy, and practice of nursing services.
2. Adherence to national standards for improving the quality of patient care services.
3. Leadership of the nurse administrator in supporting professional practice and continued competence of nurses.
4. Understanding and respecting the cultural and ethnic diversity of patients, their significant others, and healthcare providers (Urden, 2006, 25)

Basic criteria, or "forces of magnetism," include quality of nursing leadership, organizational structure, management style, personnel policies and programs, professional models of care, quality improvement, consultation and resources, autonomy, community supportive partnerships, nurses as teachers, image of nursing, collegial nurse-physician relationships, and professional development. Magnet hospitals have consistently scored high on support to nursing practice, nursing workload, and nurse satisfaction (Lacey et al., 2007). Application of Magnet principles has spread abroad (Aiken, Buchan, Ball, & Rafferty, 2008; Chen & Johantgen, 2010) but has yet to move to practice settings outside hospitals.

Another example of a specific external measure of quality for hospitals is the Malcolm Baldrige National Quality Award, a federal award to healthcare organizations that seek to meet particular standards on leadership; strategic planning; customer and market focus; measurement, analysis, and knowledge management; human resource focus; process management; and results (American Society for Quality, 2006). The standards include strategic business principles, core values, and role modeling of leaders in principles that ultimately promote quality, such as "planning, communication, coaching, development of future leaders, review of organizational performance, and staff recognition" (Baldrige National Quality Program, 2008; Goonan & Stoltz, 2004; Kurtzman & Jennings, 2008, p. 241).

Also, the NQF is a private, nonprofit organization that develops strategies for quality measurement and reporting in health care. Its mission is to set national priorities and goals for performance improvement, endorse national consensus standards for measuring and publicly reporting on performance, and promote the attainment of national goals through education and outreach programs (NQF, 2009). It has exerted considerable recent influence on performance, influencing initiatives of pay-for-performance, which is a paradigm that began with the Centers for Medicare and Medicaid Services whereby third parties reimburse healthcare providers based on quality and efficiency rather than on services and procedures only. It requires healthcare agencies to monitor and report data on specific measures with standards that must be met in order to receive payment reimbursement (Gelinas, 2008). Third parties are beginning to withhold payment for conditions related to poor care quality and paying for performance on safety and quality. The movement has begun to change the culture of quality in patient care.

Brooks (2008, p. 146) further proposed four key trends that will shape the future of quality and safety in nursing practice: "(1) transparency; (2) 100K Lives Campaign and standards of care; (3) pay-for-performance/pay-for-reporting; and (4) patient centeredness and coordination of care" (Reinertsen, 2006). Transparency refers to the trend of healthcare agencies toward publishing outcome data. Such publication is thought to increase competition on measures of quality. The 100K Lives Campaign refers to an initiative begun in 2005 of more than 2,600 healthcare organizations to reduce national hospital deaths by 100,000. It is part of the move toward transparency to improve quality of care. Patient centeredness and coordination of care include accountability for quality processes within entire patient care systems and coordination of patient care across settings.

A variety of individual demonstration movements across the country have begun to make a difference. One example is the Hospital Quality Incentive Demonstration, where hospitals are rewarded financially for top performance on specific outcomes. The Physician Group Practice Demonstration provides for physician groups to be rewarded for innovative proactive patient care and disease management in specific areas to reduce healthcare costs. Also, the Hospital Consumer Assessment of Health Plans Survey is designed to measure and standardize data on patient satisfaction. Private healthcare systems and advocate organizations have joined the movement, with a variety of initiatives to change the culture toward incentives for quality and efficiency.

The recent Transforming Care at the Bedside project (IHI, 2010) was a major national effort to address issues of quality, safety, and reliability; vitality of nursing engagement and teamwork; patient-centered care; and value-added care processes in hospitals. It specifically targeted medical-surgical units in a large number of hospitals across the country (Anonymous, 2004, 2005; IHI, 2010; Rutherford, Lee & Greiner, 2004). Specific, broad targets were impressive (Rutherford et al., 2004, p. 4):

1. No unanticipated deaths.
2. No needless pain and suffering.
3. Clinicians, staff, and students will say, "I contribute to an effective care team within a supportive environment that nurtures my professional career/growth and continually strives for excellence."
4. Patients will say, "They give me exactly the help I want (and need) exactly when I want (and need) it."
5. Unnecessary documentation is eliminated, reducing total documentation by 50%.
6. Clinicians spend 70% of their time in direct patient care.

Measures to monitor achievement of targets include "adverse events, unanticipated deaths, patient falls, unplanned returns to the intensive care unit, pressure ulcer prevalence, hospital-acquired pneumonia prevalence, care team satisfaction, voluntary turnover, patient and family satisfaction, percentage of time spent in direct patient care, percentage of time spent in documentation, percentage of time spend in value-added work, and costs per diagnosis related group for the top three diagnoses of patients" (Rutherford et al., 2004, p. 4). Results have been highly positive and vary from situations of critical care (Donahue, Rader, & Triolo, 2008) to general medical-surgical patient care (Lorenz, Greenhouse, Miller, Wisniewski, & Frank, 2008; Upenieks, Needleman, et al., 2008; Viney, Batcheller, Houston, & Belcik, 2006), focusing on specific patient choices (Scott-Smith & Greenhouse, 2007) as well as multihospital systems (Martin et al., 2007).

Such trends toward quality offer important opportunities for leadership, particularly in nursing. Similar initiatives need to be tested in settings beyond hospitals. Transformational nurse leaders must have a foundation in understanding the interdisciplinary aspects of care in continuous quality improvement processes, and in patient-centered care. The next challenge is to create systems in which quality of care is integrated as second nature into all aspects of health care, including primary care and community health care. As the leader, remember that tools for quality management are "means, not the end." Kibort (2005, p. 54) reminded, "Remember they are just tools. Learn to use a few of them well. And stick to the fundamentals."

Nearly always, an initiative for quality improvement means leadership in change and change management, whether it is a change of procedure or process, change of product, or change of culture. Weber and Joshi (2000) noted that understanding change is most critical to successful quality improvement initiatives. It is important for the leader to understand the following eight critical strategies to manage change for quality improvement:

1. Develop a vision for change.
2. Focus on the change process.
3. Analyze which individuals in the organization must respond to the proposed change and what barriers exist.
4. Build partnerships between physicians and administration.
5. Create a culture of continuous commitment to . . . [quality].
6. Ensure that . . . [quality] begins with leadership.
7. Ensure that change is well communicated.
8. Build in accountability for change [and quality]. (Weber & Joshi, 2000, p. 388)

As noted in the discussion of patient safety, we must be continually aware in an environment of increased public and regulatory scrutiny and associated reporting requirements to distinguish between competence in compliance and excellence. Every other industry is moving toward customized service. Patients are becoming accustomed to know what they want and to expect care specific to their needs. Nursing leadership, in particular, can create new paradigms and care models that frame productivity as value-added care. This vision of care "goes beyond direct care activities and includes team collaboration, physician rounding, increased . . . communication, and patient centeredness . . . [in order to] improve efficiency, quality, and service," for example (Upenieks, Akhaven, & Kotlerman, 2008, p. 394). Excellence in quality represents not only a minimum standard of care but also superb care.

Kurtzman and Jennings (2008, p. 241) suggested the need to develop "quality literacy," calling for leaders to acquire and advance understanding of principles of quality, "both conceptually and practically." This includes the development of a business case that includes a set of standard performance measures to highlight nursing's influence on quality. The business case must provide "clear, unambiguous, quantifiable evidence of the primacy of nursing's contribution." Evidence is the rule of the day. As a leader, you must speak the language and provide the data to support the work that you know leads to excellence.

An innovative study of leaders in 370 hospitals in all 50 states revealed that specific attributes of transformational leadership are related to both quality improvement and knowledge management, resulting in better patient outcomes (Gowen, Henagan, & McFadden, 2009). Another study in England found that specific leadership activities of training personnel, team working, and appraisal of hospital staff were directly related to patient mortality (West et al., 2002). To lead the charge in authentic quality of care, leaders must create and communicate a specific plan, gather appropriate data, use the data in specific evidence-based decision making, provide training and education to all members of the work team, and reward excellent performance (Kurtzman & Jennings, 2008).

Knowledge and processes of quality improvement in health care have expanded to become recognized as a science with its own emerging body of knowledge. Cronenwett (2010) outlined its characteristics. It "considers local context, or what outcomes are achieved in what settings with what roles and processes, and it requires knowledge of [the specific] discipline, local culture, quality improvement methods and measures, and how to manage change." Furthermore, specific methods for reporting and publishing work on quality improvement have been proposed (see Davidoff et al., 2009).

In all the efforts to accelerate quality initiatives, we must not forget the viewpoint of patients themselves. Jennings and associates (Jennings & McClure, 2006; Kurtzman & Jennings, 2008, p. 241) warned that since most current indicators of quality in all of our lists and recommendations are developed and driven by data needs for compliance to "payers and purchasers, accreditors, and other policymakers":

> . . . The aspects of care that are most meaningful to clinicians, patients, and family members may not be reflected in these measures. Consequently, while there may be enormous measurement "activity" taking place, nurse executives must ask themselves, "What are we gaining from this activity and does it reflect the aspects of care that are most vital? How can we use the findings from the measurement efforts to make improvements in the quality of patient care?"

Quality and customized service are the currency of consumers across society today. People have become accustomed to demanding quality and to have service fit particular individual needs. A service such as health care cannot afford to overlook the personal meaning of that service to those who need it and receive it.

Although most of the published work on quality reflects practice in acute care, in any position or any setting, as a leader, you will devote considerable attention to quality. The public now demands it. There is an amazing array of resources for leaders in standards, structures, and processes to test, evaluate, and improve quality. The vigilance and hard work required to sustain formal activities in quality improvement are enormous. In the midst of all the work, remember that you are the transformational leader. Look beyond the work "activity" to the vision and meaning of improving lives and promoting healing. Quality "work" can be exhausting if it is not ultimately meaningful to patients and providers and born from passion and inspiration. That reflects the true challenge to leaders. You must share your own wise energy as leader.

ASSESSING AND MANAGING RISK

Risk is the other side of safety and quality. There are two aspects to risk management. One is to reduce risk to patients in particular situations, such as taking measures to reduce infection transmission or to prevent pressure ulcers. The other part of risk management is to prevent incidents for which the institution may be held liable or to provide an environment for patients and workers that reduces loss to the organization (Pozgar, 2007). Risk management most often refers to risk to the healthcare institution. Risk management is defined by the Joint Commission on Accreditation of Healthcare Organizations (2006) as "clinical and administrative activities undertaken to identify, evaluate, and reduce the risk of injury to patients, staff, and visitors, and the risk of loss to the organization itself," which appears to be largely a statement to avoid liability. With the increased attention to patient safety, risk to patients and to organizations has risen to the forefront of health care. Legal issues can become entangled with risk management. Risk managers have become invaluable in helping to assess issues, develop interventions, and evaluate outcomes to prevent and reduce risks to patient safety and to the organization as well as to interpret legal implications. Risk management encompasses an entire body of knowledge and experts. The effective leader will recognize and work effectively with others who have such expertise.

Depending on the size of the organization, either the risk manager or you as leader are responsible for developing and enforcing systems to identify, report, and communicate incidents that expose risk. Risk managers develop policies and procedures that address issues related to risk, such as confidentiality, informed consent, product performance, and sentinel events. They work closely with clinicians, managers, and quality management experts. Major areas of stewardship in risk management include loss prevention and reduction, claims management, financial risk, and compliance with regulatory and accrediting organizations (Dearman, 2009).

It has become the responsibility of the leader to assure effective systems and to change the culture toward a systems perspective and transparency. Most important to reduce adversarial and litigious responses to risk is transparency, to be genuine with patients and families, and to meet their expectations. This often boils down to simply showing up when they expect and responding in a compassionate professional manner.

Key components of effective risk management include effective policies and procedures, documentation of patient care and other clinical activities, as well as timely and transparent reporting of critical incidents. Effective risk management requires leadership at the highest level of ethical behavior. The transformational leader will engage the expertise of risk managers and lawyers as appropriate to manage and contain risk for patients, employees, and the organization. Such a leader will also have the values and principles that provide the foundation for effective assessment, management, and reduction of risk.

PATIENT AND PROVIDER SATISFACTION

Risk to the organization and litigation related to liability are often related to simple satisfaction with service. Ultimately, patient, family, and provider satisfaction relates to perceptions and expectations of quality and value. Regardless of your perspective of a leader or your belief that your organization is performing famously, it means nothing if you are not in touch with expectations and the actual experiences of the people you serve.

Patient Satisfaction

The activities of seeking patient perceptions of value and actually measuring patient satisfaction are often so highly related that distinctions may be blurred. How is value defined? What do patients and families value? Business suggests customer value models, which are data-driven representations of the worth of what the business does or could do for its customers. Value is the worth of service to the customer in exchange for the price the customer pays. More simply, value is what the customer gets in exchange for a price paid (Anderson & Narus, 1998). In business, value is measured in monetary terms, but in health care, it is much more complicated. Value is more than price. Perhaps, because of its complexity, we have avoided framing satisfaction in terms of value. Womack and Jones (2005, pp. 60–61) referred to "lean consumption" or providing full value expected or desired by the customer "with the greatest efficiency and least pain." They outlined the following six principles of lean consumption:

1. Solve the customer's problem completely by ensuring that all the goods and services work, and work together.
2. Do not waste the customer's time.
3. Provide exactly what the customer wants.
4. Provide what is wanted exactly where it is wanted.
5. Provide what is wanted where it is wanted exactly when it is wanted.
6. Continually aggregate solutions to reduce the customer's time and hassle.

Can you imagine the healing benefits to patients and families if we achieved such principles in daily acts of care? One method used to assess value is patient and family focus groups. Members of the focus groups need to include a true sample of the patients you serve. Questions must be crafted to uncover actual perceptions of value, and then you must listen from the perspective of the patient and family. It is often easy to continue to see the world from your perspective within the system. Another sure way for a leader to see the patient's perspective is to actually *be* the patient or family member, but not where you are known and receive even subtle special attention. Healthcare providers gain invaluable lessons when they actually become the patient.

Anderson and Narus (1998) suggested that you formally list the value elements of your organization. Such elements might be basic technical elements such as safety, economic, service oriented, or social and will vary in how tangible they might be. The more comprehensive the list, the better able you are to tease out areas of value that determine satisfaction. What is most valued in your system? What are your best qualities? Where do you need to improve? Would your patients agree with your list? Still, another method is benchmarking with similar facilities regarding elements and scores of patient satisfaction. Unfortunately, our healthcare systems are so vast and varied, with little integration or data sharing across systems, that this is a challenge, particularly in settings outside hospitals. Regardless of the method you use to seek information on value and satisfaction, service and care decisions need to be based on data. Too often, in health care, we have made internal assumptions regarding value. We need to know what our patients really want.

Identifying and securing valid and useful data on patient satisfaction are challenges. As a leader, I often wish we had a "secret shopper" way to glimpse into the realities of the patient experience. What could we learn about patient satisfaction from an authentic behind-the-patient-scene? How might we integrate principles of customer service to assure satisfaction? Born, Rizo, and Seeman (2009) proposed the idea of understanding patient satisfaction from data available by social media such as patient stories on social networking and social rating Web sites. The data are patient generated, publicly available, generous in authenticity, and directly from the patient's perspective. Think about how you might seek actual patient stories. When I am in any public setting, such as riding on an airplane, and the stranger next to me learns I am a nurse, the person *always* has a story. And the story always includes elements of personal satisfaction or dissatisfaction that are not measured in our systems. How might we harness those stories to identify ways to improve value and satisfaction?

Provider Satisfaction

Regardless of the organization you lead, you will deal with a range of providers including physicians, nurses, other professionals, and support personnel. Perceptions, expectations, and experiences among these groups can differ vastly. Satisfaction among all types of providers is critical to retain valuable personnel, to create a positive caring environment, and to accomplish the mission of the organization. Retention of nurses and other providers is directly correlated with the general work environment, which is heavily influenced by the characteristics of the leader (Rondeau, Williams, & Wagar, 2008; Thomas, Thompson, & Koch, 2009). A "healthy, healthful, and healing environment" is "imperative" to satisfaction and positive patient outcomes (Stichler, 2009, p. 176). Providers need to feel valued, to believe they are making a difference, to believe they have control over the care they provide, and to feel able to provide care in the manner they believe their patients deserve (Thomas et al., 2009). Role discrepancy is a growing problem for physicians and nurses. Generally, healthcare providers invest in their preparation and enter their disciplines with an expectation of the role they will play in caring for others. When the job they are actually required to do does not match the role they expected, dissatisfaction leads to frustration, cynicism, and even despair (Takase, Maude, & Manias, 2006). They either stay on and complain or leave. We cannot afford to lose the very people with the most idealistic expectations to help others.

Thomas et al. (2009) outlined some organizational strategies to assure retention and satisfaction for nurses. These include appointing a nurse retention coordinator who deals with the daily issues in the work environment, such as schedule negotiation, position reassignment, exit and transfer interviews, team building, and recognition (Clevenger, 2007). Internal career planning opportunities have also been shown to improve the work environment to retain nurses. Examples include career ladders and career development programs. These programs provide recognition and advancement based on performance. Another approach is to promote job variety or job sharing, allowing nurses to have positive stimulation and convenience. To be effective, such options need to be perceived as opportunities rather than imposed mandates (Erenstein & McCaffrey, 2007).

Sheer demographics can bring challenge or opportunity to the leader working to promote retention and satisfaction. The intergenerational nature of current providers presents unique challenges. Physicians, nurses, and other healthcare workers may represent senior, Gen-X, Millennial, or other cultural groups trying to work together. One study revealed that younger nurses tend to be less satisfied than older ones, and Millennial nurses are more likely to be planning to leave their current job in the near future (Wieck, Dols, & Landrum, 2010). As the healthcare workforce generally ages, issues of retaining experienced workers are important. Creative personnel policies that recognize worker realities, such as offering elder day care and/or child day care for providers, recognizes the real-life experience of workers on both ends of the family caregiver life experience.

Few studies have examined satisfaction among providers in rural and underserved areas. One study found that rural nurses preferred work variety and autonomy in practice. Rural nurses also confirmed the findings of other studies that younger nurses report less intention to stay in their current job and that personal lifestyle is increasingly important in retention and job satisfaction (Molinari & Monserud, 2008). Another study also found higher levels of burn-out among younger nurses (Kanai-Pak, Aiken, Sloane, & Poghosyan, 2008). Still, other works have pointed to the importance of professional social support for nurses in rural and community settings (MacPhee & Scott, 2002). Furthermore, we have little experience dealing with issues of interprofessional satisfaction such as between physicians and nurses when actually working together as a team.

An important part of your job as a leader is to develop leaders within your organization. Satisfaction of managers who report to you is an important indicator of your effectiveness in leadership development. Lee and Cummings (2008) found that frontline nurse managers value autonomy and span of control over their work and sense of organizational support and empowerment in decision making. More than once I have heard the adage that valuable workers are attracted to *come* to the *organization*, but they *leave* because of dissatisfaction with a *leader*.

IMPROVING PATIENT AND HEALTHCARE OUTCOMES

Patient and healthcare outcomes generally refer to the results of our practices on structure, process, or products. The modern origin of the concept of outcomes management is attributed to Paul Ellwood (1988), who referred to outcomes management as "a technology of the patient experience." His basic principles included an emphasis on established standards, measurement of patient functional status and well-being and disease-specific clinical outcomes, collecting outcome data from the broadest reach, and analysis and dissemination to healthcare decision makers.

In the last 20 years, Ellwood's work has been quoted and emulated broadly. In the beginning, outcomes referred to the "five Ds of death, disability, disease, discomfort, and dissatisfaction" (American College of Emergency Physicians, 2009; Health Services Research Group, 1992; White, 1967). They have evolved to include clinical outcomes, functional status, satisfaction, and cost (American College of Emergency Physicians, 2009; Lonborg, 1995; Nelson, Mohr, Batalden, & Plume, 1996).

Unfortunately, even with all the rhetoric and guidelines, the focus on outcomes in health care continues to be relatively new to our daily operational activities. Kibort (2005, p. 53) complained:

I don't believe we, as an industry, truly know our "core business." The prime example comes when someone asks us what our outcomes are, and we are unable to articulate them. . . . We may know a few select outcomes for this program or that condition, but if you ask nine out of ten administrators . . . they couldn't tell you their organization's overall mortality rates, infection rate, or complication rates without really struggling for days to get the information. Very few other industry leaders would be this naïve about their business. Heck, they would be embarrassed.

Hopefully, current efforts on safety and quality are changing this outlook. Never underestimate the influence of the quality of leadership on patient outcomes. West et al. (2002) found significant correlations between leaders' management of employees and patient mortality in hospitals. Positive leadership practices included clarifying work objectives, identifying training needs, and providing feedback on performance, with focus on achieving organizational goals and improving individual performance and satisfaction. Wong and Cummings (2007) reviewed studies attempting to relate nursing leadership and patient outcomes, finding positive relationships between transformational leadership styles and patient satisfaction and reduced adverse events. But research on leadership in health care has been largely descriptive and related to the styles or traits of the leaders. Unfortunately, there are little empirical data on leadership and healthcare outcomes. We need more information on patient care and organizational outcomes and leadership (Vance & Larson, 2002).

Meade (2005, p. 1) reported the results of a study of seven healthcare facilities identified as "high-performing" organizations. High performance was defined as showing statistically significant progress sustained over 3 years on the following criteria: "increases in patient satisfaction ratings, increases in employee satisfaction ratings, reductions in employee turnover, increases in market share, financial return, or other growth indicators, and improvements on self-selected quality indicators."

Meade (2005, p. 3) identified the most influential factors in the success of high-performing healthcare organizations. The most important factor was commitment of executive and senior leadership. Achievement of positive healthcare outcomes requires vision, passion, and example at the highest levels. Next was leadership evaluation and accountability. Meade argued for a "no excuses" environment where leaders were evaluated and rewarded according to outcomes performance. Third was support for leadership development throughout the organization. You cannot expect leaders and managers at all levels to function without development as leaders themselves. This is part of the stewardship of generativity of leaders. Managers benefit from development specifically focused to prepare them as leaders. The fourth factor to achieve positive outcomes was open communication and formal opportunities for such communication throughout the organization. Finally, high-performing organizations nurtured a culture where everyone knew that patient-centered care and positive patient outcomes were the "right thing to do," that they "should" be doing what made sense for patients. Such organizations also reported a more friendly and helpful atmosphere, more collaboration and teamwork, and more regard for each other within the organization as well as for patients themselves.

Barriers to involving an entire organization into monitoring patient-centered outcomes are generally culture related. They include cultural cynicism that outcomes measurement is another fad, resistance to change, beliefs that the status quo is sufficient, lack of accountability, and poor leadership skills among managers (Meade, 2005).

With few exceptions, outcomes systems have been confined to acute care settings, although the concept of healthcare outcomes actually probably began in public health with community reporting systems. Clardy, Booth, Smith, Nordquist, and Smith (1998) provided a model to measure public health mental health services across an entire state. We need more of such models.

Outcomes has become the language of education and health care. Whenever an idea or concept grows in organizations, it develops theories; coins its own language, jargon, and meanings; attracts structures; and soon becomes a world of its own. Soon, citizens of that world begin to use only the language of the new world, speak only to each other, and build systems and processes around themselves. Do not let this happen to the endeavor of pursuit of positive outcomes in health care. Allow some positive deviance to break open the thinking once in a while. Allow independent examples of success to flourish, and learn from them to improve the entire organization. Sometimes, solutions are in plain sight but just need a new way of looking at them. We need new practices outside the tradition. Look at old problems in new ways. To do that is a hallmark of complexity theory and transformational leadership. Sternin (2007) argued that such positive deviance has changed some of the world's most pressing problems. The unfortunate rhetorical assumption related to outcomes is that there *is* actually an *outcome*, or destination, to care. The reality is that health care is an ongoing, iterative process to promote health, relieve suffering, and encourage healing. The inspiring leader keeps that vision ahead of the work with a healthy perspective that outcomes are markers on a continuing road toward excellence and improved health.

HEALTHCARE INDUSTRY WORKFORCE ISSUES

Challenges of providing care that meets the needs of the population and efforts to assure that care is safe and reflects high quality are paralleled by challenges within the entire workforce of all healthcare professionals. For many years, health care has led other industries in its need for well-qualified professionals who reflect the diversity of society. There is not a single component of the healthcare industry that does not suffer a need for people to do the work and leaders to guide them.

Shortages of Professionals

Personnel shortages abound in all aspects of health care. Over the last couple of decades, physicians have moved toward specialty training, leaving a gap in primary care. Although advanced practice nurses are well poised to fill that need, this gap continues because (1) state regulations vary widely on scope of practice, (2) payment gaps for nurse practitioner services continue, and (3) shortages in nurse practitioners themselves also persist. An aging population, the growing prevalence of chronic conditions, the increased use of technology, and a range of other realities contribute to a general shortage among all healthcare professionals including care providers, technicians, and workers in specialty and support disciplines.

A major factor in the growing crisis in health care is the serious worldwide shortage of nurses. Experts tell us that this shortage is different and more critical than previous deficits. It is projected to be of unprecedented severity and to endure long into the future. One nursing leader noted:

> We are on the brink of a health care disaster. With millions of Baby Boomers marching their way toward Alzheimer's disease, our nation will see a major long-term care work force shortage and dramatic drop in care quality unless we address this problem immediately. (Charity Wire, 2005)

At the same time our general population gets older, lives longer, and needs more nursing care, nurses themselves are getting older and more tired. The average age of practicing nurses is 45 years old.

Reflecting current economic challenges, some settings report little or no shortage of nurses, especially in acute-care settings. This appears to be largely due to responses to a poor economy: institutions maximize resources by reducing workforces, nurses working part-time change to full-time, older nurses delay retirement, These responses are temporary reflecting hard times. They do not reflect the larger picture of the growing need for highly-qualified nurses.

Current upheaval and needs of the healthcare system challenge the survival of professional nursing as we have known it. The knowledge, skills, and responsibilities of nurses have steadily increased over time. However, ironically, throughout modern history, the profession of nursing has accommodated immediate demands of the system by maintaining or even lowering educational requirements. And more than half of practicing nurses do not hold even a bachelor's degree. This has challenged the influence and stature of nursing as a discipline, diminished its attractiveness to young people as a profession, and affected the quality of care for patients. Nurses are now virtually the only "professionals" among healthcare practitioners who have significant responsibility for critical care in illness and injury, health maintenance, and health promotion for whom college graduation is not a prerequisite. The public expects a sophisticated healthcare workforce composed of nurses prepared as college graduates. The need for more highly prepared nurses, especially as leaders, matches the need for public confidence.

Physicians, nurses, and patients voice increasing dissatisfaction with health care, largely from their own personal experience. We all want the latest technology at the lowest cost in the shortest time from people with the greatest knowledge and skill who treat us in the most caring manner.

The next generation of physicians and nurses will require courageous, creative thinkers with compassionate hearts. We need leaders. We need not only leaders who continue to manage personnel and resources, but also, we need knowledgeable, clear-thinking, caring leaders who can turn around a failing system, slipping in the ranks of healthcare systems throughout the developed world. Further, we will need to recognize that the work of health care from the provider perspective will change and the way we prepare professional nurses must change (Benner, Sutphen, Leonard, & Day, 2010; Bosher & Pharris, 2008). Monroe (2006, p. 431) reminded, "How nursing work changes, while remaining true to our distinct core of caring, to use new approaches is the challenge that is most complex and holds the greatest potential to affect the availability of nursing care." We cannot change the work of providers without effectively changing the physical, political, and social structures and environments in which they practice. Creating new ways to provide care without changing the work environment is futile. Porter-O'Grady and Malloch (2008, p. 182) chided, "Clinical executives should be less panicked and preoccupied with staff shortages and more concerned with staff support." In other words, at the level of your own leadership, there is a vast range of creativity and inspiration you can offer to recruit, retain, and promote the abundance of caring providers needed for care within your stewardship.

The Value of Diversity

One of the most important current issues facing leaders in healthcare organizations and education of healthcare professionals is the need for diversity of the workforce. Wheatley (2001) taught that successful organizations rely on diversity in order to adapt to change, "If a system becomes too homogenous, it becomes vulnerable to environmental shifts," and added the following:

> Our organizations and societies are now so complex, filled with so many intertwining and diverging interests, personalities, and issues, that nobody can confidently represent anybody else's point of view. . . . No matter how hard we try to be understanding of differences, there is no possibility that we can adequately represent anybody else. But there is a simple solution to this dilemma. We can ask people for their unique perspective. We can invite them in to share the world as they see it. We can listen for the differences. And we can trust that together we can create a rich mosaic from all our unique perspectives.

One of the champions of nurses in healthcare leadership, Porter-O'Grady (2001, pp. 61–62), candidly shared his own experience of breaking the barriers of the stereotypes of nursing to diversity:

> It is hard for a man to "get into" nursing. All the images and language are directed toward women. The whole framework for caring and care giving is based on feminine notions. The overriding notion is that nursing is women's work and that there must be something wrong or "funny" if a man shows an interest in nursing. . . . The goodness-of-fit between what nursing is and who I am has never been in doubt for me from the foundations of nursing school to the present complexities. I have not always found that my colleagues have agreed with this understanding.

Disparities in gender and racial diversity in the current healthcare workforce have been framed as a contributing factor in the crisis of disparities in health care for the American population and, perhaps, even an issue of safety (Sullivan Commission, 2004). Providers cannot adequately care for a population that is not recognized within their own professional community.

Cummings et al. (2009) examined the influence of nursing leadership styles on factors related to nursing work, workforce, and work environments. Among their findings were a positive relationship between leadership styles that focused on people and relationships (such as transformational or resonant styles) and higher nurse job satisfaction. Similar trends were found related to nurses' role and pay, staff relationships, work environment factors, productivity, and effectiveness. The leader has the greatest power to influence the environment of work and caring. You can create the climate that sets the tone for a positive culture that supports the best work and retains the desirable number and diversity of healthcare workers.

ETHICAL ISSUES FOR THE LEADER OF THE NEXT CENTURY

Ethics in health care, in its best and broadest sense, may be the most important challenge to the transformational leader. In his *New York Times* column, Stanley Fish (2010) explored the difference between the "right" answer and the "true" answer. In complex systems, the right answer is "the answer required by the system," or the answer "a system invested in its own machinery will recognize no matter what the true facts may be." For example, a right answer might be the score on a standardized patient satisfaction score when the true answer is the actual experience of the patient that is not reflected in the score. To make a lasting positive difference, you must have the courage to question the right answers in favor of the true answers. To be ethical is to act consistently with what is moral, right, and true. To behave ethically is to consider societal norms and moral right and wrong and to do right. It requires public trust, basic honesty, recognition of conflicts of interest, and procedural fairness. To make ethical decisions requires the ability to recognize ethical issues and to consider ethical consequences of decisions, the ability to consider alternative points of view, and the ability to deal with uncertainty (National Defense University [NDU], n.d.).

From the beginning, identify and live your own mission statement, clearly articulate and integrate your values into all aspects of your life, and make all decisions based on principles preceding policies or procedures. Pointing to Morrison's (2000, p. 203) lament, "Organ and body functions are restored while the whole patient is ignored. The system is failing to serve." Vlasses and Smeltzer (2007, p. 379) responded, "Nursing must become the guardian of the values that bring dignity and respect to the patient and to humanize care as we go through the transformation and build beyond it . . . nurse executives are challenged to manage ambiguity, uncertainty, and conflicts during the transitions while sustaining a focus on transformation and innovation."

Guido (2006, p. 79) reviewed the following well-known list of ethical principles for the nurse leader:

1. Autonomy: The right to select a course of action.
2. Beneficence: The actions that promote "good" or appropriate outcomes.
3. Nonmaleficience: The duty to avoid harm.
4. Veracity: Telling the truth about decisions to the persons affected.
5. Justice: Treating all persons fairly and equally.
6. Paternalism: Assisting persons to make difficult decisions.
7. Fidelity: Keeping promises.
8. Respect: Treating all others with equal respect and concern.

At the heart of ethical leadership is commitment to your personal values. Values are "those things that are most important," what you believe to be right, "more than words . . . the moral, ethical, and professional attributes of character" (NDU, n.d.). Values are both personal and organizational. Vision and mission must be grounded in values.

Quinn (2005) described the difference between a "normal" state of leadership and the "fundamental" state of leadership. He asserted that when you are at your best, you are not trying to emulate anyone else. In a crisis, you draw from your fundamental values and abilities. Think about when you faced the most difficult trial of your life either at work or personally. You followed the instinct of your core values, and you found the best within yourself. You responded beyond your own usual abilities and likely surprised others by your wisdom and strength. That is the state of fundamental leadership. Quinn described the contrasts: (1) Fundamental leadership is results centered rather than comfort centered, as in a normal state. A focus on results invites you to move beyond a comfort zone to explore new possibilities and new outcomes. (2) Fundamental leadership is internally directed toward personal values rather than compliance with expectations of others. (3) Fundamental leadership is others focused rather than self focused. And, (4) fundamental leadership is externally open to needs and opportunities rather than internally closed to stay on the immediate task and avoid risk. The key is to know your values, set high standards, focus on others, be open to possibilities, and lead courageously.

One ironic ethical concern related to the nursing workforce is the appropriate response to a continuing nursing shortage. Halloran (2008) proposed that "Leaders in the nursing profession have pandered to cries of nurse shortages by preparing new entrants with beginning skills to support the existing hospital and physician dominated health system." He argued, "Were there to be investments in graduate education for clinical nurses who would compete for patients, more care would be given at less cost," that:

> Nurses are too important to be used to shore up an existing, fragmented, expensive system. Leadership is needed to see that patients have access to the services of nurses in primary care in more than token numbers. Nurses can contribute to the solution of health care financing by collaborating in the provision of primary care . . . or competing with doctors and hospitals for access to patients. As it is now, nurses are seen as part of the problem of financing health care in the United States. (Halloran, 2008, pp. 232–233)

The primary, essential, central moral principle ethics in nursing leadership is the doctrine of intrinsic human dignity (Perkins, 2008). It is codified in an official code of ethics adopted by the American Nurses Association (2001, p. 7):

> The nurse, in all professional relationships, practices with compassion and respect for the inherent dignity, worth and uniqueness of every individual, unrestricted by considerations of social or economic status, personal attributes, or the nature of health problems.

Leaders in health care are continually confronted with new and more complex ethical questions, but the core principle to protect human dignity remains at the center of the moral compass. Modern issues of disparities in access and care, vulnerable populations, end-of-life care and issues of assisted suicide, patients in persistent vegetative states, infectious diseases, chronic illness, and homeless and migrant populations will test the ethical decision making of all members of the healthcare system.

Leaders in health care encounter ethical issues that truly affect lives. Shale (2008) reminded that although the entire reason for being for healthcare systems is to provide the best care for the individual, and leaders are confronted with the paradox of managing limited resources to provide care for entire populations, which may not always be consistent with serving the individual. Other sources of paradox and dilemmas pervade the work of the transformational leader. Curtin (2006) gave the simple example in hospital leadership:

A staff nurse has an obligation to request more help when staffing on [his or] her unit is inadequate, and a right to expect that administration will respond to this need. [He or] she need not be concerned about the staffing on other units. The nurse manager, however, must judge the conflicting needs of other units to determine which has the greater need and allocate staff accordingly. [He or] she has an obligation not to base decisions on who complains the loudest, but rather on a fair assessment of needs. Such decisions do not deny the needs of the one, but rather recognize the greater need of the other.

Curtin (2006) further suggested that leaders facing difficult and ethic issues ask the following questions: (1) What is the case? (2) What criteria should be used to make the decision? (3) Who is best qualified to make the decision? (4) Is the decision a group decision? (5) Who should benefit most from the decision? And she reminded that for the leader, issues of "professional standards, self-regulation, and self-discipline assume different" and greater proportions and significance.

In a study by Redman and Fry (2003, p. 153), nurse leaders reported their most difficult ethical issues. They included staffing patterns that reduce patient access to care, inappropriate prolonging of the process of dying, working with incompetent or unethical colleagues, implementing mandated care practices that threaten quality, measures that do not consider patient quality of life, and caring for patients and/or families who are uninformed or misinformed about diagnosis, prognosis, treatments, or alternatives. These reflect the challenging realities of current systems. Future leaders must resolve these difficult issues.

Beyond making specific decisions, the leader has the responsibility to build an ethical climate. The first step to create an environment of ethics is to model ethical behavior. It requires a commitment to integrate personal, professional, and organizational values throughout the work environment. Informal models of ethical behavior have been found to be more effective than formal policies (Cooper, Frank, Gouty, & Hansen, 2003). Next is to establish policies and procedures that reflect fairness and ethical values. Then, communicate those values and policies throughout the organization. Finally, monitor all systems to know when and where ethical issues may arise in order to support ethical behavior and manage risk in decisions (NDU, n.d.).

Secretan (1986) suggested the primary values of mastery (or consistent action at the highest standard of which you are capable), chemistry (or "relating so well with others that they actively seek to associate themselves with you"), and delivery (or "identifying the needs of others and meeting them"). He further proposed leader behaviors to learn and seek wisdom, to empathize with the perspective of others, and to listen.

The challenges explored in this chapter certainly do not represent all major issues facing healthcare leadership. Perhaps, there is some topic you think that should have been discussed here. Perhaps, you are devoted to one of these or another cause just as important. Other significant issues related to patient populations include genetic testing issues care of the elderly, reaching underserved and uninsured children, the effects of poverty on health, access to care for mental health, palliative and end-of-life care, women's health, and health care provider coverage for all. There are also other systems issues such as access in rural areas, issues related to niche providers, private and public systems, financing health care, system models, the role of government in health care, and a world of other concerns. The challenges described here represent but a sample of issues that cross all populations of patients and concerns within systems at the moment. All require the leader with personal values who sets high standards and aspires to wisdom. Such leaders inspire trust and credibility.

It is most vexing that many of these challenges really ought not to be. For example, it is most unfortunate that we continue to discuss the need for and laud initiatives for patient-centered care. Shouldn't it be self-evident in a modern healthcare system as rich in resources as that of our country that patient-centered care would be the very fiber and practice of our system—that it would already be integrated into every aspect of care? You must be the leader to take us to that next most important level of caring. There are certainly other problems not listed here, but creating a longer list would not diminish the significance of these. What will you do as a leader to solve them?

REFERENCES

Advisory Board. (2004). *Enhancing nursing business performance* (pp. 2–24). Washington, D.C.: The Advisory Board Company.

Agency for Healthcare Research & Quality (AHRQ). (2000, February). *Addressing racial and ethnic disparities in health care* [fact sheet]. Rockville, MD: AHRQ. AHRQ Publication No. 00-PO41.

Agency for Healthcare Research & Quality (AHRQ) (2004, February). *National health care disparities report: Summary*. Rockville, MD: AHRQ.

Aiken, L. H., Buchan, J., Ball, J., & Rafferty, A. M. (2008). Transformative impact of Magnet designation: England case study. *Journal of Clinical Nursing, 17*(24), 3330–3337.

Alexander, G. R. (2008). Cultural diversity. In H. R. Feldman, M. Jaffe-Ruiz, M. L. McClure, M. J. Greenberg, & T. D. Smith (Eds.), *Nursing leadership: A concise encyclopedia* (pp. 154–155). New York: Springer.

Alliance for Health Reform (AHR). (2006, November). *Racial and ethnic disparities in health care*. Washington, D.C.: AHR.

American Academy of Nursing (AAN). (2008). *Disparities in health care initiative*. Retrieved February 2, 2010, from http://www.aannet.org/i4a/pages/index.cfm?pageid=3296

American College of Emergency Physicians (ACEP). (2009). *Quality of care and outcomes management movement*. Retrieved September 3, 2009, from http://www.acep.org/practres.aspx?id=30166

American Nurses Association (ANA). (2001). *Code of ethics for nurses with interpretive statements*. Washington, D.C.: ANA.

American Society for Quality (ASQ). (2006). *Malcolm Baldrige National Quality Award*. Retrieved September 1, 2009, from http://www.asq.orglearn-about-quality/malcolm-baldrige-award/pverview/overview.html

Anderson, J. C., & Narus, J. A. (1998, November–December). Business marketing: Understand what customers value. *Harvard Business Review, 76*(6), 53(76(=–64.

Anonymous. (2004). Program enables 50 new initiatives in four months: "Transforming care at the bedside" program. *Healthcare Benchmarks & Quality Improvement, 11*(9), 100–101.

Anonymous. (2005). Transforming care at the bedside: Using a team approach to give nurses—and their patients—new voices in providing high-quality care. *Quality Letter in Healthcare Leadership, 17*(11), 1–8.

Arnold, L., Campbell, A., Dubree, M., Fuchs, M. A., Davis, N., Hertzler, B., et al. (2006). Priorities and challenges of health system chief nursing executives: Insights for nursing educators. *Journal of Professional Nursing, 22*(4), 213–220.

Baldrige National Quality Program, National Institute of Standards and Technology. (2008). *Health care criteria for performance excellence*. Gaithersburg, MD: National Institute of Standards & Technology. Retrieved January 29, 2010, from http://www.quality.nist.gov/PDF_files/2008_Healthcare.Criteria.pdf

Beecher, E. C. (2001). Improving the quality of health care: Who will lead? *Health Affairs, 20,* 164–172.

Benner, P., Sutphen, M., Leonard, V., & Day, L. (2010). *Educating nurses: A call for radical transformation*. San Francisco, CA: Jossey-Bass/Carnegie Foundation for the Advancement of Teaching.

Berens, M. J. (2000, 10 September). Nursing mistakes kill, injure thousands. *Chicago Tribune.*

Berry, L. L., Seiders, K., & Wilder, S. S. (2003). Innovations in access to care: A patient centered approach. *Annals of Internal Medicine, 139*(7), 568–574.

Born, K., Rizo, C., & Seeman, N. (2009). Participatory storytelling online: A complementary model of patient satisfaction. *Healthcare Quarterly, 12*(4), 105–110.

Bosher, S. D., & Pharris, M. D. (2008). *Transforming nursing education: The culturally inclusive environment.* New York: Springer.

Brewington, K. (2009, 18 September). Cost of racial disparities in health care put at $229 billion between 2003, 2006. *The Baltimore Sun.* Retrieved February 15, 2010, from http://www.commondreams.org/print/47177

Brooks, J. (2008). Continuous quality improvement. In H. R. Feldman, M. Jaffe-Ruiz, M. L. McClure, M. J. Greenberg, & T. D. Smith (Eds.), *Nursing leadership: A concise encyclopedia* (pp. 145–149). New York: Springer.

Carmona, R. H. (2006). Health literacy: A national priority. *Journal of General Internal Medicine, 21*, 803.

Charity Wire. (2005). *Long term care workforce crisis is looming: Millions with Alzheimer's disease at risk.* Retrieved January 29, 2010, from http://www.charitywire.com/charity3/00080.html

Chen, Y. M., & Johantgen, M. E. (2010, 1 February). Magnet hospital attributes in European hospitals: A multilevel model of job satisfaction. *International Journal of Nursing Studies.* Epub ahead of print.

Cipriano, P. (2008). Improving health care with systems thinking. *American Nurse Today, 3*(9), 6.

Clardy, J. A., Booth, B. M., Smith, L. G., Nordquist, C. R., & Smith, G. R. (1998). Implementing a statewide outcomes management system for consumers of public mental health services. *Psychiatric Services, 49*, 191–195.

Clevenger, K. (2007). The role of a nurse retention coordinator: One perspective. *Nursing Management, 38*, 8–10.

Committee on Health Literacy (CHL) for the Council on Scientific Affairs. (1999). Health literacy: Report of the Council on Scientific Affairs. *Journal of the American Medical Association, 281*(6), 552–557.

Committee on Health Literacy of the Institute of Medicine (CHL, IOM). (2004). *Health literacy: A prescription to end confusion.* Washington, DC: National Academies Press.

Cooper, R. W., Frank, G. L., Gouty, C. A., & Hansen, M. M. (2003). Ethical helps and challenges faced by nurse leaders in the healthcare industry. *Journal of Nursing Administration, 33*(1), 17–23.

Cronenwett, L. (2010). *Quality and safety implications for doctoral programs in nursing.* Paper presented at the meetings of the American Association of Colleges of Nursing, Captiva Island, FL.

Cronenwett, L., Sherwood, G., Barnsteiner, J., Disch, J., Johnson, J., Mitchell, P., et al. (2007). Quality and safety education for nurses. *Nursing Outlook, 55*(3), 122–131.

Crowley, C. F., & Nalder, E. (2009, 10 August). Within health care hides massive, avoidable death toll. *Hearst Newspapers.* Retrieved August 17, 2009, from http://www.chron.com/fdcp?1250519170391

Cummings, G. G., Macgregor, T., Davey, M., Lee, H., Wong, C. A., Lo, E., et al. (2009, 23 September). Leadership styles and outcome patterns for the nursing workforce and work environment: A systematic review. *International Journal of Nursing Studies.* Epub ahead of print.

Curtin, L. (2006). Ethics in management: A framework for analysis. *Curtin Calls.* Retrieved June 14, 2006, from http://curtincalls.xillioninc.com/processor/posting/displayposting.asp?selwebsection=ethics

Davidoff, F., Batalden, P., Stevens, D., Ogrine, G., Mooney, S., McAvoy, J., et al. (2009). *SQUIRE: Standards for Quality Improvement Reporting Excellence.* Retrieved January 31, 2010, from http://squire-statement.org/

Davis, T. C., Dolan, N. C., Ferreira, M. R., Tomori, C., Green, D., Sipler, A. M., et al. (2001). The role of inadequate health literacy skills in colorectal cancer screening. *Cancer Investigation, 19*, 193–2000.

De Castro, A. B. (2004). Handle with care: The American Nurses Association's campaign to address work-related musculoskeletal disorders. *Online Journal of issues in Nursing, 9*(3), 45–54.

Dearman, V. (2009). Risk management and legal issues. In L. Roussel & R. C. Swansburg (Eds.), *Management and leadership for nurse administrators* (5th ed.). (pp. 470–493). Sudbury, MA: Jones & Bartlett.

DeWalt, D. A., Berkman, N. D., Sheridan, S., Lohr, K. N., & Pignon, M. P. (2004). Literacy and health outcomes. *Journal of General Internal Medicine, 19*, 1228–1239.

Donahue, L., Rader, S., & Triolo, P. K. (2008). Nurturing innovation in the critical care environment: Transforming care at the bedside. *Critical Care Nursing Clinics of North America, 20*(4), 465–469.

Donelle, L., Arocha, J. F., & Hoffman-Goetz, L. (2008). Health literacy and numeracy: Key factors in cancer risk comprehension. *Chronic Diseases in Canada, 29*, 1–8.

Ellwood, P. M. (1988). Outcomes management: A technology of patient experience. *New England Journal of Medicine, 318*(23), 1549–1556.

Erenstein, C. F., & McCaffrey, R. (2007). How healthcare work environments influence nurse retention. *Holistic Nursing Practice, 21*, 303–307.

Fish, S. (2010, 11 January). The true answer and the right answer. Opinionator Column. *The New York Times.* Retrieved January 13, 2010, from http://opinionator.blogs.nytimes.com/2010/01/11/the-true=answer-and-

Friedman, D. B., & Hoffman-Goetz, L. (2008). Literacy and health literacy as defined in cancer education research: A systematic review. *Health Education Journal, 67*, 285–304.

Gelinas, L. S. (2008). National Quality Forum. In H. R. Feldman, M. Jaffe-Ruiz, M. L. McClure, M. J. Greenberg, & T. D. Smith (Eds.). *Nursing leadership: A concise encyclopedia* (pp. 392–397). New York: Springer.

Gerardi, D. (2010). *Conflict management training for health care professionals.* Retrieved January 3, 2010, from http://www.mediate.com/articles/gerardi4.cfm

Goonan, K. J., & Stoltz, P. K. (2004). Leadership and management principles for outcomes-oriented organizations. *Medical Care, 42*(4 Suppl.), III31–III38.

Gowen, C. R., Henagan, S. C., & McFadden, K. L. (2009). Knowledge management as a mediator for the efficacy of transformational leadership and quality management initiatives in U.S. health care. *Health Care Management Review, 34*(3), 129–140.

Guido, G. W. (2006). Fostering legal and ethical practices. In P. S. Yoder-Wise & K. E. Kowalski (Eds.), *Beyond leading and managing: Nursing administration for the future* (pp. 77–95). St. Louis, MO: Mosby.

Halloran, E. J. (2008). Financing health care. In H. R. Feldman, M. Jaffe-Ruiz, M. L. McClure, M. J. Greenberg, & T. D. Smith (Eds.), *Nursing leadership: A concise encyclopedia* (pp. 229–234). New York: Springer.

Health Services Research Group (HSRG). (1992). Outcomes and the management of health care. *Canadian Medical Association Journal, 147*, 1775–1780.

Herrin, D., Jones, K., Krepper, R., Sherman, R., & Reineck, C. (2006). Future nursing administration graduate curricula, part 2: Foundation and strategies. *Journal of Nursing Administration, 36*(11), 498–505.

Hollingsworth, N. (2008). Benchmarking. In H. R. Feldman, M. Jaffe-Ruiz, M. L. McClure, M. J. Greenberg, & T. D. Smith (Eds.), *Nursing leadership: A concise encyclopedia* (pp. 69–71). New York: Springer.

Institute for Healthcare Improvement. (2010). *Transforming care at the bedside.* Retrieved January 31, 2010, from http://www.ihi.org/IHI/Programs/Collaboratives/TransformingCareattheBedside.htm?TabId=0

Institute of Medicine (IOM). (2000). *To err is human: Building a safer health system.* Washington, D.C.: National Academies Press.

Institute of Medicine (IOM). (2001). *Crossing the quality chasm: A new health system for the 21st century.* Washington, D.C.: National Academies Press.

Institute of Medicine (IOM). (2003). *Unequal treatment: Confronting racial and ethnic disparities in health care.* Washington, DC: National Academies Press.

Institute of Medicine (IOM). (2004). *Keeping patients safe: Transforming the work environment of nurses.* Washington, D.C.: National Academies Press.

Institute of Medicine (IOM). (2006). *Preventing medication errors.* Washington, D.C.: National Academies Press.

Jennings, B. M., & McClure, M. L. (2004). Strategies to advance health care quality. *Nursing Outlook, 52*(1), 17–22.

Joint Commission on Accreditation of Healthcare Organizations (JCAHO). (2006). *Sentinel event glossary of terms.* Retrieved January 31, 2010, from http://www.jointcommission.org/sentinelevents/se_glossary.htm

Kanai-Pak, M., Aiken, L. H., Sloane, D. M., & Poghosyan, L. (2008). Poor work environments and nurse inexperience are associated with burnout, job dissatisfaction and quality deficits in Japanese hospitals. *Journal of Clinical Nursing, 17*(24), 3324–3329.

Kibort, P. M. (2005, November–December). I drank the Kool-Aid—And learned 24 key management lessons. *Physician Executive, 31*(6), 52–55.

Kurtzman, E. T., & Jennings, B. M. (2008). Capturing the imagination of nurse executives in tracking the quality of nursing care. *Nursing Administration Quarterly, 32*(3), 235–246.

Lacey, S. R., Cox, K. S., Lorfing, K. C., Teasley, S. L., Carroll, C. A., & Sexton, K. (2007). Nursing support, workload, and intent to stay in Magnet, Magnet-aspiring, and non-Magnet hospitals. *Journal of Nursing Administration, 37*(4), 199–205.

Lee, C. (2006, October 25). Studies look for reasons behind racial disparities in health care. *The Washington Post*. Retrieved February 15, 2010, from http://www.washingtonpost.com/wp-dyn/content/article/2006/10/24/

Lee, H., & Cummings, G. G. (2008). Factors influencing job satisfaction of front line nurse managers: A systematic review. *Journal of Nursing Management, 16*(7), 768–783.

Lonborg, R. (1995). *Measuring patient satisfaction over the entire episode of care*. Washington, D.C.: Congress on Health Outcomes and Accountability.

Lorenz, H. L., Greenhouse, P. K., Miller, R., Wisniewski, M. K., & Frank, S. L. (2008). Transforming care at the bedside: An ambulatory model for improving the patient experience. *Journal of Nursing Administration, 38*(4), 194–199.

MacPhee, M., & Scott, J. (2002). The role of social support networks for rural hospital nurses: Supporting and sustaining the rural nursing work force. *Journal of Nursing Administration, 32*(5), 264–272.

Martin, S. C., Greenhouse, P. K., Merryman, T., Shovel, J., Liberi, C. A., & Konzier, J. (2007). Transforming care at the bedside: Implementation and spread model for single-hospital and multihospital systems. *Journal of Nursing Administration, 37*(10), 444–451.

Matzke, B., Machtmes, K., & Marshall, E. S. (2007, November). *Health literacy: An evidence-based program for baccalaureate nursing students*. Paper presented at the meetings of the American Association of Colleges of Nursing Baccalaureate Education Conference, New Orleans, LA.

Matzke, B., Marshall, E. S., Melton, B., & Chopak-Foss, J. (2009, February). *Health literacy knowledge and perceptions among college students*. Poster presented at the meetings of the Southern Nursing Research Society, Baltimore, MD.

Meade, C. M. (2005). *Organizational change processes in high performing organizations: In-depth case studies with health care facilities*. Gulf Breeze, FL: Alliance for Health Care Research.

Molinari, D. L., & Monserud, M. A. (2008). Rural nurse job satisfaction. *Rural & Remote Health, 8*(4), 1055.

Monroe, L. (2006). Emerging and high-stake issues of the workforce. In P. S. Yoder-Wise & K. E. Kowalski *Beyond leading and managing: Nursing administration for the future* (pp. 427–442). St. Louis, MO: Mosby Elsevier.

Morrison, I. (2000). *Health care in the new millennium: Vision, values, and leadership*. Hoboken, NJ: Jossey-Bass.

National Center for Education Statistics (NCES). (2006). *The health literacy of America's adults: Results from 2003 National Assessment of Adult Literacy*. Washington, D.C.: NCES.

National Defense University (NDU). (n. d.). *Strategic leadership and decision making: Values and ethics*. Retrieved September 22, 2009, from http://www.au.af.mil/au/awc/awcgate/ndu/strat-ldr-dm/pt4ch15html

National Quality Forum (NQF). (2004). *National voluntary consensus standards for nursing-sensitive care: An initial performance measure set*. Washington, D.C.: NQF. Retrieved August 5, 2009, from http://www.qualityforum.org

National Quality Forum (NQF). (2009). Mission and vision. Retrieved September 2, 2009, from http://www.qualityforum.org/About_NQF/Mission_and_Vision.aspx

Nelson, E., Mohr, J. J., Batalden, P., & Plume, S. (1996). Report cards or instrument panels: Who needs what? *Journal on Quality Improvement, 21*, 155–166.

Parker, R. M., Baker, D. W., Williams, M. V., & Nurss, J. R. (1999). Patients with limited health literacy. In W. B. Bateman, E. J. Kramer, & K. S. Glassman (Eds.), *Patient and family education in managed care and beyond* (pp. 63–71). New York City: Springer.

Perkins, I. (2008). Human dignity and ethical decisions in nursing. In H. R. Feldman, M. Jaffe-Ruiz, M. L. McClure, M. J. Greenberg, & T. D. Smith (Eds.), *Nursing leadership: A concise encyclopedia* (pp. 278–282). New York: Springer.

Pignone, M., DeWalt, D. A., Sheridan, S., Berkman, N., & Lohr, K. N. (2005). Interventions to improve health outcomes for patients with low literacy: A systematic review. *Journal of General Internal Medicine, 20*, 185–192.

Plexus. (2007, 11 January). Appreciative inquiry insights transform relationships and boost patient safety. *PlexusNews*. Retrieved March 24, 2007, from http://www.plexusinstitute.org

Porter-O'Grady, T. (2001). Beyond the walls: Nursing in the entrepreneurial world. *Nursing Administration Quarterly, 25*(2), 61–68.

Porter-O'Grady, T., & Malloch, K. (2008). Beyond myth and magic: The future of evidence-based leadership. *Nursing Administration Quarterly, 32*(3), 176–187.

Pozgar, G. (2007). *Legal aspects of health care administration* (10ᵗʰ ed.). Sudbury, MA: Jones & Bartlett.

Quinn, R. E. (2005, July–August). Moments of greatness: Entering the fundamental state of leadership. *Harvard Business Review 83*(7/8), 75–83.

Redman, B. A., & Fry, S. T. (2003). Ethics and human rights issues experienced by nurses in leadership roles. *Nursing Leadership Forum, 7*(4), 150-156.

Reinertsen, J. L. (2006). Quality and safety: Quality is now strategic. In Society for Healthcare Strategy & Market Development of the American Hospital Association, & American College of Healthcare Executives. *Futurescan: Healthcare trends and implications 2006–2011* (pp. 20–24). Chicago, IL: Health Administration Press.

Rogers, B. (1997). As I see it: Is health care a risky business? *The American Nurse, 29*, 5–6.

Rondeau, K. V., Williams, E. S., & Wagar, T. (2008). Turnover and vacancy rates for registered nurses: Do labor market factors matter? *Healthcare Management Review, 33*, 69–78.

Rutherford, P., Lee, B., & Greiner, A. (2004). *Transforming care at the bedside. IHI Innovation Series White Paper*. Boston, MA: Institute for Healthcare Improvement.

Sack, K. (2008, 10 June). Doctors miss cultural needs, study says. *The New York Times*. Retrieved February 15, 2010, from http://www.nytimes.com/2008/06/10/health/10study.html?_r=1&page

Scott-Smith, J. L., & Greenhouse, P. K. (2007). Transforming care at the bedside: Patient-controlled liberalized diet. *Journal of Interprofessional Care, 21*(2), 179–188.

Secretan, L. (1986). *Assessment tools: Values-centered leadership*. Retrieved September 16, 2009, from http://www.secretan.com/freetools_assessment_vcl_definition.php

Shale, S. (2008). Managing the conflict between individual needs and group interests—Ethical leadership in health care organizations. *Keio Journal of Medicine, 57*(1), 37–44.

Smedley, B. D., & Stith, A. Y. (2002). *Unequal treatment, confronting racial and ethnic disparities in health care*. Washington, D.C.: National Academies Press.

Sternin, J. (2007). *Positive deviance: Moving from intractable problems to successful outcomes*. Allentown, NJ: Plexus Institute.

Stichler, J. F. (2009). Healthy, healthful, and healing environments: A nursing imperative. *Critical Care Nursing Quarterly, 32*(3), 176–188.

Sullivan Commission. (2004). *Missing persons: Minorities in the health professions*. Washington, D.C.: Sullivan Commission.

Takase, M., Maude, P., & Manias, E. (2006). The impact of role discrepancy on nurses' intention to quit their jobs. *Journal of Clinical Nursing, 15*(9), 1071–1980.

Thomas, E., Thompson, K. S., & Koch, R. W. (2009). Human resource development: Recruitment, retention, and managing conflict. In L. Roussel & R. C. Swansburg (Eds.), *Management and leadership for nurse administrators* (5ᵗʰ ed., pp. 260–287). Sudbury, MA: Jones & Bartlett.

Upenieks, V. V., Akhaven, J., & Kotlerman, J. (2008). Value-added care: A paradigm shift in patient care delivery. *Nursing Economic$, 26*(5), 394–301.

Upenieks, V. V., Needleman, J., Soban, L., Pearson, M. L., Parkerton, P., & Yee, T. (2008). The relationship between the volume and type of transforming care at the bedside innovations and changes in nurse vitality. *Journal of Nursing Administration, 38*(9), 386–394.

Urden, L. (2006). Transforming professional practice environments: The Magnet Recognition Program. In P. S. Yoder-Wise & K. E. Kowalski (Eds.), *Beyond leading and managing: Nursing administration for the future* (pp. 23–39). St. Louis, MO: Mosby.

Vance, C., & Larson, E. (2002). Leadership research in business and health care. *Journal of Nursing Scholarship, 34*(2), 165–171.

Viney, M., Batcheller, J., Houston, S., & Belcik, K. (2006). Transforming care at the bedside: Designing new care systems in an age of complexity. *Journal of Nursing Care Quality, 21*(2), 143–150.

Vlasses, F. R., & Smeltzer, C. H. (2007). Toward a new future for healthcare and nursing practice. *Journal of Nursing Administration, 37*(9), 375–380.

Weber, V., & Joshi, M. S. (2000). Effecting and leading change in health care organizations. *Joint Commission Journal on Quality Improvement, 26*(7), 388–399.

Weiss, B. D., Mays, M. Z., Martz, W., Castro, K. M., DeWalt, D. A., Pignone, M. P., et al. (2005). Quick assessment of literacy in primary care: The newest vital sign. *Annals of Family Medicine, 3*, 514–522.

Weitz, T. A. (2000, November). *Developing a definition of "underserved populations."* Paper presented at the 128th Annual Meeting of the American Public Health Association, Boston, MA. Retrieved February 1, 2010, from http://apha.confex.com/apha/128am/techprogram/paper_8347.htm

West, M. A., Borrill, C., Dawson, J., Scully, J., Carter, M., Anelay, S., et al. (2002). The link between the management of employees and patient mortality in acute hospitals. *International Journal of Human Resource Management, 13*(8), 1299–1310.

White, K. (1967). Improved medical statistics and health services systems. *Public Health Reports, 82,* 847–854.

Wolf, F., Triolo, P., & Ponte, P. R. (2008). Magnet recognition program: The next generation. *Journal of Nursing Administration, 38*(4), 200–204.

Womack, J. P., & Jones, D. T. (2005, March). Lean consumption. *Harvard Business Review 83*(3), 58–68.

Wong, C. A., & Cummings, G. G. (2007). The relationships between nursing leadership and patient outcomes: A systematic review. *Journal of Nursing Management, 15*(5), 508–521.

Wheatley, M. J. (2001). Innovation means relying on everyone's creativity. *Leader to Leader.* Retrieved October 7, 2009, from http://www.margaretwheatley.com/articles/innovationmeans.html

Wieck, K. L., & Dols, J., & Landrum, P. (2010). Retention priorities for the intergenerational nurse workforce. *Nursing Forum, 45*(1), 7–17.

World Health Organization (WHO). (2000a). *World health reports.* Geneva, Switzerland: WHO.

World Health Organization (WHO). (2000b). *The World Health Organization's ranking of the world's health systems.* Retrieved August 25, 2009, from http://www.photius.com/rankings/healthranks.html

7

Practice Design and Management

> The task of the leader is to get his people from where
> they are to where they have never been.
>
> —*Henry Kissinger*

Leaders in health care must accept the mandate of the future to design, guide, and manage models of care for the future. The old ones are not working. We must think in new ways. We must analyze our current models and find ways to assess them from an organizational perspective for systemwide improvement. This must be done using the best evidence and technology. We must identify new ways to promote health and to care for the suffering, with an eye on productivity and effectiveness. If we meet these challenges, we will enter a new era that requires a new kind of leadership.

MODELS OF CARE ON THE HORIZON: EMBRACING THE ENTREPRENEURIAL SPIRIT OF INNOVATION

Healthcare redesign is a theme and a byword in healthcare reform. Providers are reexamining structures, processes, personnel, technology, and outcomes of the entire American healthcare system, including interactions among patients, consumers, insurers, providers, and other members of the community. In addition, nearly $200 billion will be spent on the construction of new and revisioned facilities. Such activities must "ensure optimal patient outcomes, enhance the work environment for healthcare providers, and improve organizational performance" (Stichler, 2007, p. 527). Creative models of care will be critical to successful innovation and transformational change of health care.

A model is a graphic scheme or map of a phenomenon or enterprise. It explains relationships or processes among key concepts, variables, structures, and activities. The first idea of healthcare modeling is attributed to Donebedian (1966), who proposed the model of structure, process, and outcomes related to care. Structures represent the existing organization or setting of how things are, processes are what happens, and outcomes represent resulting achievements (Wolf & Greenhouse, 2007). Care models are helpful to communicate what needs to happen to achieve the organization's mission, highlighting planning, decisions, assessments, and activities to promote optimal structures, processes, and outcomes. A model depicts the work purpose and flow and promotes team unity of purpose and direction to do the work.

Models of Care for Nursing Practice

Nursing models of care traditionally refer to the work of nursing in hospital settings. Florence Nightingale designed the first modern Western care delivery model by distinguishing head nurse from staff, or "floor" nurse and establishing a hierarchy of governance of nursing care. At the beginning of the 20th century, her model spread throughout the industrialized Western world, eventually adding student labor to the structure. Student nurses, already living and learning inside the walls of the hospital, provided much of the human resources for patient care, leaving graduates to hire out for private duty, often through a registry. A few brave nurses also struck out to the new independent practice of public health nursing. Hard economic times and growth of hospitals of the 1930s effectively ended families' abilities to pay for private-duty nurses, which sent graduate nurses back to hospital practice. As hospitals continued to evolve, nursing continued as a subordinate occupation. As nursing education moved toward the university setting after the midcentury, a myriad of theories and models to distinguish nursing as a professional discipline were born of the now grande dames of nursing like Virginia Henderson, Martha Rogers, Dorothea Orem, Sister Callista Roy, Betty Neuman, Margaret Newman, Madeleine Leininger, Jean Watson, and a dozen others. Most of their models defined or distinguished *nursing* rather than outline specific models of care.

In the last 25 years, a variety of nursing care models has grown across the country. Early models included versions of team nursing, functional nursing care, total patient care, primary nursing (Nelson, 2008), and primary care nursing (Aroian, Maservey, & Crockett, 1996). More recent models have examined shared governance, nursing environments, differentiated practice, patient-focused care, and still others using the clinical nurse leader and Magnet hospital models (Seago, 2001). Some entrepreneurs have even launched consulting and commercial ventures to promote specific models (see examples: Dingman, 2005; Dingman, Williams, Fosbinder, & Warnick, 1999, Manthey, 2009; Planetree, 2010; Wesorick, 2002, 2008). Depending on your age, you will recognize the model under which you worked as a student, new graduate nurse, or perhaps even your work today, especially if you work in a hospital.

More recent versions of nursing care models include parish nursing, community-based nursing centers, patient- and family-centered care, as well as more innovative models such as a collaborative patient management model, a partnership clinical model, and a hospital at home model (Danna, 2009). With few exceptions, these models have focused largely on the work of nursing in acute care hospital settings, focusing on such issues as nurse-patient ratios, various staffing mixes, and measuring nurse and patient satisfaction.

Professional Practice Models

Another relatively recent movement in nursing is that of professional practice models. Such models came of age with the development of Magnet hospitals, and thus also refer largely to nursing practice within hospitals. Foundational elements of professional practice are nursing autonomy and control over practice as well as collaborative relationships with physicians. Hoffart and Woods (1996) proposed five basic characteristics of a nursing professional practice model: professional values, professional relationships, a specific care delivery model, management or governance, and professional recognition and rewards. Historically, professional practice models have been invented by nurses and for nurses working in hospitals.

New professional practice models have moved beyond describing the work of nursing. They have begun to align nursing with other professional practice disciplines, including medicine. They have enhanced opportunities across many institutions to develop their own brand of professional nursing practice. The advent of the doctor of nursing practice (DNP) offers the promise to promote environments of professional practice for nurses as colleagues in multidisciplinary approaches to care. To assure a truly professional practice paradigm for nurse leaders requires vigilance, promotion of the appropriate environment to assure professional practice, and lifting of some of the restrictions on scope of practice for advanced practice nurses that remain inconsistent across the 50 states. When nursing truly becomes a professional practice, we must ask ourselves if it will even be necessary to develop and proclaim models for professional practice. When will professional practice be self-evident, embodied within the system, the practitioners, and the leaders themselves, and simply a way of being?

Innovative Practice Models

Currently, some research is examining the relationship between nursing care delivery models and patient outcomes, such as safety or satisfaction (Hall & Doran, 2004; Seago, 2001). Across history, such models have mostly focused on rearranging the definition, structure, processes, and the general work of nurses, all claiming to transform care. The Institute for Healthcare Improvement recently launched a large collaborative project funded by the Robert Wood Johnson Foundation to "transform care at the bedside" in hospitals. Already, several positive outcomes have been reported, and the project has provided a foundation for continued work toward "safe and reliable care, vitality and teamwork, patient-centered care, and value-added care processes" (Institute for Health care Improvement, 2010). Specific outcomes have been positive (see Anonymous, 2004, 2005; Donahue, Rader, & Triolo, 2008; Lorenz, Greenhouse, Miller, Wisniewski, & Frank, 2008; Martin et al., 2007; Scott-Smith & Greenhouse, 2007; Upenieks et al., 2008; Viney, Batcheller, Houston, & Belcik, 2006).

Joynt, Kimball, and associates (Joynt & Kimball, 2008, pp. 3–5; Kimball, Joynt, Cherner, & O'Neil, 2007) performed a large-scale study of innovative care delivery models throughout the United States. Most of the criteria for inclusion in themselves provide a guide for evaluation of effective new models for nursing. They include innovation in provider roles and teams, interdisciplinary activities, sustainability and replicability, and demonstrated impact on patient or business outcomes. Joynt and Kimball (2008) examined 60 new care delivery models, the majority of which were in acute care and hospital settings, located in urban or suburban areas, and mostly not-for-profit. From these 60 models, they identified eight common elements: (1) elevated roles for nurses with nurses as care integrators, (2) migration to interdisciplinary care with a team approach, (3) bridges across a continuum of care, (4) movement toward recognition of the home as setting for care, (5) targeting high users of health care, such as the elderly, (6) sharpened focus on the patient, (7) high use of technology in care delivery, and (8) focus on results such as outcomes, quality of care, and cost. The study represents a beginning of the important dialogue to examine, invent, and share care delivery models that work. A key challenge reflected in current research is to move beyond the focus mainly on the work of nursing toward the interdisciplinary work of patient care.

Arguably, the time has come for new more effective models. New models must include recognition of a set of interdisciplinary values and relationships among representatives of all disciplines of respect as peers. They need to include patients and consumers as integral members of planning teams. New models will consider all care settings, including community-based and home environments. Finally, models will recognize use of evidence and technology and focus beyond productivity and effectiveness toward excellence. What might be on the horizon? It will depend on you and the new generation of transformational leaders.

Care Model Design and System Change

Wang, Hyun, Harrison, Shortell, and Fraser (2006) found the following factors to be critical to successful care design in a context of system change: (1) directly involve all leaders at all levels; (2) strategically align and integrate improvement efforts with organizational mission and priorities; (3) systematically establish infrastructure, processes, and performance appraisal systems for continuous improvement, and (4) actively develop champions, teams, and staff.

Various professional healthcare organizations have also proposed models. For example, the American Association of Critical Care Nurses and the American College of Chest Physicians developed two complementary initiatives, the Standards for Establishing and Sustaining Health Work Environments and the Patient-Focused Care Project. Both projects propose processes to create new interdisciplinary practice environments. They call for new practice and education structures to integrate selected aspects of medical and nursing education in order to promote respect and knowledge about each other's discipline, new ethics committees, and creating structures to position medical directors and nurse managers as peers with equal accountability for clinical outcomes and team performance (McCauley & Irwin, 2006; Reineck, 2007). Implementation would include interdisciplinary patient rounds, mechanisms for respectful interdisciplinary approaches to competence issues, and team building. Parsons (2004; Reineck, 2007) also proposed a Health Promoting Organizations Model for systems change that includes unit-shared leadership, participatory management, and empowerment of staff nurses.

The care designs of the next generation will likely continue to recognize structures, processes, and outcomes of provider interactions with each other and with patients, but they must genuinely reflect care across disciplines and settings. Silos of medicine, nursing, and other healthcare disciplines simply will not work anymore. As systems become more integrated, "The old compartmentalized and segmented system of the 20th century is no longer viable to the content and mechanics of a complex and technologically driven healthcare infrastructure. The emerging realities of a 21st century model of health care are changing all the rules for service delivery and clinical relationships" (Porter-O'Grady, 2001, p. 64; Porter-O'Grady & Wilson, 1999). Interprofessional collaborative practice promotes team identity, conserves energy by a unity in direction, and invites harmony of efforts. Respect and peer collaboration promote a complementary matrix of authority and shared purpose (Ives Erickson & Ditomassi, 2008; Senge, 1995).

Essential elements to successful implementation of innovative care models also include continued intentional communication and a sensible business plan. Poor or inadequate communication within the organization and among outside constituents can quickly kill any new idea. Furthermore, any new model must also exhibit a healthy respect for business. It must be strong, formal, and rigorous. The plan should include analysis of assumptions, strategy, operations, resources and management, evaluation, and even a contingency plan (Morjikian, Kimball, & Joynt, 2007). The business plan must show a mechanism for projecting and evaluating cost savings and organizational mission support. Some examples of such models of care include the Primary Care Team in Austin, TX, that showed a reduction in staff turnover by 64% (Batcheller, Burkman, Armstrong, Chappell, & Carelock, 2004; Morjikian et al., 2007) and the Transitional Care Model in Pennsylvania that reduced readmission rates, inpatient costs, medical complications, and mortality while improving patient and physician satisfaction (Morjikian et al., 2007; Naylor, et al., 1999, 2004).

When creating a team to implement change, it is especially important to include as many views and as many representatives as possible. Any group or faction that is not included will surely emerge at some point to resist or sabotage. Wheatley (2001a) further admitted, "I haven't become insistent on broad-based participation just to avoid resistance. . . . I've learned that I'm not smart enough to design anything for the whole system. None of us these days can know what will work inside the dense networks we call organizations. We can't see what's meaningful to people, or even understand how they get their work done. We have no option but to ask them into the design process."

Practice redesign that really works can happen only when it is done by a community. A group of people with shared interests and a desire to solve a problem can do anything. I am still looking for us to find the courage and creativity to include actual patients in the design of our care and practice models. Kerfoot (1998) quoted Kao (1996, p. 194), "Change is the sum of a thousand acts of re-perception and behavior change at every level of the organization." Wheatley (2001a) further observed:

> Every change, every burst of creativity, begins with the identification of a problem or opportunity that somebody finds meaningful. As soon as people become interested in an issue, their creativity is instantly engaged. If we want people to be innovative, we must discover what is important to them, and we must engage them in meaningful issues. The simplest way to discover what's meaningful is to notice what people talk about and where they spend their energy.

To engage a community in the creative design of care systems, it is most helpful for the leader to work beside, rather than above, those most involved. Wheatley (2001a) confirmed, "I need to be working alongside a group of individuals to learn who they are and what attracts their attention. As we work together and deepen our relationship, I can then discern what issues and behaviors make them sit up and take notice. As we work together, doing real work, meaning always becomes visible."

To survive as the creative leader who designs new care systems from an entrepreneurial perspective, you must choose a work environment that will support and encourage your efforts, and you must know your organization. Kerfoot (1998, p. 181) warned, "Creativity does not exist in hostile environments where all of one's time is spent thinking about survival." Part of your job as leader is to develop a culture and context that fosters creativity. Kerfoot (p. 181) outlined some basic functions of the leader to promote a fertile environment for creative thinking and invention: "promoting conversations and dialogue; providing access to information; building relationships across disciplines; teaching, re-perceiving, rethinking, questioning, innovating; creating a culture of innovation; orchestrating and executing." Beyond such characteristics, some "organizational agility" is helpful to understand the culture and strategize what will actually work in the specific organization (Morjikian et al., 2007).

Care redesign requires an attitude of entrepreneurial innovation. Some think that this is simply a personality style among creative thinkers. But innovation actually happens much more systematically from the recognition of a problem crying for a solution or an opportunity for positive change.

Drucker (1998) outlined four areas of opportunity for innovation: unexpected occurrences, incongruities, process needs, and industry and market changes. Others include demographic changes, changes in community perceptions, and new knowledge that changes circumstances. Unexpected occurrences include unexpected failures as well as successes. Drucker shared the example of the Ford Edsel, which is the most famous failure of a carefully designed car in the modern automotive industry. Analyzing that failure, the people at Ford realized that the American market had moved from the expected income-group basis to the unexpected lifestyle focus, so they recovered by developing the Mustang and thus resumed, at that time, their leadership in the industry. An example of the inability to recognize an unexpected opportunity for success is the German scientist Einhorn who, in about 1904, developed novocaine, the first nonaddictive narcotic. He intended its use in major surgical procedures such as amputation. Surgeons continued to prefer general anesthesia, but dentists quickly adopted the new novocaine. Nevertheless, Einhorn spent his life as a traveling preacher from dental school to dental school warning to stop "misusing his noble invention in applications for which he had not intended it" (Drucker, 1998, p. 152).

Incongruities in practice also provide opportunities for invention. Drucker (1998) gave the example of the surgical procedures of removing cataracts. A major incongruity of the procedure was the step of cutting a ligament—so incongruous with the rest of the procedure that surgeons reportedly dreaded it. Although they knew of an enzyme that could dissolve the ligament, it was unusable. Alcon laboratories simply found a way to add a preservative to the enzyme to make it usable to the surgeon, immediately making the procedure more congruous with the processes of the operation, the operation became more common, and Alcon subsequently became the wealthy monopoly of the relatively simple drug (Drucker, 1998).

Other simple, but perplexing, realities of the work can promote invention. Process needs invite innovation, and healthcare leaders are experts at recognizing them. There are dozens of examples within your own healthcare setting. Do we work around them, or do we take them up as opportunities for innovative models? Industry and market changes continually provide opportunities for innovative approaches to healthcare delivery and leadership. A mere count of new and emerging healthcare provider settings in the last couple of decades provides a good example: independent centers for imaging, surgery, and instant care; health maintenance organizations; and new models of free-standing psychiatric hospitals and clinics are some examples (Drucker, 1998), as well as nurse-managed clinics and community health centers.

Care models should endure beyond a time enough that they are not simply trendy responses to current practices; they should fit within the mission and strategic plan of the organization and be based on evidence (Wolf & Greenhouse, 2007). One of the biggest challenges to design a new care model is the ongoing 7-day 24-hour consistent patient care that must be sustained through the midst of change. O'Reilly and Tushman (2004) suggested that an organization might separate exploratory innovation units from other existing traditional units to allow for different processes, structures, and cultures. Thus, it is possible to sustain one unit of service by gentle tweaking at the same time another team is diving into full-speed change and redesign. The authors referred to such an organization as "ambidextrous," but warned that the units must be tightly integrated at the executive leadership level. In other words, we cannot be running two businesses at the same time, but we also do not have to do everything at once. We can recognize a variety of processes and cultures within the stewardship of our leadership.

Finally, leaders of new models of care must always pursue the perspective of the broader organizational culture, mission, and strategic planning; they will identify champions for success of the plan and extend creative authority, will engage internal and external interdisciplinary team members and allies, and will identify opportunities for internal and external formal partnerships. They will take care to prepare contingency plans for resistance (Morjikian et al., 2007), and they will take the perspective of the entire organization and system.

ASSESSING ORGANIZATIONS, IDENTIFYING SYSTEM ISSUES, FACILITATING SYSTEM-WIDE IMPROVEMENT

Perhaps, there is not a single person in the United States who will argue that our health-care system does not need change or redesign at some level. Our system is ranked among the highest in cost and lowest on outcomes on almost any scale among those of developed countries. The American healthcare system has been the brunt of criticism from popular media to the federal government itself (Hacker, 2007; Oberlander, 2007). A myriad of factions, each with its own self-interest, and the mere weight of the complexity of all aspects of the system, seem to overwhelm hopes of immediate or fundamental change. A full decade after the report by the Institute of Medicine (2001) calling for system-wide changes to transform healthcare systems, we are still working on assessing organizations and identifying system issues, and are frustrated with the slow progress on system-wide improvement.

Challenges in Taking the Organizational or Systems Perspective

At the outset, it is important to recognize that we do not even have a specific definition of organization or system. We sometimes refer to system as the entire national endeavor of health care and other times to some specific enterprise. We most often refer to organization, or system, as a specific facility or microsystem. We need definition.

The other truth is that leaders are individuals, and it is a supreme challenge for even the most global conceptual-thinking leader to fully embrace the idea of an entire system. Celebrated business thinkers Clayton Christensen and Michael Overdorf (2000) observed that no matter how talented the leader or manager, most lack the habit of thinking about the capabilities of the entire organization, as they deal with the capacity of the individual person. Nevertheless, they asserted that organizations themselves, independent of the people within them, have characteristics and capabilities. Thus, the task of the leader is to continually evaluate not only people but also the entire organization. They remind that three key areas affect organizational capabilities and achievements: resources, processes, and values. Resources include finances, facilities, equipment, and people. Other less considered resources are information, brand value, and relationships with customer or community. Processes refer to patterns of human interactions, coordination, communication, and decision making, both formal and informal. Finally, values include principles, standards by which workers set priorities, how ideas are evaluated, and metrics for good management.

In its early stages, an organization or systemic endeavor within an organization relies heavily on resources. Loss of funding or loss of key personnel can devastate outcomes. But as the organization matures, processes and values sustain institutional activities, and resources and/or people may flow in and out without seriously undermining the work and mission of the organization (Christensen & Overdorf, 2000).

Current healthcare systems are actually composed of a variety of subsystems, called microsystems (Godfrey, Melin, Muething, Batalden, & Nelson, 2008; McKinley et al., 2008; Nelson et al., 2008; Wasson et al., 2008), each trying to negotiate the transition between a traditional industrial age to an age of technology, information, and innovation. Formella and Rovin (2004, p. 264) bravely admitted, "Nursing is perfectly designed to be in its current state: a mess. A mess is a complex system of interacting problems that must be addressed as a whole or systemically if it is to be treated effectively."

Assessing Environments for Professional Practice

Nearly as important as environment for patient care is the concept of the work environment for the clinician. For the past 30 years ago, leaders in nursing have been investigating work environments that support nursing practice, recruitment, and retention. We are beginning to identify how such factors are important to patient outcomes (see Aiken, Sochalski, & Lake, 1997; Ives Erickson et al., 2004; Kramer & Hafner, 1989; Lake, 2002; McClure, Poulin, Sovie, & Wandelt, 2002). From some of this work has emerged the concept of Magnet hospitals, which have been officially recognized to provide positive environments for professional nursing practice.

The American Association of Colleges of Nursing (2002) outlined the specific characteristics of the environment that supports professional nursing practice:

1. Manifests a philosophy of clinical care emphasizing quality, safety, interdisciplinary collaboration, continuity of care, and professional accountability.
2. Recognizes the contributions of nurses' knowledge and expertise to clinical care quality and patient outcomes.
3. Promotes executive-level nursing leadership.
4. Empowers nurses participating in clinical decision making and organization of clinical care systems.
5. Maintains clinical advancement programs based on education, certification, and advanced preparation.
6. Demonstrates professional development support for nurses.
7. Creates collaborative relationships among members of the healthcare provider team.
8. Utilizes technological advances in clinical care and information systems.

Danna (2009, p. 235) proposed the following areas for evaluating environments for professional nursing practice models:

1. Create the environment of practice.
2. Establish and ensure the standards of nursing care delivery.
3. Coordinate patient care with inputs from all types of health professionals.

4. Select and develop the nursing workforce.
5. Evaluate and plan the work of nursing to meet patient requirements for care.
6. Provide adequate staffing.
7. Evaluate and develop relationships within and external to hospital services.

Like many models before, these criteria focus on the work of nursing within the hospital. The next generation of leaders needs to open the perspective to include all settings beyond the hospital.

Perspectives for Organizational Assessment

There are several perspectives from which to assess the structures, processes, and outcomes of an organization. A well-worn classic model to assess an organization is the Six-Box model of Weisbord (1976). It proposes six interrelated "boxes" or areas to evaluate the health and effectiveness of the organization. At the center of the boxes is *Leadership*, with the key question, "Who balances the boxes?" Leadership is the key to defining purposes, guiding the translation of purposes into programs, defending the integrity of the organization, and ordering internal relationships. The second box is *Purpose*, asking, "What business are we in?" It concerns goal clarity and goal agreement. Third is *Structure*, which asks, "How do we divide up the work?" It examines the fit between goals and structure and the way the work actually gets done. The fourth box is *Relationships*. Questions include "How do we relate as individuals and groups?" "How do we collaborate or coordinate?" and "How do we manage conflict?" The fifth box is *Rewards*, asking, "Do all tasks have the needed rewards or incentives?" Finally, *Helpful Mechanisms* asks about processes of planning, stewardship, budgeting, communication, and co-ordination of technologies. Although Weisbord's boxes were created at a time of orientation and language toward the traditional mechanistic system of the industrial age, it does provide a structure to begin to think about organizational assessment.

Another classic and popular perspective for assessing an organization is through Peter Senge's (1990) lens of "the learning organization." Senge asserted that because people are designed for learning, so must be the organizations in which they work. He suggested that the first level of organizational learning is adaptive learning, which is about coping. However, a higher level of learning is generative learning, which is about expanding capacities and capabilities. Generative learning requires a broader perspective, where leaders are not the authoritative "charismatic decision makers" but rather "designers, teachers, and stewards" (p. 9). Senge outlined a principle of creative tension where members of the organization are able to see the idealistic vision of where and what they want to be, while at the same time recognizing the "current reality" and telling the truth about where they are. Senge explained that leading in an environment of creative tension is different than traditional problem solving. Rather than trying to escape, avoid, or reduce some aspect of the current reality by solving a problem, the leader in a learning organization uses the creative tension to create positive change in the current realities according to the direction of the organizational vision. In other words, it is a difference in perspective that moves the leader and the organization from repairing what is wrong to inventing what works.

Still, another perspective is offered by Bulger (2003), who called for a vision of "healer-clinicians" in "the therapeutic institution." He developed an assessment tool called the Organization Therapeutic Index for healthcare institutions that measures the following constructs: (1) scientific and technical competence; (2) understanding suffering and pain, death, and dying; (3) appreciating the placebo effect; (4) expanding healthcare roles and responsibilities; (5) communicating dignity and respect; (6) demonstrating organizational loyalty to patients; (7) making the patient part of the healthcare team; (8) emphasizing teamwork and collaboration; (9) taking the environment into account; (10) affirming cultural sensitivity and workforce diversity; and (11) working with the community. Unfortunately, the assumptions of the measure are based almost exclusively on the discipline of medicine in large hospital systems.

Lukas et al., (2007, p. 309) evaluated 12 American healthcare systems to identify essential elements necessary for enduring transformation of patient care. They found the following five critical factors:

1. Impetus to transform.
2. Leadership commitment to quality.
3. Improvement initiatives that actively engage staff in meaningful problem solving.
4. Alignment to achieve consistency of organization goals with resource allocation and actions at all levels of the organization.
5. Integration to bridge traditional intraorganizational boundaries among individual components.

Another perspective to consider is that organizations are living systems. Regardless of whether you view the system as a living organism, a more helpful view may be as an organization of living beings. Wheatley (2001a) suggested that we need go no deeper, that life processes apply to both people and systems.

Innovation may happen within or external to the system. Four key elements can drive change within the system by affecting its components:

1. Mission, vision, and strategies that set its direction and priorities.
2. Culture that reflects its informal values and norms.
3. Operational functions and processes that embody the work done in patient care.
4. Infrastructure such as information technology (IT) and human resources that supports the delivery of patient care (Lukas et al., 2007).

Transformational change within the system is iterative and happens over time across the organization.

Christensen (1997) referred to evolutionary changes as "sustaining innovations." Sustaining innovations are usually introduced by current industry leaders who continue to develop and focus on improved processes consistent with their established values. They develop improved products and services within the context of their history and tradition. More challenging is radical and revolutionary change called "disruptive innovations." Examples of these include the telephone disrupting the telegraph, semiconductors disrupting vacuum tubes, cellular phones disrupting fixed telephone lines, and perhaps retail medical clinics disrupting the traditional physician's office. Healthcare systems are poised to be ambushed by disruptive innovation. As leaders in health care, we need to brace ourselves for disruptive innovations that will threaten the way we have been doing business.

Some hope is on the horizon for organizations that are prepared. First, they must create new organizational structures or capabilities within their own boundaries to develop new processes. Second, they could spin out independent organizations to develop new processes and values to solve new problems. Or, finally, they might acquire or collaborate with a different organization whose processes and values match the need of the new task (Christensen & Overdorf, 2000). These further underscore the urgency for interdisciplinary and cross-discipline collaboration in health care. We need to collaborate, not only nurses with physicians, but also nurses with engineers, nurses with humanists, and physicians with who-knows-who-else. Christensen and Overdorf (2000, p. 74) warned:

> In our studies of this challenge, we have never seen a company succeed in addressing a change that disrupts its mainstream values without the personal, attentive oversight of the CEO—precisely because of the power of values in shaping the normal resource allocation process. Only the [leader] can ensure that the new organization gets the required resources and is free to create processes and values that are appropriate to the new challenge.

A writer for the *New York Times* (Rae-Dupree, 2009) reminded that two key factors in current healthcare systems, the general hospital and the physician's practice, are largely based on business models over 100 years old. These systems are built on a foundation of fee-for-service based on treating illness. "Hospitals and doctors are paid by insurers and the government for the healthcare equivalent of piecework; hospitals profit from full beds, and doctors profit from repeat visits." Some integrated systems are preparing to deal with disruptive innovations that will fundamentally change healthcare practice. Take this warning: place your best sentinel at the watchtower on night duty. Some major disruptive innovations are on the horizon to change health care forever. Be ready, watch for it, be part of it.

INSPIRING EVIDENCE-INFORMED PRACTICE: USING EVIDENCE FROM ALL DISCIPLINES

No organizational or systemwide change can be enduring or effective without the wise and appropriate use of evidence. By now, evidence-based practice should be a way of life. Its value has been well demonstrated in all aspects of health care and proven to be so critical to patient care outcomes that the leader who does not inspire its universal application is irresponsible. It is fundamental to clinical practice, and it is an essential role for leaders to assure its universal implementation. The basic tenets of effective use of evidence must be part of the daily discourse of the transformational leader. Despite such bold statements, still, a relatively low proportion of healthcare providers actually practice from a base of evidence. It is time for a call to action by both leaders and clinicians (Shirey, 2006). Furthermore, it is time for examination and use of evidence from all disciplines that might make a positive contribution. No single profession, practice, or area of study owns all helpful information for health care.

Using Evidence for Practice

To review the basics of evidence-based practice, sources of evidence for clinical decision making include empirical research, patient assessment, clinical expertise, and patient preferences and values. Evidence may be positivistic or interpretive, drawn from quantitative or qualitative data. The level of existing knowledge determines the level of evidence and the clinical question to obtain or examine the evidence. The first-level, or descriptive, question is "What is it?" when little is known and you simply need to identify or explore. The next level is "What is the relationship between X and Y?" for observational and correlation inquiries. In the third level, "What happens if . . . ?" describes an experimental approach. Finally, the randomized controlled trial (RCT) answers the question "How to make it happen?"

The distinctive activity of evidence-based practice begins with a question in the PICOT format: P = population of interest, I = intervention to be investigated, C = the comparison group, O = the outcome, and T = the time period of the phenomenon. Steps in evidence-based practice are the following: (1) ask the PICOT question; (2) search and collect the evidence; (3) appraise and synthesize the evidence; (4) integrate the evidence with patient assessment, clinical expertise, and patient preferences and values; (5) translate the evidence to practice; and (6) evaluate outcomes (Melnyk & Finout-Overholt, 2005).

Levels of evidence are usually ranked. The lowest level includes expert opinions based on authority, clinical experiences, descriptive studies, or reports from expert committees. Higher levels include well-designed cohort or case-controlled studies, and RCTs are considered the highest level of evidence. Obviously, not all information or evidence for practice has or even can come from RCTs. Most important is that the leader inspires practice from the highest level of available evidence rather than from tradition, provider preference, or other factors without a basis in evidence.

Unfortunately, despite universal recognition of the importance of evidence-based practice, it continues to require the vigilance of a bold leader to implement and ensure its practice throughout the entire organization. Marchionni and Ritchie (2008) outlined specific organizational factors needed to support the implementation of evidence-based practice, including a culture of learning and transformational leadership. Practice leaders and managers can support specific evidence-based projects and decision making, facilitate measurement of quality and safety, use outcome measures to evaluate quality, and support exemplars at the point-of-service level of care (Newhouse & Johnson, 2009). Smooth and pervasive use of evidence in practice requires some degree of change or transformation of the entire system, culture, leadership characteristics, evaluation methods, and professional environment (Cummings, Estabrooks, Midodzi, Wallin, & Hayduk, 2007; Newhouse, 2007, 2009).

Leaders in clinical practice can inspire and promote the use of evidence in practice by linking with academic settings that foster collaboration with students and faculty as well library resources. Advanced practice nurses can model the use of evidence in daily patient care. Furthermore, there are models that can be useful in clinical settings to support the use of evidence.

Each setting has its unique characteristics that must be considered in the application of evidence. Implications of context and culture are especially important, since evidence-based practice is not a solitary act of practice but an initiative that requires an entire community of committed clinicians. For example, conditions in rural and community hospitals may require unique and inventive infrastructures to support evidence-based practice (Burns, Dudiak, & Greenhouse, 2009; Sossong et al., 2009; Vratny & Shriver, 2007).

A number of models has been proposed for systematic implementation of evidence-based practice in healthcare settings (Marchionni & Ritchie, 2008; Stetler, 2003; Stetler, Ritchie, Rycroft-Malone, Schultz, & Charns, 2007). One example is the Advancing Research and Clinical Practice Through Close Collaboration model that provides a standard process for clinical implementation of evidence. Stetler and colleagues (Stetler, McQueen, Demakis, & Mittman, 2008; Stetler, Ritchie, Rycroft-Malone, Schultz, & Charns, 2009) suggested that operational implementation of evidence-based practice requires a formal strategic approach and role models.

Recruit everyone at all levels into the role of implementing evidence-based practice in a context of shared accountability and shared governance (Melnyk, 2007; Melnyk & Fineout-Overholt, 2002, 2005; Newhouse, 2009; Waddell, 2009). Although pervasive use of evidence in practice certainly requires the support of leadership, it must also be claimed, integrated, and practiced with a sense of autonomy and creativity at the point of care (Schulman, 2008; Strout, Lancaster, & Schultz, 2009) and throughout the system.

Although significant descriptive work has been done to highlight the strategic role of leaders and managers, and the literature offers abundant case examples (Cullen, Greiner, Greiner, Bombei, & Comried, 2005; MacRobert, 2008; Marchionni & Richer, 2007), there is little empirical hypothesis testing or theory testing regarding the best practice for leadership oversight or strategies to implement and sustain evidence-based practice (Gifford, Davies, Edwards, Griffin, & Lybanon, 2007).

The advent of the DNP launches the opportunity for the clinician prepared at the highest level to guide other healthcare providers in practice inquiry. DNPs are prepared to lead systematic inquiry regarding the realities and complexities of practice, the challenges of translating discovery research into practice, and effective integration of evidence into individual, community, and population-based health care. In addition, the DNP is uniquely poised, and sorely needed, to translate evidence into needed policy that makes a difference (Magvary, Whitney, & Brown, 2006).

Practice-Based Evidence

A growing methodological turn on the concept of evidence-based practice is practice-based evidence. Horn and Gassaway (2007, p. S50) described practice-based evidence as a "rigorous, comprehensive" research methodology "that fills gaps in information needed by clinical and health policy decision makers." Horn and colleagues (Tunis, Stryer, & Clancy, 2003; Westfall, Mold, & Fagnan, 2007) have led the charge to point out weaknesses in traditional methods of evidence-based practice to answer all clinical, leadership, and policy questions. Rather than performing RCTs, practice-based evidence proposes the use of practical clinical trials. Characteristics include comparing clinically based, existing alternative interventions actually in practice rather than introducing new interventions; large and diverse study populations rather than selected criterion-based samples; recruitment of samples from heterogeneous practice settings rather than from matched, controlled settings; and data collection from a broad and vast range of outcomes rather than selected, isolated variables. In other words, methods of practice-based evidence study what is actually practiced in a large number of situations, collecting huge datasets of detailed data on as many variables as possible to compare the effectiveness of interventions to identify what actually works in practice. Furthermore, variables of study are drawn from the perspective of an inclusive multidisciplinary team of researchers, practitioners, and others who have direct experience with the issues to be studied, and the method depends on local knowledge. Rather than *efficacy* measured by evidence-based approaches, practice-based methods measure *effectiveness*. What might be considered confounding and irrelevant variables in an RCT would be considered relevant, included, and controlled statistically in the practice-based method. The method resembles a kind of epidemiological method largely within institutional acute care environments. From the method have been developed several measures of severity indices used in clinical practice (Horn et al., 2002). The practice-based evidence approach has demonstrated effectiveness in identifying best practices on a range of clinical situations, including pediatric bronchiolitis (Willson, Landrigan, Horn, & Smout, 2003), stroke rehabilitation (Conroy, DeJong, & Horn, 2009), and pressure ulcer treatment (Bergstrom et al., 2005). To date, formal practice-based research methods have been confined to large hospital systems or groups of institutional settings. Although it shows promise in public health and certainly is helpful to policy leaders, the practice-based evidence method needs to be further developed in those areas.

Using Evidence for Leadership

Just as research indicates the need to integrate evidence-based practice throughout healthcare practice, conventional wisdom suggests that evidence can drive leadership. But that is not always the case. Likely in no other area of clinical practice are individual characteristics, preferences, and situations more complex and unique than in the context of leadership. Rather, evidence informs leadership.

Indeed, a growing number of healthcare leaders prefer reference to evidence-*informed*, rather than evidence-*based*, practice in leadership and policy (Best et al., 2009; Bowen & Zwi, 2005; Chalkidou, Walley, Culyer, Littlejohns, & Hoy, 2008; Fretheim, Oxman, Lavis, & Lewin, 2009; Lavis, Oxman, Moynihan, & Paulsen, 2008; Lavis, Paulsen, Oxman, & Moynihan, 2008a, 2008b; Rycroft-Malone, 2008). Certainly, appropriate evidence and use of data are critical to most aspects of leadership practice (Brandt et al., 2009), but caution is warranted in wholesale development or use of formal protocols for leadership. First, empirical evidence based on controlled trials is simply not available or sufficient to mandate a particular formula for a specific leader's decision making in a particular situation or setting. Second, leadership is both objective and artful, intellectual and emotional, evidence based and creative risk taking. There are helpful guidelines, studies, experts, cases, and anecdotes, but effective leadership will not flow neatly from a database of clinical trials and outcomes (Arndt & Bigelow, 2009). Leadership is both empirical and metaphysical, positivistic and interpretive. It happens always in the natural setting rather than a controlled environment. Data are important to successful leadership, but leading is often about meaning more than measurement. People function in a place of context, meaning, and stories. Thus, the wise leader balances use of data from evidence, appropriate technologies, and educated talents of instinct.

TECHNOLOGY: INFORMATICS, ELECTRONICS, AND OTHER TOOLS OF THE FUTURE

Modern use of evidence always includes some aspect of technology. Sometimes, the very word *technology* feels like either some wolf in the wilderness waiting to ambush our comfort in the status quo or the next great gadget to make life easier. Indeed, in too many cases, technologies continue to be "underused, misused, or overused" (Fitzpatrick et al., 2010, p. 16). The truth is that technology has always been part of the work of leadership in health care. Although we all seem to have an image of what technology means, there is not a clear definition. It generally refers to the application of science and scientific invention to practice. It includes the tools and machines we use to monitor, care for, and treat patients; clinical information systems; communication systems; databases for patient classification; education systems; clinical evidence; and even personnel management.

Informatics and Health Care

Informatics is the science and application of gathering, using, manipulating, storing, retrieving, and classifying information. Broadly, it may include artificial intelligence, computer science, information science, cognitive science, social sciences, and healthcare sciences. It focuses on how data are structured and organized to support knowledge building and decision making. The goal of informatics is to store and integrate data in order to provide accurate, accessible, and useful information. Just as it is hard to imagine professional leadership and practice without using informatics, it is nearly impossible to imagine future possibilities for applications of informatics to support leadership and health care.

Informatics and technology for consumers already provide information access, distance support groups, communication resources, and direct care by tele-health. New areas of expertise continue to emerge among health care providers. One can only imagine what the future may hold for consumer healthcare using informatics. On the horizon are personal access to medical records and databases, customized diagnosis, and personalized prescriptions and treatments. Informatics is critical to define, represent, and apply nursing and healthcare knowledge across care settings, as well as to provide large datasets to promote the discovery of new knowledge. Kossman and Brennan (2008, p. 417) described the significance of health information technology (IT) for nursing leaders:

> Effective [health information technology] systems support nurse leaders by collecting and analyzing data pertinent to nursing practice, quality, and outcomes. This fosters benchmarking and best practices identification. Financial and administrative databases offer useful information but are not sufficient for nursing decisions. [For example], the Nursing Minimal Data Set and Nursing Management Minimal Data Set identify essential data necessary to characterize nursing practice.

Such datasets collect, identify, and provide information related to demographics, service, and healthcare data; environment and financial elements; and other provider-sensitive data to improve patient outcomes. Access and management of information have broken down barriers across countries, across distance, across disciplines, and across roles. But as a leader, never forget that it is human beings who create knowledge, and *knowledge* is very different from *information*.

Although technology and informatics are pervasive throughout health care, the industry continues to fall well behind others in the effective, cross-disciplinary, or global use of available technologies. Porter-O'Grady and Malloch (2008, p. 81) further chided:

> It is a travesty of both time value and duplication that each healthcare institution establishes its own policies, practices, protocols, and procedures without access either to each other or to regional and national databases where a repository of this information is available to all.

There is simply no hope of establishing regional or national standards of excellence in practice and clinical care if no one accesses the virtual community where these processes can be located.

Historically, neither healthcare providers nor business or leadership experts have been prepared with competencies in informatics. That will change for the next generation of advanced clinicians, especially among nurses with a DNP degree (Trangenstein, Weiner, Gordon, & McArthur, 2009). Westra and Delaney (2008) have begun the work to identify the unique knowledge and skills required for the healthcare leader. The list should certainly include some degree of computer skills, informatics knowledge, and some informatics skills. At this point, leaders must recognize the significance of informatics to health care, identify specific needs and opportunities for their applications, and develop new expertise and collaborate with experts specifically qualified to support desired outcomes.

Electronic Health Records

One important aspect of the use of informatics in health care that has lagged far behind is the emerging electronic health record (the electronic medical record, or EMR). It is ironic and unfortunate that health care is among the last industries to effectively use electronic technology for client records. It is truly incredulous that through technology, as an ordinary consumer, we can research what is the best kitchen appliance, like a toaster, then order it, pay for it, and have it delivered nearly anywhere in the world. However, in too many parts of the country, we still struggle to read someone's handwriting to determine a drug dosage and work in an industry that does not yet provide a consistent, portable, accessible patient record. The next generation of leaders must change that. The history of resistance to the EMR among some healthcare providers reminds of Western Union's legendary response in 1876 when offered the opportunity to purchase rights to the telephone: "This 'telephone' has too many shortcomings to be seriously considered as a means of communication. The device is inherently of no value to us" (Nova, 2000).

Computerized medical records were available over 40 years ago (Ausman, 1967; Schenthal, Sweeney, & Nettleton, 1961; Thompson, Classen, & Haug, 2007). Analysis of early studies revealed that use of the EMR saved 24% of documentation time of nurses in hospitals, but did not reduce documentation time especially for physicians (Poissant, Pereira, Tamblyn, & Kawasumi, 2005), apparently hampering its adoption. Other studies have demonstrated as much as 90% reduction in medication errors associated with transcription, and 30% to 50% reduction in errors associated with prescribing. Other evidence indicates that such record systems increase use of preventive care, reduce use of laboratory tests, track drug utilization, improve detection of infections, reduce patient length of stay in hospitals, and even reduce mortality risks (Thompson et al., 2007). Of course, the electronic record will not eliminate errors altogether. Already, we have identified errors of data entry and data retrieval (Ash, Berg, & Coiera, 2004), but if we are able to generalize the use of an electronic record, a whole new range of opportunities would likely open to transform care in ways yet unknown. Possibilities to improve access to patient information across settings, to develop electronic decision support measures to improve safety and care, and to create entirely new care models await the full implementation of the electronic health record.

Tele-health and Tele-medicine

Tele-health and *tele-medicine* are also commonly used terms often without specific definition. Tele-health has been defined as "the use of electronic information and tele-communications technologies to support long-distance clinical health care, patient and professional health-related education, public health, and health administration" (Health Resources and Services Administration, 2001). Tele-medicine is now generally considered synonymous with tele-health. Tele-health is still in its infancy, with amazing promise to extend the benefits of excellent health care to populations without access and to extend educational opportunities to clinicians beyond restraints of distance and resources. In rural, underserved areas, tele-health can offer immediate feedback, decrease isolation, and extend health and life-saving benefits not otherwise possible. As the promise of tele-health becomes reality, it will require the most creative and effective leaders to maneuver through a variety of challenges, such as licensure and practice across state or national boundaries, access and insurance coverage to patients, fair reimbursement to providers, scrutiny of liability and other legal issues, patient privacy, fair distribution of resources and services, assurance of interprofessional collaboration, patient documentation systems, and a world of other issues yet unknown. Tele-health must be practiced outside traditional paradigms, so all of our thinking related to what we have always done will be challenged. This will require thoughtful and effective leadership. Rae-Dupree (2009) observed that the idea that technology decreases the provider-patient relationship is a myth. It actually enhances it.

Technology and Simulation

Use of simulation for clinical preparation as well as practitioner development is another mode to continue to grow. Simulation laboratories are popping up all over the country in medical and nursing schools as well as healthcare organizations. These expensive extensions of practice preparation and development are an attractive focus for community donors since they provide a tangible product of the investment and an impressive "high-tech" image of the future. They are used to train practitioners in skills. At first, such laboratories were directed toward teaching skills and procedures on individual high-fidelity mannequins. Now, the trend is to create specific simulated clinical sites, such as the simulated intensive care unit, labor and delivery unit, or even homes and community centers. The centers provide safe environments for skill practice and feedback. Although these are often shared among disciplines, we have yet to see much truly integrated, collaborative use. There is a growing movement toward using such centers to train care teams in collaboration and communication. The future waits for the use of such simulation centers to promote leadership development.

Technologies on the Horizon

Regardless of its form, it is clear that technology will continue to change the face of healthcare practice and leadership. It will provide entrepreneurial opportunities beyond current imagination. Patient assessment, interventions, and communications will become more technological than mechanical, and mass customization will become as prevalent in health care as it is in current online shopping. As technology continues to advance and change communication modes, choice and access will shift control of health care decisions toward the patient and community, and finally, we will begin to see consumers as central members of our professional care teams.

Our models of care of the future will move away from traditional clinical practice, practitioner-based designs to information-based, consumer-access models "that inform, empower, and actualize the consumer to take individual action with regard to his or her health status" (Porter-O'Grady, 2001, p. 66).

Other technology and tools of the future that will change health care as we know it are out there, about to happen, and yet unknown. Ellis (2003, p. 2) summarized our impotence in predicting which innovations will change health care by the following observations:

> It is easy to predict that innovation will occur, harder to predict what the successful innovations will be. . . .. If a healthcare enterprise or profession is to stay in business, it must accurately predict the future, because the future is as close as tomorrow; and there may not be time to recover from the sort of major predictive failures made by Lord Kelvin (discoverer of absolute zero), former IBM chairman Tom Watson, DEC founder Ken Olson. . . and one of the original Warner Brothers, who said, respectively that X-rays would prove to be a hoax, there was a world market for maybe five computers, there was no reason anyone would want a computer in their home. . ., and "Who the hell wants to hear actors talk?"

Innovative technologies on the immediate horizon include the legacy of the Human Genome Project that will forever change the timing, processes, and ethics of the entire process of care, from history and diagnosis to prevention, therapies, and interventions. Other advances are the nearly incredible work on artificial limbs, biochip technologies, the artificial bionic retina, and islet cell transplantation for diabetes (Ellis, 2003, p. 3). We have only to imagine (or perhaps cannot even imagine) the technologies that will change health care, change how we manage health care, and change us as leaders.

Implications of Technology for Leadership

Technology and information access and management have changed the lives of leaders. Leaders play a critical role in the selection and adoption of technology in care services. For example, the clinical leader must collaborate and interact closely with providers at the point of care to first learn what technology is needed and then to assure that the appropriate technology is employed. This requires orchestration of input and feedback from staff nurses and other direct care providers. Furthermore, the leader must cultivate close relationships with IT experts and personnel as well as technology vendors to assure the appropriate integration and support for technology. Finally, the leader must be the frontline translator of the needs, uses, and outcomes of technology to the highest levels of healthcare administration to assure understanding and resources for the use of technology. Indeed, the leader must interpret such data across disciplines as well as up and down from patient to care provider to business administrator. Always, the purpose of technology in health care is, first, to improve the quality of care and, second, to assure effective business performance of the organization.

Instant access and communication have blurred the lines between personal and professional lives and expectations. Leaders are called upon to guide organizations through overwhelming information and incredible velocity of change. "Organizations need to be incredibly smart, fast, agile, responsive" (Wheatley, 2001b, p. 29), and they depend upon their leaders to support them. Furthermore, the leader's promotion and management of the use of technology can be an important recruitment factor as nurses and other healthcare workers are drawn to work environments that effectively employ technology (Fitzpatrick et al., 2010). On the other hand, Wheatley (p. 29) warned:

> Unlike past organizational change efforts, knowledge management is truly a survival issue. Done right, it can give us what we so desperately need—organizations that act with intelligence. Done wrong, we will, like lemmings, keep rushing into the future without using our intelligence to develop longer-term individual and organizational capacity. To continue blindly down our current path, where speed and profits are the primary values, where there is no time to think or reflect, is suicidal.

We have learned how to retrieve, store, and manage information. We are learning how to convert information to knowledge. It is the human capacities to apply and wisely use the technologies and information, to reflect on what matters, to project how things can be better. When will we learn how to transform information to knowledge to wisdom?

PRODUCTIVITY AND EFFECTIVENESS

We use technology to seek, store, and measure results. But measurement of productivity in health care is a special challenge. Although we are in the business of healing, health care is an industry, a business that measures outcomes and expects accountability and productivity. Increases in cost, wide variations in quality, more diverse and better informed patients and consumers, and public and business concerns regarding value for investment have provoked a greater interest in productivity and effectiveness in health care in general across the United States (Shortell, n.d.). Value is what the customer receives for the price paid. To promote efficiency and productivity, Womack and Jones (2005, p. 60) proposed the concept of "lean consumption," which is when a business provides the full value that customers expect with the "greatest efficiency and least pain." It requires integrated and streamlined processes and attention to meeting the needs of the customer or patient.

Traditionally, productivity refers to the amount or quality of output per unit of input, a return on investment, or worker efficiency. It is easy to measure the productivity of a machine or even the productivity of labor to produce a product. Healthcare outputs are more vexing. To a large healthcare system in today's market-oriented culture, productivity may mean its margin of the market. To a hospital worker, productivity may be the timely accomplishment of the day's duties. Ultimately, the productivity of a national healthcare system must be measured by the health of all its citizens.

From a management and human resources perspective, productivity usually refers to productive hours of human labor, most often referred to as full-time equivalents, or FTEs, or staff workload used in some formula of output. In acute-care systems, outputs are usually measured in some measure related to patient census, acuity levels, patient throughputs, or procedures performed. Other measures include staff turnover related to manager effectiveness.

There is current interest in various formal quality and productivity programs. Among the most popular are Six Sigma and Lean. These programs are focused toward manufacturing production but are growing in use in large healthcare systems and hospitals (American Society for Quality, 2009). Their hope is based in improving quality and decreasing cost, with a focus on work processes. Six Sigma is "a disciplined data-driven approach and methodology for eliminating defects" (Six Sigma, 2010). The program uses jargon such as titles of "champion" for leaders and awards of "belts," such as "green belt" and "master black belt" status. The management approach is driven by outcomes data, usually financial, and based on projects to improve processes by controlling variation and improving predictability. Lean is "a systematic approach to identifying and eliminating eight "wastes" through continuous improvement by flowing the product at the 100% pull of the customer" (Lean, 2005). Systems measure productivity by reducing waste of time and human resources for a "lean" journey of the patient across care settings facilitated by efficient coordination of care (Kim, Spahlinger, Kin, Coffey, & Billi, 2009). Principles are that all work is process, that process flow can be optimized, and that employee flexibility increases productivity and reduces waste. The eight wastes of lean are waiting, defects, extra processing, inventory, excessive motion, transportation, over-production, and under-utilized employees. An increasing number of such outcomes-based measures are considered in a context of productivity. The long-term value of such programs in human healing organizations remains to be determined. Effectiveness is reflected by accomplishment of mission, goals, and outcomes and satisfaction by all concerned, including and especially the people we serve. The danger of a focus on efficiency, in its usual sense, in health care is its potential effects on quality and patient satisfaction, not to mention pushing out the goals of healing and well-being, which have some human subjective, reflective, and social characteristics that challenge productivity measurement. Productivity and effectiveness must ultimately refer to a focus on value.

The Mayo Clinic Policy Center (2007) identified six action principles to assure productivity in health care for the future: (1) develop a definition of value based upon the needs and preferences of patients, measureable outcomes, safety, and service, compared with the cost of care over time; (2) pay providers based on value and develop a methodology for allocating finite resources; (3) create competition around results through pricing and quality transparency; (4) hold all sectors in health care accountable for reducing waste inefficiencies; (5) create a trusted mechanism to synthesize scientific and clinical information in an impartial and rigorous way for both consumers and providers; and (6) encourage formation of integrated systems to deliver effective and appropriate care.

The future will require increased knowledge, facility, and creativity by all leaders in health care regarding how to integrate important business and market principles into the enterprise of healing. We will need to move beyond safety and efficiency toward value and excellence.

The leader who promotes productivity and fosters effectiveness continually sends a message of clear intention and expectations of what is expected and when it must be produced. He or she instills a sense of ownership of goals, processes, and outcomes. Even detractors must know what are the goals, the work, and the desired outcomes of the organization. In business, effectiveness is often associated with the concept of execution. Execution is the action of getting things done. It requires careful match of people with processes and tasks that come together for highest performance and best results. All does not always go as planned, but the leader guides the team through continuous improvement and recovery. The leader is also the key person to clearly articulate desired outcomes in a manner that can be identified and measured.

Why do some good organizations fall short of acceptable productivity and effectiveness? Leaders, beware of some habits that can quash the spirit to produce. Overplanning and overmeasuring can kill the spirit, especially in health care. We are in it because we want to help people. We need time to reflect, to cherish our contact with those we serve, and to create. Overplanning, overprocessing, and overproceduring can be devastating. Good leaders hold people accountable, then guide them toward success, recognize that success, and celebrate it.

Effective practice design and management for the future will consider innovative models, embracing an entrepreneurial context. Such designs must include continual assessment at the local unit and entire systems level, decisions based on evidence, effective use of technology in all areas of patient care, and creative ways of measuring effectiveness that improve the efficiency of the system while promoting environments of healing.

REFERENCES

Aiken, L., Sochalski, J., & Lake, E. (1997). Studying outcomes of organizational change in health services. *Medical Care, 35*(11 Suppl.), NS6–NS18.

American Association of Colleges of Nursing (AACN). (2002). *Hallmarks of the professional nurse practice environment.* Washington, D.C.: AACN. American Society for Quality (ASQ). (2009). *Hospitals see benefits of Lean and Six Sigma.* Retrieved February 20, 2010. from http://www.asq.org/mediaroom/press-releases/2009/20090318-hospit

Anonymous. (2004). Program enables 50 new initiatives in four months: "Transforming care at the bedside" program. *Healthcare Benchmarks & Quality Improvement, 11*(9), 100–101.

Anonymous. (2005). Transforming care at the bedside: Using a team approach to give nurses—and their patients—new voices in providing high-quality care. *Quality Letter in Healthcare Leadership, 17*(11), 1–8.

Arndt, M., & Bigelow, B. (2009). Evidence-based management in health care organizations: A cautionary note. *Health Care Management Review, 34*(3), 206–213.

Aroian, J., Maservey, P. M., & Crockett, J. G. (1996). Developing nurse leaders for today and tomorrow, part 1: Foundations of leadership in practice. *Journal of Nursing Administration, 26*(9), 18–26.

Ash, J. S., Berg, M., & Coiera, E. (2004). Patient care information system-related errors. *Journal of the American Medical Informatics Association, 11*(2), 104–112.

Ausman, R. K. (1967). Automated storage and retrieval of patient data. *American Journal of Surgery, 114,* 159–166.

Batcheller, J., Burkman, K., Armstrong, D., Chappell, C., & Carelock, J. A. (2004). A practice model for patient safety: The value of the experienced registered nurse. *Journal of Nursing Administration 34*(4), 200–205.

Bergstrom, N., Horn, S. D., Smouth, R. J., Bender, S. A., Ferguson, M. L., Taler, G., et al. (2005). The National Pressure Ulcer Long-term Study: Outcomes of pressure ulcer treatments in long-term care. *Journal of the American Geriatric Society, 53*(10), 1721–1729.

Best, A., Terpstra, J. L., Moore, G., Riley, B., Norman, C. D., & Glasgow, R. E. (2009). Building knowledge integration systems for evidence-informed decisions. *Journal of Health Organization Management, 23*(6), 627–641.

Bowen, S., & Zwi, A. B. (2005). Pathways to "evidence-informed" policy and practice: A framework for action. *Public Library of Science Medicine, 2*(7), e166.

Brandt, J. A., Reed, Edwards, D., Cos Sullivan, S., Zehler, J. K., Grinder, S., et al. (2009). An evidence-based business planning process. *Journal of Nursing Administration, 39*(12), 511–513.

Bulger, R. J. (2003). *The quest for therapeutic institutions.* Washington, D.C.: Association of Academic Health Centers.

Burns, H. K., Dudiak, L., & Greenhouse, P. D. (2009). Building an evidence-based practice infrastructure and culture: A model for rural and community hospitals. *Journal of Nursing Administration, 39*(7–8), 321–325.

Chalkidou, K., Walley, T., Culyer, A., Littlejohns, P., & Hoy, A. (2008). Evidence-informed evidence-making. *Journal of Health Services Research & Policy, 13*(3), 167–173.

Christensen, C. (1997). *The innovator's dilemma.* Boston: Harvard Business School.

Christensen, C. M., & Overdorf, M. (2000, March–April). Meeting the challenge of disruptive change. *Harvard Business Review, 78*(2), 67–76.

Conroy, B. E., DeJong, G., & Horn, S. D. (2009). Hospital-based stroke rehabilitation in the United States. *Topics in Stroke Rehabilitation, 16*(1), 34–43.

Cullen, L., Greiner, J., Greiner, J., Bombei, C., & Comried, L. (2005). Excellence in evidence-based practice: Organizational and unit exemplars. *Critical Care Nursing Clinics of North America, 17*(2), 127–142, x.

Cummings, G. G., Estabrooks, C. A., Midodzi, W. K., Wallin, L., & Hayduk, L. (2007). Influence of organizational characteristics and context on research utilization. *Nursing Research, 56*(4 Suppl.), S24–S39.

Danna, D. (2009). Organizational structure and analysis. In L. Roussel & R. C. Swansburg (Eds.), *Management and leadership for nurse administrators* (5th ed., pp. 184–259). Sudbury, MA: Jones & Bartlett.

Dingman, S. K. (2005). The caring model. Retrieved January 22, 2010, from http://thecaringmodel.com/info.html

Dingman, S. K., Williams, M., Fosbinder, D., & Warnick, M. (1999). Implementing a caring model to improve patient satisfaction. *Journal of Nursing Administration, 29*(12), 30–37.

Donahue, L., Rader, S., & Triolo, P. K. (2008). Nurturing innovation in the critical care environment: Transforming care at the bedside. *Critical Care Nursing clinics of North America, 20*(4), 465–469.

Donebedian, A. (1966). Evaluating the quality of medical care. *Millbank Quarterly, 44,* 166–203.

Drucker, P. F. (1998, November–December). The discipline of innovation. *Harvard Business Review, 76*(6), 149–157.

Ellis, D. (2003). *The acceleration of innovations.* Retrieved January 20, 2010, from http://www.Healthfuturesdigest.com/

Fitzpatrick, M. A., Grant, S., McCue, P., O'Rourke, M. W., Reck, D. L., Shaffer, F. A., et al. (2010). Nurse leaders discuss the nurse's role in driving technology decisions. *American Nurse Today, 5*(1), 16–19.

Formella, N., & Rovin, S. (2004). Creating a desirable future for nursing, part 2: The issues. *Journal of Nursing Administration, 134*(6), 264–267.

Fretheim A., Oxman, A. D., Lavis, J. N., & Lewin, S. (2009). SUPPORT tools for evidence-informed policymaking in health 18: Planning, monitoring, and evaluation of policies. *Health Research Policy & Systems, 16*(7), S18.

Gifford, W., Davies, B., Edwards, N., Griffin, P., & Lybanon, V. (2007). Managerial leadership for nurses' use of research evidence: An integrative review of the literature. *Worldviews on Evidence Based Nursing, 4*(3), 126–145.

Godfrey, M. M., Melin, C. N., Muething, S. E., Batalden, P. B., & Nelson, E. C. (2008). Clinical microsystems, part 3: Transformation of two hospitals using microsystem, mesosystem, and macrosystem strategies. *Joint Commission Journal on Quality & Patient Safety, 34*(10), 591–603.

Hacker, J. S. (2007). Healing our *Sicko* health care system. *The New England Journal of Medicine, 357*(8), 733–735.

Hall, L. M., & Doran, D. (2004). Nurse staffing, care delivery models, and patient care quality. *Journal of Nursing Care Quality, 19*(1), 27–33.

Health Resources and Services Administration (HRSA). (2001). *Report to Congress on telemedicine.* Retrieved September 3, 2009, from http://www.hrsa.gov/telehealth/pubs/report2001.htm

Hoffart, N., & Woods, C. (1996). Elements of a nursing professional practice model. *Journal of Professional Nursing, 12*(6), 354–364.

Horn, S. D., & Gassaway, J. (2007). Practice-based evidence study design for comparative effectiveness research. *Medical Care, 45*(10), S50–S57.

Horn, S. D., Torres, A., Jr., Willson, D., Dean, J. M., Gassaway, J., & Smout, R. (2002). Development of a pediatric age- and disease-specific severity measure. *Journal of Pediatrics, 141*(4), 496–503.

Institute for Healthcare Improvement. (2010). *Transforming care at the bedside.* Retrieved January 31, 2010, from http://www.ihi.org/IHI/Programs/Collaboratives/TransformingCareattheBedside.htm?TabId=0

Institute of Medicine. (2001). *Crossing the quality chasm: A new health system for the 21st century.* Washington, DC: National Academies Press.

Ives Erickson, J., & Ditomassi, M. (2008). Professional practice model. In H. R. Feldman, M. Jaffe-Ruiz, M. L. McClure, M. J. Greenberg, & T. D. Smith (Eds.), *Nursing leadership: A concise encyclopedia* (pp. 467–470). New York: Springer.

Ives Erickson, J., Duffy, M., Gibbons, P., Fitzmaurice, J., Ditomassi, M., & Jones, D. (2004). Development and psychometric evaluation of the professional practice environment scale. *Journal of Nursing Scholarship, 36*(3), 279–284.

Joynt, J., & Kimball, B. (2008). *Innovative care delivery models: Identifying new models that effectively leverage nurses* [white paper]. Princeton, NJ: Robert Wood Johnson Foundation.

Kao, J. (1996). *Jamming: The art and discipline of business creativity.* New York: HarperBusiness.

Kerfoot, K. (1998). On leadership: Leading change is leading creativity. *Pediatric Nursing, 24*(2), 180–181.

Kim, C. S., Spahlinger, D. A., Kin, J. M., Coffey, R. J., & Billi, J. E. (2009). Implementation of lean thinking: One health system's journey. *Joint Commission Journal on Quality & Patient Safety, 35*(8), 406–413.

Kimball, B., Joynt, J., Cherner, D., & O'Neil, E. (2007). The quest for new innovative care delivery models. *Journal of Nursing Administration, 37*(9), 392–398.

Kossman, S. P., & Brennan, P. F. (2008). Nursing informatics. In H. R. Feldman, M. Jaffe-Ruiz, M. L. McClure, M. J. Greenberg, & T. D. Smith (Eds.), *Nursing leadership: A concise encyclopedia* (pp. 416–419). New York: Springer.

Kramer, M., & Hafner, L. P. (1989). Shared values: Impact on staff nurse job satisfaction and perceived productivity. *Nursing Research, 38*, 58–64.

Lake, E. (2002). Development of the practice environment scale of the nursing work index. *Research in Nursing & Health, 25*, 176–188.

Lavis, J. N., Oxman, A. D., Moynihan, R., & Paulsen, E. J. (2008). Evidence-informed health policy 3: Interviews with the directors of organizations that support distribution in British Columbia. *Implementation Science, 17*(3), 55.

Lavis, J. N., Paulsen, E. J., Oxman, A. D., & Moynihan, R. (2008a). Evidence-informed health policy 1: Synthesis of findings from a multi-method study of organizations that support the use of research evidence. *Implementation Science, 17*(3), 53.

Lavis, J. N., Paulsen, E. J., Oxman, A. D., & Moynihan, R. (2008b). Evidence-informed health policy 1: Survey of organizations that support the use of research evidence. *Implementation Science, 17*(3), 54.

Lean. (2005). *What is lean?* Retrieved February 20, 2010, from http://www.6sigma.us/what-is-lean.php

Lorenz, H. L., Greenhouse, P. K., Miller, R., Wisniewski, M. K., & Frank, S. L. (2008). Transforming care at the bedside: An ambulatory model for improving the patient experience. *Journal of Nursing Administration 38*(4), 194–199.

Lukas, C. V., Holmes, S. K., Cohen, A. B., Restuccia, J., Cramer, I. E., Schwartz, M., et al. (2007). Transformational change in health care systems: An organizational model. *Health Care Management Review, 32*(4), 309–320.

MacRobert, M. (2008). A leadership focus on evidence-based practice: Tools for successful implementation. *Professional Case Management, 13*(2), 97–101.

Magvary, D., Whitney, J. D., & Brown, M. A. (2006). Advancing practice inquiry: Research foundations of the practice doctorate in nursing. *Nursing Outlook, 54*(3), 139–151.

Manthey, M. (2009). *Creative health care management.* Retrieved January 22, 2010, from http://www.chcm.com

Marchionni, C., & Richer, M. C. (2007). Using appreciative inquiry to promote evidence-based practice in nursing: The glass is more than half full. *Nursing Leadership, 20*(3), 86–97.

Marchionni, C., & Ritchie, J. (2008). Organizational factors that support the implementation of a nursing best practice guideline. *Journal of Nursing Management, 16*(3), 266–274.

Martin, S. C., Greenhouse, P. K., Merryman, T., Shovel, J., Liberi, C. A., & Konzier, J. (2007). Transforming care at the bedside: Implementation and spread model for single-hospital and multihospital systems. *Journal of Nursing Administration, 37*(10), 444–451.

Mayo Clinic. (2007). *Improving productivity in health care: Executive summary.* Retrieved January 22, 2010. from http://www.mayoclinic.org/healthpolicycenter/forum2-summary.html

McCauley, K., & Irwin, R. (2006). Changing the work environment in intensive care units to achieve patient-focused care: The time has come. *American Journal of Critical Care, 15*(6), 541–548.

McClure, M., Poulin, M., Sovie, M., & Wandelt, M. (2002). *Magnet hospitals: Attraction and retention of professional nurses*. Kansas City, MO: American Nurses Association.

McKinley, K. E., Berry, S. A., Laam, L. A., Doll, M. C., Brin, K. P., Bothe, A., et al. (2008). Clinical Microsystems, part 4: Building innovative population-specific mesosystems. *Joint Commission Journal on Quality & Patient Safety, 34*(11), 655–663.

Melnyk, B. (2007). The evidence-based practice mentor: A promising strategy for implementing and sustaining EBP in healthcare systems. *Worldviews on Evidence Based Nursing, 4*(3), 123–125.

Melnyk, B., & Fineout-Overholt, E. (2002). Putting research into practice. Rochester ARCC. *Reflections on Nursing Leadership, 28*(2), 22–25.

Melnyk, B., & Finout-Overholt, E. (2005). *Evidence-based practice in nursing & health care: A guide to best practice*. Philadelphia: Lippincott Williams & Wilkins.

Morjikian, R. L., Kimball, B., & Joynt, J. (2007). Leading change: The nurse executive's role in implementing new care delivery models. *The Journal of Nursing Administration, 37*(9), 399–404.

Naylor, M., Brooten, D., Campbell, R., Jacobsen, B. S., Mezey, M. D., Pauly, M. V., et al. (1999). Comprehensive discharge planning and home follow-up of hospitalized elders: A randomized clinical trial. *JAMA: Journal of the American Medical Association, 281*(7), 613–620.

Naylor, M., Brooten, D., Campbell, R., Maislin, G., McCauley, K., & Schwartz, S. (2004). Transitional care of older adults hospitalized with heart failure: A randomized, controlled trial. *Journal of the American Geriatric Society, 52*, 675–684.

Nelson, E. C., Godfrey, M. M., Batalden, P. B., Berry, S. A., Bothe, A. E., McKinley, K. E., et al. (2008). Clinical microsystems, part 1: The building blocks of health systems. *Joint Commission on Quality & Patient Safety, 34*(7), 367–378.

Nelson, M. J. (2008). Patient care delivery models. In H. R. Feldman, M. Jaffe-Ruiz, M. L. McClure, M. J. Greenberg, & T. D. Smith (Eds.), *Nursing leadership: A concise encyclopedia* (pp. 443–445). New York: Springer.

Newhouse, R. P. (2007). Creating infrastructure supportive of evidence-based nursing practice: Leadership strategies. *Worldviews on Evidence Based Nursing, 4*(1), 21–29.

Newhouse, R. P. (2009). Nursing's role in engineering a learning healthcare system. *Journal of Nursing Administration, 39*(6), 260–262.

Newhouse, R. P., & Johnson, K. (2009). A case study in evaluating infrastructure for EBP and selecting a model. *Journal of Nursing Administration, 39*(10), 409–411.

Nova. (2000). Traveling through time. Retrieved January 20, 2010, from http://www.pbs.org/wgbh/nova/time/throughz.html

Oberlander, J. (2007). Learning from failure in health care reform. *The New England Journal of Medicine, 357*(17), 1677–1680.

O'Reilly, C., & Tushman, M. L. (2004, April). The ambidextrous organization. *Harvard Business Review, 82*(4), 74–83.

Parsons, M. (2004). Capacity building for Magnetism at multiple levels: A healthy workplace intervention. Part 1. *Topics in Emergency Medicine, 26*(4), 287–295.

Planetree. (2010). *Planetree patient-centered care*. Retrieved January 22, 2010, from http://www.innovativecaremodels.com/care_models/4/overview

Poissant, L., Pereira, J., Tamblyn, R., & Kawasumi, Y. (2005). The impact of electronic health records on time efficiency of physicians and nurses: A systematic review. *Journal of the American Medical Informatics Association, 12*(5), 505–516.

Porter-O'Grady, T. (2001). Beyond the walls: Nursing in the entrepreneurial world. *Nursing Administration Quarterly, 25*(2), 61–68.

Porter-O'Grady, T., & Malloch, K. (2008). Beyond myth and magic: The future of evidence-based leadership. *Nursing Administration Quarterly, 32*(3), 176–187.

Porter-O'Grady, T., & Wilson, C. (1999). *Leading the revolution in health care*. Gaithersburg, MD: Aspen.

Rae-Dupree, J. (2009, February 1). Disruptive innovation applied to health care. *The New York Times*. Retrieved January 18, 2010, from http://www.nytimes.com/2009/02/01/business/01unbox.html?_r=1&p

Reineck, C. (2007). Models of change. *Journal of Nursing Administration, 37*(9), 388–391.

Rycroft-Malone, J. (2008). Evidence-informed practice: From individual to context. *Journal of Nursing Management, 16*(4), 404–408.

Schenthal, J. E., Sweeney, J. W., & Nettleton, W. J. (1961). Clinical application of electronic data processing apparatus II: New methodology in clinical record storage. *JAMA: Journal of the American Medical Association, 178*, 267–270.

Schulman, C. S. (2008). Strategies for starting a successful evidence-based practice program. *American Association of Critical Care Nurses (AACN) Advances in Critical Care, 19*(3), 301–311.

Scott-Smith, J. L., & Greenhouse, P. K. (2007). Transforming care at the bedside: Patient-controlled liberalized diet. *Journal of Interprofessional Care, 21*(2), 179–188.

Seago, J. A. (2001). Nurse staffing, models of care delivery, and interventions. In R. M. Wachter, K. G. Shojania, B. W. Duncan, & R. M. Wachter (Eds.), *Making health care safer: A critical analysis of patient safety practices*. Washington, D.C.: Agency for Healthcare Research & Quality (AHRQ). Retrieved January 22, 2010 from http://www.ahrq.gov/clinic/ptsafety/

Senge, P. (1990). The leader's new work: Building learning organizations. *Sloan Management Review, 32*(1), 7–23.

Senge, P. (1995). *The fifth discipline*. New York: Doubleday.

Shirey, M. R. (2006). Evidence-based practice: How nurse leaders can facilitate innovation. *Nursing Administration Quarterly, 30*(3), 252–265.

Shortell, S. M. (n. d.). *Integrated health systems: Promise & Performance*. Berkeley, CA: University of California Berkeley. Retrieved January 22, 2010, from http://www.hks.harvard.edu/m-rcbg/hcdp/readings/Integrated%20Health%20Systems%20-%20Promise%20and%20Performance.pdf

Six Sigma. (2010). *Six Sigma: What is Six Sigma?* Retrieved February 13, 2010, from http://www.isixsigma.com/sixsigma/six_sigma.asp.

Sossong, A. E., Cullen, S., Theriault, P., Stetson, A., Higgins, B., Roche, S., et al. (2009). Renewing the spirit of nursing: Embracing evidence-based practice in a rural state. *Nursing Clinics of North America, 44*(1), 33–42.

Stetler, C. B. (2003). Role of the organization in translating research into evidence-based practice. *Outcomes Management, 7*(3), 97–103.

Stetler, C. B., McQueen, L., Demakis, J., & Mittman, B. S. (2008). An organizational framework and strategic implementation for system-level change to enhance research-based practice: QUERI Series. *Implementation Science, 29*(3), 30.

Stetler, C. B., Ritchie, J., Rycroft-Malone, J., Schultz, A., & Charns, M. (2007). Improving quality of care through routine, successful implementation of evidence-based practice at the bedside: An organizational case study protocol using the Pettigrew and Whipp model of strategic change. *Implementation Science, 31*(2), 3.

Stetler, C. B., Ritchie, J. A., Rycroft-Malone, J., Schultz, A. A., & Charns, M. P. (2009). Institutionalizing evidence-based practice: An organizational case study using a model of strategic change. *Implementation Science, 30*(4), 78.

Stichler, J. F. (2007). Leadership roles for nurses in healthcare design. *Journal of Nursing Administration, 37*(12), 527–530.

Strout, T. D., Lancaster, K., & Schultz, A. A. (2009). Development and implementation of an inductive model for evidence-based practice: A grassroots approach for building evidence-based practice capacity in staff nurses. *Nursing Clinics of North America, 44*(1), 93–102.

Thompson, D. I., Classen, D. C., & Haug, P. J. (2007). EMRs in the fourth stage: The future of electronic medical records based on the experience at Intermountain Health Care. *Journal of Healthcare Information Management, 21*(3), 49–60.

Trangenstein, P. A., Weiner, E. E., Gordon, J. S., & McArthur, D. (2009). Nursing informatics for future nurse scholars: Lessons learned with the doctorate of nursing practice (DNP). *Studies in Health Technology & Informatics, 146*, 551–555.

Tunis, S. R., Stryer, D. B., & Clancy, C. M. (2003). Practical clinical trials: Increasing the value of clinical research for decision making in clinical and health policy. *Journal of the American Medical Association, 290*, 1624–1632.

Upenieks, V. V., Needleman, J., Soban, L., Pearson, M. L., Parkerton, P., & Yee, T. (2008). The relationship between the volume and type of transforming care at the bedside innovations and changes in nurse vitality. *Journal of Nursing Administration, 38*(9), 386–394.

Viney, M., Batcheller, J., Houston, S., & Belcik, K. (2006). Transforming care at the bedside: Designing new care systems in an age of complexity. *Journal of Nursing Care Quality, 21*(2), 143–150.

Vratny, A., & Shriver, D. (2007). A conceptual model for growing evidence-based practice. *Nursing Administration Quarterly, 31*(2), 162–170.

Waddell, A. W. (2009). Cultivating quality: Shared governance supports evidence-based practice. *American Journal of Nursing, 109*(11), 53–57.

Wang, M. C., Hyun, J. K., Harrison, M., Shortell, S. M., & Fraser, I. (2006). Redesigning health systems for quality: Lessons from emerging practices. *Joint Commission Journal on Quality & Patient Safety, 32*(11), 599–611.

Wasson, J. H., Anders, S. G., Moore, L. G., Ho, L., Nelson, E. C., Godfrey, M. M., et al. (2008). Clinical microsystems, part 2: Learning from micro practices about providing patients the care they want and need. *Joint Commission Journal on Quality & Patient Safety, 34*(8), 445–452.

Weisbord, M. R. (1976). Organizational diagnosis: Six places to look for trouble with or without a theory. *Group & Organizational Studies, 1*(4), 430–447.

Wesorick, B. (2002). 21st Century leadership challenge: Creating and sustaining healthy healing work cultures and integrating service at the point of care. *Nursing Administration Quarterly, 26*(5), 18–32.

Wesorick, B. (2008). *Clinical practice model resource center* (CPM). (2008). Retrieved January 22, 2010, from http://www.cpmrc.com

Westfall, J. M., Mold, J., & Fagnan, L. (2007). Practice-based research: "Blue highways" on the NIH roadmap. *Journal of the American Medical Association, 297*, 403–406.

Westra, B. L., & Delaney, C. (2008). Informatics competencies for nursing and healthcare leaders. *AMIA Annual Symposium Proceedings, 6*, 804–808.

Wheatley, M. J. (2001a, Spring). Innovation means relying on everyone's creativity. *Leader to Leader.* Retrieved October 7, 2009, from http://www.margaretwheatley.com/articles/innovationmeans.html

Wheatley, M. J. (2001b). The real work of knowledge management. *IHRIM [International Association for Human Resources Information Management] Journal, 5*(2), 29–33.

Willson, D. F., Landrigan, C. P., Horn, S. D., & Smout, R. J. (2003). Complications in infants hospitalized for bronchiolitis or respiratory syncytial virus pneumonia. *Journal of Pediatrics, 143*(5 Suppl.), S142–S149.

Wolf, G. A., & Greenhouse, P. K. (2007). Blueprint for design: Creating models that direct change. *Journal of Nursing Administration, 37*(9), 381–387.

Womack, J. P., & Jones, D. T. (2005, March). Lean consumption. *Harvard Business Review, 83*(3), 58–68.

8

Culture and Practice Environments

There are two ways of being creative. One can sing and dance.
Or one can create an environment in which singers and dancers flourish.

— *Warren G. Bennis*

Environment and culture matter. They matter to patients and to healthcare workers. The importance of *place* and *culture* as dynamic aspects of health care is attracting growing interest among scholars in anthropology, architecture, geography, and the social sciences who have begun to explore the "landscapes" for health care (Dixon & Durrheim, 2000; Williams, 2002). Human geographers and environmental psychologists recognize that *who we are* (Dixon & Durrheim, 2000, p. 27) is inextricably related to *where we are*, and likewise related to *who receives care* and *who are the caregivers*. As settings for care expand beyond the traditional places like the hospital, healthcare leaders are challenged to assure that care is appropriate to meaning of place and that culture and place enhance health and healing.

Just as environment is important to patients and their families, healthy work environments are critical for healthcare providers. Preliminary evidence indicates that the effectiveness of transformational leaders may be related to place, size of the organization, nature and commitment of the chief executive officer, and amount of time at the helm of a particular organization (Ling, Simsek, Lubatkin, & Veiga, 2008). Conclusions are unclear at this point, but what is known is that environment makes a difference. A study in Denmark showed transformational leadership style as closely related to healthcare workers' perceptions of environmental working conditions as well as opportunities for involvement, sense of influence, meaningfulness, and sense of well-being. The authors concluded that to simply study leadership style and employee responses gives an incomplete picture, that work environment must be considered to understand positive leadership behaviors and outcomes (Nielsen, Yarker, Brenner, Randall, & Borg, 2008).

Among the most important factors related to environment is culture. Culture reflects who we are as human beings. Cultural sensitivity promotes understanding of human beings in environments of work and caring. Such environments include complex healthcare systems, primary care practices, community settings and rural communities, patient and family homes, international and global settings, and beyond to environments for care and healing yet to be imagined.

THE PRIMACY OF CULTURE AND CULTURAL SENSITIVITY

Culture is everything. The power of culture in all aspects of leading and caring for others cannot be overstated. Culture represents the great gestalt of human social phenomena. It is the whole: the constellation of values, knowledge, beliefs, and attitudes. It includes patterns of behavior, ways of living, roles, language and ways of communicating, myths, and meanings. It is time and space, objects and artifacts, traditions, stories, symbols, and metaphors. It is the whole of who we are in our families, ethnicities, regions, religions, and work. It embodies the entire portfolio of who we are as individuals in human communities. Each of us represents our own constellation of cultures from the family who raised us, our ethnic and regional background, our work, and a myriad of other human experiences. Your culture does not determine your behavior or attitudes, but it provides the background and repertoire of who you are.

Cultural Competence, Sensitivity, and Humility

Recognizing the importance of culture, competence, and sensitivity to culture are obviously desirable qualities in a leader. Cultural competence is a recent predominant theme in professional healthcare education and practice (Ballantye, 2008; Watts, Cuellar, & O'Sullivan, 2008). It is commonly accepted that an important step toward elimination of health disparities among diverse populations is to better prepare healthcare leaders and providers in cultural competence (De Leon Siantz, 2008). Although the concept is commonly accepted, definitions are numerous and vague and often associated with diversity. Part of one definition is to have the capacity to "1) value diversity, 2) conduct self-assessment, 3) manage the dynamics of difference, 4) acquire and institutionalize cultural knowledge, and 5) adapt to diversity and the cultural contexts of the communities [served]" (Georgetown University Center for Child & Human Development, n. d.). Cultural competence involves "the attitudes, knowledge, and skills necessary for providing quality care to diverse populations" (California Endowment, 2003). A key aspect of cultural competence is reflected in professional communication. Teal and Street (2009) proposed to prepare healthcare providers in the following areas to improve cultural competence: communication repertoire, situational awareness, adaptability, and knowledge about core cultural issues.

The American Association of Colleges of Nursing (AACN, 2008, p. 2) promoted five competencies essential for nurses to provide culturally competent care:

1. Apply knowledge of social and cultural factors that affect nursing and health care across multiple contexts.
2. Use relevant data sources and best evidence in providing culturally competent care.
3. Promote achievement of safe and quality outcomes of care for diverse populations.
4. Advocate for social justice, including commitment to the health of vulnerable populations and the elimination of health disparities.
5. Participate in continuous cultural competence development.

Often, when we discuss culture in health care and community affairs in general, we actually refer to ethnic or racial diversity of cultures. Alexander (2008, p. 155) observed, "Every patient encounter is a cultural encounter and therefore a significant encounter."

Cultural diversity continues to be a significant issue in health care. For example, the vast majority of nurses are women (94.23%) and mostly White (89.3%), while 25% of Americans represent an ethnic or racial minority, and nearly 20% do not speak English as their native language (Minority Nurse, 2009). Cultural sensitivity is a mandate in health care, and the standard must be set by those in leadership. The U.S. Office of Minority Health (2000) defined, "Cultural and linguistic competence is the ability of health care providers and health care organizations to understand and respond effectively to the cultural and linguistic needs brought by patients to the health care encounter."

The concept of cultural competence has been scrutinized and critiqued in favor of concepts of cultural sensitivity or cultural humility (Carpenter-Song, Nordquest Schwallie, & Longhofer, 2007; Foster, 2009; Hunt, 2001; Johnson & Munch, 2009; Tervalon & Murray-Garcia, 1998). Cultural sensitivity is the expression of respect and appreciation for the diversity of another person or group. Cultural humility is said to go beyond cultural competence, encouraging people not only to learn about and appreciate the culture of others but also to examine their own biases and cultural limitations (Levi, 2009).

While cultural competence implies a goal of familiarity with aspects of other cultures, which is certainly desirable, cultural humility goes beyond to imply a willingness to acknowledge that it is impossible to know enough about another culture. Instead of "mastery of lists of 'different'. . . beliefs and behaviors supposedly pertaining to certain groups," the healthcare provider and leader are sensitive to a *relationship* between two perspectives (Hunt, 2001). Thus, it is less about knowing and more about relating, although both are critical.

Cultural humility is a willingness to assess one's self with an openness to new ideas and new cultures while acknowledging the limitations of one's own cultural perspective. It is the difference between *knowing about* another culture and being willing and able to relate to it while recognizing *the inability to know about*, with full knowledge, another's culture. It implies an understanding that one will interact with others from a variety of cultures, that cultural differences will affect those relationships, but that, ultimately, each person is a unique individual. Cultural humility invites one to commit to lifelong self-reflection and sensitivity to cultural imbalances in power in provider-patient relationships (Tervalon & Murray-Garcia, 1998). It also invites a more sensitive self-reflection to strengthen international collaborative relationships (Foster, 2009). Clinical leaders and care providers must know that differences will always exist, that no one can know everything about another culture. Thus, leaders commit to recognize, appreciate, and promote differences and lead as models of cultural humility.

Culture most often refers to diverse personal ethnic and community contexts. But we all know that culture also is highly evident and important in organizations.

Organizational Culture of Healthcare Environments

One of the primary, and most challenging, responsibilities of the transformational leader is to understand, interpret, and shape the organizational culture. The culture of the environment in which health care resides, whether the hospital, clinic, community center, or the family home, is important to support those who give their lives to promote health and care for the suffering. The environment must be just as healthy for those who work as it is for those who are served. Such a culture supports workers and promotes performance.

Regardless of the qualifications of the leader, no proposed mission, vision, or strategy for change that is not consistent with the organizational culture has a chance of success. First, as leader, you must recognize that the organization has a culture and that its characteristics, strengths, and challenges have likely been in place for longer than your life as the leader. Kibort (2005, p. 55) exclaimed, "Culture eats strategy for lunch." Most organizations reside within powerful longstanding cultures. People devoted to the history and culture of the place will defend against anything that changes its tradition or comfort even when aspects of the culture are so ingrained that there is not even a conscious awareness of them. Values, assumptions and beliefs, and patterns of behaviors and relationships are often woven deeply into the organization. In addition, there are likely to be both delightful and vexing subcultures within the larger culture of the organization.

In any organizational culture, there are specific areas that resist change. So choose wisely as a leader which changes are critical because they will require all your attention and energy. First are the institutional mission, philosophy, and political climate. Sometimes, these are indicated by formal statements, and sometimes, they are more subtle parts of the fiber of the organization. Second are the existing structure and processes, which have likely been there for a long time. It is a challenge to overcome "this-is-the-way-we-do-it here" and "this-is-the-way-we-have-always-done-it" syndromes. Third may be the facilities and physical space. It is amazing how location, arrangement of rooms, and even light sources can make either a positive or negative difference in culture. I remember an experience consulting to evaluate an academic department that had been famous for years of internal strife. The department was located in an old building with nearly all of the staff offices in a long hall on a basement level. The very appearance was of an oppressive institution of confinement. Apparently unnoticed by staff, but obvious to anyone from outside, the cantankerous social environment was highly related to the unfortunate physical configuration. Years later, the department was relocated to a new building enlightened by windows on all sides and warmed by inviting social areas among offices on various levels. It was no surprise that, eventually, the social climate changed from distrust to collegiality. Perhaps, it was not due solely to the change in physical environment, but I will never be convinced that the change of environment was not a major factor in the culture improvement. Finally, any organization has history, legends, stories, and heroes. As a new leader, you must learn them, value them, and then build on them.

There is no correct or incorrect organizational culture. Leaders can influence the organizational culture by how they build or change structure, where they focus their attention, how they deal with critical incidents and crisis, how they model teaching and coaching, and how they handle the people issues like recruitment and development.

Savage (2003) suggested that resistant organizational cultures can confine leaders to tactical and operational decisions, preventing energy toward vision or strategic decisions. Daily aspects of the local care culture draw leaders to solve immediate problems. A firmly enmeshed organizational culture can also pull a leader from important reflective aspects of leadership.

Individuals and populations of patients, indeed the very experience of being a patient, contribute their own subculture to the entire gestalt of the organization. The significant interchange, characterized by an intimacy and urgency known only to healthcare cultures among leaders, caregivers, and patients, creates a supernal uniqueness of culture.

Such a culture merits the most rigorous scrutiny, best thinking, and most devoted commitment to its truly becoming a culture of caring and healing.

Porter-O'Grady and Malloch (2007 p. 51) further explained,

> Culture rules. The point of service is driven by the culture of the patient population, and the system is driven by the culture of its community, which gives it purpose, and the culture of its members or workers, who give it focus. These constituencies converge to drive the system to thrive.

The Institute of Medicine (2001) proposed 10 rules of performance in a sensitive, redesigned healthcare system. These rules are critical to a culture of caring:

1. Care is based on continuous healing relationships. Health professionals should provide care whenever patients need it and in many forms, not just face-to-face visits. Health professionals should be responsive at all times (24 hours a day, every day) and provide care over the internet, by telephone, and by other means in addition to face-to-face visits.
2. Care is customized based on patient needs and values. Health professionals have the capability to respond to individual patient choices and preferences.
3. The patient is the source of control. Health professionals should be able to accommodate differences in patient preferences and encourage shared decision making.
4. Knowledge is shared, and information flows freely. Health professionals should support patients' unfettered access to their own medical information and to clinical knowledge, and communicate effectively and share information with patients.
5. Decision making is evidence based. Health professionals should provide care based on the best available scientific, standardized knowledge.
6. Safety is a system property. Health professionals should ensure safety by, paying greater attention to systems that help prevent and mitigate errors.
7. Transparency is necessary. Health professionals should make information available to patients and their families that allows them to make informed decisions about all aspects of care.
8. Needs are anticipated. Health professionals should be able to anticipate patient needs through planning.
9. Waste is continuously decreased. Health professionals should make efforts not to waste resources or patient time.
10. Cooperation among clinicians is a priority. Health professionals should actively collaborate and communicate to ensure an appropriate exchange of information and coordination of care.

Nursing leaders have long promoted a culture of caring. The concept of caring is the hallmark of the culture and stories of nursing. Koerner and Wesley (2008, p. 56) performed a series of studies within the culture of healthcare systems and hospitals that focused on understanding the personal values of professional nurses and how they affected the political environment of the organizational culture. They concluded that a cultural focus on the values of the "healing disciplines" in a caring culture carries more influence for enhancing the culture than any amount of "political maneuvering." Kilpatrick (2009) further called for a greater culture of "humanism" as an essential, primary focus in healthcare management and leadership. Humanism would include serving and caring about patients and their families, organizational members, and the community. She chided that such an environment does not yet exist, and if such were better facilitated by healthcare leaders, patients and families would be supported and uplifted and clinicians would be empowered by positive support.

Regardless of the history or persistence of the organizational culture, you can make a positive difference as a leader. Indeed, as a leader who may be new to the organization or to your position, you will find that colleagues in the organization will be anxiously awaiting your influence. You will enjoy a brief honey-moon period when you can unfreeze the most entrenched issues and begin to make the most difference. Yoder-Wise and Kowalski (2006, p. 146) noted critical questions outlined by Muller (2004, p. 4). If you begin the dialogue with sincere interest in honest exchange, these questions can invite the entire organization to examine its culture:

> Who are we?
> What is our business and purpose?
> What is our role as citizens of the organization?
> What is our uniqueness and what values drive our decisions?
> What is our passion?

As you engage all members of the organization in conversations about culture, pay attention to issues of time perspective, such as how time is used and what is considered urgent. Notice the expressions of values, listen to the stories, identify the rituals, and learn who the heroes are. Treasure the clues and honor the history and positive aspects of the culture, then set your mark and add your own story.

COMPLEX HEALTHCARE SYSTEMS

Although managing organizational culture may be critical to transform complex healthcare systems, there is little help regarding definition of or how to execute successful culture change in such organizations (Scott, Mannion, Davies, & Marshall, 2003). "Health systems and healthcare institutions are among the most complex and interdependent entities known to society" (Charns & Tewksbury, 1993; Kodner, 2002, p. 3). One persistent prevailing fallacy is that a *complicated* system is a complex adaptive system. The natural tendency of complicated systems is to become more complex, which has helped to generate the complexity perspective (Clancy, 2007). But not every complex healthcare system functions according to theories of complex adaptive systems.

The perspective of complex adaptive systems provides a useful framework to look at the "whole" of healthcare systems and how they function (Holden, 2005). A complex adaptive system is "a collection of individual agents with freedom to act in ways that are not always totally predictable and whose actions are interconnected" (Holden, 2005, p. 651) from which order emerges (Clancy, Effken, & Pesut, 2008). The chaos theory is closely related to the theory of complex adaptive systems.

Many of the ingrained cultural aspects of large complex healthcare systems may originate in their history as hospitals. American hospitals are laden with history and cultural stories. Throughout most of the 20th century, hospitals were powerful symbols of progress and modern society's affinity for science, technical procedures, and efficiency. In midcentury Western cities, the edifice of the hospital became temple in the center of the community where people came as disciples of the art and science of medicine and submitted to its secular-divine authority. Patients remained confined for weeks under the daily oversight and care of physicians and nurses (Marshall, 2005, 2008). Hospitals and healthcare systems are now much more corporate and complex. But behind the reality of complex healthcare systems is the embellished nostalgia for the hospital we remember with fondness as a an authoritarian but caring community landmark.

We have yet to face the reality of the future that point-of-service in health care continues to move away from the hospital. This challenges our traditional thinking that persists in viewing hospitals as the center of healthcare system infrastructure. To successfully adapt to the future, transformational leaders must recognize and facilitate that "the delivery system must become fluid, efficient, fast, and effective in a highly mobile context for service. Much of the leadership of hospitals must now dismantle much of the infrastructure many of them spent their careers building" (Porter-O'Grady, 2001, p. 66). Complex systems are moving beyond hospital centers.

Leading within a complex healthcare organization requires a kind of "complex leadership" (Ford, 2009), including facility and flexibility with business practices, beginning with an understanding of terminology. Leaders must be facile with issues of competition, the technological sector, the regulatory sector, the economic sector, and the sociocultural sector (National Defense University, n. d.). Taking the perspective of complex adaptive systems helps to "focus less on prediction and control and more on fostering relationships and creating conditions" to promote positive creative outcomes (Burns, 2001, p. 474). Burns (2001) surveyed healthcare leaders to find that they intuitively support principles of complexity science in their leadership patterns.

Current focus on healthcare reform has revealed the growing trend toward integrated healthcare systems. Integrated care has become a buzzword of the industry in current discussion of healthcare reform (Kodner, 2002). Growing from managed care, there is no consistent definition of an integrated system and limited evidence on effectiveness. An integrated system may be the answer in one sector, but likely not the one and only solution for health care (Armitage, Suter, Oelke, & Adair, 2009). Generally, integrated systems link a variety of services and systems, including physician groups, coordinated care systems, quality management and outcome data systems, organized oversight, and financial strength (Boone & Maley, 2000), providing the capacity to offer quality care and coordinated services at controlled costs. Actual financial performance is unclear (Boone & Maley, 2000), and discussion of the role for nursing leadership is often silent. Such systems are becoming increasingly competitive in a social environment that demands improved safety, quality, and values-based clinical performance (Englebright & Perlin, 2008). It is clear that now is the time for nursing leaders to be prepared to take key leadership roles at the highest levels of such systems.

Within complex environments, including integrated systems, are unique challenges for nurse leaders and for professional nursing practice. Over a decade ago, Dunham and Klafehn (1990) found nurse executives in hospitals across the United States to score high on measures of transformational leadership. One challenge is to inspire nurses in complex environments to become empowered and engaged in structure and governance. Penprase and Norris (2005, p. 127) suggested that the complex adaptive systems theory "integrates easily with nursing values and beliefs" and, thus, that nurse leaders should expect to thrive in the complex environment of health care. They asserted that a complexity perspective "frees nurse leaders from previous prescribed behaviors that stressed prediction, forecasting, and control to behaviors that aim to build strong relationships with the freedom to produce creative outcomes." Gokenbach (2007) suggested professional nurse councils within the environment to increase a sense of value and productivity. Such councils can be the center of modeling creativity, collaboration, and confidence in a complexity approach to the healthcare system. A supportive group can let go of notions of control and predictability in favor of innovation, flexibility, and trust that patterns of stability emerge from chaos.

Unfortunately, although some complex systems have begun the journey toward a humanistic evolving perspective of complex adaptive systems, progress has been slow. Stordeur, Vandenberghe, and D'hoore (2000) found transformational leadership characteristics of idealized influence, vision, intellectual stimulation, and individual consideration among leaders at the highest levels of hospitals, but were not able to demonstrate any "cascading effect" or transfer of such characteristics to leaders and managers at lower levels. They attributed this to the traditional hierarchical, mechanistic structure of the hospitals as institutions. They concluded that transformational change is not likely to happen until complex structures themselves can change. Nevertheless, some nurse leaders have identified successful dissemination of transforming unit changes across an entire hospital system. Although they described several different approaches from centralized to bottom-up approaches, such success required careful planning, engineering, coordination, and collaboration. It also only happened with clear support from leaders at the highest levels (Pearson, Upenieks, Yee, & Needleman, 2008).

The AACN examined work environments for nurses, especially in complex healthcare systems. The organization identified characteristics of practice that support professional nursing practice (AACN, 2002):

1. Manifests a philosophy of clinical care emphasizing quality, safety, interdisciplinary collaboration, continuity of care, and professional accountability.
2. Recognizes contributions of nurses' knowledge and expertise to clinical care quality and patient outcomes.
3. Promotes executive level nursing leadership.
4. Empowers nurses' participation in clinical decision making and organization of clinical care systems.
5. Maintains clinical advancement programs based on education, certification, and advanced preparation.
6. Demonstrates professional development support for nurses.
7. Creates collaborative relationships among members of the healthcare provider team.
8. Utilizes technological advances in clinical care and information systems.

The complex environment of health care can provide the leader with new strategies to guide professionals and patients through chaos and uncertainty. It requires a clear vision, a few simple rules, and the extension of freedom to support adaptation, evolution, and emergence (Penprase & Norris, 2005). Also, be cautious to remember that a complex health center is only one place of so many for leadership in practice.

PRIMARY CARE ENVIRONMENTS

Primary care is the growing focus of crisis in American healthcare systems. First, the shortage of primary care physicians is well recognized (Bodenheimer, Grumbach, & Berenson, 2009; Cooper, 2007; Kane et al., 2009; Nusbaum, 2009; Steinbrook, 2009). Beyond national healthcare reform movements, states and regions continue to struggle with primary care needs at the policy level (Craven & Ober, 2009). Second, a major hope of health care reform is that, eventually, all Americans will have insurance coverage and access to primary care. When that goal is realized, whenever that moment comes, the current healthcare system will be overwhelmed and unable to accommodate the primary health care demands of our citizens. Third, primary care is an area of increasingly entrepreneurial, and sometimes controversial, efforts such as retail clinics (Rudavsky & Mehrotra, 2010), instant-care centers, and nursing-managed care centers. Finally, at the same time, although advanced practice nurses are poised with the preparation to alleviate the shortage in primary care, the profession suffers serious disparities in scope of practice across the country (Pearson, 2009), as it continues to struggle for full political parity with medicine.

Some examples of nurses leading in primary care come from outside the United States. McKenna, Keeney, and Bradley (2004) invited views of community nurses, general practice physicians, members of the public, and key policymakers regarding the role and function of nurses in primary care in England. They found agreement that strong leadership was needed to develop the role for nurses in primary care, citing the traditional subservient culture and view of nurses in the community as the major barriers to the development of nursing leadership in primary care. In Canada, researchers found ambiguity in the role of the nurse in primary care and the need for trust in the role of the nurse specifically in settings of interprofessional collaboration (Akeroyd, Oandasan, Alsafar, Whitehead, & Lingard, 2009).

Extreme needs in primary care present opportunities for entrepreneurial responses from all healthcare leaders. Models for care, for access, and for payment that really work have yet to be invented. It is time for communities to come together to identify workable solutions. The easy things have been done, and leaders on the horizon must deal with these difficult issues. Primary care will be the next great challenge for healthcare leaders.

COMMUNITY AND RURAL SETTINGS

Community nursing leadership claims an inspiring history from the moment Lillian Wald set out to establish Henry Street Settlement and officially launched public health nursing. Today's community-based nursing centers represent the legacy of that history. Such centers serve the poor and underserved in both urban and rural areas. Community nursing centers are found in school-based clinics, faith-based organizations, and academic outreach centers. The need for such centers will only increase through the foreseeable future and the need for leaders is critical.

Bender, Clune, and Guruge (2009) explored the meaning of place in home and community from the perspective of geography of care and community nursing practice, inviting nurse leaders to examine health care in community settings with specific attention to the power of the nurse, the meaning of marginalized places as determinants of health, and how to care for people who live in diverse community settings.

When we think of complex systems of health care, it is important to remember that much of population of the country and the world resides in rural environments. Such settings present unique implications for leadership. Most rural practice areas require a generalist approach along with inventiveness, and flexibility and a broad knowledge base (Montour, Baumann, Blythe, & Hunsberger, 2009). Distance technologies have begun to make a difference in staff and leadership development, communication, and improved care but have not reached optimal use in most rural regions.

Rural hospitals, often revered by members of the community, continue to face decreasing ability to survive financially. Leaders face unique and significant challenges. Newhouse (2005) interviewed nurse executives of rural hospitals, revealing the following themes: (1) challenges from the external environment, including physical isolation, unique patient populations, needed services, and legislation; (2) internal organizational issues such as patient acuity, patient volume issues, technology needs, financial margins and strategies, staffing, leadership, culture, and resources; and (3) nursing infrastructure, which included staffing issues, salary challenges, nurse-physician conflicts, needs for continuity of care, healthcare provider competency, culture issues, politics, and leadership. Other challenges include patient transport, implementation and support for technology, communication among agencies, and demographics of aging communities, as well as older healthcare providers (Montour et al., 2009).

Other considerations include cultural factors of rural living. In many parts of the world, rural residents generally have poorer health status and less access to professional care than do urban families (Forbes & Janzen, 2004). Nevertheless, personal cultural and family attachments to rural communities are often strong. Norris-Baker and Scheidt (1994) noted unique attachment to land and community among older residents of the rural American Midwest. Hayes (2006) also found older women living alone in rural American Appalachia defined their health and use of healthcare services in terms of their attachment to a sense of home.

Leading in rural settings brings many special challenges not addressed in common discussions of health care or leadership. Practitioners and leaders are often isolated by distance between areas of service and between colleagues for mutual support in leadership. One group in Canada addressed such issues by bringing leaders together from various rural settings who had similar issues. The specific purpose of the gathering was to identify successful leadership strategies, to collaborate with each other and with academic leaders, and to develop and enhance individual leadership qualities. This team effort, although separated by distance, facilitated leadership development and enhanced mutual support among leaders (Hall, Weaver, Handfield-Jones, & Bouvette, 2008).

Robertson and Cockley (2004, p. 329) developed core competencies for leaders in rural health environments. They include adaptation and "application of health management tools to rural settings, understanding designated reimbursement mechanisms for financing rural facilities, and development of leadership skills for dealing with multidisciplinary management teams and evaluation of small organizations."

As long as a significant portion of underserved populations reside in rural communities, the need for healthcare leadership is enormous. Such leadership must meet needs unique to the environments, communities, and healthcare conditions.

HOME AS PLACE FOR CARE

The patient or family home is another environment of care where leadership seeks definition. Home is where health care began. Throughout most of human history, home was the place where babies were born, where the sick received care, and where the dying and bereaved were comforted. Physicians and nurses ministered as guests in homes, and family members were the primary caregivers (Marshall, 2005, 2008). Eventually, progress in science and technology formalized health care, and it moved from home to the institution. Hospitals have been the center of care through most of the 20th century. But increasing costs and efficiency of medical treatments have shortened hospital stays. Changes in delivery of healthcare services, an aging population, increasing informal treatment of chronic illness and disabilities, decreased institutionalization for mental illness and physical disabilities, and the growing palliative care and hospice movements have shifted the setting of care to the home (Marshall, 2005; Williams, 2002).

Ironically, although care has moved to the home, with few exceptions (see Brooten et al., 1986, 2002; Naylor, 2004, Naylor, Bowles, & Brooten, 2004; Naylor et al., 2004), there has been little attention to the needs or care of patients and families in the transition from institutional care to home. This has been most blatant in the lack of policy to support such care. In healthcare research and practice, the home environment has remained background artifact, with little attention to home as a specific dynamic environment calling for healthcare leadership, with its own characteristics, concepts, variables, and implications for unique aspects of care. Although home as a term is abundant in healthcare literature and practice, it is most often left as latent backdrop (Allen, 2003, 2005) or the unknown destination of referral in discharge planning or transition planning. Such neglect of home as essential to the entire healthcare experience has precluded the development of effective planning, interventions, or policy to optimize health care in the setting of the home. This is especially ironic in view of the major move of care from institution to home.

As early as 1975, Hayward defined home in context of five dimensions: (1) home as a physical structure, (2) home as territory, (3) home as locus in space, (4) home as self and self-identity, and (5) home as social and cultural unit. Studies of the 1980s affirmed the meaning of home as physical locus, as territory or community, and as a personal psychological construct with attributes of privacy, security, and sense of belonging (Sixsmith, 1986). Among the areas of meaning of home identified by Despres (1991) were security and control, reflections of one's ideas and values, permanence and continuity, relationships with family and friends, and refuge from the outside world. Other meaning clusters attributed to the home setting include retreat, independence, and self-expression (Sommerville, 1997). Roush and Cox (2000, p. 391) proposed a model that recognizes home as central to home health care and includes the following aspects of home:

1. *Home as Familiar*: The place where one is comfortable and at ease because of the habitual nature of routines and physical arrangements.
2. *Home as Center*: The place that is the center of everyday experience of space, time, and social life.
3. *Home as Protector*: A place where privacy, identity, and safety can be preserved and protected.

4. *Home as Locator* (added by Williams, 2004, p. 333): A place that locates the patient and caregiver within a larger context, including how the home reflects socioeconomic status, degree of community integration, and service access and regional geography.

Missing, however, is a definition of home as a center for health care and caregiving.

There is growing research on the meaning of home in specific areas such as long-term care and among the elderly (Angus, Kontos, Dyck, McKeever, & Poland, 2005), in childbearing (Lock & Gibb, 2003), among people with disabilities (Hagner, Snow, & Klein, 2006), among specific cultural groups (Jahnke, 2002), among the homeless (Baumann, 1993), and in social migration (Stoller & Longino, 2001). In order for leaders in health care to understand the significance of home as a setting for care, it is also important to understand related issues, such as the absence of home in homelessness, or the cultural meaning of home among migrant or refugee families (Becker, 2002; Stoller & Longino, 2001); placement of family members in out-of-home care, such as children with disabilities (Baker & Blacher, 1993; Bruns, 2000); or the elderly in residential care or assisted-living facilities (DePaola & Ebersole, 1995; Evans & Welge, 1991). Finally, leaders must be sensitive to the issues related to the meaning of home and hospice at the end of life (Brazil, Howell, Bedard, Krueger, & Heidebrecht, 2005; Gott, Seymour, Bellamy, Clark, & Ahmedzai, 2004; Grande, McKerral, Addington-Hall, & Todd, 2003; Teno et al., 2004).

Even with our models of care that include a continuum of care, discharge planning, transition care, homecare, and community-based care, the gap in the practice of professional care between institution and home is well documented (Driver, Hinegardner, Rea, Reed, & Ward, 2001; Priest, 2006; Satzinger, Courte-Wienecke, Wenng, & Herkert, 2005; Tyburski, 2000). We try to provide homelike atmospheres in our institutions, while at the same time, we often require family caregivers in the home to assume institution-like regimens, procedures, equipment, and care in the home. In homecare, we ask family members to adjust to new people (nurses, therapists, and other formal healthcare providers) coming in and out of private physical and social space. We intrude with new social interactions, schedules, and rearrangement of the physical environment. Arras and Dubler (1994, p. S20) reminded of the ethical and social implications of moving hospital to home for high-tech homecare that effectively "medicalizes" the home, that it may "improve life for many while threatening to erode for others" important issues like "nurturing home life, with its intimacy, privacy, and freedom from the bureaucratic and rationalized trappings of institutions." They asked, "Under what conditions a household might cease to become a genuine home to anyone." Leiter (2004, p. 837) also questioned the implementation of so-called "family-centered" approaches to professional homecare of children with disabilities that superimposes "therapeutic imperatives" on already burdened mothers. Furthermore, two reviews of trials of early hospital discharge to care at home reported satisfaction among patients but mixed responses from family caregivers burdened with care (Shepperd & Iliffe, 2005; Ward, Sever, Dean, & Brooks, 2003).

Although healthcare economics and even patient preferences favor homecare over institutional care, leaders and policymakers must be aware of the implications of shifting financial and social cost to families as well as other effects of the alteration of home spaces and social interactions for patients and families. The transfer of health care from institution to home, not only assumes access to adequate care in the home, but without concurrent reallocation of funding results in a cost increase to families for informal care. Furthermore, we have no formula by which to determine actual family cost and little or no healthcare policy that recognizes such costs. Current reimbursement policies that focus on institutional care by physicians do not adequately promote innovative care models, such as transitional care (see Brooten et al., 2002; Naylor, 2004) by other providers such as advanced practice nurses. Innovative transitional care may actually save costs both to formal sources of reimbursement and to patients and families.

Furthermore, a substantial portion of that cost is borne by the woman in the family who often leaves employment, loses income, and assumes social and physical burdens of caregiving. These costs are most often not calculated in analysis of health care cost.

These issues are especially difficult for the leader who guides care model designs and represents the organizational mission. Among the 24 innovative care delivery models reviewed by Joynt and Kimball (2008, p. 6), only 6 extended care into the patient's home as the primary care setting for acute care. Some of those models provided the option for "hospital-level" care within the home. It is the challenge of the sensitive and creative leader to promote the most effective care in these situations. When that care is within the home of patients and families, the leader must guide modes of care that conserve resources from all sources, and preserve the privacy and sanctity of that place called home.

Another key consideration is the cultural implication of home as setting for care. Home has special meaning within each social, ethnic, and cultural group. Furthermore, home as location may not be confined to domicile but perceived as family, neighborhood, community, cultural or ethnic group, or nation. An example is Becker's (2002) study of Cambodian and Filipino Americans who told poignant stories of their hopes to die in their homelands. Such desires were mediated by the presence of absence of family members, memories of the homeland, and engagement in traditional cultural rituals within their homes in the United States.

Implications of health care in the home environment are significant to leaders in all other settings. The patient or family home is part of the whole consideration of care far beyond clinicians working in homecare, community health, or hospice. As a leader, you must assure that care providers who consider the entire spectrum of patient care and healing pay close attention to the home situation of patients and families. Indeed, such attention should be part of strategic planning, financial planning, care models, and provider orientation and support in any care setting.

Never underestimate the power of place for the person who is suffering. Illness and dying naturally call the most primitive inclination toward a space, a nest, home. It is in the heart of the patient and family regardless of the care setting. Healthcare providers in any setting are already allowed into the most private and intimate of human experiences. We are taken in on trust that we will help, that we will care. We covenant to honor the privacy, culture, and personal needs when we promote personal health and care for the sick. Home is a powerful representation of privacy, security, and sanctuary to nearly everyone, even when its history is negative or painful. When one suffers, that person is drawn to both an idea and reality of home. Leaders are critical models to enhance sensitivity to home in any situation where we care for patients and families.

Thus, the implications of the home environment for care are greater than one might imagine for healthcare leaders. Understanding and integration of the geographical, psychological, social, and medical elements of place pose enormous challenges and exciting promise. It requires extraordinary interdisciplinary creativity, sensitivity, and collaboration. Attention to the complexity of the implications of home environment for care is an imperative to promote clinical practice interventions, policy, and leadership that recognizes all aspects of family and health environment, recognizes all aspects of the patient and family experience, supports patient and family strength and resilience, reduces informal caregiver burden, and promotes the general health of all members of the community. How the leader addresses the patient's home is an indicator of vision and sensitivity to all environments for care.

INTERNATIONAL AND GLOBAL PERSPECTIVES

Well on the other side of the concept of home, but no less important, is the international and global context of care. Globalization of communication, information, and business in general sets a context for special challenges. It must begin with the difficult task to shed the blinders of Western thought. Although travel and service in foreign countries are common, the capacity for cultural humility combined with genuine and effective collaborative endeavors with the perspective of an entire global community is rare. There is a variety of opportunities to join a growing movement in the international and global perspective for healthcare leadership.

Several international institutions provide opportunities to join international health efforts. Among the best known organizations for international health care is the World Health Organization. It is a component of the United Nations, whose purpose is to monitor health issues across the world. Its headquarters are in Geneva, Switzerland, and it has regional offices all over the world. It develops and promotes regular priorities, such as control and prevention of infectious diseases, decreasing infant mortality and childhood illness, improvement of maternal health and outcomes, and emergency disaster response.

Official organizations in nursing with some emphasis on international issues include the International Council of Nurses, which advances the profession of nursing worldwide. Sigma Theta Tau International promotes learning, nursing knowledge, and professional development of nurses. Current global issues in nursing include the worldwide shortage of professional nurses and the related international migration of nurses (Mintz-Binder, Lewis, & Fitzpatrick, 2008). Nurse leaders also need to focus on larger issues of malnutrition and hunger, infectious diseases, lack of healthcare services, need for potable water, disaster response, and other issues of health particularly in developing countries.

Mintz-Binder et al., (2008. p. 317) suggested:

> International leaders in nursing focus on health planning and decision making, professional development of nurses, promoting the contributions of nurses in health care, promoting nurse entrepreneurship, defining nursing roles and scope of practice, and promoting the legislative involvement of nurses in their home countries. They seek to increase nursing influence globally by building cooperative coalitions to effect change in local communities. Significant and ongoing issues of concern among global nursing groups have been gender disparity and working conditions for women.

The need for effective leadership in health care is a worldwide problem. For example, McKenna et al., (2004) interviewed community nurses, physicians, and senior policymakers regarding nursing leadership in primary care in Northern Ireland. Finding un-fortunate traditional cultural issues related to respect for nurses, they concluded that strong leadership was needed among nurses in community and primary care.

Experience with healthcare issues in other countries of the world offers insights into our own systems as well as a greater understanding of global leadership issues and contribute to a sense of world citizenship. For example, we can gain insights into the regional implications of our own national community by learning about urban versus rural residents in other parts of the world, such as Canada (Forbes & Janzen, 2004), Japan (Asahara, Momose, & Murashimia, 2002), and Russia (Struyk, Alexandrova, Belyakov, & Chagin, 2006). It is amazing to observe current debates regarding healthcare reform in the Unites States to note the relative lack of discussion across national borders to identify what works in the dozens of developed countries who outrank the U.S. in healthcare costs and outcomes.

How refreshing and forward-moving we will be when leaders truly engage in inter-national collaborative efforts on health care and when nurses are international leaders rather than international nursing leaders, focusing less on issues of nursing and more on issues of relief of suffering and promoting health in the global arena. Experience with health and human issues in both advanced and developing countries enlightens, gives perspective, and opens opportunities for creative thinking for health care in all settings and environments.

CLINICAL ENVIRONMENTS AND BEYOND

Beyond clinical environments of complex healthcare systems, primary care, community settings, rural communities, care in the home, and international perspectives, there are dozens of other environments where the expert clinician is highly valued as an influen-tial leader. Bahadori and Fitzpatrick (2009) noted that with increased knowledge of legal and political issues, advanced practice nurses are in a position to shape national and international health policy. Nurses prepared at the highest level of practice are poised to be the leaders needed for policy development and other areas of public service. Indeed, it is only leadership informed by clinical practice that will make a significant difference in healthcare reform that will meet the needs of American citizens.

Doctoral-prepared advanced clinicians with expertise in application and translation research have yet to break real paths into academic leadership, for example. The tradi-tional routes of discovery research are most appropriate for research centers, but it is unreasonable to assume that many of the hundreds of other academic settings would not benefit from the doctor of nursing practice–prepared leader.

Entrepreneurial opportunities abound in areas not yet even imagined for expert clin-ical leaders. As we enter the next generation with extensions of customized services, self-service, information access and utilization, electronic and distance education and tele-health care, unconventional settings for care, who knows what is on the horizon? Emerging health issues, such as chronic illness prevention and care, infectious disease, and emergency disaster response, call for new thinking and leadership. Prepare yourself with all the tools and wisdom of leadership to create, manage, and help others to realize the best innovative ways to promote health and relieve suffering. Whole new industries, settings, models, and environments wait to be invented for healing.

REFERENCES

Akeroyd, J., Oandasan, I., Alsafar, A., Whitehead, C., & Lingard, L. (2009). Perceptions of the role of the registered nurse in an urban interprofessional academic family practice setting. *Nursing Leadership, 22*(2), 73–84.

Alexander, G. R. (2008). Cultural diversity. In H. R. Feldman, M. Jaffe-Ruiz, M. L. McClure, M. J. Greenberg, & T. D. Smith (Eds.), *Nursing leadership: A concise encyclopedia* (pp. 154–155). New York: Springer.

Allen, S. (2003). *Voluntary intra-national migration and the process of creating a place called home* (doctoral dissertation). Ontario, Canada : University of Guelph.

Allen, S. (2005, November). *Where is the home in family studies?* Paper presented at the 35th Annual Theory Construction and Research Methodology Workshop of the National Council on Family Relations, Phoenix, AZ.

American Association of Colleges of Nursing (AACN). (2002, January). *Hallmarks of the professional nursing practice environment.* Washington DC: AACN.

American Association of Colleges of Nursing (AACN). (2008). *Tool kit of resources for cultural competent education for baccalaureate nurses.* Washington, DC: AACN.

Angus, J., Kontos, P., Dyck, I., McKeever, P., & Poland, B. (2005). The personal significance of home: Habitus and the experience of receiving long-term home care. *Sociology of Health & Illness, 27*(2), 161–187.

Armitage, G. D., Suter, E., Oelke, N. D., & Adair, C. E. (2009). Health systems integration: State of the evidence. *International Journal of Integrated Care, 17*(9), e82.

Arras, J. D., & Dubler, N. N. (1994). Bringing the hospital home: Ethical and social implications of high-tech home care. *Hastings Center Report, 24*(5, Suppl), S19–S28.

Asahara, K., Momose, Y., & Murashimia, S. (2002). Family caregiving of the elderly and long-term care insurance in rural Japan. *International Journal of Nursing Practice, 8*(3), 167–172.

Bahadori, A., & Fitzpatrick, J. J. (2009). Level of autonomy of primary care nurse practitioners. *Journal of the American Academy of Nurse Practitioners, 21*(9), 513–519.

Baker, B. L., & Blacher, J. B. (1993). Out-of-home placement for children with mental retardation: Dimensions of family involvement. *American Journal of mental Retardation, 98*(3), 368–377.

Ballantye, J. E. (2008). Cultural competency: Highlighting the work of the American Association of Colleges of Nursing-California Endowment advisory group. *Journal of Professional Nursing, 24*(3), 133–134.

Baumann, S. L. (1993). The meaning of being homeless. *Scholarly Inquiry for Nursing Practice: An International Journal, 7*(1), 59–70.

Becker, G. (2002). Dying away from home: Quandaries of migration for elders in two ethnic groups. *The Journal of Gerontology: Series B, Psychological Sciences & Social Sciences, 57*(2), S79–S95.

Bender, A., Clune, L., & Guruge, S. (2007). Considering place in community health nursing. *Canadian Journal of Nursing Research, 39*(3), 20–35.

Bodenheimer, T., Grumbach, K., & Berenson, R. A. (2009). A lifeline for primary care. *New England Journal of Medicine, 360*(26), 2693–2696.

Boone, B., & Maley, R. (2000). *Integrated health care delivery systems' challenges.* Retrieved January 26, 2010, from http://irmi.com/expert/articles/2000/boone06.aspx

Brazil, K., Howell, D., Bedard, M., Krueger, P., & Heidebrecht, C. (2005). Preferences for place of care and place of death among informal caregivers of the terminally ill. *Palliative Medicine, 19*(6), 492–499.

Brooten, D., Kumar, S., Brown, L. P., Butts, P., Finkler, S. A., Bakewell-Sachs, S., et al. (1986). A randomized controlled trial of early hospital discharge and home follow-up of very-low-birth-weight infants. *New England Journal of Medicine, 315*(15), 934–939.

Brooten, D., Naylor, M. D., York, R., Brown, L. P., Munro, B. H., Hollingswoth, A. O., et al. (2002). Lessons learned from testing the quality cost model of advanced practice nursing transitional care. *Journal of Nursing Scholarship, 34*(4), 369–374.

Bruns, D. A. (2000). Leaving home at an early age: Parents decisions about out-of-home placement for young children with complex medical needs. *Mental Retardation, 38*(1), 50–60.

Burns, J. P. (2001). Complexity science and leadership in healthcare. *Journal of Nursing Administration, 31*(10), 474–482.

California Endowment. (2003). *Principles and recommended standards for cultural competence education of health care professionals.* Woodland, CA: California Endowment.

Carpenter-Song, E. A., Nordquest Schwallie, M., & Longhofer, J. (2007). Cultural competence reexamined: Critique and directions for the future. *Psychiatric Services, 58*(10), 1362–1365.

Charns, M., & Tewksbury, L. (1993). *Collaborative management in health care: Implementing the integrative organization.* San Francisco: Jossey-Bass.

Clancy, T. R. (2007). Organizing: New ways to harness complexity. *Journal of Nursing Administration, 37*(12), 534–536.

Clancy, T. R., Effken, J. A., & Pesut, D. (2008). Applications of complex systems theory in nursing education, research, and practice. *Nursing Outlook, 45*(5), 248–256.

Cooper, R. A. (2007). New directions for nurse practitioners and physician assistants in the era of physician shortages. *Academic Medicine, 82*(9), 827–828.

Craven, G., & Ober, S. (2009). Massachusetts nurse practitioners step up as one solution to the primary care access problem: A political success story. *Policy & Politics in Nursing Practice, 10*(2), 94–100.

De Leon Siantz, M. L. (2008). Leading change in diversity and cultural competence. *Journal of Professional Nursing, 24*(3), 167–171.

DePaola, S. J., & Ebersole, P. (1995). Meaning in life categories of elderly nursing home residents. *International Journal of Aging & Human Development, 40*(3), 227–236.

Despres, C. (1991). The meaning of home: Literature review and directions for future research and theoretical development. *Journal of Architectural and Planning Research, 8*(2), 96–115.

Dixon, J., & Durrheim, K. (2000). Displacing place-identity: A discursive approach to locating self and other. *British Journal of Social Psychology, 39*(Pt. 1), 27–41.

Driver, H. G., Hinegardner, C. L., Rea, M. R., Reed, P. H., & Ward, K. K. (2001). Whose patient is it anyway? Coordinating nursing and case management services. *Lippincott's Case Management, 6*(6), 256–262.

Dunham, J., & Klafehn, K. A. (1990). Transformational leadership and the nurse executive. *Journal of Nursing Administration, 20*(4), 28–34.

Englebright, J., & Perlin, J. (2008). The chief nurse executive role in large healthcare systems. *Nursing Administration Quarterly, 32*(3), 188–194.

Evans, M., & Welge, C. (1991). Trends in the spatial dimensions of the long term care delivery system: The case of New York State. *Social Science & Medicine, 33*(4), 477–487.

Forbes, D. A., & Janzen, B. L. (2004). Comparison of rural and urban users and non-users of home care in Canada. *Canadian Journal of Rural Medicine, 9*(4), 227–235.

Ford, R. (2009). Complex leadership competency in health care: Towards framing a theory of practice. *Health Services Management Research, 22*(3), 101–114.

Foster, J. (2009). Cultural humility and the importance of long-term relationships in international partnerships. *Journal of Obstetrical, Gynecological, and Neonatal Nursing, 38*(1), 100–107.

Georgetown University Center for Child & Human Development (Georgetown UCCHD). (n. d.). *National Center for Cultural Competence.* Washington, D.C.: Georgetown University. Retrieved January 24, 2010, from http://www11.georgetown.edu/research/gucchd/nccc/

Gokenbach, V. (2007). Professional nurse councils: A new model to create excitement and improve value and productivity. *Journal of Nursing Administration, 37*(10), 440–443.

Gott, M., Seymour, J., Bellamy, G., Clark, D., & Ahmedzai, S. (2004). Older people's views about home as a place of care at the end of life. *Palliative Medicine, 18*(5), 460–467.

Grande, G. E., McKerral, A., Addington-Hall J. M., & Todd, C. J. (2003). Place of death and use of health services in the last year of life. *Journal of Palliative Care, 19*(4), 263–270.

Hagner, D., Snow, J., & Klein, J. (2006). Meaning of homeownership for individuals with developmental disabilities: A qualitative study. *Mental Retardation, 44*(4), 295–303.

Hall, P., Weaver, L., Handfield-Jones, R., & Bouvette, M. (2008). Developing leadership in rural interprofessional palliative care teams. *Journal of Interprofessional Care, 22*(Suppl. 1), 73–79.

Hayes, P. A. (2006). Home is where their health is: Rethinking perspectives of informal and formal care by older rural Appalachian women who live alone. *Qualitative Health Research, 16*(2), 282–297.

Hayward, G. (1975). Home as an environmental and psychological concept. *Landscape, 20,* 2–9.

Holden, L. M. (2005). Complex adaptive systems: Concept analysis. *Journal of Advanced Nursing, 52*(6), 651–657.

Hunt, L. J. (2001). Beyond cultural competence. *The Part Ridge Center Bulletin, 24.* Retrieved January 24, 2010, from http://www.parkridgecenter.org/Page1882.html

Institute of Medicine (IOM). (2001). *Ten rules of performance in a redesigned health care system.* Washington, D.C.: National Academies Press.

Jahnke, H. T. (2002). Towards a secure identity: Maori women and the home-place. *Women's Studies International Forum, 25*(5), 503–505.

Johnson, Y. M., & Munch, S. (2009). Fundamental contradictions in cultural competence. *Social Work, 54*(3), 220–221.

Joynt, J., & Kimball, B. (2008). *Innovative care delivery models: Identifying new models that effectively leverage nurses: White paper*. Princeton, NJ: Robert Wood Johnson Foundation.

Kane, G. C., Grever, M. R., Kennedy, J. I., Kuzma, M. A., Saltzman, A. R., Wiernik, P. H., et al. (2009). The anticipated physician shortage: Meeting the nation's need for physician services. *American Journal of Medicine, 122*(12), 1156–1162.

Kibort, P. M. (2005, November–December). I drank the Kool-Aid—And learned 24 key management lessons. *Physician Executive, 31*(6), 52–55.

Kilpatrick, A. O. (2009). The health care leader as humanist. *Journal of Health & Human Services Administration, 42*(4), 451–465.

Kodner, D. L. (2002, October–December). Integrated care: Meaning, logic, applications, and implications: A discussion paper. *International Journal of Integrated Care,* e12. Retrieved January 26, 2010, from http://www.ncbi/nlm.nih.gov/pmc/articles/PMC1480401/

Koerner, J., & Wesley, M. L. (2008). Organizational culture: The silent political force. *Nursing Administration Quarterly, 32*(1), 49–56.

Leiter, V. (2004). Dilemmas in sharing care: Maternal provision of professionally driven therapy for children with disabilities. *Social Science & medicine, 58*(4), 837–849.

Levi, A. (2009). The ethics of nursing student international clinical experiences. *Journal of Obstetric, Gynecologic, & Neonatal Nursing, 38*(1), 94–99.

Ling, Y., Simsek, Z., Lubatkin, M. H., & Veiga, J. F. (2008). The impact of transformational CEOs on the performance of small-to-medium-sized firms: Does organizational context matter? *Journal of Applied Psychology, 93*(4), 923–934.

Lock, L. R., & Gibb, H. J. (2003). The power of place. *Midwifery, 19,* 132–139.

Marshall, E. S. (2005). Home: A place for health, caring, and healing. In S. R. Klein & E. J. Hill (Eds.), *Creating home as a sacred center: Principles for everyday living* (pp. 183–194). Provo, UT: BYU Academic Press.

Marshall, E. S. (2008). Home as place for healing. *Advances in Nursing Science, 31*(3), 259–267.

McKenna, H., Keeney, S., & Bradley, M. (2004). Nurse leadership within primary care: The perceptions of community nurses, GPs, policy makers, and members of the public. *Journal of Nursing Management, 12*(1), 69–76.

Minority Nurse. (2009). *Minority nursing statistics.* Retrieved January 27, 2010, from http://www.minoritynurse.com/minority-nursing-statistics

Mintz-Binder, R., Lewis, K. L. C., & Fitzpatrick, J. J. (2008). International leadership in nursing. In H. R. Feldman, M. Jaffe-Ruiz, M. L. McClure, M. J. Greenberg, & T. D. Smith (Eds.), *Nursing leadership: A concise encyclopedia* (pp. 315–316). New York: Springer.

Montour, A., Baumann, A., Blythe, J., & Hunsberger, M. (2009). The changing nature of nursing work in rural and small community hospitals. *Rural & Remote Health, 9*(1), 1089.

Muller, R. (2004). Time, narrative and organizational culture: A corporate perspective. *Journal of Critical Postmodern Organization Science, 3*(1), 4.

National Defense University (NDU). (n. d.). *Strategic leadership and decision making: Systems thinking and learning organizations.* Retrieved September 22, 2009, from http://www.au.af.mil/au/awc/awcgate/ndu/strat-ldr-dm/pt1ch4.html

Naylor, M. D. (2004). Transitional care for older adults: A cost-effective model. *LDI Issue Brief, 9*(6), 1–4.

Naylor, M. D., Bowles, K. H., & Brooten, D. (2000). Patient problems and advanced practice nurse interventions during transitional care. *Public Health Nursing, 17*(2), 94–102.

Naylor, M. D., Brooten, D. A., Campbell, R. L., Maislin, G., McCauley, K. M., & Schwartz, J. S. (2004). Transitional care of older adults hospitalized with heart failure: A randomized controlled trial. *Journal of the American Geriatric Society, 52*(7), 1228.

Newhouse, R. P. (2005). Exploring nursing issues in rural hospitals. *Journal of Nursing Administration, 35*(7), 350–358.

Nielsen, K., Yarker, J., Brenner, S. O., Randall, R., & Borg, V. (2008). The importance of transformational leadership style for the well-being of employees working with older people. *Journal of Advanced Nursing, 63*(5), 465–475.

Norris-Baker, C., & Scheidt, R. J. (1994). From "our town" to "ghost town?" The changing context of home for rural elders. *International Journal of Aging and Human Development, 38*(3), 181–202.

Nusbaum, N. J. (2009). Commentary: Physician retirement and physician shortages. *Journal of Community Health, 34*(5), 353–356.

Office of Minority Health (OMH). (2000). *Assuring cultural competence in health care: Recommendations for national standards and an outcomes-focused research agenda.* Retrieved August 26, 2009, from http://www.omhrc.gov.clas/finalpo.htm

Pearson, L. J. (2009). The Pearson report. *American Journal for Nurse Practitioners, 13*(2), 8–82.

Pearson, M. L., Upenieks, V. V., Yee, T., & Needleman, J. (2008). Spreading nursing unit innovation in large hospital systems. *Journal of Nursing Administration, 38*(3), 146–152.

Penprase, B., & Norris, D. (2005). What nurse leaders should know about complex adaptive systems theory. *Nursing Leadership Forum, 9*(3), 127–132.

Porter-O'Grady, T. (2001). Beyond the walls: Nursing in the entrepreneurial world. *Nursing Administration Quarterly, 25*(2), 61–68.

Porter-O'Grady, T., & Malloch, K. (2007). *Quantum leadership: A resource for health care innovation* (2nd ed.). Sudbury, MA: Jones & Bartlett.

Priest, A. (2006). Bridging the gap between acute care and community care. *Nursing BC: Registered Nurses Association of British Columba, 38*(4), 16–19.

Robertson, R., & Cockley, D. (2004). Competencies for rural health administrators. *Journal of Health Administration Education, 21*(3), 329–341.

Roush, C. V., & Cox, J. E. (2000). The meaning of home: How it shapes the practice of home and hospice care. *Home Healthcare Nurse, 18*(6), 388–394.

Rudavsky, R., & Mehrotra, A. (2010). Sociodemographic characteristics of communities served by retail clinics. *Journal of the American Board of Family Medicine, 23*(1), 42–48.

Satzinger, W., Courte-Wienecke, S., Wenng, S., & Herkert, B. (2005). Bridging the information gap between hospitals and home care services. Experiences with a patient admission and discharge form. *Journal of Nursing Management, 13*(3), 257–264.

Savage, C. M. (2003, July/August). Nursing leadership: Oxymoron or powerful force? *AAACN Viewpoint.* Retrieved July 8, 2009, from http://findarticles.com/p/articles/mi_qa4022/is_200307/ai_n9259744/

Scott, T., Mannion, R., Davies, H. T., & Marshall, M. N. (2003). Implementing culture change in health care: Theory and Practice. *International Journal of Quality in Health Care, 15*(2), 111–118.

Shepperd, S., & Iliffe, S. (2005). Hospital at home versus in-patient hospital care. *Cochrane Database System Review, 20*(3), CD000356.

Sixsmith, J. (1986). The meaning of home: An exploratory study of environmental experience. *Journal of Environmental Psychology, 6,* 281–298.

Sommerville, P. (1997). The social construction of home. *Journal of Architectural & Planning Research, 14*(3), 226–245.

Steinbrook, R. (2009). Easing the shortage in adult primary care: Is it all about money? *New England Journal of Medicine, 360*(26), 2696–2699.

Stoller, E. P., & Longino, C. F., Jr. (2001). "Going home" or "leaving home"? The impact of person and place ties on anticipated counterstream migration. *Gerontologist, 41*(1), 96–102.

Stordeur, S., Vandenberghe, C., & D'hoore, W. (2000). Leadership styles across hierarchical levels in nursing departments. *Nursing Research, 49*(1), 37–43.

Struyk, R., Alexandrova, A., Belyakov, I., & Chagin, K. (2006). Client satisfaction with home care services in rural Russia. *Journal of Aging & Social Policy, 18*(1), 87–105.

Teal, C. R., & Street, R. L. (2009). Critical elements of culturally competent communication in the medical encounter: A review and model. *Social Science & Medicine, 68*(3), 533–543.

Teno, J. M., Clarridge, B. R., Casey, F., Welch, L. C., Wetle, T., Shield, R., et al. (2004). Family perspectives on end-of-life care at the last place of care. *Journal of the American Medical Association, 291*(12), 88–93.

Tervalon, M., & Murray-Garcia, J. (1998). Cultural humility versus cultural competence: A critical distinction in defining physician training outcomes in multicultural education. *Journal of Health Care for the Poor & Underserved, 9*(2), 117–125.

Tyburski, L. A. (2000). Transition from acute care to home care nursing: How can management help? *Home Healthcare Nurse Manager, 17*(9), 17–19.

Ward, D., Severs, M., Dean, T., & Brooks, N. (2003). Care home versus hospital and own home environments for rehabilitation of older people. *Cochrane Database System Review, 2,* CD003164.

Watts, R. J., Cuellar, N. G., & O'Sullivan, A. L. (2008). Developing a blueprint for cultural competence education at Penn. *Journal of Professional Nursing, 24*(3), 136–142.

Williams, A. (2002). Changing geographies of care: Employing the concept of therapeutic landscapes as a framework in examining home space. *Social Science & Medicine, 55,* 141–154.

Williams, A. M. (2004). Shaping the practice of home care: Critical case studies of the significance of the meaning of home. *International Journal of Palliative Nursing, 10*(7), 333–342.

Yoder-Wise, P. S., & Kowalski, K. E. (2006). *Beyond leading and managing: Nursing administration for the future.* Philadelphia: Mosby Elsevier.

9

Building the Team

If your actions inspire others to dream more, learn more,
do more and become more, you are a leader.

—*John Quincy Adams*

Leadership by team is the common functional structure and expectation across business and health care. The power of a leader is magnified by an effective team, and the leader who empowers team members expands the capacity of the whole. In the ideal context of complexity science, self-organizing interprofessional teams work on significant issues across systems to accomplish specific goals of the organization. Such a structure has enormous potential to release energy, encourage commitment and accountability, and promote creativity. New interest in interprofessional collaboration, along with technological possibilities for virtual team membership (Majchrzak, Malhotra, Stamps, & Lipnack, 2004), offer the promise to expand the concept of teamwork to include consulting experts, community members, patients, and others. The full potential of teamwork has yet to be realized.

It is the work of the leader to build the team. Leadership by team can be inspiring and fulfilling to team members. The leader must balance efforts between building team member satisfaction and pushing for team productivity. It is often tempting to focus on building team processes and dynamics while losing sight of the actual work to be accomplished by the team. Evidence-based practice and current outcomes perspectives require that the primary evaluation of the team must be in terms of its productivity, patient outcomes, and the difference its work makes (Porter-O'Grady & Malloch, 2007). Individual commitment, team satisfaction, or impressive team processes cannot substitute for positive effects on clinical outcomes. Thus, the transformational leader always carries a vision not only for team spirit and activities, but also for the actual accomplishments of the team to improve the lives of the people we serve.

Teamwork is messy. Reality does not resemble the diagrams of the inspiring consultant you heard at your last professional retreat on team building. Leading a successful team is not for the faint hearted.

BAD LEADERS, TOXIC FOLLOWERS

This entire book has been devoted to a tone of positive expectation and optimism. However, the unfortunate reality is that there are instances of bad leaders or toxic followers. It would be deceptive and unfair to avoid those topics as if they did not exist. Barbara Kellerman (2004) wrote an article in *Harvard Business Review* that boldly chided leadership authors and theorists for "telling stories" by only describing leadership and leaders in a positive frame. Furthermore, she placed much of the responsibility for our sometimes overstated optimism and positive framing of leadership at the feet of scholars of transformational leadership theory. She said:

> Good stories make the world more bearable. Inevitably, therefore, we want to tell—and be told—stories that make us feel better, even if that means that we don't get as complete a picture as we need. People who study leaders have fallen victim to this instinct in a big way. In the leadership literature of the past several decades, almost all successful authors have fed into their readers' (and perhaps their own) yearnings for feel-good stories. (p. 40)

It is easy to recall world leaders gone bad—Hitler, Stalin, and Pol Pot—or leaders in business found to be corrupt or dishonest. We know their names. But seldom do we hear about villains in health care, although each of us likely knows someone who has done damage. Kellerman continued:

> It is impossible to deny that bad or at least unworthy people often occupy and successfully fill top leadership positions, and it is high time leadership experts acknowledge the fact. For, contrary to the expectations of these experts, we have as much to learn from people we would regard as bad examples, as we do from . . . numerous examples we're presented with these days. (p. 42)

She reminded us to ask the questions "Why do leaders behave badly? Why do followers follow bad leaders? How can bad leadership be slowed or even stopped?" (p. 45). These are important questions for which at this time we have no answers. But you can be vigilant in your own experience. Neither your career nor your life is long enough to spend any of your finite time working with a bad leader. When you recognize that you are in a bad situation, do not stay. This kind of "bad" situation is not one in which you simply do not like the leader, or that you have a disagreement or grudge, or that he or she is not like the previous leader you knew and loved. Those are *your* problems that will follow you wherever you go. Get over them and become the follower who gets the job done. I am talking about the situation where there is no hope, no dealing with a person who is irrational and unable to take a healthy leadership perspective, where the person is truly doing harm. So first, you must honestly evaluate the situation. If it is truly a condition of bad leadership, then do not become beguiled by the idea that you can rescue coworkers, or patients, or the system. And do not entrap yourself with the thought that you do not have a choice, that you cannot get out, that you have no other options, and least of all, because you must stay for some insurance or retirement benefit. You always have options.

You may not be able to change a bad leader, but you must make sure you do not become a bad leader. From a bad situation, you have a chance to learn what does not work. What is it about the leader that you do not want to emulate? What will you remember from this situation to improve your own leadership? How will others benefit from what you have learned from a negative situation? Remember that this learning must be without a grudge and from an authentic perspective of examination of both the situation and of your own responses. Ultimately, it must be a learning experience.

Bad leaders are not the only problem. Challenges of difficult followers are probably more common. "Sometimes good leaders end up making poor decisions because well-meaning followers are united and persuasive about a course of action. This is a particular problem for leaders who attract and empower strong followers" (Offermann, 2004, p. 54). Offermann (2004) described several situations where followers take the wheel and steer in the wrong direction or impede the success of leaders and the organization. Consider, for example, leaders who attract followers "who fool them with flattery and isolate them from uncomfortable realities" (p. 54). Charismatic leaders may be especially vulnerable to such situations. Such Rasputin-like followers may or may not have malicious intent, but their keeping hard realities from you as the leader eventually dooms success. Thus, leaders must seek honest feedback from a variety of sources and be willing to move beyond the usual protected space of power to face difficult issues. When you become the leader, almost immediately, you feel some doors to "street talk" shut closed. You enter a different category, so it requires a different kind of behavior and relationships to stay in touch with the realities of the people who work for you. Many leaders report that "leadership by walking around" is a most effective way to keep the reality perspective. Do not become isolated within the walls of your office or within your administrative tasks and meetings.

A different example of a difficult follower is the manipulative person who has informal power, sometimes by sheer longevity in the institution, and continually diminishes your authority. Such workers are difficult to deal with and may appear in any setting for any leader. Offermann (2004) suggested that straightforward, honest leaders are less likely to attract manipulative followers. Disarm them with transparency, resilience, and absolute honesty. When you err, be the first to notice and the first to seek forgiveness. Do not leave a moment's space for the deceptive person to fill with manipulative gossip. Move forward with fairness and confidence.

Other individuals may simply not be responsive or productive, or may not be professionally mature. Maccoby (2004) demonstrated that such followers commonly indulge in "transference." They perceive the leader from personal life experience into projected roles like an "all-knowing father figure," "authoritative yet loving mother figure," or "as a brother or sister who isn't necessarily a model of good behavior" (p. 76). The best way to manage such "transferential ties" is to expose them, discuss them, and facilitate mutual understanding. And do not forget humor. An occasional lighthearted self-deprecation goes a long way to share your humanness and endear yourself to other human beings.

When you are in the position of power as a leader, you can help to rehabilitate many poor followers. When you identify a problem, face it. Make sure your own motives are appropriate, then find the best way to confront the issue. It may be face-to-face conversation and confrontation, developing a change contract, or ultimate reassignment.

Finally, do not assume that someone who appears to be a difficult team member is a poor follower. Do not overlook the true value of what some call "depressive realists," or those curmudgeon-like sages planted in the end-of-the-hall offices of any great organization. They may appear to be cranky, grumpy, and negative because they have been around long enough to see the cycles and patterns of initiatives, successes, and failures repeating themselves across time. But they hold institutional memory and wisdom that have gone unnoticed and unheralded. They may appear to threaten your vision and progress, but they may be your best listening ear and guide. Include them in your contemplations and private plans; consult them as your best ally and mentor. There is room for the loyal pessimist aside the strategic optimist. Indeed, some studies have shown that thoughtful people with negative mood may have better eyewitness recall of facts than do optimists, and demonstrate greater social influence by persuasive messages (Forgas, 2007; Forgas & Locke, 2005; Norem, 2001). In other words, there is room on an effective team for constructive pessimism. The "defensive pessimist" is likely to think through worst-case scenarios and can motivate or influence others for caution. Leaders are best served by listening to the loyal opposition. One of my most valuable consultant-informants was an assistant with years of history with many leaders who had preceded me in my position. She had an amazing ability to stall at just the right moment. Just when I was most frustrated with what I perceived to be negative resistance, she saved me from running backward off the edge of a cliff—the cliff she had seen before—thus saving the organization from some error I was just about to make.

Some entire work cultures are simply not healthy. It may not be about a particular person or style or environment. Rather, a constellation of factors come together to create an entire scene of negativity. Often, such cultures have endured over time, steeped in history and tradition of unfortunate relationships. It is usually about the relationships: how people treat each other and how people relate to the work and the environment. Trust diminishes and people settle into an inertia of unhealthy habits. Ineffective efforts seem to flow in unfortunate patterns: consultants on team building move in and out, agendas of staff meetings list communication issues, memories of well-meaning retreats and their refreshments become stale. Things get better for awhile, then return to the uneasy state of tension. You can try to open the windows to invite a sunshine breeze of culture change, but it is might simply be easier to leave the environment.

It is possible to transform a culture. When it happens, it can be inspiring. Baker, Beglinger, King, Salyards, and Thompson (2000) outlined actions that transformed a culture. They constructed several deliberate productive steps. First, leadership teams were invested in the process. They began by showing a genuine interest in listening—then that is just what they did. They interviewed every staff member, identified themes, and shared the themes to validate individual and group struggles. Next, they identified and reaffirmed a vision for the unit. They remodeled the physical environment to create fresh space and to assure staff of their value by providing attractive work areas. They created a working structure for shared governance and staff empowerment, providing opportunities for genuine control by staff clinicians. Finally, they recognized that even as progress ensued toward a positive transformation, the environment required constant tending, listening, and investment to sustain the newly established healthy work culture.

When you are faced with a person or situation that threatens the health of the work culture, if you do not leave; you must act. The first step in dealing with difficult people or improving an unhealthy work culture is to acknowledge that problems exist. You cannot solve a problem that you avoid or deny. Then seek help from a compassionate third party who may act as your coach as you embark on what may be a long or difficult journey to heal the relationship or the environment. Study what has worked and not worked for others, include everyone involved in the process, and listen, listen, listen. Involve the entire group in planning and be bold in executing change. Ignite interest in a vision and articulate group values. Change the physical environment if it is a problem. I know a leader who simply painted each staff office a wonderful soothing color. But the truth is changing a culture can be a long and challenging process. Do not take yourself too seriously, and always keep a sense of goodwill and good humor. Understand what you can do as a leader and what you do not do—like take on the problems or personal responsibilities of others. Be wise in recognizing where you put your trust, but at the same time assume good intention from others. Sustain a central idea of value for positive health. It requires energy and commitment. You need to care about the organization and the individuals within it, and care for yourself.

CREATING THE CARING COMMUNITY

Team building is so common in organizations that it sometimes seems trite. Team has many meanings. Here, we refer to team in its best and broadest sense, referring to any group of professionals and others working toward a purpose of service in health care. Numerous studies provide rationale for teams in health care (Chen, Kirkman, Kanfer, Allen, & Rosen, 2007; Clark, 2009; Clements, Dault, & Priest, 2007; DiMeglio et al., 2005; Humphrey, Morgeson, & Mannor, 2009; Kearney & Gebert, 2009; Mohr, Burgess, & Young, 2008; Oandasan, 2007; Rafferty, Ball, & Aiken, 2001). Recent reports from the Institute of Medicine (IOM) have underscored the power and hope that healthcare reform can happen only if healthcare professionals learn how to work effectively in interdisciplinary teams. The 2000 report noted, "People make fewer errors when they work in teams" (IOM, 2000). The 2001 report noted, "The current system shows too little cooperation and teamwork . . . under the new rule cooperation in patient care is more important than professional prerogatives and roles" (IOM, 2001). And in 2003, the institute reported the following five competencies for health professions, (1) patient-centered, (2) interdisciplinary teams, (3) evidence-based practice, (4) quality improvement, and (5) informatics (IOM, 2003).

A large part of the job of any leader is to build the team. By building the team, you are building a community that becomes the culture of the organization. Caring communities are not convened by magic. Building the effective team requires planning, training, and constant effort (Salas, DiazGranados, Weaver, & King, 2008). The very complexity and pace of healthcare organizations demand team approaches to problem solving, and leaders who understand and promote team achievement. Five important functions of the leader are: (1) environmental monitoring to provide resources and support to the team, (2) organizing activities to enhance team activities, (3) teaching and coaching team members, (4) motivating the team, and (5) intervening appropriately and collaboratively in team activities (Hackman & Wageman, 2005; Morgeson, 2005; Klein, Zeigert, Knight, & Xiao, 2006).

Recruiting, Retaining, and Reassigning

Among the most important roles for the leader are recruitment, development, and retention of team members. Indeed, in hospitals, poor management of human resources has actually been linked to patient mortality (West et al., 2002). Team is often discussed in the context of acute care hospital environments. But in reality, some of the most effective team models are found in other settings, such as community health and primary care. Interprofessional collaboration is often stronger and healthier in community environments (Jones & Way, 2007).

Regardless of the setting, a recruitment plan is critical. The plan should include clear objectives, long-term projections, analysis of potential pools of candidates, and specific strategies to attract and keep the best candidates. Personnel recruitment is one area where there is a fine dance between immediate needs for effective management and long-term investments in human capital for the future.

One of the most winning race horse trainers, interviewed by editors at *Harvard Business Review*, compared recruitment and team building to horse training. He described recruiting and selecting the best horse, "First you have to find out what he does best and what he can do best. Is he a sprinter? Can he run a middle distance? Does early speed confuse him? Or does he like early speed, and that builds his heart up and makes him bolder? Horses that prefer to follow, you sometimes have to train them to lead; those that want to lead, you sometimes have to train them to follow.... The biggest thing ... is to be very observant. You must pick up on the little things" (Lukas & Kirby, 2004, p. 50).

Best-selling leadership author Jim Collins (2001, p. 13) used the well-known bus analogy: "First [get] the right people on the bus, the wrong people off the bus, and the right people in the right seats—and *then* ... figure out where to drive it."

Recruiting talented people is important, but more important is retaining highly talented people. Once you have recruited good people and identified the right person for the right job, do what you can to keep them. The best organizations have potential leaders they cannot afford to lose. They are committed to the work, they know the culture, and they know their jobs. Keeping them can save enormous resources in searching, training, and hoping for another good match. Professional development is your next important step. Reward appropriately, consistently, and personally. Get to know people personally and be generous to extend opportunities for growth. Some experts have noted that it is more important to reward and retain your own good people who know and function well within your organizational culture than to recruit "stars" from the outside (Groysberg, Nanda, & Nohria, 2004).

One mechanism that helps retention of nurses appears to be Magnet designation. For more than two decades in hospitals, retention of nurses has been linked to the professional recognition of Magnet status (American Nurses Association Academy of Nursing Task Force on Nursing Practice in Hospitals, 1983). For the leader, it is most important to note that the dimensions of Magnetism that attract and retain professional nurses are directly related to leadership. They include quality of nursing leadership, organizational structure, management style, personnel policies and programs, quality of care, professional models of care, level of autonomy, quality assurance, consultation and resources, community and the hospital, nurses as teachers, image of nursing, nurse-physician relationships, and professional career development.

After all your efforts, sooner or later, every leader faces the unfortunate task of accepting the resignation of or terminating an employee. Each situation requires uncommon altruism. First, when you receive the notice that a valuable worker is leaving, it is not helpful to spill out a long liturgy of your needs or the organization's shortages. Simply offer genuine gratitude and wishes of good will. When someone leaves in anger, also do your best to show good will. You do not need to be "right" in the argument, but generous of heart. It is unbecoming to you as a leader to do anything but assume a stature of charity and generosity. Finally, the involuntary termination of a subordinate should not be a surprise to the person. If possible, it should be preceded by your investment in time and coaching to improve inadequacies, contracts for improvement of performance, and time lines to improve. When all of such activities have been in vain, the notice of discharge should be planned, professional, honest, and compassionate. In a personal conversation, the person should be provided with a letter documenting the issues, then end with wishes of good will. If termination follows the sudden discovery of an egregious act, the person will not be surprised but may react from his or her own guilt or displeasure at being caught. Handle the situation with the same grace as you would by announcing unfortunate downsizing or need for reassignment. You need to make a decision on how you will handle requests for recommendation for subsequent job searches by the individual you have terminated. Of course, it depends on circumstance, but it is sometimes wise to share simply that the person-environment fit was not appropriate. Most employers will understand the meaning of that message.

Leading the Team

Despite the prevailing culture of teams, naysayers remind us of their challenges, particularly in complex healthcare organizations. Gerardi (2010) threw the following cold water on our ideal of the healthcare team:

> Despite the descriptor, "health care team," there are relatively few times throughout the day when members of the interdisciplinary team function as a team. Most often, they are working as individual advocates for the patient through their role and only in rare instances, such as clinical emergencies, do they step out of the role and truly work together as a synergistic team. Turf battles, differences of knowledge level and experience, and rare opportunities for group conversation lead to a competitive atmosphere where everyone is struggling to do the right thing.

Weiss and Hughes (2005) further criticized traditional teamwork training programs for not making a difference in actually promoting collaboration.

One of the challenges to successful team building is potential discrepancy of perceptions and expectations among team members. This may be between team members and the leader (Gibson, Cooper, & Conger, 2009) or among team members, as between physicians and nurses (Sexton & Helmreich, 2003), or among other representatives of distinct different disciplines.

Nevertheless, transformational leadership in health care can hardly be done in solitude. Team effectiveness has become a basic component of the evaluation of any healthcare system (Davidson, Griffith, Sinioris, & Carreon, 2005). It requires enormous energy and investment in others by effective collaborative connections, relationships with the entire community, and building teams within the organization. Team leadership is a fine art commonly discussed and uncommonly done in excellence. The work of the team needs to be seamless and with a synthesis whose results are greater than the sum of the efforts of individual members. The leader is critical to set the tone, to ensure that each member clearly understands his or her role, and has the resources to perform that role. Expectations and communication should be clear and open in all directions. Each team member should have full accountability for decision making within his or her work role, and the entire team must be included in larger strategic decision making. The leader is the guardian of both the welfare of team members and the effectiveness of the work. That requires setting the standard for acceptance of diversity, focus on goal achievement, and sustenance of health of the team.

Creating a community is about belonging. It requires leader attention to the details of supporting a sense of belonging: design of the environment, location, and process for conversations and relationships. Block (2008) observed that in order to build community, conversations should be structured around questions that do not necessarily evoke answers but rather commitment, accountability, and the possibility for transformation. Block asserted that such questions are of "invitation" rather than mandate or persuasion, "possibilities," "ownership" that guides people to accept responsibility, "dissent" that allows constructive conflict and safe authentic doubt, "commitment" that promotes kept promises and results, and "gifts" that appear when members of the community come together.

Teams function best in organizations that value broad-based governance structures. Regardless of the size or type of organization, there is usually some need for a team. It may be for management and governance, for some specific project or organized action, or an advisory role. The purpose of the team needs to be clear to its members. Team governance and decision making need to be well planned and executed. Some teams make decisions by simple majority vote. This method carries the risk of being less about team and more about a collection of individuals. In this case, it is important that once the vote is taken, all team members support the decision. Other teams are able to work by consensus, which is more challenging but often more effective. Consensus requires team members to work together until a decision is crafted that reflects the entire team membership without a vote. It has the advantage of team members coming to mutual decisions. It requires discussion, listening, and compromise. At some point, the entire team must be behind all decisions. A good decision means nothing without the support of the team.

Effective teams have a purpose. Members understand their roles and the priorities of their work. They feel appreciated for their contribution. Norms for behavior and conflict management are understood. The decision-making authority of the team is clear, and team members have a vision for what constitutes success. Team members feel free to contribute, recognize, and appreciate differences among members, and they participate. High-performance teams are aligned on purpose, participation, responsibility, and accountability. They focus on tasks efficiently and productively (National Small Business Association, n.d.). Wheatley (2001a, p. 32) proposed the following "non-negotiable" terms for teams: "People must understand and value the objective or strategy, people must understand how their work adds value to the common objective, people must feel respected and trusted, people must know and care about their colleagues, and people must value and trust their leaders."

Although much has been said about the preferred characteristics of teams and team members, little evidence has correlated team characteristics with strategies, outcomes, innovations, or decisions in healthcare environments (Holleman, Pot, Mintjes-de Groot, & van Achterberg, 2009). There is no such thing as the "correct" or "perfect" team member. The very reason we work in teams is that a combination of a variety of individuals with individual characteristics and gifts is better than the perfect individual. Certainly, team members need to have the basic character qualities of honesty, respect, and accountability and be willing to participate, but teams do not benefit by selected personality styles.

On the other hand, leader characteristics do seem to be important. Several studies have confirmed that transformational qualities in the leader contribute to more effective team function (Eisenbeiss, van Knippenberg, & Boerner, 2008; Keller, 2006; Lim & Ployhart, 2004; Schaubroeck, Lam, & Cha, 2007).

Although we continue to promote team governance, as we recruit leaders, we have few effective measures for team function, and we continue to evaluate individual leader's characteristics and competencies, rather than individual capacity for successful team-work (Leggat, 2007). Leader preparation and supportive coaching have been shown to be important to team member perceptions of leader effectiveness (Morgeson, 2005). We do not know what are the specific skills of a leader needed to empower teams to lead.

Communication and information sharing are probably the most important aspects of team leading and teamwork. It is critical to success that team members individually and collectively use all available sources of information, including members of the team itself. Mesmer-Magnus and Dechurch (2009) performed a meta-analysis of 72 independent studies, totaling 4,795 work teams and a total of 17,279 individuals. The studies all explored team information sharing. They found information sharing to be critical to team performance, cohesion, decision satisfaction, and knowledge integration. Information sharing positively predicted team performance across all levels of related factors. Furthermore, in a study among Israeli soldiers, friendship networks within the team (or platoon) was the single mediator of the positive relationship between transformational leadership and climate strength, or agreement among platoon members regarding social climate (Zohar & Tenne-Gazit, 2008).

The truth is that from a transformational perspective, we have not even begun to think creatively about teams. In a learning organization, why don't we see more truly inter-professional teams with clinicians of all kinds, including staff nurses, nurse practitioners, physicians, leaders, community members, patients, and students? Why don't learning organizations have more inclusive teams of learning where team members learn from each other (Allan, Smith, & Lorentzon, 2008)? Teams have such potential in any setting and under any form of governing structure, although teams function best in areas of broad-based governance such as shared governance.

Shared Governance

Shared governance has become common terminology in health care, although its implementation varies widely. One definition of shared governance is "an organizational frame for configuring accountable professional decision making that fully engages the stakeholders by placing right decisions made by the right people in the right place at the right time for the right purposes" (Golanowski, Beaudry, Kurz, Laffey, & Hook, 2007, p. 352; Porter-O'Grady, 2008, p. 497; Prince, 1997). Shared governance is built on accountability and collaboration. Governance is without power if there is no specific accountability. Accountabilities (such as for resources, personnel, decision making, or productivity) must be clearly delineated and sustained. Shared governance "encourages professional autonomy, effective communication, and development of leadership" (Force, 2004, p. 262). It is often the model for nursing in hospitals with Magnet status and is associated with patient, nurse, and physician satisfaction as well as retention of nurses (Force, 2004).

The concept of shared governance was championed and set firmly into the discipline of nursing by Tim Porter-O'Grady (2001, p. 63). Reflecting on the origins of shared governance, he listed the following promises it provided:

1. Nurses had a clinical model of governance that reflected nurses' ownership of decisions that affected their own practice.
2. There was a clear framework for decision making that placed nurses at the table where decisions affecting what they did were made.

3. For the first time, there was a clear organizational mandate that clinical nurses be involved at the highest levels of the organization—from unit to boardroom.

4. Unlike collective bargaining, which uses adversarial tactics to obtain advantage, shared governance invested and involved all the stakeholders in essential dialogue around issues that affected their work and organization.

5. A clear formal set of professional bylaws described the structure and operation of the nursing profession within the organization, becoming a legal and functional framework for the professional activities of nurses in the healthcare organization.

I suspect from your own experience in practice that you recognize that these values or characteristics are still a bit idealistic and do not reflect all practice settings today. From the beginning, we have not seen a consistent commitment to sustain genuine shared governance across settings in health care (see Dunbar et al., 2007; Frith & Montgomery, 2006; Havens, 1994; Kennerly, 1996; Stewart, Stansfield, & Tapp, 2004). Porter-O'Grady (2001, pp. 63–64) himself critically lamented historical concerns precluding its broad implementation, and listed the barriers of shared governance in current contexts :

1. The shift in the locus-of-control to the point-of-service, where 90% of the decisions in a service-driven organization should be made.

2. Locating accountability and authority for clear and specific decisions in the clinical staff in a way that precludes managers from controlling these decisions.

3. The unwillingness of the nursing staff to take hold of their empowerment and engage it as a fundamental part of their practice and as their way of doing the business of nursing.

4. The cost-cutting undercurrent that has failed to value nursing practice to the extent of endangering patient care and driving nurses away from hospitals, exacerbating the shortage of nursing professionals.

5. Fear of nurses' power and an inability to harness the energy of nurses to integrate all professionals across the system within the continuum of care.

6. A slavish attachment to hierarchical models of decision making without any evidence of the efficacy and viability and substantial evidence to the contrary.

Shared governance provides a model beyond nursing for interdisciplinary governance but has yet to be applied to its full extent. To share decision-making processes across professional disciplines requires support of leadership and redistribution of resources, time, and personal investment (Golanowski et al., 2007).

IT IS ABOUT HEALING

Leaders in health care have the special stewardship to see that others receive care. Thus, the leader must be caring. Never forget that the mission and purpose of health care are to promote health and care for the suffering. Health care is about healing. Seek and sustain some sanctity to that mission and work to develop caring communities. The history and legacy of caring for the sick represent healing. Caring and restoring health and wholeness are the core of what we do in health care (Swanson & Wojnar, 2004).

Although healing is central to healthcare disciplines, it is not commonly recognized in our daily work environments. Indeed, Wicks (1995, p. 122) called the discourse of healing an "alternative knowledge or practice framework . . . unrecognized in the actual daily work." Indeed, "though healthcare disciplines are eager to own philosophies that embrace the idea of healing, realities of practice sometimes lack evidence of healing it its deepest and most meaningful sense" (Marshall, 2008, p. 259). Hopefully, that is changing. Marshall (2008) reminded that healing is grounded in suffering; thus, not for one moment should we forget that health care is about helping others who suffer. After all our talk of teams and leading, it is all about alleviating suffering. Leadership in health care carries a unique importance. We serve those who serve the suffering at the most intimate or difficult moments of their lives. The transformational leader holds that reality somewhere in his or her mind and heart always. It informs the vision, energy, thoughts, strategies, and realities of every moment. In health care especially, transformational leadership is about healing.

Healing is not cure. Cure is quick and passive, but healing requires recognition of the need for mending, intention toward wholeness, and resolution to embark on the journey and positive actions. Healing is an iterative process that takes time. Healing requires presence (Marshall, 2008). Perez (2004) explained the dimensions of presence: communication (listening and speaking), connection (space, safety, and sacredness), and communion. The transformational leader who understands the significance of healing is hopeful, empathetic, attentive, intentional, nourishing, and present. The transformational leader invites others to experience the private spiritual experience of caring for others. Healing leadership invites serenity, optimism (Day & Maltby, 2003), and beneficence (Milton, 2000).

The words of Jean Watson (1990, p. 15), spoken over two decades ago, continue as a warning:

> My plea is for informed passion, passion that is informed by thought, reflection, and contemplation, giving rise to moral landscapes and contexts of human and nature relational concerns. If not thoughtful, reflective, and contemplative about our knowledge, we become accomplices in stifling freedom, staying behind. Then knowledge development takes a simplified approach; we reduce humans and caring-healing health processes to problems to diagnose. Problems become laws, and we begin to empower problems as foci for study and external intervention void of the human and natural landscape, which results in purely technical, mechanical nursing interventions.

Healing begins with you—you create the personal space to sustain your own journey to become and remain whole. Hallowell (2005, p. 56) identified an unfortunate syndrome of busy leaders called "attention deficit trait." Symptoms include a sense of inner frenzy, anxiety, distractibility, and impatience. Leaders with attention deficit trait have problems staying organized and managing time. The person gradually takes on more and more task assignments and responsibilities to the point of overload. Then, the person continues to try to handle the load gracefully, "pretending everything is fine," laden with panic and guilt, and "facing a tidal wave of tasks." The person becomes "hurried, unfocused, impatient, and curt." Physiological responses kick into crisis mode. The person loses flexibility, sense of humor, and vision. Peace disappears, and the person struggles simply to keep up. If this sounds familiar, you need help. Find a trusted colleague and connect with some nurturing person at least daily; make the time to sleep and exercise; eat sensibly; keep one sacred space in your office, or just clear a place on your desk;

listen to music; make some space in your schedule (Hallowell, 2005). Do what you need to bring yourself back to healing.

Transformational leaders in any setting work to create healing environments for the people who serve. Shirey (2006) explored healthy work environments, and concluded that they are created by "authentic leaders." They are characterized by respect and fairness, trust, communication and collaboration, and a "feeling tone" of physical and emotional safety (Shirey, 2006, p. 258). Healing work environments are internally and externally consistent in that policies and systems, interpersonal relationships, and patient care environments are positive and humane and represent the mission of the institution (Disch, 2002; Kerfoot & Neumann, 1992; Shirey, 2006). Indeed, they must be "joyful" places (Shirey, 2006; Whiley, 2001).

Delegation or the Gift of Authorship

The issue of delegation to team members is always a subject of management training. Bolman and Deal (2001, pp. 110–111) elevated the term to "authorship." Authorship reflects an environment for healing. The traditional management approach is to give people jobs, tell them how to do them, "look over their shoulders to make sure they do the jobs right," and reward or punish according to performance. This long-held process sets up disappointment and blame. But giving authorship "provides space within boundaries," allowing workers to own, interpret, create, connect, and find pride in their work. Trust is deepened and motivation is ignited. Work and client satisfaction improve, and the leader's influence is expanded. It requires a confident, creative leader to develop conditions that invite the gift of authorship. By giving authorship, as a leader, you share and expand power.

Bolman and Deal (2001) distinguished between the gift of authorship and the gift of power. Authorship and power are related but distinct. Both require confidence and trust as well as space and freedom. Authorship is about having autonomy and ownership over performance and productivity. Power is about having influence. Authorship may not involve relationships with others, but power always involves relationships with others. It is a capacity to influence and make things happen. Bolman and Deal (p. 115) clarified, "Authorship without power is isolating and splintering. Power without authorship can be dysfunctional and oppressive. Each of these two gifts is incomplete. Together, their impact on organizational spirit is extraordinary."

Identify, Loyalty, and the Gift of Significance

You need the loyalty of the members of your organization, and those members need a sense of identity with the organization. Bolman and Deal (2001, pp. 116–119) also described the "gift of significance." Individuals must feel that they matter to the mission and work of the organization, and the entire organizational community must have a sense that what they are about is important. Significance has both internal and external implications. Inside, it feeds unity, cohesiveness, and a true sense of "team" and community—sometimes, even a sense of family. When members of the organization have a sense of significance, externally, they also have a sense of pride in contributing to something larger than themselves, something uniquely valuable to society at large. There are specific ways in which a leader may offer the gift of significance. Authentic and expressive use of symbols is most important: traditions, rituals, ceremonies, celebrations, logos, music, and stories. There is a kind of unifying magic when people come together around symbols in which they believe. Identify analogies and metaphors that represent your work. Shared metaphors are more powerful than strategic objectives. Analogies can open creativity and build community. Gavetti and Rivkin (2005, p. 54) noticed that "Managers who pay attention to their own analogical thinking will make better strategic decisions and fewer mistakes."

Create special occasions and weave history and tradition with future dreams. Encourage the sharing of stories "about people, events, triumphs, and tragedies" (Bolman & Deal, 2001, p. 116). Eventually, but only if authentic, such traditions transcend time and urgencies and become a source of community strength and energy.

The value of storytelling to leadership is increasingly recognized. Throughout history, narratives, both mythical and factual, have been a part of all aspects of society. Bolman and Deal (2001, p. 148) asserted, "Successful organizations are storied organizations. One does not have to be there long or go very far to learn the lore." An organization needs constructive inspiring myths that ground its realities; they are the foundation of the shared mission. Bolman and Deal continued, "Without story and myth, there is no public dream. Without shared dreams, organizations falter and perish" (p. 149). They suggested that when we put stories into each other's memories, we help people to care for themselves. From the stories, a history grows along with symbols and icons for celebration.

The Art of Followership

Nearly as important as leadership is the art of followership. It does not take long after you are appointed to a position of leadership to repent from your past sins as a follower. I remember thinking, "When the time comes again that I am not in charge, I will be a much better follower!" It is an art. It requires adopting the role of engaged apprentice: watching, responding to, and learning from the leader. It means to take initiative, to become engaged in supportive, productive activities. Do not wait to be asked or assigned to do good work. Do not ask about minimum expectations; give maximum engagement. Surprise your leader by producing the best. When you have an issue, thoughtfully challenge the leader, not from a personal, self-centered, perspective (that is called whining), but from the sensitive sharing of the perspective of your unique view point of the direction of the organization. From that perspective, an effective follower can invigorate and contribute to the entire organization. Practice seeing yourself in an important role as follower. Who are you? What is your role? What do you contribute? What is the best you can be in the role of follower (Grossman & Valiga, 2005)?

The Gift of Healing Leadership

Drucker (2001, p. 81) reminded, "One does not 'manage' people. The task is to lead people. The goal is to make productive the specific strengths and knowledge of each individual."

Garrison, Morgan, and Johnson (2004, p. 25) described team building, or the relationship between leader and followers: "Rather than being 'subordinates,' the knowledge workers of today are 'associates'; for the organization to work effectively, the knowledge workers must actually know more about their jobs than their supervisor. The relationship is more like that of an orchestra leader and the musicians, than the traditional concept of the superior-subordinate dyad."

Transformational leadership has been linked to team member health and well-being. One study in Denmark demonstrated that perceptions of healthcare workers of their leader as transformational helped to ensure job satisfaction and psychological well-being (Nielsen, Yarker, Randall, & Munir, 2009). A similar study in Kuwait linked transformational leadership to hospital workers' perceptions of leadership effectiveness, and concluded that qualities of transformational leadership style were directly related to quality of care, employee satisfaction, increased productivity, and employee perceptions of leader efficacy (Al-Mailam, 2004). Another study in the United States among 236 leaders and 620 team members in mental health care showed transformational leadership to be positively related to a cohesive organizational culture and negatively associated with staff burnout. Furthermore, transformational leaders viewed themselves more positively, reflecting confidence and a sense of competence (Corrigan, Diwan, Campion, & Rashid, 2002). Transformational leadership has the effect of giving followers a sense of competence, control, and a sense of direction. Team members engage because they feel they are a part of something effective and worthwhile. Liao and Chuang (2007) found that managers' characteristics of transformational leadership predicted employee service performance, which, in turn, positively predicted customer satisfaction and intention to sustain a relationship with the employee. Transformational leadership was positively related to general service climate, manager-employee relations, and employee service performance.

Wheatley (2001b) inspired:

There is no substitute for human creativity, human caring, and human will. We can be incredibly resourceful, imaginative, and open-hearted. We can do the impossible, learn and change quickly, and extend instant compassion to those who are suffering . . .

After so many years of being bossed around, of working within confining roles, of unending reorganization, reengineering, down-sizing, mergers and power plays, most people are exhausted, cynical, and focused only on self-protection. Who wouldn't be? But it's important to remember that we created these negative and demoralized people. We created them by discounting and denying our best human capacities.

But people are still willing to come back; they still want to work side by side with us to find solutions, develop innovations, make a difference in the world. We just need to invite them back. We do this by using simple processes that bring us together to talk to one another, listen to one another's stories, reflect together on what we're learning as we do our work. We do this by developing relationships of trust . . . . These processes and relationships have already been developed by many courageous companies, leaders, and facilitators. Many pioneers have created processes and organizations that depend on human capacity and know how to evoke our very best.

In my experience, people everywhere want to work together, because daily they are overwhelmed by problems that they can't solve alone. People want to help. People want to contribute. Everyone wants to feel creative and hopeful again.

At the end of the day, if you are truly to be a transformational leader, you will guard the health and welfare of your team members. You will remember that they are people with lives. At any moment, you will be working with someone who is struggling. Someone is going to graduate school part-time to advance in your organization; someone is facing his or her own chronic illness; someone leaves a precious child at daycare on the way to work; someone is in the middle of a divorce; someone is caring for an aging parent; someone has recently lost a loved one. But they all come to work for you. They attend your meetings. For the most part, they admire your leadership and are loyal to you. They are willing to follow your vision and create where you give space for their creation. Just as you are, they are trying to balance complex and demanding personal lives with their work. Just as you are, they are trying to figure it all out. You will worry about them, check in, and show interest in their personal struggles, and you will guard their confidences. You will create cushions of tolerance and understanding between colleagues when they inadvertently invade tender territory. You will be the leader they will remember who advanced their best at work and understood them. You will be their hero. It is about healing.

FROM STRATEGY TO ACTION

Effective strategy is built on the organization's mission, vision, and values. Those three words have become the well-worn currency of strategic planning. First, remember that mission, vision, and values *represent* what you do. They are important symbols and expressions. They are the voice of your organization—but they are not what you actually do. Consultant Jane Logan (2004) reminded us not to take ourselves too seriously:

> Mission, vision, and values are supposed to be the North Star of strategic planning. . . . But let's face it, the prospect of attending a visioning session is not always greeted with enthusiasm by the conscripts.
> We've all been there. Held captive in a windowless room, hallucinating slowly from a) too much coffee; b) uncapped magic markers and c) the glaring blankness of the flip charts. We've word-smithed with a warring group of colleagues well beyond the point of caring. The result is a mission statement that looked much like our last one—and like everyone else's. Or else we've crafted a vision so lofty, outrageous, or abstract (save the world, conquer the world . . .) that seeds of doubt are planted before we leave the room. . . . Is this really worth the effort?

Regardless of their overuse, mission, vision, and values retain their position as the foundation for the strategic direction of organizations. They are the currency of the day. So they are reviewed here to help you avoid cynicism within your own organization. It is in your best interest as a leader to make them yours and make them live.

The mission clearly identifies what you do, what is your purpose, and why you do it as an organization. It is your vision put to work. Keep it simple and keep to the basics of the essential activities of the organization. Following is a homemade example: "Shawfield Community Care is a community-based agency of professional nurses and volunteers who provide compassionate home health and support services to Smith county adults and children suffering chronic or life-threatening illness."

A vision is the picture of your ideal future. It is idealistic, elegant, and ambitious but reflects the work and mission of the organization. It sets a standard of excellence; reflects the purpose, direction, and uniqueness of the organization; and it inspires. It should be simple enough to be easily understood by anyone (National Defense University, n. d.). It is most often an internal statement that announces your dream of a better future that you want to create. It should reflect the essence of who you are as an organization and unite members of the organization. For example, "To become the first choice of families in Smith county to promote health and create a haven of hope in every home."

Values are the guides for conduct and principles of behavior in performing the mission and following the vision. Examples are compassion, caring, quality, respect.

Strategic Planning

Strategic planning is a useful process to guide the organization into your preferred future. It is just an exercise if you are not committed to it. It can only be effective if you are a strategic leader. The strategic leader continually thinks of the organization at higher levels, taking a larger perspective of analysis and looking into the future. You must think conceptually and creatively, always examining internal applications in a context of the larger community. Strategic thinking is to look forward. Thus, it always carries some challenges and risks. It is a challenge to think large and into the future while attending to the local immediate issues.

Strategic planning has been defined as a "process of identifying directions and facilitating the alignment of purpose, people, plans, and actions with the aim of serving a cocreated, value driven, desired outcome" (Pesut, 2008). It is not an option for the healthcare leader. It is a mandate. Strategic planning is one of your most important activities.

As organizations have become more complex, so has the process of strategic planning (Young & Gubanc-Anderson, 2009). But the basic steps are simple. Schaffner (2009, p. 152) encouraged, "Start simple, but start." Thoughtful planning and effective execution are imperative (Young, 2008). Unfortunately, it is not always done well. Kibort (2005, p. 52) lamented:

> Strategy is in high demand but short supply. I see very little strategic differentiation going on in health care . . . the same thousand organizations continue to do exactly the same things, in exactly the same way. . . . Very few . . . systems are actually using strategic differentiating factors. . . . Rather, they are all playing the same games. There is very little creative, truly "out-of-box thinking". . . . Few places are creating new rules.

While the optimist hopes this is not true, it is a common view point crying for creative leaders to make it live with relevance.

Strategic planning refers to long-range visioning and planning for the entire organization. It is expansive and conceptual, whereas tactical or operational planning involves goal setting or objective development for shorter-term or more targeted or local plans that are part of the larger strategic plan. Both kinds of planning are necessary and critically important to include all stakeholders in the organization. Some kind of strategic planning is helpful at the team, group, unit, or system level. Indeed, a version of strategic planning is helpful to an enterprise at any level (Drenkard, 2001). Although some have described strategic planning in a context of competition and "winning" by being first, faster, or better than competitors (Pietersen, 2002), strategic planning from a transformational perspective involves visioning, planning, and executing in the best possible manner to fulfill the purpose or principles for which the organization stands. Deliberate and careful planning helps the transformational leader to define and crystallize goals for the organization and the people involved. It allows the opportunity to affirm values, define principles, and break the path toward a more effective organization with high personal satisfaction for all involved in the enterprise. It requires precision of expression and innovative thinking.

Beyond goal setting and measurement, strategic planning is "a systematic process through which an organization builds commitment among key stakeholders to goals and priorities which are essential to its mission and vision, and responsive to the operating environment" (Gelinas, 2003, p. 11).

A strategic plan is a roadmap to the desired future, so it may address a future of 1, 3, 5, or even more years, but it must project into the future. Baker, Beglinger, Bowles et al. (2000, p. 98) outlined significant purposes of the strategic plan:

1. Represents a long-range vision for improving organizational performance.
2. Provides a model for planning and implementing structures and processes for the management of outcomes.
3. Reflects and shapes the organizational culture and customer focus.
4. Provides decision support for difficult operational choices day by day.
5. Integrates and aligns the work of the organization.

Schaffner (2009) outlined 10 steps for success in strategic planning for nursing from which we shall draw here and adapt to the larger healthcare perspective. Schaffner's work provides the framework and foundation for the following discussion:

1. Appoint a strategic planning steering committee. This team should include the appropriate number of key personnel and stakeholders of the organization. Think about who should be included. You need some visionary thinkers, some realists, and some representatives from all corners of your influence as an organization, and you must have the support of higher administration. Orient members of the committee to their roles and to the process of strategic planning itself.
2. Use strategic analysis to guide the planning, using key indicators. Schaffner proposed that this step may be done "behind the scenes" (p. 153). Collect data on the organization and the larger community in which it resides to provide the committee with baseline and rationale for their work. The data may include information related to finances, personnel, satisfaction and quality metrics, community demographics, and whatever is important in planning.
3. Conduct key stakeholder interviews to assess perceptions regarding the enterprise. This step is often overlooked in strategic planning activities. Schaffner suggested the use of a standard set of questions, but spread the net wide for the interviews. Include all who have any vested interested in your enterprise. Include surveys of the broader population. Most important is to develop a data-based picture of the perceptions of the current situation and visions of the future.
4. Share key stakeholder interview and analytical data. Everyone involved in planning needs the benefit of all baseline data.

5. Conduct a SWOT analysis. This is a critical step in any strategic planning process: examination of strengths, weaknesses, opportunities, and threats related to effective performance or to the fulfillment of the vision of the organization. The SWOT analysis can be valid only to the degree that all players are involved in the process. Thus, from the highest administrators to the valuable people who provide care must be involved to some degree. Ultimately, key operational decisions must be made at the point of contact (Garrison et al., 2004), so those involved where the organization actually meets the client must be included. Evaluation of strengths and weaknesses must be honest and done within an environment where all discussion is safe. It helps the leader and members of the organization to identify internal capabilities and challenges. Looking at strengths and weaknesses is largely an internal analysis. Evaluation of opportunities and threats includes consideration of possibilities and challenges outside the organization. It requires analysis of issues within the community and the entire industry, and identification of signs of future or emerging issues outside the realm of the organization. To use the term *threats* is sometimes not precise because it often does not refer to actual threats to the mission or success of the organization in a pejorative manner. Threats may include challenges in the community, changes in the external environment, or technological innovations that the organization should consider.

6. Brainstorm potential strategies. The first part of this step needs to be wide open and free. Allow time and space for dreaming. Record all possibilities; let no idea be withheld or precluded. Then, the next step, usually by multi-voting, is to narrow the strategies to less than half a dozen strategic actions or goals that are aligned with the mission and goals of the organization and speak to its vision. Strategies are stated within a framework of a roadmap or goals for the future. The strategies need to imply that their accomplishment will change the organization toward its desired future.

7. Complete a gap analysis around the strategies. Analyze the difference between the newly designed strategies and the current state of the organization. This helps the group to develop tactical goals or objectives.

8. Develop a tactical plan. Usually, a handful of specific tactical objectives are identified under each strategy.

9. Develop metrics for the strategic plan. Metrics are the measures that reflect success or failure on each objective and strategy. They need to produce outcome data. In addition to specific measures, an evaluation plan needs to outline what the data sources are, when and how often measurements are taken, who is responsible, and to whom the results will be reported.

10. Communicate a strategic plan. The plan should be broadly communicated at all stages. It can become a vehicle for sharing your mission and direction as well as to elicit internal and external support.

Once the strategic planning process is in place, obviously, it will do no good if it is put on the shelf until the next committee meeting, annual retreat, or accreditation visit. It really is possible for a well-developed strategic plan to guide the direction of the organization. But it is up to you as the leader to make it work. It can be a helpful roadmap for you to refer and check in on where you are going. It becomes a public document for everyone to understand the purpose and direction of the organization. It should be a living entity updated and revisioned over time into the future.

Strategy needs to be clearly stated and focused. It must be understood by clients, customers, patients, employees, and all stakeholders. Mission and strategic plans must be based on values rooted in the mission. Strategy must also include realistic appraisals of capacities.

Moving the Plan Into Action

The strategic plan is launched from the vision, which is the inspiring banner that reflects the loftiest identity and dream of the organization. The plan begins with broad but achievable and measurable goals. They may relate to strategic leadership, systems, and specific aspects of the work of the organization. Under each of the strategic goals are listed more local, specific, and measurable objectives. In addition, the responsible team or person who is accountable for the achievement of the objectives is identified. The process to achieve the objectives is usually mapped out by some sort of time line or logic model.

Effective planning begins with the strategic plan, but moves beyond to establish the business plan and the implementation plan (Gelinas, 2003). It is well-known that personality types best at planning are not always the best at implementing, which is precisely why you need a team that reflects a range of skills.

Implementation of the strategic plan requires its own set of actions. From the beginning, the plan needs to be conducive to action. Baker, Beglinger, Bowles, et al., (2000, p. 98) outlined appropriate conditions and goals for a workable plan:

1. To develop a strategic plan that is meaningful and part of daily work life at all levels of the organization.
2. To make the plan practical and realistic through incremental building.
3. To locate and articulate accountability for each step.
4. To build in a process for checking progress toward goal achievement and re-adjusting the plan as necessary.

To implement the strategic plan, begin by communicating it broadly. It is helpful to outline the plan in a specific format or template (Schaffner, 2009). Templates are likely available within your organization and certainly can be found by looking at the strategic plans of other organizations.

EFFECTIVE EVALUATION

Achievement of goals of the strategic plan is documented by an evaluation plan. Most evaluation plans follow some sort of logic model that includes inputs, activities, outputs, intermediate outcomes, and end outcomes. End outcomes must reflect tangible results that represent the success or failure of the organization. In other words, evaluation requires data, and the results of data and analyses should reflect the mission and purpose of the work. Intermediate outcomes reflect the success of strategies to achieve the end outcomes. Beside the strategic plan, evaluation plans may map performance plans, accountability tracking, or other data collection and data tracking plans. All major aspects of the organization should be included somewhere on the overall organizational evaluation plan. Such components may include performance management, financial management, information technology and management, and management of activities related to the mission of the organization. Mission activities include patient outcome and satisfaction data.

Each objective should be measurable, and the evaluation plan should include specific tools or measures with accountability and designated time intervals for taking measurements on each objective. Avoid too many tools or a plan that measures process instead of outcomes. Also, if there is general resistance to an outcomes orientation or an evaluation plan, it will be meaningless. So you have some motivation, clarification, and invitations to engagement to do as part of your evaluation activities. The organization must invest in evaluation and use the results to improve its work.

In today's culture of outcomes, evaluation is much more than measures related to the strategic plan. Evaluation is a part of every activity of health care. Entire volumes, courses, and experts are available and should be consulted as you set out to develop and sustain an evaluation plan. We evaluate resources, personnel, patient outcomes, satisfaction, processes, and everything else we care about. As a leader, always think about how you will evaluate what you are doing and/or who is responsible to do it. Have an overall plan for data collection to provide evidence for the evaluation decisions you make. Evaluation should be done as systematically as research, with a plan, specific questions, data, analysis, and use of the data to make informed decisions. This pertains to processes outcomes, and people.

Evaluating people is a special case. Invite workers to articulate their performance goals alongside your expectations for their performance. Document and measure achievement of expectations. Track progress with data. Provide opportunities for improvement and follow-up. Use personnel evaluations not only as performance reviews for retention or advancement, but for teaching and growth.

A chief executive officer of a major advertizing agency reminded, "No matter how much time you spend thinking about, worrying about, focusing on, questioning the value of, and evaluating people, it won't be enough. People are the only thing that matters, and the only thing you should think about, because when that part is right, everything else works." She continued, "Who do I have to worry about? Who needs another challenge? Who seems a little stale? Who needs a new view on life or a new country to run?" (Wademan, 2005). People who do the work, people who lead, and the people who are served are most important. Make sure all team activities and evaluation measures reflect what is most important.

REFERENCES

Allan, H. T., Smith, P. A., & Lorentzon, M. (2008). Leadership for learning: A literature study of leadership for learning in clinical practice. *Journal of Nursing Management, 16*(5), 545–555.

Al-Mailam, F. F. (2004). Transactional versus transformational style of leadership: Employee perception of leadership efficacy in public and private hospitals in Kuwait. *Quality Management in Health Care, 13*(4), 278–284.

American Nurses Association (ANA) Academy of Nursing Task Force on Nursing Practice in Hospitals. (1983). *Magnet hospitals: Attraction and retention of professional nurses.* Kansas City, MO: ANA.

Baker, C., Beglinger, J., King, S., Salyards, M., & Thompson, A. (2000). Transforming negative work cultures: A practical strategy. *Journal of Nursing Administration, 30*(7–8), 357–363.

Baker, C., Beglinger, J. E., Bowles, K., Brandt, C., Brennan, K. M., Engelbaugh, S., et al. (2000). Building a vision for the future: Strategic planning in a shared governance nursing organization. *Seminars in Nursing Management, 8*(2), 98–106.

Block, P. (2008). *Community: The structure of belonging.* San Francisco: Berrett-Koehler.

Bolman, L. G., & Deal, T. E. (2001). *Leading with soul: An uncommon journey of spirit.* San Francisco: Jossey-Bass.

Chen, G., Kirkman, B. L., Kanfer, R., Allen, D., & Rosen, B. (2007). A multilevel study of leadership, empowerment, and performance in teams. *Journal of Applied Psychology, 92*(2), 331–346.

Clark, P. R. (2009). Teamwork: Building healthier workplaces and providing safer patient care. *Critical Care Nursing Quarterly, 32*(3), 221–231.

Clements, D., Dault, M., & Priest, A. (2007). Effective teamwork in healthcare: Research and reality. *Healthcare Papers, 7 Spec No.,* 26–34.

Collins, J. (2001). *Good to great.* New York: HarperCollins.

Corrigan, P. W., Diwan, S., Campion, J., & Rashid, F. (2002). Transformational leadership and the mental health team. *Administrative Policy & Mental Health, 30*(2), 97–108.

Davidson, P. L., Griffith, J. R., Sinioris, M., & Carreon, D. (2005, 20 November). Evidence-based leadership development for improving organizational performance. *Joint Commission Journal on Quality & Patient Safety,* 1–31. Retrieved April 20, 2010 from http://www.ph.ucla.edu/hs/HS422_Davidson_Griffith_article_W06.pdf

Day, L., & Maltby, J. (2003). Belief in good luck and psychological well-being: The mediating role of optimism and irrational beliefs. *Journal of Psychology, 137*(1), 99–110.

DiMeglio, K., Padula, C., Piatek, C., Korber, S., Barrett, A., Ducharme, M., et al. (2005). Group cohesion and nurse satisfaction: Examination of a team-building approach. *Journal of Nursing Administration, 35*(3), 110–120.

Disch, J. (2002). Creating healthy work environments. *Creative Nursing, 8*(2), 3–4.

Drenkard, K. N. (2001). Creating a future worth experiencing: Nursing strategic planning in an integrated healthcare delivery system. *Journal of Nursing Administration, 31*(7–8), 364–376.

Drucker, P. F. (2001). *The essential Drucker.* New York: HarperCollins.

Dunbar, B., Park, B., Berger-Wesley, M., Cameron, T., Lorenz, B. T., Mayes, D., et al. (2007). Shared governance: Making the transition in practice and perception. *Journal of Nursing Administration, 37*(4), 177–183.

Eisenbeiss, S. A., van Knippenberg, D., & Boerner, S. (2008). Transformational leadership and team innovation: Integrating team climate principles. *Journal of Applied Psychology, 93*(6), 1438–1446.

Force, M. V. (2004). Creating a culture of service excellence: Empowering nurses within the shared governance councilor model. *Health Care Management, 23*(3), 262–266.

Forgas, J. P. (2007). When sad is better than happy: Negative affect can improve the quality and effectiveness of persuasive messages and social influence strategies. *Journal of Experimental Social Psychology, 43,* 513–528.

Forgas, J. P., & Locke, J. (2005). Affective influences on causal differences: The effects of mood on attributions for positive and negative interpersonal episodes. *Cognition & Emotion, 19,* 1071–1081.

Frith, K., & Montgomery, M. (2006). Perceptions, knowledge, and commitment of clinical staff to shared governance. *Nursing Administration Quarterly, 30*(3), 273–284.

Garrison, D. R., Morgan, D. A., & Johnson, J. G. (2004). Thriving in chaos: Educating the nurse leaders of the future. *Nursing Leadership Forum, 9*(1), 23–27.

Gavetti, G., & Rivkin, J. W. (2005). How strategists really think: Tapping the power of analogy. *Harvard Business Review, 83*(4), 54–63, 132.

Gelinas, M. A. (2003). Strategic planning: The first step in the planning process. *Journal of Oncology Management, 12*(3), 11–14.

Gerardi, D. (2010). *Conflict management training for health care professionals.* Retrieved January 3, 2010, from http://www.mediate.com/articles/gerardi4.cfm

Gibson, C. B., Cooper, C. D., & Conger, J. A. (2009). Do you see what we see? The complex effects of perceptual distance between leaders and teams. *Journal of Applied Psychology, 94*(1), 62–76.

Golanowski, M., Beaudry, D., Kurz, L., Laffey, W. J., & Hook, M. L. (2007). Interdisciplinary shared decision-making: Taking shared governance to the next level. *Nursing Administration Quarterly, 31*(4), 341–353.

Grossman, S. C., & Valiga, T. M. (2005). *The new leadership challenge: Creating the future of nursing.* Philadelphia: FA Davis.

Groysberg, B., Nanda, A., & Nohria, N. (2004, May). The risky business of hiring stars. *Harvard Business Review, 82*(5), 92–100.

Hackman, J. R., & Wageman, R. (2005). When and how team leaders matter. *Research in Organizational Behavior, 26,* 37–74.

Hallowell, E. M. (2005, January). Overloaded circuits: Why smart people underperform. *Harvard Business Review, 83*(1), 55–62.

Havens, D. S. (1994). Is governance being shared? *Journal of Nursing Administration, 24*(6), 59–64.

Holleman, G., Poot, E., Mintjes-de Groot, J., & van Achterberg, T. (2009). The relevance of team characteristics and team directed strategies in the implementation of nursing innovations: A literature review. *International Journal of Nursing Studies, 46*(9), 1256–1264.

Humphrey, S. E., Morgeson, F. P., & Mannor, M. J. (2009). Developing a theory of the strategic core of teams: A role composition model of team performance. *Journal of Applied Psychology, 94*(1), 48–61.

Institute of Medicine (IOM). (2000). *To err is human: Building a safer health system.* Washington, D.C.: National Academies Press.

Institute of Medicine (IOM). (2001). *Crossing the quality chasm: A new health system for the 21st century.* Washington, D.C.: National Academies Press.

Institute of Medicine (IOM). (2003). *Health professions education: A bridge to quality.* Washington, DC: National Academies Press.

Jones, L., & Way, D. (2007). Healthy workplaces and effective teamwork: Viewed through the lens of primary health care renewal. *Healthcare Papers, 7*(Spec No. 92-7), 109–119.

Kearney, E., & Gebert, D. (2009). Managing diversity and enhancing team outcomes: The promise of transformational leadership. *Journal of Applied Psychology, 94*(1), 7–89.

Keller, R. T. (2006). Transformational leadership, initiating structure, and substitutes for leadership: A longitudinal study of research and development project team performance. *Journal of Applied Psychology, 91*(1), 202–210.

Kellerman, B. (2004, January). Leadership: Warts and all. *Harvard Business Review, 82*(1), 40–45, 112.

Kennerly, S. M. (1996). Effects of shared governance on perceptions of work and work environment. *Nursing Economics, 14*(2), 111–116.

Kerfoot, K., & Neumann, T. (1992). Creating a healing environment: The nurse manager's challenge. *Nursing Economic$, 10,* 423–425.

Kibort, P. M. (2005, November–December). I drank the Kool-Aid—And learned 24 key management lessons. *Physician Executive, 31*(6), 52–55.

Klein, K., Zeigert, J. C., Knight, A. R., & Xiao, Y. (2006). Dynamic delegation: Hierarchical, shared, and deindividualized leadership in extreme action teams. *Administrative Science Quarterly, 51,* 590–621.

Leggat, S. G. (2007, 7 February). Effective healthcare teams require effective team members: Defining teamwork competencies. *BMC Health Services Research, 7,* 7–17.

Liao, H., & Chuang, A. (2007). Transforming service employees and climate: A multilevel, multisource examination of transformational leadership in building long-term service relationships. *Journal of Applied Psychology, 92*(4), 1006–1019.

Lim, B. C., & Ployhart, R. E. (2004). Transformational leadership: Relations to be five-factor model and team performance in typical and maximum contexts. *Journal of Applied Psychology, 89*(4), 610–621.

Logan, J. (2004, March). *Mission, vision, values.* The Canadian Association, Association Xpertise Inc. Retrieved February 16, 2010, from http://www.axi.ca/TCA/mar2004/associatearticle_1.shtml

Lukas, D. W., & Kirby, J. (2004, May). Passion for detail. *Harvard Business Review, 82*(5), 49–54.

Maccoby, M. (2004, September). Why people follow the leader: The power of transference. *Harvard Business Review, 82*(9), 76–85, 136.

Majchrzak, A., Malhotra, A., Stamps, J., & Lipnack, J. (2004, May). Can absence make a team grow stronger? *Harvard Business Review, 82*(5), 131–137.

Marshall, E. S. (2008). Home as place for healing. *Advances in Nursing Science, 31*(3), 259–267.

Mesmer-Magnus, J. R., & Dechurch, L. A. (2009). Information sharing and team performance: A meta-analysis. *Journal of Applied Psychology, 94*(2), 535–546.

Milton, C. L. (2000). Beneficence: Honoring the commitment. *Nursing Science Quarterly, 13*(2), 111–115.

Mohr, D. C., Burgess, J. F., Jr., & Young, G. J. (2008). The influence of teamwork culture on physician and nurse resignation rates in hospitals. *Health Services Management Research, 21*(1), 23–31.

Morgeson, F. P. (2005). The external leadership of self-managing teams: Intervening in the context of novel and disruptive events. *Journal of Applied Psychology, 90,* 497–508.

National Defense University (NDU). (n. d.). *Strategic leadership and decision making: Strategic vision.* Retrieved September 16, 2009, from http://www.au.af.mil/au/awc/awcgate/ndu/strat-ldr-dm/pt4ch18.html

National Small Business Association (NSBA). (n. d.) *Leadership teams.* Retrieved October 27, 2009, from http://www.nsba.org/sbot/toolkit/LeadTeams.html

Nielsen, K., Yarker, J., Randall, R., & Munir, F. (2009, April). The mediating effects of team and self-efficacy on the relationship between transformational leadership and job satisfaction and psychological well-being in healthcare professionals: A cross-sectional questionnaire survey. *International Journal of Nursing Studies, 46,* 1236–1244.

Norem, J. K. (2001). *The positive power of negative thinking.* Cambridge, MA: Basic Books.

Oandasan, I. (2007). Teamwork and healthy workplaces: Strengthening the links for deliberation and action through research and policy. *Healthcare Papers, 7 Spec No.,* 98–103, 109–119.

Offermann, L. R. (2004, January). When followers become toxic. *Harvard Business Review [Inside the Mind of the Leader],*82(1), 54–63.

Perez, J. C. (2004). Healing presence. *Care Management Journal, 5*(1), 41-46.

Pesut, D. (2008). Strategic planning. In H. R. Feldman, M. Jaffe-Ruiz, M. L. McClure, M. H. Greenberg, & T. D. Smith (Eds.), *Nursing leadership: A concise encyclopedia* (pp. 518–520). New York: Springer.

Pietersen, W. (2002). *Reinventing strategy: Using strategic learning to create and sustain breakthrough performance.* New York: Wiley.

Porter-O'Grady, T. (2001). Beyond the walls: Nursing in the entrepreneurial world. *Nursing Administration Quarterly, 25*(2), 61–68.

Porter-O'Grady, T. (2008). Shared governance is structure not process. In H. R. Feldman, M. Jaffe-Ruiz, M. L. McClure, M. H. Greenberg, & T. D. Smith (Eds.), *Nursing leadership: A concise encyclopedia* (pp. 497–500). New York: Springer.

Porter-O'Grady, T., & Malloch, K. (2007). *Quantum leadership: A resource for health care innovation.* 2nd. Ed. Sudbury, MA: Jones & Bartlett.

Prince, S. (1997). Shared governance: Sharing power and opportunity. *Journal of Nursing Administration, 27*(3), 28–35.

Rafferty, A. M., Ball, J., & Aiken, L. H. (2001). Are teamwork and professional autonomy compatible, and do they result in improved hospital care? *Quality in Health Care, 10*(Suppl. 2), ii32–ii37.

Salas, E., DiazGranados, D., Weaver, S. J., & King, H. (2008). Does team training work? Principles for health care. *Academy of Emergency Medicine, 15*(11), 1002–1009.

Schaffner, J. (2009). Roadmap for success: The 10-step nursing strategic plan. *Journal of Nursing Administration, 39*(4), 152–155.

Schaubroeck, J., Lam, S. S., & Cha, S. E. (2007). Embracing transformational leadership: Team values and the impact of leader behavior on team performance. *Journal of Applied Psychology, 92*(4), 1020–1030.

Sexton, T. E. J., & Helmreich, R. L. (2003). Discrepant attitudes about teamwork among critical care nurses and physicians. *Critical Care Medicine, 31*(3), 956–959.

Shirey, M. R. (2006). Authentic leaders creating healthy work environments for nursing practice. *American Journal of Critical Care, 15*(3), 256–267.

Stewart, J., Stansfield, K., & Tapp, D. (2004). Clinical nurses' understanding of autonomy: Accomplishing patient goals through interdependent practice. *Journal of Nursing Administration, 34*(10), 443–450.

Swanson, K. M., & Wojnar, D. M. (2004). Optimal healing environments in nursing. *Journal of Alternative & Complementary Medicine, 10*(Suppl. 1), 543–548.

Wademan, D. (2005, January). The best advice I ever got. *Harvard Business Review, 83*(1), 35–44.

Watson, J. (1990). Caring knowledge and informed moral passion. *Advances in Nursing Science, 13,* 15–24.

Weiss, J., & Hughes, J. (2005, March). Want collaboration? Accept and actively manage conflict. *Harvard Business Review, 83*(3), 93–101.

West, M. A., Borrill, C., Dawson, J., Scully, J., Carter, M., Anelay, S., et al. (2002). The link between the management of employees and patient mortality in acute hospitals. *International Journal of Human Resource Management, 13*(8), 1299–1310.

Wheatley, M. J. (2001a). The real work of knowledge management. *IHRIM Journal, 5*(2), 29–33.

Wheatley, M. J. (2001b, Spring). Innovation means relying on everyone's creativity. *Leader to Leader.* Retrieved October 7, 2009, from http://www.margaretwheatley.com/articles/innovationmeans.html

Whiley, K. (2001). The nurse manager's role in creating a healthy work environment. *AACN Clinical Issues, 12,* 356–365.

Wicks, D. (1995). Nurses and doctors discourses of healing. *Australian & New Zealand Journal of Sociology, 31*(3), 122–139.

Young, C. (2008). Establishing a nursing strategic agenda: The whys and wherefores. *Nursing Administration Quarterly, 32*(3), 200–205.

Young, C., & Gubanc-Anderson, D. (2009). The nursing strategy officer: A new and evolving role. *Nursing Administration Quarterly, 32*(3), 195–199.

Zohar, D., & Tenne-Gazit, O. (2008). Transformational leadership and group interaction as climate antecedents: A social network analysis. *Journal of Applied Psychology, 93*(4), 744–757.

Economics and Finance

Brenda Talley, RN, PhD

> Transformational leaders motivate others to do more than they
> originally intended and often even more than they thought
> possible.
>
> —*Ronald Riggio and Bernard Bass*

Effectively dealing with scarce resources is the perennial problem and, perhaps, the first sentence in the job description of the healthcare leader. Financial pressures are among the most significant challenges that have provoked a recent wave of departures of leaders, particularly from hospitals (Carlson, 2009; Carlson, Evans, Lubell, Rhea, & Zigmond, 2009). This exodus marks an unfortunate loss of experience but offers the opportunity for new talent with new ways of thinking about health care and finance.

Early financing of health care was provided mostly by charitable organizations, "religious groups, ethnic organizations, philanthropists, women's associations," and others. As modern hospitals developed with advances in technology, treatment procedures, and the healthcare professions, models of fees-for-service governed payment for health care, leading to payment by "third parties," insurance, and public sources (Halloran, 2008, pp. 229–230).

Furthermore, for much of the history of nursing education, budget and fiscal management was not seriously considered or taught. Never underestimate the power of the one who knows where the money is. Kibort (2005, p. 53) warned, "There is no doubt about it, the people who get the most response are the ones who create most of the wealth in the organization.... Because these groups generate the contribution margins for the system, they are the ones who get listened to first. It takes a lot of fortitude to balance this phenomenon and give heed to the smaller players."

Although health care is recognized as unique among service industries and, as such, has unique issues related to resource management, "everyone can affirm that some foundation for financial stewardship is long overdue" (Porter-O'Grady, 2001, p. 64). The purpose of this chapter is simply to introduce selected topics related to financial resources and essential concepts of financial management for the leadership role. Entire texts, courses, and experts are devoted to teaching economics, finance, accounting, and budgeting. No attempt is made here to include every aspect of financial management that you will need as a healthcare leader. Instead, this chapter will attempt to connect the skills of financial management with your role as leader.

CULTIVATING CONFIDENCE IN MONEY MATTERS

Because financial matters are not often emphasized in the educational preparation of nurses, they are sometimes intimidated by financial management. But the days are long gone that nurses may come forward with good ideas simply because they are good for patients or clinicians. Transformational leaders always make a strong business case for new models of care.

Must a successful leader have the skills of a manager? While those who describe successful leaders cite the ability to create a vision, to communicate that vision, and to support and motivate others to accomplish that vision, descriptions of managers include controlling resources, interpreting and implementing policies, organizing work, and focusing on short-term goals (Yoder-Wise, 2007).

Moseley (2009, p. 296) identified the critical connection between financial management and a leader's ability to meet strategic goals. Lack of such connection may result in:

1. Failing to integrate the strategic planning and capital allocation process. This can result in inefficiency, missed opportunities, and failure to meet targets.
2. Defaulting from a strategic financial planning process to a budgeting process. Budgets tend to be year to year, while strategic visions may require 3 to 5 years or more.
3. Spending more on strategic initiatives than is justified by the strategies' financial prospects and the organization's credit rating. Strategic plans that are not appropriately budgeted and do not generate acceptable return can expend critical capital reserves.
4. Inadequately monitoring strategic financial performance. An effective mechanism for monitoring financial performance is necessary to avoid wasted capital, cash flow problems, and failure to reach objectives.

Power struggles over resources have consumed the purpose of individual's lives, divided families and friends, initiated wars and rebellions, and resulted in upheavals of social, political, and economic systems. It is no small wonder then that conflict can erupt over how an organization can best allocate resources. Priorities differ, and poor communication among disciplines and specialties exacerbates problems. The considerations of the business manager may conflict with those of the clinician. Values may not differ so much as perspectives.

Effective leadership requires creativity and the ability to work with others in order to fulfill a vision. While doctoral-prepared nurses may or may not actually be developing the budget, there is much to know about overseeing or supporting the process, validating the inputs, setting priorities, enabling evaluative mechanisms, or responding to variances and deviants from financial and output goals.

Financial management and planning tools provide the vehicle by which vision can be realized. The ability to communicate effectively with healthcare providers *and* with financial experts on knowledgeable levels is a powerful means toward providing both efficient and effective health care.

Understanding the Language of Finance

While it is not necessary for you to *be* an accountant, in order to take the initiative in financial matters as the leader, it may be wise to seek the counsel of experts in finance. As in any profession, there are helpful key terms used by financial officers. These are shown in Exhibit 10.1. Knowledge of basic terms demonstrates an ability and willingness to learn about finance, and can convey an intention to be "hands on" in making decisions. Frankly speaking, knowledge of basic accounting concepts and terms is empowering. Once you simply learn the terminology and its meaning, your confidence will soar and your role in the financial matters of the institution will become increasingly significant.

EXHIBIT 10.1 | *U.S. Small Business Administration (SBA) Glossary of Terms*

ACCOUNTS PAYABLE: Trade accounts of businesses representing obligations to pay for goods and services received.

ACCOUNTS RECEIVABLE: Trade accounts of businesses representing moneys due for goods sold or services rendered evidenced by notes, statements, invoices, or other written evidence of a present obligation.

ACCOUNTING: The recording, classifying, summarizing, and interpreting in a significant manner and in terms of money, transactions, and events of a financial character.

BREAKEVEN POINT: The break-even point in any business is that point at which the volume of sales or revenues exactly equals total expenses—the point at which there is neither a profit nor loss—under varying levels of activity. The break-even point tells the manager what level of output or activity is required before the firm can make a profit; reflects the relationship between costs, volume, and profits.

BUSINESS PLAN: A comprehensive planning document which clearly describes the business developmental objective of an existing or proposed business applying for assistance in SBA's 8(a) or lending programs. The plan outlines what and how and from where the resources needed to accomplish the objective will be obtained and utilized.

CAPITAL: Assets less liabilities, representing the ownership interest in a business; a stock of accumulated goods, especially at a specified time and in contrast to income received during a specified time period; accumulated goods devoted to the production of goods; accumulated possessions calculated to bring income.

CAPITAL EXPENDITURES: Business spending on additional plant equipment and inventory.

CAPITALIZED PROPERTY: Personal property of the agency which has an average dollar value of $300.00 or more and a life expectancy of one year or more. Capitalized property shall be depreciated annually over the expected useful life to the agency.

CASH DISCOUNT: An incentive offered by the seller to encourage the buyer to pay within a stipulated time. For example, if the terms are 2/10/N 30, the buyer may deduct 2 percent from the amount of the invoice (if paid within 10 days); otherwise, the full amount is due in 30 days.

CASH FLOW: An accounting presentation showing how much of the cash generated by the business remains after both expenses (including interest) and principal repayment on financing are paid. A projected cash flow statement indicates whether the business will have cash to pay its expenses, loans, and make a profit. Cash flows can be calculated for any given period of time, normally done on a monthly basis.

CHARGE-OFF: An accounting transaction removing an uncollectible balance from the active receivable accounts.

CORPORATION: A group of persons granted a state charter legally recognizing them as a separate entity having its own rights, privileges, and liabilities distinct from those of its members. The process of incorporating should be completed with the state's secretary of state or state corporate counsel, and usually requires the services of an attorney.

COSTS: Money obligated for goods and services received during a given period of time, regardless of when ordered or whether paid for.

EARNING POWER: The demonstrated ability of a business to earn a profit, over time, while following good accounting practices. When a business shows a reasonable profit on invested capital after fully maintaining the business property, appropriately compensating its owner and employees, servicing its obligations, and fully recognizing its costs, the business may be said to have demonstrated earning power. Demonstrated earning power is the foremost test of the business risk in pressing upon an application for a loan.

ENTREPRENEUR: One who assumes the financial risk of the initiation, operation, and management of a given business or undertaking.

EQUITY: An ownership interest in a business.

FINANCIAL REPORTS: Reports commonly required from applicants request for financial assistance, e.g.:
- Balance Sheet—A report of the status of a firm's assets, liabilities and owner's equity at a given time.
- Income Statement—A report of revenue and expense which shows the results of business operations or net income for a specified period of time.

CASH FLOW: A report which analyzes the actual or projected source and disposition of cash during a past or future accounting period.

INNOVATION: Introduction of a new idea into the marketplace in the form of a new product or service or an improvement in organization or process.

INSOLVENCY: The inability of a borrower to meet financial obligations as they mature or having insufficient assets to pay legal debts.

MARK-UP: Mark-up is the difference between invoice cost and selling price. It may be expressed either as a percentage of the selling price or the cost price, and is supposed to cover all the costs of doing business plus a profit. Whether markup is based on the selling price or the cost price, the base is always equal to 100 percent.

NET WORTH: Property owned (assets), minus debts and obligations owed (liabilities), is the owner's equity (net worth).

NOTES AND ACCOUNTS RECEIVABLE: A secured or unsecured receivable evidenced by a note or open account arising from activities involving liquidation and disposal of loan collateral.

OBLIGATIONS: Technically defined as "amount of orders placed, contracts awarded, services received, and similar transactions during a given period which will require payments during the same or a future period."

PROPRIETORSHIP: The most common legal form of business ownership; about 85 percent of all small businesses are proprietorships. The liability of the owner is unlimited in this form of ownership.

RETURN ON INVESTMENT: The amount of profit (return) based on the amount of resources (funds) used to produce it. Also the ability of a given investment to earn a return for its use.

SERVICE CORPS OF RETIRED EXECUTIVES (SCORE): Retired and working successful business persons who volunteer to render assistance in counseling, training, and guiding small business clients.

SMALL BUSINESS DEVELOPMENT CENTERS (SBDC): The SBDC is a university-based center for the delivery of joint government, academic, and private sector services for the benefit of small business and the national welfare. It is committed to the development and productivity of business and the economy in specific geographical regions.

VENTURE CAPITAL: Money used to support new or unusual commercial undertakings; equity, risk, or speculative capital. This funding is provided to new or existing firms that exhibit above-average growth rates, a significant potential for market expansion, and the need for additional financing for business maintenance or expansion.

Source: U.S. SBA (n.d.).

As you continue your adventure to learn more about financial matters, take advantage of every opportunity and resource. Table 10.1 outlines some online resources related to financial matters.

TABLE 10.1 *Online Resources for Financial Management for the Healthcare Leader*

Accounting principles for entrepreneurs	http://www.entrepreneur.com/money/moneymanagement/bookkeeping/article21908.html
Accounting principles for nonprofit organizations	http://managementhelp.org/finance/np_fnce/np_fnce.htm
Free online management library	http://www.managementhelp.org/aboutfml/what-it-is.htm
Mind tools	http://www.mindtools.com/pages/main/newMN_TED.htm
CDC cost-benefit analysis	http://www.cdc.gov/owcd/EET/CBA/fixed/1.html
Cost-volume-profit graphs	http://software.informer.com/getfree-cost-volume-profit-graph-in-excel/
Make graphs using Microsoft Excel	http://office.microsoft.com/enus/excel/ch010003731033.aspx http://www.internet4classrooms.com/excel_create_chart.htm
Strategic planning	http://work911.com/planningmaster/faq/scan.htm
Business plans	http://www.score.org/template_gallery.html?gclid=COm-57nLrpcCFQO5GgodagL_iQ
Service Corp of Retired Executives (SCORE)	
U.S. Small Business Administration	http://www.sba.gov/smallbusinessplanner/index.html
Short courses on writing a grant proposals	http://foundationcenter.org/getstarted/tutorials/shortcourse/index.html http://www.mcf.org/mcf/grant/writing.htm
Search for grants	http://grants.nih.gov/grants/guide/index.html http://nnlm.gov/funding/grants.html http://www.ahrq.gov/

Comfort in Collaborative Financial Relationships

Rarely do individuals enter into business ventures totally alone. Even when an individual does not have business partners, he or she must collaborate with funding institutions, affiliated and associated agencies and providers, governmental agencies, or other members of the community. Nurses, especially, know the stories of health care and can make the need for services real to other collaborators. While standards of care and levels or types of services provided may not appear negotiable, they do warrant open discussion. In such negotiations, leaders must always examine and weigh the need to have control for control's sake, and the need to maintain standards and employ expertise. Developing confidence in one's own ability to listen, to contemplate, and to make informed decisions in collaboration with others will improve confidence in working with others on financial matters. Such collaboration can add to knowledge and confidence in all matters, including risks related to financial issues.

Rational Risk Taking

When resources are designated to produce a certain outcome, there is always a certain amount of inherent risk in reaching that outcome. Although you can develop skills to forecast changes affecting organizational, economic, and social environments, exact outcomes will always remain uncertain:

> All decisions and actions are rife with risk. Risk cannot be eliminated and should not necessarily be decreased because courses of action that possess great value tend to be associated with higher risk. What is important to determine is not whether the risk can be eliminated,

but whether the level of risk is appropriate for the actions undertaken and, if so, what strategies can accommodate the risk. (Porter-O'Grady & Malloch, 2007, p. 28)

Fear of risk taking can paralyze decision making and deter organizational success. Porter-O'Grady and Malloch (2007) suggested that *rational risk taking* is a leadership skill that can be learned and practiced. Rational risk taking requires shifting from the notion of risk taking as negative to developing the skills required to promote the success of a complex and rapidly changing organization. Decisions are made based on organizational values, the strategic plans of the organization, respect for others, the well-being of individuals, and availability of resources.

Assessing the Context of Care From a Financial Perspective

Effective projections and management of resources require some ability to understand history, including the business history of the organization, the history of the community or context of the business, and the history of the services of the business within the business community as well as the general social geography. It is also necessary to connect with current affairs in business and in the community, and you must be able to predict the future to some degree. There are several mechanisms that can help you in such assessments, such as the environmental scan.

Environmental Scan

An environmental scan is a critical and intentional review of information available in order to make appropriate resource decisions related to the organization. Information is categorized and used to help guide planning, decision making, and use of resources. It is a critical step in financial management and necessary for strategic planning.

For example, Cote, Lauzon, and Kyd-Strickland (2008) used critical browsing in an environmental scan to search, select, and summarize information found on the Web related to *interprofessional collaborative practice initiatives*. Twenty-seven documents were selected for additional analysis and inclusion. The information was categorized using three main parameters: source, summary, and relevance to the practice model. Five broad themes were identified: promotion, networking, evidence, resources, and linkage between interprofessional education and care. The scan helped to provide data for successful financial decisions.

Conducting a full-scale environmental scan to include national issues is time-consuming and requires skill. Many organizations regularly conduct environmental scans. The information published from such studies is applicable in many healthcare settings. One example of this is the annual environmental scan of the American Hospital Association (AHA):

> The *2010 America Hospital Association Environmental Scan* provides insight and information about market forces that have a high probability of affecting the healthcare field. It is designed to help hospital and health system executives better understand the healthcare landscape and the critical trends and issues their organizations will likely face in the foreseeable future. The *2010 AHA Environmental Scan* is compiled from 35 nationally recognized sources with recommendations from select AHA governance committees. (AHA, 2009, p. 2)

Emerging or potential problems related to resources as well as opportunities can be recognized by a critical and systematic evaluation of information from an environmental scan.

External Trends in the Community

Changes in the demographics of the local community can result in a shift in healthcare needs and affect potential revenue. For example, nearby construction of a high-rise residential building for the elderly may result in a greater demand for geriatric services. An increase in the number of manufacturing plants in the community may increase the need for services for young families with small children. Increased unemployment rates could mean that families no longer have health insurance and have fewer resources to pay for care. Changes in the economy on a local, regional, or national level can result in decreased funding or changes in reimbursement levels.

Trends Within the Organization

An environmental scan of the internal environment, in terms of past experiences, present conditions, and expressions of future expectations, is important. The internal political climate should be assessed to place appropriate issues on the "front burner." Furthermore, potential conflicts within multiple agendas may be identified, and alliances and areas of competition should be defined.

There are several points to ponder when conducting an internal scan. They include the degree of organizational stability. For example, is any instability attached to confusion or uncertainty or is the atmosphere that of positive change? Furthermore, what is the financial history of the organization? Also, consider the organization's relationship with the community and local leaders.

BUSINESS MODELS, PLANS, AND BUDGETS

Expert clinicians are not usually prepared as experts in business or finance. But in order to make a difference in any transformational manner, as a leader, you must know the language, processes, and outcomes related to fiscal matters in health care. You must be able to clearly articulate the return on investment of the important work you do, and you must be able to interpret the work of promoting health and caring for the sick to professional colleagues whose world is about providing, developing, and/or managing resources. Business models are depictions of the business, the theoretical picture, or the conceptual portrayal of the organization from a business or financial perspective. The business plan is the roadmap to project the success and contingency plans of the enterprise, and the budget is the operational record of all financial resources and management of the endeavor.

Business Models

Formal and theoretical business models have been developed using a multitude of criteria. Models may be based on relationships with other businesses, type of product or service, physical location of the infrastructure, corporate structure, and ownership, among others. Many models are complicated and seem to have little apparent application to healthcare delivery.

TABLE 10.2 *Characteristics of Archetypes for Leadership*

MIT Business Model Archetypes	Characteristics of Archetypes
Creator	■ Buys raw materials or components from suppliers and then transforms or assembles them to create a product sold to buyers ■ Predominant business model in all manufacturing industries. ■ Designs the products they sell
Distributor	■ Buys a product and resells essentially the same product to someone else ■ May provide additional value by, for example, transporting or repackaging the product or by providing customer service ■ Ubiquitous in wholesale and retail trade
Landlord	■ Sells the right to use, but not own, an asset for a specified period of time ■ Also includes lenders who provide temporary use of financial assets (like money), and contractors and consultants who provide services produced by temporary use of human assets. ■ Healthcare services would be classified as a Landlord model.
Broker	■ Facilitates sales by matching potential buyers and sellers

Source: Adapted from Weill et al. (2004).

A business model is defined simply as "consisting of two elements: (a) what the business does, and (b) how the business makes money doing these things" (Weill, Malone, D'Urso, Herman, & Woermer, 2004, p. 6). Generally, health care is considered a service model. For example, using this definition, Weill et al., (2004) derived the four basic business model archetypes: Creator, Distributor, Landlord, and Broker, shown in Table 10.2. Under this model, provision of healthcare services may be classified as Landlord-type business (which could be additionally subgrouped as Intellectual Landlord). Neither healthcare facilities nor providers are bought or sold by "customers" and "people are not 'assets' in an accounting sense"; however, "their time (and knowledge) may be 'rented out' for a fee" (Weill et al., 2004, p. 11).

The 1,000 largest public companies in the United States were categorized by archetype and evaluated for financial performance by analysis of revenue stream. Results demonstrated that selling use of assets to customers (Landlord archetype) was more profitable and more highly valued by the market than selling ownership of assets. In general, business models based on nonphysical assets were found to be more profitable than those based on physical assets (Weill et al., 2004).

This perspective of a business model is useful as it helps communicate the capital value of the healthcare professional and the services provided to those who may be the gatekeepers to funding. The willingness to support a particular type of venture is generally grounded on the perception that the business will be profitable, or at least an asset to the organization or community rather than a liability.

Business Plans

A business plan functions as a developmental "roadmap," integrating goals, resource needs, financial needs and planning, and projected outcomes to begin a business venture, clinical practice initiative, educational project, or some other innovation. It is a document most often prepared as a proposal in order to obtain funding (Baker & Baker,

2011, p. 271). As a clinical leader, you would likely develop a business plan before setting up a new practice, program, or service. This process could also be used to make decisions about choosing among several competing service or business options or even considering a new line of services or implementing a new program within the organization. Several factors should be considered before beginning such a venture. Bupert (2004) listed the following: need for the services in the community, community interest and willingness to use the services, number of potential client/patients for the service, and reimbursement for services by third-party payers.

The business plan for a proposed innovation must include more than money matters. It should include analysis of "key assumptions, strategy, operating plan and tactics, resource requirements, financial plan/analysis, evaluation/measurement plan, and contingency plans" (Morkikian, Kimball, & Joynt, 2007, p. 400). It should also be based on the best available evidence (Brandt et al., 2009). As a leader, you need to know and articulately communicate if your plan is budget neutral and why or why your plan makes business sense. Your projections and subsequent evaluation should quantify cost savings while advancing the mission of the organization. Cost savings may be reflected in the actual budget by costs, charges, or new revenue, or indirectly by reduction in worker turnover, or other employee costs such as workers' compensation. Thus, the business plan for a clinical practice initiative should reflect the best information available from those most knowledgeable on the project, good program design, evidence of practice expertise, evidence of expert economic and financial management, and strong evidence of effective leadership (Harris, 2010).

The business plan should be written and should contain many of the following sections. Consider which element is most appropriate and will be most useful and persuasive to launch your enterprise. First, always include an executive summary. If you cannot make your case clearly on one page, no one will want to hear your pitch. Next, include your vision/mission statement, background information on the initiative that reflects the rationale and need for your initiative, and specific objectives. The background and rationale should reflect a clear definition of your market and analysis of the market, including input from stakeholders, analysis of competition if appropriate, and a profile of the clients or community that your project will serve. Objectives should flow from your rationale. Include current products or services and needed research and development as appropriate. Describe your management teams, your product or service strategies, key factors in delivering your service, and what your project will accomplish, including a timeline. Specifically describe capital requirements; business risks; financial plan, including repayment plans if appropriate; and your plan to sustain the project. Finally, outline a marketing plan for communication, dissemination, advertising, promotion, and other publicity strategies (Bupert, 2004, pp. 341–342; Harris, 2010).

Two financial activities are critical components of the business plan: the break-even analysis and the projected payer mix. Simply stated, an organization's break-even point is that point after which revenues exceed costs. Both fixed costs, those costs that can be most easily predicted and tend to be stable, and variable costs, or those costs that, by their nature, can fluctuate, are considered when projecting the break-even point. Estimation of the break-even point is especially critical in financial planning for new programs, services, and beginning organizations. Until that point is reached, operations can be thought of as being in the "red"; that is, operations expend more than is received. Funds must be available to meet cost (expenses) until the revenue can at least equal expenses. Even then, it must not be assumed that revenue will continue to exceed expenses. However, accurate projection of break-even point can assist in (1) estimating acceptable risk in beginning a new service, (2) approximating the amount of funds needed for "start-up," that is, the amount of funding required to maintain operations until a profit is realized, and (3) communicating potential business success to potential funding sources.

Projection of the break-even point is also useful in determining charges for units of service, such as the charges for a clinic visit. However, the amount charge for unit of service is also influenced by market conditions including competition, by participation in third-party payer programs, by conditions set forth by funding organizations or affiliated organizations, and by other factors.

Baker and Baker (2011, p. 69) illustrated the break-even point as cost-volume-profit analysis. The break-even point is defined as the "point when the contribution margin (that is, net revenue less variable costs) equals fixed cost." In addition, the break-even point can be expressed in two ways: an amount per unit of service or as a percentage of net revenues.

Cost-volume-profit projections or portrayals are often displayed in graph form, with the horizontal axis being the volume (number of visits, for example) and the vertical axis shows cost. Low-cost or free software can assist in "plugging in" various scenarios of volume, revenue, and fixed and variable costs. Adaptation of electronic spreadsheets can be used to generate graphs showing the intersection between revenue and cost. Changing the variables can illustrate how differences in projections might produce different potential outcomes. Contingency plans can then be made to help minimize risks.

Estimating the Volume

Estimating the projected volume of units, such as clinic visits, is an inexact science. First of all, the intended recipients of the service need to be defined in terms of characteristics (i.e., emerging families, the elderly, and migrant workers) and by geographical location. This would be the targeted market. Need and demand for services then can be projected based on the demographics of the community, services already in place or gaps in services, client loyalty and satisfaction to these services, and comparison of charges to existing services. Other potential considerations may be the market conditions. Is the service considered a necessity by the potential target market? Is there a comparable alternative to the clients? How competitive to the service proposed? Is the service consistent with expectations and community norms, and is the service congruent with the culture of the target market?

Estimating the Payer Mix

The payer mix is the variety of sources that pay, or reimburse, for healthcare services. The mix of third-party payers can be estimated from information about varied demographic groups, such as the percentages of the population eligible for Medicaid, those over 65 years who would have Medicare coverage, the unemployment rates, and the age distribution of the population. The type of services provided may also provide insight to payer mix. Those services targeted toward the elderly, for example, would tend to have a higher mix of Medicare as third-party payer. Locations where poverty is prevalent likely would have a higher percentage of Medicaid recipients and other sources for subsidized care. They also may represent a higher percentage of those who do not have third-party payers and cannot afford to self-pay.

Variations in the mix of payers can have a great impact on the revenue of an organization. Shifts in payer mix or failure to project a near approximation can severely alter income projections, as seen in Tables 10.3 and 10.4. Note that both scenario A and scenario B show revenue for 100 visits. Reversing the number of visits per payer source in this payer mix results in a difference of revenue of $1,300.00 for the same number of visits.

Choosing to Participate

Some healthcare providers choose to not provide care to individuals whose services are billed to specific payers, due to the potential loss or liability incurred by decreased revenue. Others provide services but limit the percentage of patients whose payment is from a particular source. An excellent example of this is providers who refuse or limit the number of patients covered by Medicaid. In many states, the amount allowed for payment of services is much lower than payment by other sources. It is not uncommon in a community to find few or no providers for services paid by Medicaid. The decision to accept all payers or whether to restrict those accepted into care based on the payment sources is a decision based on financial, legal, and ethical considerations and on the ability to fulfill the mission of the organization.

Not-for-Profit Status and Making a Profit

Nurses tend to dislike thinking about the probability of payment and making a profit for providing healthcare services. However, staff and rent must be paid; supplies must be purchased; and in many instances, investors must be repaid. The for-profit or proprietary model of conducting business has infused some variety and innovation into the delivery of health care in the United States. The number of healthcare facilities and

TABLE 10.3 Scenario 1: Payer Mix

	Scenario 1: Volume × Reimbursement Rate = Total Reimbursement		
Third-Party Payer	Volume (Number of Visits)	Reimbursement Rate	Total Reimbursement
Payer Uni	10 visits	$55.00	$550.00
Payer Medi	25 visits	$85.00	$2,125.00
Insurance A	30 visits	$95.00	$2,850.00
Insurance B	35 visits	$105.00	$3,675.00
Total	100 visits		$9,200.00

TABLE 10.4 Scenario 2: Payer Mix

	Scenario 2: Volume × Reimbursement Rate = Total Reimbursement		
Third-Party Payer	Volume (Number of Visits)	Reimbursement Rate	Total Reimbursement
Insurance B	10 visits	$105.00	$1,050.00
Insurance A	25 visits	$95.00	$2,375.00
Payer Medi	30 visits	$85.00	$2,550.00
Payer Uni	35 visits	$55.00	$1,925.00
Total	100 visits		$7,900.00

providers who have moved to for-profit status continues to increase. A not-for-profit organization is an organization recognized by both the state and the federal government as not-for-profit and hence exempt from some specific taxes, based on documented return to the organization and/or return to the community. Actually, this does not mean that the organization does not wish to make a profit. Rather, income after expenses is reinvested by the organization rather than paid to owners or stockholders. Often, any overage of income beyond expenses is used to provide additional services or to subsidize those who cannot pay or to provide charitable services.

Projecting Revenue

When calculating projected revenue, the difference between charges and reimbursement or payment must be recognized. Only the actual reimbursement amount can be projected as potential revenue. For example, Medicare and Medicaid will pay only within specific limits. Planning and targeting marketing of services should include defining all potential payers and estimating reimbursement levels. Contracts and agreements, such as care under preferred provider agreements, rarely pay at the level of charges but rather another amount agreed upon, or a contractual charge. Some payers use the "customary and usual" guidelines for payment. Customary and usual payments are those determined by the payer by evaluating local or regional market and assessing the usual charges for like services. Currently, this method is less prevalent than are negotiated contracts, such as with preferred provider agreements. Many contracts state a maximum amount per service that can be billed to the client. Whether or not the client can be billed for any difference between the charges and the designated reimbursement depends on the contract, and this can change by service by the same provider of services. For example, a payer may not require a client copayment for an annual physical examination but have a set copayment for an illness visit. Usually, expressed deductibles can be billed to the client. In addition to set rates, discounts, contractual allowances, the likelihood of uncollectable bills, and client copayments should be considered when projecting revenues.

The time intervals between provision of services and billing and then between billing and payment for services are of significant importance when minimal operating funds are available. Scrutiny of these time intervals will reveal the impact on the organization's ability to meet financial obligations and the level of operating funds needed to meet obligations.

In undertaking a business venture that requires funding, you must consider the level of *personal* financial liability that may be assumed. The structure and legal designation of the organization provide for specific "ownership" of liability. Consultation with legal experts on such issues is imperative. For example, liability, either personal or corporate, has to be defined in the event that the organization does not generate enough revenue to meet payroll, utilities, rent, and repayment of loans or other obligations.

Budgets

Oversimplified, financial management is simply a matter of managing, balancing, and projecting resources. Most simply, a budget "is a plan with a timetable that guides an organization's activities" (Finkler & Kovner, 2000; Greenberg, 2008, p. 74):

A budget is based on *revenue* (income generated, owed, or [received] for services) and *expenses* (expenditures and costs of activities needed for the organization's operations). The difference between the projected cost and the actual cost of services is called a *variance*. The major types of budgets include the *operating budget* (the daily income and costs in one year for workload, personnel. . ., supplies, and overhead), the *capital* budget (buildings, land, long-term investments, or durable expensive equipment), the *cash* budget (actual/expected monthly income and cash disbursements), and the *long range* budget (a strategic plan of goals over a 3- to 10-year period).

A traditional budget approach is simple annual incremental increases or decreases based on revenue and expenses or "zero based," where the budget is developed and justified anew, or from zero each fiscal year.

Creating a budget, or a financial roadmap, for an organization is an ongoing process. Possibly the biggest mistake made in budgeting is to assume that once a budget is constructed and implemented, the work is done until "next year."

Generally, budgets are created at the institutional/organizational level around designated cost centers. A cost center is simply a unit or department for which a budget is created and to which expenses are "charged." A cost center may also be a designated source of revenue; however, depending on how the cost center is defined, revenue may be difficult to define. An example of this is a centralized cost center for nursing services in a hospital. The revenue for nursing services is often not detectable, but rather embedded with other services or charges. Thus, expenses can be clearly defined, but not the contribution to revenue.

Approaches to Budgeting

Approaches to budgeting can be classified by two different approaches and by variations and combinations of the two. The approaches are the incremental approach and the zero-based or objectives approach.

The historical or incremental approach. The simplest and most commonly used approach is to base the following year's budget on budgets of the past, usually the previous year, assisted by data from the current year. A certain percentage is added or subtracted based on increases or decreases in projected expenses. Investigations are conducted on more or less predictable changes, such as employee salaries, benefits, and costs for energy, supplies, and equipment. Actual expenditures of the preceding year are also considered. This expected increment or decrease (the difference between last year's budget and the expected expenses for the coming year) is added to the current year's budget and becomes the new proposed budget.

The historical approach to budgeting is attractive because it requires less time commitment and expertise for the one preparing the budget. The assumption of this approach is that business will continue into the future relatively unchanged. Therefore, it is especially useful in an organization with intentionally enduring services or programs and in a stable economy.

The downside of historical or incremental budgeting is that it tends to sustain existing departments, programs, or activities for better or worse. While change is not incompatible with this approach to budgeting, neither is it fostered by this process. A tendency toward continuing status quo may cause difficulty in aligning organizational objectives with the needs of the community, changes in the economy and in reimbursement practices, and with changes in health care delivery. This could result from a tendency to look within the organization rather than the organization's external environment.

The zero-based or budgeting by objectives approach. In contrast to the historical approach to budgeting, the zero-based or budgeting by objectives makes no assumptions regarding the continuation of specific programs of the organization or of services provided. The budget is presented as a package that includes objectives, projected outcomes, and cost and revenue. Each budget unit must be justified and have definite objectives in line with the mission of the organization. In terms of the mission and needs of the organization, priorities are assigned to each of the unit budget proposals.

One of the strengths of zero-based budgeting is that a mechanism for discontinuing ineffective or inefficient departments or programs is inherent to the process, whereas historical budgeting tends to perpetuate the status quo. If the costs of a program or department cannot be justified in terms of intended outcomes and/or ratio of cost to benefits, then deletion has to be considered. The danger is that only financial benefit to the organization is used for this determination. Care should be taken that intangible benefits are considered. Public expectations, goodwill, mission, and community needs must be considered.

An additional strength of zero-based budgeting is that new and creative programs have an equal footing in terms of possible funding as do established programs. The organization can be more responsive to changes in the social, economic, and health delivery environments. Rather than being grounded in established traditions, new creative and innovative approaches to health care delivery can be grounded in community needs, results of evidence-based practice, trials of community interventions, and opportunities for collaborative ventures.

Zero-based budgeting does have potential drawbacks. It is more time-consuming than the historical approach and requires a higher level of budgetary expertise to construct. Also, employees may feel threatened by a perceived lack of long-term stability and viability of their work environment, since continued funding will be questioned and may suffer in competition with other programs. In this same vein, a sense of negative competition may exist among departments and programs.

A department or program's continued existence may be seen to depend on the manager's ability to develop unit objectives, to assign cost to achieving defined outcomes, and to analyze the impact on the overall organization. The leader has an obligation to assist the units in best presenting their budgetary package.

Several conditions may influence the manner in which budgets are framed. Budgets are framed within a specific time period in each organization, which may include a set fiscal year or a continual rolling process over time. Budgets may be relatively fixed or flexible.

Fiscal year. Budgets most often span a fiscal year. The fiscal year for a private organization is self-defined; for example, it could be from January 1 to December 31, or from July 1 to June 30. The choice of inclusive dates is influenced by the fiscal year of funding sources and the reporting requirements of associated or governmental agencies. Public organizations would most often follow the appropriate government fiscal year.

Rolling budget. A rolling budget is a budget projected for a selected time frame in the future, for example, 3 or 6 months. While that budget is in effect, a new budget to follow that time period is developed. Thus, a budget is always in use and a new budget is always in development. Although that appears to be time-consuming (and it is), it is not as great a variation from the yearly budget as it may appear. In actuality, organizations are engaged in developing future budgets on an ongoing basis, even when employing yearly budgets. The advantage of the rolling budget is that it allows for shifts in needs and proprieties that become apparent during the current budget span, allowing for adaptation to changes in priorities and needs without having to restructure a budget or miss an opportunity due to budget constraints.

Trended budget. A trended budget is useful when there is a predictable unevenness in services over the budget year. If 20% more services are provided in September, October, and November than in June, July, and August, budget appropriation for those time periods differ by that same difference. This prevents having unnecessary budget variances in these months and having a surplus of funds in a month that might have been better utilized in a different time period.

Fixed versus flexible budget. A fixed budget assumes that both revenue and expenses will be essentially the same from month to month. The total amount allotted to an expense for the year is divided by 12 to determine the allotment for each month. A flexible budget, however, is a budget that automatically adjusts variables to reflect changes such as volume, labor costs, and capital expenditures (Barr, 2005). The same advantages apply to the flexible budget as to a trended budget but are enhanced. The ability to respond to changes in economics, patient care delivery, personnel needs, and emergencies is inherent in the flexible budgeting approach. What could be thought of as a disadvantage of flexible budgeting techniques, that is, the requirement for constant surveillance and synchronicity with both internal and external environments, is actually a business advantage. The biggest advantage to using a flexible budget is that you have an opportunity to make timely operational adjustments if possible (Sharpe, 2009). For example, a home health agency may recognize that the cost of gasoline has increased, and that travel expenditures are over budget. Using a flexible approach, alternatives could be identified immediately and set in place to mitigate the cost increases. Collaboration with those at the point of care might provide assistance in defining alternatives without diminishing quality of care. For example, in this case, it may be possible to sequence home visits more efficiently without diminishing quality.

In the past, the ability to access the data needed for successful flexible budgeting would have been impossible. But today, electronic processes and sources of information make it relatively easy. The first challenge to implementing a flexible budget is to ensure that a system is in place to collect the needed data (Sharpe, 2009). Barr (2005, p. 26) explained:

> Patient volume can be plugged into a flex budget to make it more useful. The percentage of patients participating in Medicare, Medicaid and private insurance as well as the percentage of uninsured will have varying effects on revenue and costs, and during the traditional budget preparation time those can only be estimated. A flex budget allows those numbers to be updated frequently over the year, creating new budgetary estimates of how the current year is unfolding and how the coming year looks financially based on those complicated interrelationships.

Components of the Budget

Organizations often have a format for creating the budget which includes several components. The most common components are discussed here. The operating budget is the expenditure plan for the daily "operating" activities of the organization and includes both budgets for each cost center and all expense units in the organization as well as a projection of revenue (Yoder-Wise, 2007). The personnel budget is usually the largest portion of an operating budget, accounting for about 85% of the projected expenditures (Liebler, & McConnell, 2004). Personnel costs include wage and salary for each position and for each person, anticipated compensation raises, adjustments resulting in changes in personnel status, vacation relief, overtime pay, and temporary or seasonal help (Liebler & McConnell, 2004, p. 311). Consideration is given also to the cost of recruiting and orienting new personnel. Most organizations include a separate section on the cost of benefits such as any health insurance and life insurance premiums that the employer pays, or payments made into retirement benefits by the employer on behalf of the employee. Both time worked and time paid but not worked must be included in the budget.

Personnel needs are usually calculated by full-time equivalents, which, in turn, are calculated using projections of units of service or volume of services. Usually, a full-time equivalent is equated to be working 40 hours per week for each week of a year, or 2,080 hours yearly (Yoder-Wise, 2007). The unit of service is defined by the organization (although influenced strongly by payers' definitions) and may be the number of clinic visits, admissions to service, treatments, and others. For a continuing budget, past volume and productivity can be used to estimate future needs. For new services, descriptions of expected services, examination of similar services, and expert opinion of providers are useful in projecting personnel needs. Orientation time for employees is a special consideration, and is an expense any time there is turnover in staff.

The capital budget items are those facilities or other nondisposable or high-end purchases such as land and buildings, machinery, and equipment. Each organization has its own guidelines regarding what constitutes a capital expenditure. For example, criteria may be that equipment and machinery included in the capital budget would be those items having a cost of at least $1,000 and a life expectancy of more than 5 years. Acquisition costs of equipment are calculated and pro-rated over the expected life of the equipment. Operating and depreciation costs are also calculated (Liebler & McConnell, 2004). Choices in equipment should be grounded on many factors, including the overall operating and maintenance expenses, the human resource costs in educating the staff to use the equipment, and clinical usefulness and ease of use.

Capital budget items may originate as a part of a cost center or work unit, or may be a part of the organization's strategic plan. In some instances, depending on the organization's policies, lease agreements may be subjected the same type of budget proposals. A separate budget may be developed for future planned construction and may be referred to as the building or construction budget.

The supply budget ranges from disposable office materials such as pens and paperclips to clinical supplies and is usually the most flexible component of the overall budget. Some materials may require requisition forms, while others must be immediately available. Some supply charges are considered a part of "doing business," although others may be billable patient supplies. Some of the supplies are stable in price, and others vary over time. All potential supply costs must be examined in order to adequately budgeted. Tracking systems must be able to capture the classification of supplies and their accounting to a unit budget.

The Budgeting Process

Regardless of the approach or technique used in budgeting, budget items or components must be justified. That is, it should be clear to decision makers why each proposed expenditure is necessary. All expenditures should be tied to the mission, goals, objectives, and strategic plan of the organization.

Increasing participation of stakeholders in the budgeting process increases commitment to the budget priorities and outcomes. An inclusive approach is especially important when resources may be limited. The leader can bring into the process mid-level managers and providers of care across disciplines in a workshop environment. Not only can work toward completing a budget be fruitful, but also, a forum is established for education in the budget process, discussion of missions and goals of the organization, and concerns addressed. Bradley (2008, p. 57) described the vision of a budget workshop:

> The vision for the budget workshop included streamlining and simplifying the process as follows: 1) providing access to tools and resources including finance, payroll, and decision support staff—in a single environment, 2) scheduling a specific time for related departments to attend the workshop, and 3) establishing a goal of "relevant completion" (substantial or 90% completion) at the beginning of the process.

Managing the Budget

Among the most important activities of the leader is managing the budget. Usually, expert staff handle daily operations of finances, but ultimate accountability falls to the leader.

Flexibility. The degree of flexibility of budget parameters is affected by the type of budget, the seat of power and decision making, and the policies of the organization. Decisions can be swayed by perceived inflexibility of the budget, expressed as "The budget won't let us do it!" Rigid adherence to a budget may result in dampened creativity, squelched innovation, or even perhaps averted disaster, but choices on how to expend money is a human choice. The budget is a management tool, it is not a management entity of itself. While resources must always be considered when making choices, accountability and responsibility for making a particular choice do not lie with "the budget."

Oversight and understanding budget variances. One of the most useful reports in determining if a budget is on course is the variance report. A variance means that the funds expended on certain budgetary items (such as salaries or supplies) are over or under that which was allotted. At first glance, one may think that being over budget is inherently a negative, while being under is a desired occurrence. It is critical that each occurrence be evaluated. Being over budget on supply items may be detrimental to the organization if services provided are constant. However, if that overage is matched by an increase in revenue, then it may not be a detrimental occurrence. Accordingly, revenue should also be monitored in terms of consistency with budget expenditures. It is possible that services provided can stay at the same level, revenue for units of services remains steady, but total reimbursement can decrease because supplies that could once be billed now must be absorbed into the organization. Due to efficient electronic data retrieval and management, reports can be generated in nearly "real time," providing an opportunity to correct any deficiencies.

Finkleman (2006, pp. 455–456) presented a question guide for assessing patterns in variance management: (1) What effect does the variance have? (2) Why did the variance occur? (3) What can be done to prevent its re-occurrence? (4) What needs to be done to make the best of the situation? In addition, it may be asked: What needs to be done to make the *most* of the situation?

RESOURCE DEVELOPMENT

As you advance to higher levels in leadership, you will become more responsible for acquiring resources beyond existing budgets based on revenues and expenditures. Such fund-raising is an art unto itself. To be successful, you must be committed to your organization from the heart. Donors invest where they see vision, energy, need, and the capacity to make a difference.

Philanthropy

The foundation for such fund-raising is the case statement. It is a formal document that reflects your vision statement from the perspective of those outside your organization. Its purpose is for use with potential donors, but the sheer activity of developing the case statement may help to crystallize your vision and mission from within. The case statement is told from the heart and should answer the following questions: What is the need? It should be stated in the most urgent and compelling manner. It needs to be specific and stated in a way that potential donors can identify how they can personally make a difference. How is your organization uniquely positioned to resolve the need? The idea that your organization is the best or only means to resolve the need should become clear to the donor and should draw the donor to your enterprise. What are the benefits to your action to resolve the need? Again, specific, urgent, heart-felt, but authentic rationale needs to be articulated. How much will it cost? The donor should have a clear idea of what the appropriate donation would be to resolve the need. You must articulate, what are the consequences if you are not able to fulfill the need? (Fritz, 2009; Panas, 2003).

Grant Writing

Funding sources for healthcare services, aside from the obvious reimbursement for services, may also be secured from local, regional, and national private and government grants. Grants have a wide range in monetary amounts, qualifications for grant recipients, and targeted programs. Some grants require an affiliation with a university or established healthcare organization. Some are dedicated to not-for-profit organizations only. Many require a research component, and others require a community collaborative partner. Grant sources include federal and state government agencies, private foundations and other philanthropic organizations, commercial businesses, local charities, and professional organizations.

For example, advanced practice nurses who seek to improve patient outcomes may find good matches at the U.S. Agency for Healthcare Research and Quality (Edwardson, 2006). Unlike many grants sources, such as the National Institutes of Health, where emphasis may be more targeted toward research, the U.S. Agency for Healthcare Research and Quality focuses on the effectiveness of interventions in everyday practice.

Most grant applications require a justified budget, usually in a specified format. If you are new to the grant-writing process, consider partnering with someone who has had success. But do not be deterred by inexperience. Funding sources provide considerable guidance material and are usually available for telephone consultation. Also, many organizations offer grant writing courses for minimal or no cost, and some are available online.

Other potential funding sources, of course, are lending institutions. Again, personal liability must be considered. That said, banking institutions will examine any proposal as a potential business venture. Having a well-constructed business plan and projected budget is critical. Another source may be investors for an equity position or some interest in profits. Investors are usually only considered as resources in for-profit enterprises.

Leadership and Finance

Healthcare leaders, providers, and members of our communities currently suffer many critical economic challenges, including reductions in funding, changes in budget allocations, and elimination of or reductions in programs and services. Nurses prepared at advanced levels are looking for alternative methods of care delivery and changes in practice environments. One nurse who, dissatisfied with the philosophy, approach, and financial provisions of her care environment, began her own practice. Surprising to her was the importance of the role of her business plan, not only to establish the practice but also to sustain her through the launching process:

> Unexpectedly, the business plan provided me with emotional reassurance during slow referral times in the first year. The business plan allowed analysis of the number of referrals, timing of the referrals, and from whom they came. Gradual movement into self-employment, as opposed to complete cessation of a secure, income-providing job, decreases the stress on a businessperson because revenue still comes in while the new, self-employed position reaches the point of producing a steady and sufficient cash flow. A business plan can guide that process because it helps forecast when that time will occur and the amount of business that needs to come in before an individual can work solely for himself or herself. (Muscari, 2004, p. 177)

Attention to financial planning, careful mapping of strategy, marketing that is relevant and correctly targeted, accurate estimations of revenue and expenditures, and adherence to a vision can result not only in financial success, but also in personal fulfillment as a leader. Furthermore, it can be the beginning of you personal contribution toward transforming health care.

Leaders are required to sustain the energy, keep the strategic plan fresh, and establish ongoing significant relationships with friends and stakeholders. Philanthropy and resource development are fast becoming a key element of leadership in health care. Engagement in philanthropic relationships stimulates creativity, opens the perspective of leadership, and can energize the leader. Grantors and donors give because they are drawn emotionally to your cause. It is a unique relationship between leader and donor, often profound because both believe in the dream.

REFERENCES

American Hospital Association (AHA). (2009). 2010 AHA environmental scan. *Hospitals & Health Networks, 36*(8), 83–89.

Baker, J. J., & Baker, R. W. (2011). *Health care finance: Basic tools for nonfinancial managers* (3rd ed.). Sudbury, MA; Jones & Bartlett.

Barr, P. (2005). Flexing your budget: Experts urge hospitals, systems to trade in their traditional budgeting process for a more dynamic and versatile model. *Modern Health Care, (35)*37, 24, 26.

Bradley, L. S. (2008, March). Budgeting—or refusing to budge? How budget workshops can reduce the
pain. *Healthcare Financial Management, 62*(3), 56–59.

Brandt, J. A., Reed Edwards, D., Cos Sullivan, S., Zehler, J. K., Grinder, S., Scott, K. J., et al. (2009). An
evidence-based business planning process. *Journal of Nursing Administration, 39*(12), 511–513.

Bupert, C. (2004). *Nurse practitioner's business practice and legal guide* (2nd ed., pp. 341–342). Sudbury, MA:
Jones& Bartlett.

Carlson, J. (2009). A retiring bunch. *Modern Health Care, 39*(26), 6.

Carlson, J., Evans, M., Lubell, J., Rhea, S., & Zigmond, J. (2009). The exodus continues: More executives
leaving top healthcare jobs. *Modern Health Care, 39*(28), 4.

Cote, G., Lauzon, C., & Kyd-Strickland, B. (2008). Environmental scan of interprofessional collaborative
practice initiatives. *Journal of Interprofessional Care, 22*(5), 449–460.

Edwardson, S. R. (2006). Securing successful funding for nursing research through the Agency for
Healthcare Research and Quality. *Nursing Economic$, 24*(3), 160–161.

Finkleman, A. W. (2006). *Leadership and management in nursing*. Upper Saddle River, NJ: Pearson, Prentice Hall.

Finkler, S. A., & Kovner, C. T. (2000). *Financial management for nurse managers and executives* (2nd ed.).
Philadelphia: Saunders.

Fritz, J. (2009). *Writing a great case statement*. Retrieved August 25, 2009, from http://nonprofit.about.
com/od/fundraisingbasics/a/casestatemtn.htm

Greenberg, M. J. (2008). Budget management. In H. R. Feldman, M. Jaffe-Ruiz, M. L. McClure, M. J.
Greenberg, & T. D. Smith (Eds.), *Nursing leadership: A concise encyclopedia* (pp. 74–75). New York:
Springer.

Halloran, E. J. (2008). Financing health care. In H. R. Feldman, M. Jaffe-Ruiz, M. L. McClure, M. J.
Greenberg, & T. D. Smith (Eds.), *Nursing leadership: A concise encyclopedia* (pp. 229–234). New York:
Springer.

Harris, J. L. (2010, January). *Improving healthcare outcomes: Building the business case*. Paper presented at
the meetings of the American Association of Colleges of Nursing Doctoral Education Conference,
Captiva Island, FL.

Kibort, P. M. (2005, November–December). I drank the Kool-Aid—And learned 24 key management
lessons. *Physician Executive, 31*(6), 52–55.

Liebler, J. G., & McConnell, C. R. (2004). *Management principles for health professionals* (4th ed.). Sudbury,
MA: Jones & Bartlett.

Morkikian, R. L., Kimball, B., & Joynt, J. (2007). Leading change: The nurse executive's role in implementing new care delivery models. *Journal of Nursing Administration, 37*(9), 399–404.

Moseley, G. B., III (2009). *Managing healthcare business strategy*. Sudbury, MA: Jones & Bartlett.

Muscari, E. (2004). Establishing a small business in nursing. *Oncology Nursing Forum 31*(2). 177–179.

Panas, J. (2003). *Making the case: The no-nonsense guide to writing the perfect case statement*. New York:
Institutions Press.

Porter-O'Grady, T. (2001). Beyond the walls: Nursing in the entrepreneurial world. *Nursing Administration Quarterly, 25*(2), 61–68.

Porter-O'Grady, T., & Malloch, K. (2007). *Quantum leadership: A resource for healthcare innovation* (2nd ed.).
Sudbury, MA: Jones & Bartlett.

Sharpe, M. (2009, June). New approach to budgeting can improve bottom line: Flexible budget gives a
true picture. *Hospice Management Advisor*, 67–68.

U.S. Small Business Administration (USBA). (n. d.). *Accounting Glossary*. Retrieved January 21, 2010, from
http://www.sba.gov/smallbusinessplanner/plan/getready/serv_sbplanner_gready_glossory.
html

Weill, P., Malone, T. W., D'Urso, V. T., Herman, G., & Woermer, S. (2004). Do some business models
perform better than others? A study of the 1000 largest U.S. firms'. *MIT Sloan School of Management
Working Paper*. Boston: Sloan School of Management, Massachusetts Institute of Technology. Retrieved January 21, 2010, from http://seeit.mit.edu/Publications/BusinessModels6May2004.pdf

Yoder-Wise, P. S. (2007). *Leading and managing in nursing* (4th ed.). St. Louis, MO: Mosby Elsevier.

Fluency in the System

Never assume that you see the whole picture. There is always
more. Keep looking.

— *Frank Rivers*

"Extraordinary times call for extraordinary leaders. These extraordinary times are also a call for different leadership, leadership that is more circumspect, transparent, self-controlling, and consultative," proclaimed Judy Olian, dean of the Anderson School of Management of the University of California at Los Angeles (Feinberg, 2009, p. 8). Current healthcare environments are complex, uncertain (Begun & Kaissi, 2004), and changing in ways we never imagined. O'Neil (2009) listed four key changes in American demographics that will ensure change in health care: (1) sheer growth in population, (2) increasing racial and ethnic diversity, (3) dramatic aging of the population, and (4) the epidemiology of illness and care moving from acute to chronic, and from hospital to community. We claim to forecast (see Hegarty, Walsh, Condon, & Sweeney, 2009; Robinson & Reinhard, 2009; Thomas & Hynes, 2009), but no one really knows what is next in practice or leadership.

Friedman (2005) uncovered enough surprising examples of new ways of thinking and doing business across the world to conclude "The world is flat." Even more surprises will happen in health care. For example, a large retailer has recently launched a think-out-of-the-box low-cost agreement to send all its employees, nationwide, who need heart surgery to a specific major highly ranked healthcare system. The deal includes paid travel and lodging (Associated Press, 2010). Such bold, creative moves will surely change how we think about healthcare financing, coverage, services, and systems. Some have referred to this time as "a perfect storm" (Yoder-Wise, 2007), when a constellation of factors come together in a figuratively explosive manner. How we predict and prepare for a better future will depend on how we understand each other and how we all work together.

Never has the need been greater for an army of visionary leaders to join in the transformation of health care that meets the challenges of the next generation. Supreme among the challenges for future leaders in health care is the requirement to work together and to understand each other. Leaders are serving in a time of challenge when simply understanding the language, practice, and culture of other disciplines is not enough. We must come to the table, speak each other's language, and speak with fluency.

KNOWING THE PLAYERS AND LEADERS AND TAKING THEIR PERSPECTIVE

The enterprise of health care is composed of dozens of different highly trained clinical and management experts from a broad range of preparation, theoretical perspectives, disciplinary bodies of knowledge, practice experience, and viewpoints. For the most part, we each go on our merry way inside the silos of our disciplines. Although we interact cordially with professionals from other disciplines, we approach our work in parallel play without meaningful attention to the perspective of our colleagues. Meanwhile, patients and families rightfully expect that we truly understand each other as we work together.

Throughout the history of health care, disciplines have been educated, trained, and set out to engage in practice almost solely from within the narrow perspective and traditions of the single discipline. Once we enter the real world of practice, occasionally, we run into each other where the disparities erupt. It often happens when we notice that "someone else" is doing the tasks to which we have become accustomed. It is the unfortunate history of healthcare providers. Physicians erupt when nurse practitioners write prescriptions; nurses erupt when registered care technicians care for patients; radiological technicians erupt when dental assistants take x-rays. Even within disciplines, registered nurses complained when licensed practical nurses first inserted intravenous needles, and radiologists complained when first obstetricians used the ultrasound machine. It has gone on and on. We have fought disciplinary battles over obstetrical forceps, venipuncture, ownership of the button on the x-ray machine, and, most recently, who can be addressed as "doctor." We assert authority over the skills and tools we were taught to use. For example, the American Medical Association (2009) has recently stepped forward to presume authority on the scope of advanced practice nursing and other disciplines such as audiology. Such actions are unbecoming to professions who profess healing and altruism at their core. This cannot continue. Patients, families, and the communities we serve deserve better. The next generation of leaders must respond with authentic interprofessional understanding and collaboration. Excellence in health care demands our ability to understand and work together at the most basic levels.

Do not misunderstand. Disciplinary boundaries for preparation, expertise, and scope of practice are important to confirm order, develop expertise, and provide clear public information. But they need to be informed by wisdom and not by squabbles over tools, procedures, and titles. We must work together for the good of our communities, and we must begin by cultivating the basic skill of professional perspective taking.

Perspective taking is the empathetic understanding of another's viewpoint, way of thinking, motivation, and/or feelings (Prince, 2009). It goes beyond simple understanding of the other, but includes the ability to interpret back the viewpoint from the frame of reference of the "other" as well as the ability to convey empathy. It requires reflection on your own viewpoint and practice in seeing the world through the prism of the other. From an interprofessional viewpoint, we can begin to build authentic working relationships by learning the history and traditions of each other; by reflecting on similarities, differences, and mutual priorities; by reading the literature and policies of each other; and by basic respect for and recognition of the need for each other as we work together.

It is too simple to point to "the other" discipline. First, the unbecoming behaviors of medicine and nursing to continue to point to each other have become tired. Second, we need to get beyond attempts to highlight the virtues of our own discipline over how we work together. For example, often, nurse leaders emphasize the contribution of nursing or herald the voice of nursing. Although this may be laudable within the discipline and explained reasonably by history and legitimate needs to secure autonomy of practice (Stewart, Stansfield, & Tapp, 2004), it is sometimes not helpful. Often, what is needed is to take the perspective of other healthcare disciplines to move the agenda forward for improved health care. Of course, nursing and medicine are not the only disciplines that confront tension; a kind of egocentricism is present to some degree in all professions. The wise leader is at least aware of this tendency and is willing to look at the horizon through a different frame of reference.

Another common problem in professional disciplines is to focus on the time-valued activities within the profession without considering resources or the "bottom line" for the whole. The worn phrase "Follow the money" is a truism (see Steinbrook, 2009). We need another phrase, "Follow the care to the patient." Disciplines need to come together on quality, access, and cost. These cross all boundaries.

We cannot adequately attempt to take the perspective of the other if we do not know about the other. We need to understand the basic philosophies of the knowledge and practices of each other, how and why we prepare our clinicians in the way we do, and what our values are and understand our fears, hopes, and aspirations.

Working Across Disciplines, Styles, and Models

There is hope on the horizon. Across the world, healthcare disciplines are responding to the call to work together. Burnett (2005) described a phenomenon in Scotland called the managed clinical network, which is an interdisciplinary model to provide high-quality, evidence-based, knowledge-based care. It is based on an organizational system of knowledge and information sharing, valuing, acquiring, networking, and using knowledge to improve quality of care. In Canada, authors also described successful collaborations between research and practice in health services (Brazil, MacLeod, & Guest, 2002). Other examples could be reported in all aspects of care. In the United States, we are beginning to foster collaborative ventures between medicine and nursing, especially in professional education, in learning clinical skills (Dillon, Noble, & Kaplan, 2009; Margalit, et al., 2009; Reese, Jeffries, & Engum, 2010).

Working across styles refers not only to different styles among disciplines or personalities but also to actual "styles" of practice or practice models. Shortell (n. d.) lamented, "The largest limiting factor is not lack of money or technology or information or people but, rather the lack of an organizing principle that can link money, people, technology, and ideas into a system that delivers more cost-effective care (i.e., more value) than current arrangements." It will require leaders who are multilingual across disciplines to develop and implement such organizing principles. Systems that integrate across disciplines are better able to meet population healthcare needs, link information systems between providers and patients, and coordinate care across continua (Shortell, Gillies, Anderson, Erickson, & Mitchell, 2000).

Primary care is an important example in current healthcare debates. To meet the needs for primary care, it is going to be especially important for physicians, physician assistants, and advanced practice nurses to work together to understand the perspective of the other in order to best serve the public. This will affect practice, business affairs, educational preparation of practitioners, and licensing regulations. We have not reached that level of collaboration to date (Cooper, 2007). For example, a growing new trend in primary care is the retail clinic. Clinics inside drugstores or shopping malls have attracted controversy and debate, largely because they are "different." Although their potential has been recognized as valuable for screening, prevention, and as a "safety-net provider for the poor" and underserved, they continue to be controversial (Rudavsky & Mehrotra, 2010, p. 42). Their value or contribution to the entire healthcare landscape is yet unknown, but since there are nearly 1,000 of them across the United States, they provide an opportunity for transformational leaders to collaborate across not only disciplines but also across new approaches to care.

Another model growing in discussion is the "medical home." Although the concept began over 40 years ago (Sia, Tonniges, Osterhus, & Taba, 2004), its current iteration was begun in 2007 by a consortium representing the American Academy of Family Physicians, the American Academy of Pediatrics, the American College of Physicians, and the American Osteopathic Association. It is officially named the patient-centered medical home (Kellerman & Kirk, 2007). Its principles include the provision of a personal physician to each patient, physician-directed medical practice, whole person orientation, coordinated and/or integrated care, quality and safety, enhanced access to care, and payment structures that "recognize the added value provided" (Kellerman & Kirk, 2007, p. 774–775). Although some anecdotal efforts have pursued "healthcare home" as its title, the model around physician-centered care has persisted. Although the basic principle of the medical home is needed and laudable, its focus for directing patient care by medicine at the exclusion of other disciplines, such as advanced practice nurses, is unfortunate. Indeed, there is some evidence in the literature that one purpose of the medical home may be to secure the interests of physicians (see Baron & Cassel, 2008; Dimick, 2008; Fisher, 2008; Robeznieks, 2007; Rogers, 2008; Rubinstein, 2008; Scherger, 2009). We have yet to determine its value to patients as currently proposed under sole physician authority without the broad inclusion of truly interprofessional leadership values and practices. Nevertheless, with its initial flaws, a model that values a healthcare "home" for primary care and care coordination for patients and families is highly needed. Our challenge now is to secure the broadest perspective of patients, communities, and healthcare disciplines. This will be one of the first tasks of doctors of nursing practice working with medicine and other disciplines.

Working Across Generations

As the healthcare workforce becomes more diverse, leaders will have opportunities to work with people not from only a greater variety of disciplinary backgrounds but also across the range of generations. Strauss and Howe (1991, 1997; Howe & Strauss, 2000) reminded us that as a society, we move across time among different groups born at different times, faced with different generational cultural issues, and shaped by different life experiences as a group or generation. They further asserted that there may be cycles of these generational phenomena. We now recognize some general common characteristics in various generational groups. Of course, those commonalities do not represent individuals but do provide a general guide to understand generational perspectives.

Current popular concepts recognize traditionalists, born from 1925 to 1945, who have been socialized to stay in a specific workplace, or even the same position, over an entire career and thus may be resistant to change. Baby boomers, born from 1946 to 1964, are also generally loyal to their work and to their employer. On the other hand, Generation X, born in 1965 to 1980, shows no such loyalty but rather may seek immediate rewards, advances, recognitions, and benefits. Generation Xers are individualists who search for career meaning and purpose. They are not impressed by authority or traditional hierarchical organizations. If they do not get what they seek, they will go somewhere else. We are now beginning to work with Generation Y, who were born prewired for electronic technology. They seek the immediate and customized service that technology has always provided them, and are less willing to see the value of personal sacrifice for an employer (Malleo, 2010). Only recently have we recognized generational characteristics in popular culture, although for some time, sociologists have reminded of social and generational cycles of philosophical and lifetime viewpoints and their associated cultural implications (Strauss & Howe, 1991, 1997). The informed leader will cultivate a background in such sociological and cultural information.

SUCCEEDING WITH REGULATORY ORGANIZATIONS

Within the culture of professional health care is the ever-present heavy hand of regulation. Indeed, health care has become one of the most regulated industries in modern society. Field (2007, p. 2) claimed that healthcare regulation in the United States is broad and disjointed:

> At the federal level there is the Department of Health and Human Services and its many components, including the Centers for Medicare and Medicaid Services (CMS), the Centers for Disease Control and Prevention (CDC), and the Food and Drug Administration (FDA), in addition to the Environmental Protection Agency (EPA), the Occupational Safety and Health Administration (OSHA), and numerous other agencies. In each state there are departments of health, welfare, and insurance. In cities and counties there are municipal health departments. Turning to the private side, there is the Joint Commission on Accreditation of healthcare Organizations (JCAHO), the National Committee on Quality Assurance, and numerous professional boards and societies. . . . New ones are often added with little consideration for those already in place, sometimes resulting in redundancy and conflict.

In addition, there are other specific compliance requirements, such as privacy protections from the Health Insurance Portability and Accountability Act (HIPAA), protection of human subjects in research, health information technology standards, regulations for nondiscrimination, and numerous others. To the leader at any level, these can be daunting. But they cannot be ignored.

Although they appear overwhelming, most accredited healthcare institutions have processes and personnel in place to help the organization sustain compliance with the myriad of regulations. Your job as leader is to assure that such offices and people perform to their fullest function, to support their work, to champion compliance, and to integrate compliance with your own vision as well as quality and performance within your organization.

Beyond the employer, the first level of a regulatory body for American professional nursing practice is the state board of nursing, which takes its authority from the state legislature. Each state in the United States has its own practice act that governs the scope of nursing practice and its own regulatory body, usually called the board of nursing. Practice acts outline the authority, scope, and criteria for licensure. There is considerable range of diversity across the state regulatory boards especially related to advanced practice nursing.

As a leader, it is important to be informed regarding local and state regulations. The critical issues related to autonomy and practice authority, particularly for advanced practice nurses, remain to be resolved. For example, there is a vast range of state regulations regarding prescriptive authority. Although advanced nursing practice has evolved in response to consumer demand and financial issues, the role remains constrained in some areas due to public policy challenges (Furlong & Smith, 2005).

As a leader, build relationships with the regulators, including members of boards of nursing, legislators, and other civic leaders who have influence in health care. Regarding scope of practice, legislators are often heavily influenced by professional organizations, such as the state medical association. It is critical as a transformational leader to be an integral member of the community at large. More change in legislation has happened by personal relationships than by well-written, well-reasoned proposals.

Although unions may not be considered regulatory organizations, they can exert considerable influence on regulations and practices within your organization. Unions represent 14% of all workers in the United States, and 22% of all registered nurses are represented by some labor union (United American Nurses, 2009). The best known is probably the United American Nurses, formed in 1999 as an independent affiliate of the American Nurses Association. Laws related to labor relations in public healthcare facilities vary across states. Generally, employees have the right to organize and bargain collectively, strike, and grieve and arbitrate issues. Employees have the right to advance notice of union activities and intentions and usually preclude supervisors or managers from joining union activities (Ballard, 2008).

Regardless of the regulation load, keep your perspective as the leader. Remember in the fray that such regulations and programs are designed to make your work better. Do not allow yourself to become either buried in overwhelming "stuff," or beguiled by illusions that compliance guarantees human caring. Remember your vision and your purpose to help others to promote health and care for the sick and suffering. You are the guardian of the human processes and the humanity in your organization.

WORKING WITH THE BOARD OF TRUSTEES

Working with the board of trustees of your organization can be one of the most unique and rewarding aspects of your life as a leader. Boards usually include selected members of the community representing a broad range from none to considerable actual experience in health care. Since boards have a fiduciary responsibility to represent the community, there is increasing expectation for responsibility in financial oversight. This requires considerable orientation, training, and preparation for effective service (Evans, 2009; Kazemek, Knecht, & Westfall, 2000; Nadler, 2004; Small, 2000). That is usually the job of the leader of the organization working with the director or president of the board.

During your career as a leader, you may be responsible to recruit or work directly with a board, collaborate with a board, or actually serve on a board (Jumaa, 2008). If you work for a hospital or nonprofit organization, you may work directly with your board of trustees. Nadler (2004, p. 104) boldly observed:

> Everyone knows what most boards have been: gentleman's-club-era relics characterized by ceremony and conformity. And everyone knows what boards should be: seats of challenge and inquiry that add value without meddling and make CEOs more effective but not all-powerful. A board can reach that destination only if it functions as a team.

Nadler (2004, p. 104) further asserted that the high-performance board "is competent, co-ordinated, collegial, and focused on an unambiguous goal. Such entities do not simply evolve; they must be constructed to an exacting blueprint." He further asserted that boards need the right work, the right people, the right agenda, the right information, and the right culture. He also outlined the agenda, norms, beliefs, and values for effective boards.

Some boards are compensated, and others are voluntary. You can benefit from positive personal relationships with board members to influence decision making, resource allocation, and the strategic direction of the organization (Thorman, 2004, p. 381). Each board, and each situation, is unique. If you have the opportunity to recruit members of your board, think strategically. Consider special skills, insights, background, community connections, and personality types (Mycek, 2000). Consider both needs for the make-up of the board itself, but especially the needs of your organization. All members of the board need to care deeply about your organization; loyalty is the prime qualification. If you need fund-raising, identify people who will either make significant donations or have connections with those who may. Be prepared to accommodate a range of types of participation. Mycek (2000) described a board member of a children's hospital who was a major contributor to the board, never attended a board meeting, but was essential to community networking. I served on a board where one member seldom engaged directly in board activities but had a key legislative connection. Be creative in including such board members in activities outside the board meetings, in committee subcommittees, and as well-informed advocates or representatives of your organization to the community at large. Make sure that all board members understand the mission of the organization and tell the same story—your story!

As a leader with stature, you will likely be invited to serve on the board of another agency in your community. Especially in board service, a note should be said to all leaders about conflicts of interest. Conflict of interest occurs when personal or private interests may interfere with professional or public responsibilities or interests. As a leader, at some point, you will be confronted with a potential conflict of interest. It may be the receipt of an inappropriate personal gift or the opportunity to gain personally from a professional or public endeavor. It involves the use of position, power, or influence to gain advantage for self or others, and is seldom with actual malicious intent. Such advantages may be large or small, personal, political, or financial. A conflict of interest may be actual, perceived, or potential (Greenfield, 2008). When you are in the thick of things, it may not always be easy to recognize a conflict of interest. It helps to ask the questions, "If I worked for me, would I think this was appropriate?" or "If this appeared in the newspaper, would it be something I would be proud of?" Then trust your inner voice. Confer with a wise mentor or leader. Sometimes, it is enough to simply disclose the potential conflict of interest publicly so that everyone involved is aware that you have some personal involvement in the issue. Other times, you must remove yourself from the situation, refuse the offer, or decline the opportunity. It may be helpful to consult with legal counsel within your organization if the potential conflict is significant or even ambiguous. If the conflict precludes your service on one board, be assured that other opportunities will come. Whatever your action, ethical response always offers personal peace and potential future opportunities. People notice the ethical leader.

WORKING WITH LAWYERS, LEGISLATORS, AND POLICYMAKERS

The practice and leadership of nursing are integrally related to decisions of law, government, public and private payment organizations, and a variety of other legal entities. Such groups affect standards, practices, and payment for care.

If you serve any time as a leader, you may at some point be involved directly or indirectly in some litigation. When it happens, you realize that you did not learn about this in school; no one talks about it at work; you feel totally unprepared and alone, and you think, "I must be the only one this has ever happened to." It is not true. Because of the discrete, confidential, and often distressing nature of most issues of litigation, few people talk about it. Usually, the issue will have little or nothing to do with you personally, but you may be named because you are in a specific leadership position. Regardless of the situation, the very adversarial nature of such events can be overwhelming and devastating. Seek legal help immediately. Begin with contacting legal counsel within your organization, if such exists. In a position of leadership, you should have already cultivated a positive relationship with your institutional general counsel. If you have a personal issue in the case, seek your own counsel. Remember that the organizational counsel's priority is to protect the corporation, not to protect you personally. If you are called to give a deposition or to testify in some case not related to you, still seek counsel. You need a lawyer to prepare you for giving your testimony. Do not forget the following three simple rules when you are deposed or testifying under oath: (1) listen to the question, (2) answer the question (and only the question), (3) then stop talking. Also remember that most legal cases go on for what seems like forever. You must find a way to live your life alongside the case. Let it unfold, attend to it when required, and continue your best performance as the leader you are.

Most activities in the public arena will not have direct legal implications but rather be related to influencing public policy. Public policy refers specifically to sources of such rules, actions, and decisions specifically from government agencies. Simply stated, policy is the official plan, rules, and decisions regarding how resources are allocated to a specific purpose. Health policy is the "rules, actions, and decisions by government and private bodies—which affect the delivery of health care and the processes by which health care takes place" (Keepnews, 2008, p. 270).

The transformational leader in health care must be fluent in current issues and activities related to health policy. Resources, regulations, and decision making in health care are increasingly influenced by legislative and professional policy. Policy fluency affords the leader the opportunity to provide input and be proactive rather than reactive to measures that affect healthcare organizations. To improve policy literacy, nurse leaders may participate in a number of policy training programs, graduate courses, or studies of information provided by nearly every major healthcare organization.

A long-term member of the U.S. Congress made some helpful observations and advice in communicating with legislators. First, remember your audience. The value of your favorite program may be important to you, but a legislator needs to know "What does it do to strengthen the economy or enhance competitiveness, or provide more jobs?" Show the public benefit of your program. Make your pitch in short, common, and practical terms (Sherwood Boehlert interview, 2006).

To convert your practice, research, or project to policy, observe what kinds of evidence are best accepted by legislators and policymakers and what kinds of projects are funded. Watch for examples of how health policy is developed (Lin, 2004). Identify networks within your community and become part of them. Lewis (2009, p. 125) called these "networks of influence."

Practice-based evidence (Horn & Gassaway, 2007) is a systematic method to provide data directly from what works in practice that is especially useful to influence policymakers. It uses knowledge and practices from frontline caregivers on interdisciplinary teams. It contributes to real stories to provide policymakers with images in reality of policy needs.

Always have your 30-second elevator conversation ready. Practice to yourself no more than three major points of your issue. Prepare an internal script that you can recite, with passion, in any situation. Make it short, clear, and compelling. Then watch and wait for the perfect opportunity. I knew of an influential leader who was prepared. She needed support for a major change initiative from the highest level, the president of the corporation. Without regular access or optimal timing, she simply prepared and waited. She practiced her 30-second approach. She watched and waited. Finally, she coincidentally met the president in an airport security line. When he asked the simple benign question, "How is it going?" She was ready. She literally had about 30 seconds. She did not hesitate; she did not force, mumble, fumble, or whine. She simply repeated the main points she had rehearsed for weeks. She took advantage of the "luck" of the circumstance with supreme preparation. The president responded with interest and intrigue. Soon, she was *invited* to the president's office to share her idea, which eventually culminated in full support for her plan and her inclusion as a trusted professional colleague at the highest level of the institution.

Kerfoot (2008, p. 297) suggested that nurses might also learn from legislators themselves. Create an image, "paint a picture," and "create a sense of magnetism that comes from communicating the compelling story of optimism and hope for the future." Watch the influence of politicians to gain clues about how to gain public interest and loyalty to your position.

HAVING INFLUENCE IN THE LARGER POLITICAL ARENA

Influence is power. It is the capacity to compel change in ideas, action, and results. Having influence is one of the most important and fulfilling gifts of being a leader.

Just as policy is ultimately a decision on how resources are allocated, politics is the distribution of power. Power is what decision is made to use the resources, and political power is who gets to make the decision (Gebbie, 2010). Resources may include time, people, or money. Leadership includes elements of policy and politics. In the larger arena, healthcare leadership may include effective *response* to policy and politics but must also include effective *influence on* policy and politics. Lewis (2006) analyzed the history of the influence and power of medicine on policy. From that tradition, all healthcare disciplines can learn from medicine's example to use ties of association and effective use of positional and personal influence. To be effective as a leader, you must engage in the policy arena and network with other people of influence. A recent report from the Institute of Medicine (2008) reminded healthcare providers to communicate standards, costs, and policy implications to change systems.

It is well recognized that influence on policy requires collaboration and networking across a variety of interests. "Strategic alliances" are described as a way to promote collaboration across organizations to work toward policy-related solutions to common problems. Challenges to such alliances include "commitment versus control," "mutual expectations for performance," "managing relationships," communication, and sustaining stability of the alliances (Zuckerman & Kaluzny, 1991). As leaders in health care increase such alliances, we may expect greater applications of models from business, such as "disruptive innovations" (Huang & Christensen, 2008) and others.

You are likely leading, planning, or even contemplating some extraordinary or innovative project that might be expanded beyond your organization and make a difference to the larger community. At the outset, think larger. Include policymakers on your team. Invite your local government official, state legislator, or even your congressional representative. Become active in understanding and participating in regulatory initiatives. Regulations are most often developed from bad care rather than good works (Mason, 2010). The only way to influence a change is to become involved and to involve policymakers directly in your good work.

Mason (2010) outlined barriers related to policy that restrain the advancement of innovative models of care. They include national position statements (see American Medical Association, 2009) and state regulations that limit the scope of practice of nonphysician providers (see Pearson, 2009). Other barriers include limitations on reimbursement by insurers and payers to nonphysician providers. These barriers are further extended to definitions and credentialing of the medical or health home. In many cases, such restrictions are not necessary for quality and actually interfere with access. Mason (2010) also pointed to a list of nurse-related barriers to policy that supports innovative programs. The list includes "lack of clinical and financial outcome data," limiting reports to descriptions of programs and who are served, and "failure to recognize the mandate to translate research into practice and policy." Another key barrier is the inability to translate or "scale up" creative interventions beyond its local use to larger applications (Mason, 2010).

The United States is currently embroiled in debate regarding national healthcare policy, which is likely to continue. The issues are highly entangled regarding health insurance reform, mandated health insurance coverage, healthcare structures and paradigms such as the medical or health home, education for health professionals, scope of practice and roles of various health professionals, and ongoing issues of cost, access, and quality of health care. Among the most difficult questions are how to promote health promotion and disease prevention initiatives in the face of overwhelming emphasis on acute care and large hospital systems, how to support innovation, how to manage chronic conditions, how to reach rural and underserved populations, among others. These are areas crying most for creative leadership.

Too many nurses opt out of policy discussions. Coming from educational preparation that provided little or no training in policy, and heavily involved in patient care inside the clinical setting, nurses often do not see policy involvement as a priority. Demands of health care now require that nurse leaders join other healthcare leaders to influence and implement policy. As an expert clinician moving to the role of transformational leader, you have the preparation and tools to lead, and you have the social responsibility to influence policy. Mason (2010) reminded, "Society, and nurses themselves, should have higher expectations for what nurses can achieve, and that nurses should be held accountable for not only providing quality direct patient care, but also for healthcare leadership [in policy]."

There is a vast range of opportunities to become involved in making a difference in policy and politics. Speak up and speak out on institutional and public policy. In your role as expert, communicate on specific issues with policymakers; communicate in public forums through both traditional media and emerging social media; connect and partner with other healthcare leaders. Think creatively about influencing policy from a new perspective. For example, every state land-grant institution has an agricultural extension service that provides valuable public information. What would happen if we had a health information extension service? Just a thought—what would be the policy implications? Finally, seek and take opportunities to serve on corporate boards, hospital boards, boards of health, and nonprofit organizational boards at the local, state, and national levels. Think about running for office in your local area, including boards of health, city council, or state legislature. Who knows where it will lead you, and where you will lead? Get your message to the public.

Become sensitive to your role in "public leadership" (Kellerman & Webster, 2001, p. 485). Learn from others, read widely, and study the biographies of great public leaders. Join and participate actively in national professional organizations. Collaborate broadly at every opportunity. Empower others to expand the influence of your own leadership. Think locally, nationally, and globally. Transformational leaders support others to "transcend their own self-interest" and to grow. They generate intellectual stimulation and emotional commitment (Weston, 2008). They recognize and promote the talent of others. They transcend the bureaucracy of their environments to raise all workers to higher levels. They are aware of their own image and communicate effectively (Sullivan, 2004).

TRANSFORMING PRACTICE AND POLICY IN THE LARGER COMMUNITY

Regardless of your practice or leadership role, your work environment includes the community beyond your institution. Just as individuals must lead from a collaborative interprofessional perspective, organizations within communities are interdependent and function best within the larger community perspective. There is a variety of stimulating ways to serve.

As you continue your journey as a transformational leader, you will have opportunities to work with a variety of community agencies, including nonprofit organizations. Indeed, as a respected community leader, you may be invited to serve on the board of directors of a nonprofit organization. It is important to understand the general characteristics of nonprofit organizations. Most nonprofit organizations function under a specific mission. "They rally under the banner of a particular cause" (Rangan, 2004, p. 112) such as homelessness or other underserved populations. Nonprofit organizations are particularly mission driven. Rangan (2004, p. 114) explained, "After all, the mission is what inspires founders to create the organization, and it draws board members, staff, donors, and volunteers to become involved, What's more, the founders often deliberately ensure that their original vision is embraced by the next generation of leaders." Non-profit organizations usually depend heavily on a financial base laid by private donations and grants. Thus, nonprofit organizations are closely tied to the community in which they reside, and the contribution of board members usually focuses on helping to secure donors.

Your experience with strategic planning and outcomes evaluation can be especially helpful if you serve with a nonprofit organization or any other community agency. Rangan (2004) asserted that although most nonprofit organizations are strong on mission, they are less able in translating the mission statement to an operational mission and strategy process. Because they are usually single-mission focused, there is little need to identify integration of specific programs. An operational mission can bring quantitative measurement and evaluation to the "lofty" inspiring mission. Then, specific objectives and strategies can be implemented.

Preparing to Influence

The messages of this book have been directed to expert clinicians who are launching to lead. As you think about your own preparation to influence, consider advanced preparation beyond the terminal degree. Take advantage of opportunities to engage in larger arenas where you might interact with leaders from all disciplines. Make a commitment to never stop learning or growing.

Several formal leadership development programs are designed to help you build on your current preparation and experience to enhance your influence. Some of these were mentioned in Chapter 2. Only a few will be described briefly here as examples. The Wharton Nursing Leaders Program is directed toward high-level nursing leaders preparing for the role of chief nursing officer of a healthcare organization. The program addresses the complexity of leadership in health care, strategic planning, resource management, decision making, and team building (Wharton Executive Education, 2010). The Harvard Business School (2010) offers several short- and long-term programs in leadership development including programs in managing health care delivery.

If you aspire leadership in higher education, many programs and fellowships are offered by the American Association of Colleges of Nursing (2010) and the American Council on Education (2010). The Higher Education Resource Services (2010) also provides short-term residence programs specifically for women aspiring for higher education leadership. These are located at Bryn Mawr, PA, and Denver, CO. The Center for Creative Leadership (2010) also offers a range of programs for women and members of racial minorities in management positions. Specific to healthcare and nursing leadership, among the best known programs is the Robert Wood Johnson (2010) Executive Nurse Fellows program. Several creative endeavors to promote leadership development in specific areas offer programs, consulting, or information. For example, the Robert Wood Johnson Foundation combined with the Kellogg Foundation to support the National Center for Healthcare Leadership that has created Leadership Excellence Networks, which is a platform for healthcare systems to share best practices in leadership development (Davidson, Griffith, Sinioris, & Carreon, 2005). Many highly reputable university business schools offer executive development programs. Seek out and participate in programs that may be offered at your own institution. A simple search and talking with other leaders will produce a large variety of programs and opportunities. The cost of such programs has a wide range. Choose the best and make the case at your organization for the return on their investment in your preparation and networking as a leader. Negotiation for your preparation is instructive in itself to refine skills to negotiate ideas, projects, and changes related to your larger stewardship as a leader.

By the same token, generativity is an important part of your stewardship as a leader. That includes the development of others and the creation of a learning organization. Supporting people in formal leadership development programs is not only helpful to the individual, but also powerful in the message of support for advancement and excellence in your organization, and it attracts useful networks to your work. Your influence is also critical to the next generation of leaders. Wise influence from a perspective of generativity includes succession planning at all levels. Health care has been behind other industries in succession planning in leadership (Blouin, McDonagh, Neistadt, & Helfand, 2006; Carriere, Muise, Cummings, & Newburn-Cook, 2009). Influence in succession planning requires vision, "commitment, vigilance, and engagement" (Cadmus, 2006) not only within your own job or agency but also with a view across the entire discipline and healthcare workforce.

Leading to Transform

It is important to understand various levels of influence in leadership. Within your healthcare organization, the primary goal is to support those who deliver direct care for the people or populations served by the agency. At higher levels of state, regional, or national service, your power is to influence regulations, policy, and resources. You make decisions regarding how money is allocated and for what services. At the international level, you have the influence to make recommendations for healthcare policy across nations.

Cook (2001) developed a model for leadership reflecting four elements of levels of the leadership style of the clinician leader: experience, understanding, internal environment (personal values and beliefs), and external environment. She further proposed an ascending order of style that ultimately moves from transformational to what she calls renaissance leadership that operates in the realm of holistic care, and is characterized by empowering relationships among providers and patients. As a clinical leader, you are prepared to transform practice. You also have the professional responsibility to transform policy in the larger community to reflect the best of practice.

Opportunities to advance your influence abound throughout the world. Do not limit yourself. At the international level, you can affect policy for improved health care across the world. Global issues call for leadership to solve issues of worldwide shortages of healthcare professionals, especially nurses (Oulton, 2006), and other important issues of international disaster and humanitarian services (Negus, Brown, & Konoske, 2010). Become acquainted with and involved in international efforts. The International Council of Nurses is a federation of national nursing organizations from 129 countries, representing over 13 million nurses throughout the world. One of its current initiatives is to address policy and planning related to the severe nursing worldwide shortage (Oulton, 2006). How might you become involved?

International or global influence may take the form of involvement at the global level, as with the issues of the World Health Organization or International Council of Nurses, or may take a more local foreign partnership perspective by collaborating on some specific issues with international partners. It is a fine art, and well worth it, to work with partners in another country. It opens your vision and your view to new perspectives on old problems. You gain insights into cultural influences. You learn new perspectives of time. You discover different priorities. When the needs of your partner in a developing country may be as basic as water sanitation, you learn about different resources. And you share work across different technologies.

Also, in humanitarian and disaster health care, the work of hospital ships has attracted increased recent attention (Negus et al., 2010). This is another area that will continue to provide opportunities for leaders in the future.

Today, leaders and managers who exhibit characteristics of transformational leadership hold more central positions in organizational networks of influence, and their direct reports are more influential in informal organizational networks (Bono & Anderson, 2005). In other words, transformational leaders tend to expand their influence and the influence of those whom they lead.

As you make your own transformation from expert clinician to transformational leader, especially with the terminal degree and credential for leadership, you enter a world of expectations. The world needs your expertise and preparation to improve health care. Do not forget what you have learned about clinical scholarship. It is your obligation as a leader to contribute to the discipline. That means writing and publication. In order for academic publication in health care to have any meaning or application, it must be grounded in clinical practice. That is precisely why clinical scholarship must be part of your stewardship as a leader. Take time to reflect on your practice and your leadership. Watch for influential things you are doing that might make a difference for someone else in a similar situation. Make friends with someone in an academic setting and work together to share your work with the discipline. Part of your responsibility as a leader is to share with the discipline. Provide opportunities for your staff to become involved in research or demonstration projects in meaningful ways, and be sure that their contribution is noted appropriately. You are part of something greater than your organization; help your staff to see that too. The world needs your influence, and you will be amazed at your ability to make a difference.

Among the risks of breaking open the doors to find your own place as a transformational leader are discouragement when the cold water of reality splashes back in your face. I call it the Moses-off-the-mountain syndrome. You become singularly informed, educated, and impassioned. Then you unveil your latest creation of ideas, and no one gets on board. It does not work. Review, regroup, and try again.

Leading is lonely, but you have the capacity to continue toward your vision. Feed those who understand where you are going. Some days, you simply need to solve a problem. Sometimes, you just need smart quick action and results. Other times, you need to spread innovations and new ways of thinking and acting.

When something great is happening in one part of your organization, it is sometimes difficult to spread the word and even more challenging to spread the positive action. Massoud, Nielsen, Nolan, Schall, and Sevin (2006) called this a "framework for spread" where we need a system to accelerate or elevate improvement simply by getting changes to move across the organization. Others call it diffusion of innovation (Rogers, 2003). It sometimes requires an entire change of culture to accept innovation as a way of living and serving. When you get frustrated with the slow rate of change, remember the following guidelines to promote diffusion of innovation. First, the innovation must be perceived as better than what folks are already doing, so you have some selling to do. Second, you need a reliable source or channel of communication to spread the news that the new idea is better. Third, give folks a little time to learn about the innovation, to participate in the decision, and to implement change. Make your institution a place of learning (Newhouse & Melnyk, 2009). Finally, pay attention to the general culture and other leaders of your community to be sure you have their support (Weston, 2008).

One author reflected on the characteristics of a successful leader. The list is simple but central to the transformational leader:

1. Choose to lead.
2. Be the person others choose to follow.
3. Provide vision for the future.
4. Provide inspiration.
5. Make other people feel important and appreciated.
6. Live your values. Behave ethically.
7. Set the pace through your expectations and example.
8. Establish an environment of continuous improvement.
9. Provide opportunities for people to grow, both personally and professionally.
10. Care and act with compassion (Heathfield, n.d.).

You have prepared and you cultivated the characteristics and habits of a transformational leader. You are able to function as a leader in a broad range of contexts and you understand the power of culture. You embrace challenge. You know when to sustain tradition and when to be bold with innovation. You build and nurture your team. You understand economics and finance. You have prepared to become the leader the world needs.

You will have the greatest positive influence as a transformational leader if you are authentic and speak the truth. Authenticity means that you know and understand yourself. You are aware of your influence and effects on others. You are able to take the perspective of another. You are aware of your own values and strengths, and you are able to recognize the values and strengths of others. You are sensitive to the context in which you work and you are "confident, hopeful, optimistic, resilient, and of high moral character" (Avolio, Gardner, Walumbwa, Luthans, & May, 2004, p. 804). People can believe you and count on you, and they want to work with you and for you. You live your values. If you feel like you are not this person described, you can be. You can practice every day. Reflect on your progress at the end of the day, identifying what was the best part of each day. You bring the credibility of experience in expert clinical practice to the joyful places you create as environments for healing.

> . . . For what you are . . . yet more for what you are going to be . . . not so much for your realities as for your ideals. I pray for your desires that they may be great, rather than for your satisfactions, which may be so hazardously little. . . . Not always shall you be what you are now. You are going forward toward something great. And I am on the way with you.
>
> – *Carl Sandburg*

REFERENCES

American Association of Colleges of Nursing. (2010). *American Association of Colleges of Nursing: Advancing higher education in nursing*. Retrieved February 2, 2010, from http://www.aacn.nche.edu/

American Council on Education (ACE). (2010). *American Council on Education.* Retrieved February 2, 2010, from http://www.acenet.edu/AM/Template.cfm?Section=Home

American Medical Association (AMA). (2009, October). *Scope of practice data series.* Chicago: AMA.

Associated Press. (2010). Lowes workers offered Cleveland Clinic heart care. *Business Week.* Retrieved February 19, 2010, from http://www.businessweek.com/ap/financialnews/D9DTVOBG3/htm

Avolio, B. J., Gardner, W. L., Walumbwa, F. O., Luthans, F., & May, D. R. (2004). Unlocking the mask: A look at the process by which authentic leaders impact follower attitudes and behaviors. *Leadership Quarterly, 15,* 801–823.

Ballard, K. A. (2008). Collective bargaining and unions. In H. R. Feldman, M. Jaffe-Ruiz, M. L. McClure, M. J. Greenberg, & T. D. Smith (Eds.), *Nursing leadership: A concise encyclopedia* (pp. 116–117). New York: Springer.

Baron, R. J., & Cassel, C. K. (2008). 21st-century primary care: New physician roles need new payment models. *Journal of the American Medical Association, 299*(13), 1595–1597.

Begun, J. W., & Kaissi, A. (2004). Uncertainty in health care environments: Myth or reality? *Health Care Management Review, 29*(1), 31–39.

Blouin, A. S., McDonagh, K. J., Neistadt, A. M., & Helfand, B. (2006). Leading tomorrow's healthcare organizations: Strategies and tactics for effective succession planning. *Journal of Nursing Administration, 36*(6), 325–330.

Bono, J. E., & Anderson, M. H. (2005). The advice and influence networks of transformational leaders. *Journal of Applied Psychology, 90*(6), 1306–1314.

Brazil, K., MacLeod, S., & Guest, B. (2002). Collaborative practice: A strategy to improve the relevance of health services research. *Healthcare Management Forum, 15*(3), 18–24.

Burnett, S. (2005). Knowledge support for interdisciplinary models of healthcare delivery: A study of knowledge needs and roles in managed clinical networks. *Health Informatics Journal 11*(2), 146–160.

Cadmus, E. (2006). Succession planning: Multilevel organizational strategies for the new workforce. *Journal of Nursing Administration, 36*(6), 298–303.

Carriere, B. K., Muise, M., Cummings, G., & Newburn-Cook, C. (2009). Healthcare succession planning: An integrative review. *Journal of Nursing Administration, 39*(12), 548–555.

Center for Creative Leadership (CCL). (2010). *Center for creative leadership.* Retrieved February 2, 2010, from http://www.ccl.org/leadership/about/index.aspx

Cook, M. J. (2001). The renaissance of clinical leadership. *International Nursing Review, 48,* 38–46.

Cooper, R. A. (2007). New directions for nurse practitioners and physician assistants in the era of physician shortages. *Academic Medicine, 82*(9), 827–828.

Davidson, P. L., Griffith, J. R., Sinioris, M., & Carreon, D. (2005, 20 November). Evidence-based leadership development for improving organizational performance. *Joint Commission Journal on Quality and Patient Safety,* 1–31.

Dillon, P. M., Noble, K. A., & Kaplan, L. (2009). Simulation as a means to foster collaborative interdisciplinary education. *Nursing Education perspectives, 30*(2), 87–90.

Dimick, C. (2008). Home sweet medical home: Can a new care model save family medicine? *Journal of the American Health Information Management Association, 79*(8), 24–28.

Evans, M. (2009). Raising the bar for boards. *Modern health care, 39*(9), 1, 6–7, 16.

Feinberg, P. (2009, Fall). Q and Anderson: Kenneth Chenault on leadership. *Assets: UCLA Anderson School of Management,* 8–9.

Field, R. I. (2007). *Health care regulation in America: Complexity, confrontation, and compromise.* Oxford, England: Oxford University Press.

Fisher, E. S. (2008). Building a medical neighborhood for the medical home. *New England Journal of Medicine, 359*(12), 1202–1205.

Friedman, T. L. (2005). *The world is flat: A brief history of the twenty-first century.* New York: Farrar, Strauss, & Giroux.

Furlong, E., & Smith, R. (2005). Advanced nursing practice: Policy, education and role development. *Journal of Clinical Nursing, 14*(9), 1059–1066.

Gebbie, K. M. (2010, January). *Preparing doctoral students for health policy leadership.* Paper presented at the meetings of the American Association of Colleges of Nursing, Captiva Island, FL.

Greenfield, D. (2008). Conflict of interest. In H. R. Feldman, M. Jaffe-Ruiz, M. L. McClure, M. J. Greenberg, & T. D. Smith (Eds.), *Nursing leadership: A concise encyclopedia* (pp. 125–128). New York: Springer.

Harvard Business School (HBS). (2010). *Executive education: Managing healthcare delivery.* Retrieved February 2, 2010, from http://www.exed.hbs.edu/programs/mhcd/

Heathfield, S. M. (n. d.). *Leadership vision.* Retrieved August 20, 2009, from http://humanresources.about.com/od/leadership/a/leader_vision.htm

Hegarty, J., Walsh, E., Condon, C., & Sweeney, J. (2009). The undergraduate education of nurses: Looking to the future. *International Journal of Nursing Education Scholarship, 6*(1), 17.

Higher Education Resource Services (HERS). (2010). *Higher Education Resource Services.* Retrieved February 2, 2010, from http://www.hersnet.org/

Horn, S. D., & Gassaway, J. (2007). Practice-based evidence study design for comparative effectiveness research. *Medical Care, 45*(10), S50–S57.

Howe, N., & Strauss, W. (2000). *Millennial rising: The next generation.* New York: Random House.

Huang, J., & Christensen, C. M. (2008). Disruptive innovation in health care delivery: A framework for business-model innovation. *Health Affairs, 27*(5), 1329–1335.

Institute of Medicine (IOM). (2008). *Knowing what works in health care: A roadmap for the nation.* Washington, D.C.: National Academies Press.

Jumaa, M. O. (2008). The F.E.E.L. good factors in nursing leadership at board level through work-based learning. *Journal of Nursing Management, 16,* 992–999.

Kazemek, E. A., Knecht, P. R., & Westfall, B. G. (2000). Effective boards: Working smarter to meet the challenge. *Trustee, 53*(5), 1, 18–23.

Keepnews, D. M. (2008). Health policy. In H. R. Feldman, M. Jaffe-Ruiz, M. L. McClure, M. J. Greenberg, & T. D. Smith (Eds.), *Nursing leadership: A concise encyclopedia* (pp. 269–273). New York: Springer.

Kellerman, B., & Webster, S. W. (2001). The recent literature on public leadership reviewed and considered. *The Leadership Quarterly, 12,* 485–514.

Kellerman, R., & Kirk, L. (2007, 15 September). Principles of the patient-centered medical home. *American Family Physician, 76*(6), 774–776.

Kerfott, K. M. (2008). Leadership and learning from the politicians. *Urologic Nursing, 28*(4), 297–298.

Lewis, J. M. (2006). Being around and knowing the players: Networks of influence in health policy. *Social Science & Medicine, 62*(9), 2125–2136.

Lewis, J. M. (2009). Understanding policy influence and the public health agenda. *New South Wales Public Health Bulletin, 20*(7–8), 125–129.

Lin, V. (2004). From public health research to health promotion policy: One the 10 major contradictions. *Society of Preventive Medicine, 49*(3), 179–184.

Malleo, C. (2010). Each generation brings strengths, knowledge to nursing field: A nurse's journal. Plain Dealer guest column. *Everything Cleveland.* Retrieved February 15, 2010, from http://blog.cleveland.com/health_impact/print.html?entry=/2010/02/ea

Margalit, R., Thompson, S., Visovsky, C., Geske, J., Collier, D., Birk, T., & Paulman, P. (2009). From professional silos to interprofessional education: Ca mpuswide fouc on quality of care. *Quality Management & Health Care, 18*(3), 165–173.

Mason, D. (2010, 28 January). *Nursing's visibility in the national health care reform agenda.* Paper presented at the meetings of the American Association of Colleges of Nursing Doctoral Education Conference, Captiva Island, FL.

Massoud, M. R., Nielsen, G. A., Nolan, K., Schall, M. W., & Sevin, C. (2006). *From local improvements to system-wide change. IHI Innovation Series white paper.* Cambridge, MA: Institute for Healthcare Improvement.

Mycek, S. (2000). The right fit: Recruiting for your board. *Trustee, 53*(8), 1, 12–15.

Nadler, D. A. (2004, May). Building better boards. *Harvard Business Review, 82*(5), 102–111.

Negus, T. L., Brown, C. J., & Konoske, P. (2010). Determining medical staff requirements for humanitarian assistance missions. *Military Medicine, 175*(1), 1–6.

Newhouse, R. P., & Melnyk, B. M. (2009). Nursing's role in engineering a learning healthcare system. *Journal of Nursing Administration, 39*(6), 260–262.

O'Neil, E. (2009). Four factors that guarantee health care change. *Journal of Professional Nursing, 25*(6), 317–321.

Oulton, J. A. (2006). The global nursing shortage: An overview of issues and actions. *Policy & Politics in Nursing Practice, 7*(3 Suppl.), 34S–39S.

Pearson, L. J. (2009). The Pearson report. *American Journal for Nurse Practitioners, 13*(2), 8–82.

Prince, R. E. C. (2009). Social perspective-taking: A multi-dimensional approach. *Harvard Graduate School of Education Usable Knowledge.* Retrieved February 19, 2010, from http://www.uknow.gse.harvard.edu/teaching/TC104-607.html

Rangan, V. K. (2004, March). Lofty missions, down-to-earth plans. *Harvard Business Review, 82*(3), 112–119.

Reese, c. E., Jeffries, P. R., & Engum, S. A. (2010) Learning together: Using simulations to develop nursing and medical student collaboration. *Nursing Education Perspectives,31*(1), 33-37.

Robert Wood Johnson (RWJ). (2010). *Robert Wood Johnson executive nurse fellows program.* Retrieved February 2, 2010, from http://futurehealth.ucsf.edu/Public/Leadership-Programs/Home.aspx?pid=34

Robeznieks, A. (2007). Of primary importance: Primary-care physicians seek to legitimize the "medical home" concept to improve quality, costs—but will insurers buy it? *Modern Health Care, 37*(45), 1, 6–7.

Robinson, K. M., & Reinhard, S. C. (2009). Looking ahead in long-term care: The next 50 years. *Nursing Clinics of North America, 44*(2), 253–262.

Rogers, E. M. (2003). *Diffusion of innovations* (5ᵗʰ ed.). New York City: Free Press.

Rogers, J. C. (2008). The patient-centered medical home movement: Promise and peril for family medicine. *Journal of the American Board of Family Medicine, 21*(5), 370–374.

Rubinstein, H. G. (2008). Medical homes: The prescription to save primary care? *America's Health Insurance Plans Coverage, 49*(1), 44–47.

Rudavsky, R., & Mehrotra, A. (2010). Sociodemographic characteristics of communities served by retail clinics. *Journal of the American Board of Family Medicine, 23*(1), 42–48.

Scherger, J. E. (2009). Future vision: Is family medicine ready for patient-directed care? *Family Medicine, 41*(4), 285–288.

Sherwood Boehlert interview. (2006). Explaining science to power: Make it simple, make it pay. *Science, 314*(5803), 1228–1229.

Shortell, S. M. (n. d.). *Integrated health systems: Promise and performance.* Berkeley, CA: UCB.

Shortell, S. M., Gillies, R. R., Anderson, D. A., Erickson, K. M., & Mitchell, J. B. (2000). *Remaking health care in America: The evolution of organized delivery systems* (2ⁿᵈ ed.). San Francisco: Jossey-Bass.

Sia, C., Tonniges, T. F., Osterhus, E., & Taba, S. (2004). History of the medical home concept. *Pediatrics, 113*(5 Suppl.), 1473–1478.

Small, J. E. (2000). Making boards more effective: In too many cases, boards of trustees ore "incompetent groups of competent people." *Health Progress, 81*(3), 2–32.

Steinbrook, R. (2009). Easing the shortage in adult primary care: Is it all about money? *New England Journal of Medicine, 360*(26), 2696–2699.

Stewart, J., Stansfield, K., & Tapp, D. (2004). Clinical nurses' understanding of autonomy: Accomplishing patient goals through interdependent practice. *Journal of Nursing Administration, 34*(10), 443–450.

Strauss, W., & Howe, N. (1991). *Generations: The history of America's future 1584–2069.* New York: William Morrow.

Strauss, W., & Howe, N. (1997). *The fourth turning: What the cycles of history tell us about America's next rendezvous with destiny.* New York: Broadway.

Sullivan, E. J. (2004). *Becoming influential: A guide for nurses.* Upper Saddle River, NJ: Pearson.

Thomas, M., & Hynes, C. (2009). The times they are a changin'. *Journal of Nursing Management, 17*(5), 523–531.

Thorman, K. E. (2004). Nursing leadership in the boardroom. *Journal of Obstetrical, Gynecological, & Neonatal Nursing, 33*(3), 381–387.

United American Nurses (UAN). (2009, March). *RN unionization in comparison.* Retrieved August 25, 2009, from http://www.uannurse.org/research/pdfs/Registered-Nurse-Unionization.pdf

Weston, M. J. (2008, August). Transformational leadership at a national perspective. *Nurse Leader, 6*(4), 38–40, 45.

Wharton Executive Education. (2010). *Wharton nursing leaders program.* Retrieved January 31, 2010, from http://executiveeducation.wharton.upenn.edu/open-enrollment/health-ca

Yoder-Wise, P. S. (2007). Key forecasts shaping nursing's perfect storm. *Nursing Administration Quarterly, 31*(2), 115–119.

Zuckerman, H. S., & Kaluzny, A. D. (1991). Strategic alliances in health care: The challenges of cooperation. *Frontier Health Services Management, 7*(3), 3–23, 35.

APPENDIX

Classic Books for the Library of the Transformational Leader

The transformational leader reads widely and is informed, interested, and engaged in issues of health care, science, the arts, history, biography, current events, and popular culture. The transformational leader reads regularly from professional journals in medicine, nursing, and other healthcare disciplines, as well as business and the biological, physical, and social sciences. Following is a list of classic books on leadership, life, and health care:

Abshire, D. M. (2004). *The grade and power of civility: Commitment and tolerance in the American experience.* Kalamazoo, MI: Fetzer Institute.

Ashley, J. A. (1976). *Hospitals, paternalism, and the role of the nurse.* New York, NY: Teachers College Press.

Babcock, L., & Laschever, S. (2007). *Women don't ask: The high cost of avoiding negotiation—and positive strategies for change.* New York: Bantam.

Badaracco, J. L., Jr. (2002). *Leading quietly.* Boston: Harvard Business School Press.

Baker, N. B. (1952). *Cyclone in calico: The story of Mary Ann Bickerdyke.* Boston: Little, Brown, & Company.

Barnard, C. I. (1938). *The functions of the executive.* Cambridge, MA: Harvard University Press.

Bass, B. M. (1985). *Leadership and performance beyond expectations.* New York: Free Press.

Bass, B. M., & Riggio, R. E. (2006). *Transformational leadership.* 2nd Ed. Mahwah, NJ: Lawrence Erlbaum.

Bennis, W. (2000). *Managing the dream: Reflections on leadership and change.* New York: Perseus.

Bennis, W. (2002). *Geeks and geezers.* Boston: Harvard Business School Press.

Bennis, W. (2003). *On becoming a leader: The leadership classic.* New York: Basic Books.

Ben-Shahar, T. (2007). *Happier: Learn the secrets to daily joy and lasting fulfillment.* New York: McGraw-Hill.

Bennis, W., Spreitzer, G. M., & Cummings, T. (2001). *The future of leadership: Today's top leadership thinkers speak to tomorrow's leaders.* San Francisco: John Wiley & Sons.

Berry, L. L. (1999). *Discovering the soul of service.* New York: Free Press.

Blake, R., & Mouton, J. (1978). *The new managerial grid.* Houston, TX: Gulf.

Bolman, L. G., & Deal, T. E. (2001). *Leading with soul: An uncommon journey of spirit.* San Francisco: John Wiley.

Bolman, L. G., & Deal, T. F. (1991). *Reframing organizations: Artistry, choice, and leadership*. San Francisco: Jossey-Bass.

Bossidy, L., & Charan, R. (2002). *Execution: The discipline of getting things done*. New York: Crown.

Brown, J., & Duguid, P. (2002). *The social life of information*. Boston: Harvard Business School Press.

Bryant, J. H. (2009). *Love leadership: The new way to lead in a fear-based world*. San Francisco: Jossey-Bass.

Buckingham, M., & Coffman, C. (1999). *First, break all the rules: What the world's greatest managers do differently*. New York: Simon & Schuster.

Burns, J. M. (1978). *Leadership*. New York: HarperCollins.

Burns, J. M. (2003). *Transforming leadership: The pursuit of happiness*. New York: Atlantic Monthly Press.

Capra, F. (1982). *The turning point*. Toronto: Bantam.

Capra, F. (1997). *The web of life: A new synthesis of mind and matter*. London: HarperCollins.

Cialdini, R. B. (2007). *Influence: The psychology of persuasion*. New York: William Morrow.

Cilliers, P. (1998). *Complexity and postmodernism: Understanding complex systems*. London: Routledge.

Clawson, J. G. (1999). *Level three leadership: Getting below the surface*. Upper Saddle River, NJ: Prentice-Hall.

Cochlan, G. (2008). *Love leadership: What the world needs now*. New York: New Voices Press.

Collins, J. (2001). *Good to great*. New York: HarperCollins.

Covey, S. R. (1989). *The 7 habits of highly effective people: Powerful lessons in personal change*. New York: Simon & Schuster.

Covey, S. R. (2004). *The eighth habit: From effectiveness to greatness*. New York: Simon & Schuster.

De Pree, M. (2004). *Leadership is an art*. New York: Doubleday.

Diamond, J. (1997). *Guns, germs, and steel: The fates of human societies*. New York: W. W. Norton.

Drucker, P. (1996). *The leader of the future*. San Francisco: Jossey-Bass.

Drucker, P. F. (2006). *The effective executive: The definitive guide to getting the right things done*. New York: HarperCollins.

Drucker, P. F. (2008). *The essential Drucker: The best of sixty years of Peter Drucker's essential writings on management*. Collins.

Duck, J. D. (2001). *The change monster*. New York: Crown.

Fairman, J. (2008) *Making room in the clinic: Nurse practitioners and the evolution of modern health care*. Princeton, NJ: Rutgers University Press.

Feldman, H. R., Jaffe-Ruiz, M., McClure, M. L., Greenberg, M. J., & Smith, T. D. (Eds.). (2008). *Nursing leadership: A concise encyclopedia*. New York: Springer.

Feldman, H. R., & Lewenson, S. B. (2000). *Nurses in the political arena: The public face of nursing*. New York: Springer.

Fiedler, F. E. (1967). *A theory of leadership effectiveness*. New York: Harper & Row.

Finney, M. (2002). *In the face of uncertainty: 25 top leaders speak out*. New York: American Management Association.

Foster, J. (2001). *Ideaship: How to get ideas flowing in your workplace*. San Francisco: Berrett-Koehler.

Foster, R., & Kaplan S. (2001). *Creative destruction.* New York: Currency.

Fox, J. J. (2000). *How to become a rainmaker: The rules for getting and keeping customers and clients.* New York: Hyperion.

Friedman, T. L. (2005). *The world is flat: A brief history of the twenty-first century.* New York: Farrar, Strauss, & Giroux.

Gardner, H. (2004). *Changing minds: The art and science of changing our own and other people's minds.* Boston: Harvard Business School Press.

Gardner, J. W. (1989). *On leadership.* New York: HarperCollins.

Gawande, A. (2007). *Better: A surgeon's notes on performance.* New York: Henry Holt.

George, B. (2003). *Authentic leadership: Rediscovering the secrets to creating lasting value.* San Francisco: Jossey-Bass.

Gladwell, M. (2002). *The tipping point: How little things can make a big difference.* New York: Little, Brown, & Co.

Gladwell, M. (2009). *Outliers: The story of success.* New York: Little, Brown, & Co.

Gleick, J. (1987). *Chaos: Making a new science.* New York: Penguin.

Goad, T. W. (2002). *Information literacy and workplace performance.* Westport, CT: Quorum Books.

Goleman, D. (1995). *Emotional intelligence.* New York: Bantam.

Goleman, D. (2006). *Emotional intelligence: Why it can matter more than IQ.* New York: Bantam.

Goleman, D., McKee, A., & Boyatzis, R. E. (2002). *Primal leadership: Realizing the power of emotional intelligence.* Boston: Harvard Business School Press.

Gordon, S. (2005). *Nursing against the odds.* New York: Cornell University Press.

Graham, K. (1998). *Personal history.* New York: Vintage Books.

Green, L., & Kreuter, M. (2005). *Health promotion planning: An educational and ecological approach.* Mountain View, CA: Mayfield.

Greene, R., & Elffers, J. (1998). *The 48 laws of power.* New York: Viking.

Greenleaf, R. (1977). *Servant leadership.* Maywah, NJ: Paulist Press.

Greenleaf, R., Spears, L. C., & Covey, S. R. (2002). *Servant leadership: A journey into the nature of legitimate power and greatness.* 25th Anniversary edition. Mahwah, NJ: Paulist Press.

Greenleaf, R. K. (2002). *Servant leadership: A journey into the nature of legitimate power and greatness.* Mahwah, NJ: Paulist Press.

Halpern, B. L., & Lubar, K. (2003). *Leadership presence: Dramatic techniques to reach out, motivate, and inspire.* New York: Gotham.

Harwell, R. B. (Ed.) (1959). *Kate: The journal of a confederate nurse.* Baton Rouge, LA: Louisiana State University Press.

Heifetz, R. A., & Linsky, M. (2002). *Leadership on the line.* Boston: Harvard Business School Press.

Henry, B., Arndt, C., Di Vincenti, M., & Marriner-Tomey, A. (1989). *Dimensions of nursing administration: Theory, research, education, practice.* Boston: Blackwell.

Hersey, P., & Blanchard, K. H. (1977). *The management of organizational behavior.* Upper Saddle River, NJ: Pearson Education.

Hersey, P., Blanchard, K., & Johnson, D. (2008). *Management of organizational behavior: Leading human resources* (9th ed.). Upper Saddle River, NJ: Pearson Education.

Herzberg, F. (1966). *Work and the nature of man.* New York: World Publishing.

Houser, B. P., & Player, K. N. (2004). *Pivotal moments in nursing: Leaders who changed the path of a profession.* Indianapolis, IN: Sigma Theta Tau International.

Hughes, R., Ginnett, R. C., & Curphy, G. C. (2001). *Leadership: Enhancing the lessons of experience.* New York: McGraw-Hill.

Institute of Medicine. (2000). *To err is human: Building a safer health system.* Washington, D.C.: National Academies Press.

Institute of Medicine. (2001). *Crossing the quality chasm: A new health system for the 21ˢᵗ century.* Washington, D.C.: National Academies Press.

Institute of Medicine. (2003). *Health professions education: A bridge to quality.* Washington, D.C.: National Academies Press.

Jaworski, J. (1998). *Synchronicity: The inner path of leadership.* San Francisco: Berrett-Koehler.

Johnson, S. (1998). *Who moved my cheese?* New York: G. P. Putnam's Sons.

Johnson, S. (2006). *The ghost map: The story of London's most terrifying epidemic—and how it changed science, cities, and the modern world.* New York: Riverhead.

Kao, J. (1996). *Jamming: The art and discipline of business creativity.* New York, NY: HarperBusiness.

Kegan, R. (1982). *The evolving self.* Boston: Harvard University Press.

Kegan, R., & Lahey, L. L. (2002). *How the way we talk can change the way we work: Seven languages for transformation.* San Francisco: Jossey-Bass.

Kelley, T., & Littman, J. (2001). *The art of innovation.* New York: Doubleday.

Klein, G. (2004). *The power of intuition: How to use your gut feelings to make better decisions at work.* New York: Doubleday.

Koegel, T. J. (2007). *The exceptional presenter.* Austin, TX: Greenleaf Book Group.

Kotter, J. P. (1996). *Leading change.* Boston: Harvard Business School Press.

Kotter, J. P. (1999). *On what leaders really do.* Boston: Free Press.

Kouzes, J. M., & Posner, B. Z. (2007). *The leadership challenge* (4ᵗʰ ed.). New York: Jossey-Bass.

Kovner, A. R., Fine, D. J., & D'Aquila, R. (2009). *Evidence-based management in health care.* Chicago: Health Administration Press.

Lansing, A. (1959). *Endurance: Shackleton's incredible voyage.* New York: Carroll & Graf.

Lawrence, D. (2002). *From chaos to care: The promise of team-based medicine.* Cambridge, MA: Perseus.

Lencioni, P. (2002). *The five dysfunctions of a team: A leadership fable.* New York: Jossey-Bass.

Lewenson, S. (1996). *Taking charge: Nursing, suffrage and feminism in America, 1873–1920.* New York: National League for Nursing.

Linsky, M., & Heifetz, R. (2002). *Leadership on the line: Staying alive through the dangers of leading.* Boston: Harvard Business School Press.

Loehr, J., & Schwartz, T. (2003). *The power of full engagement: Managing energy, not time, is the key to high performance and personal renewal.* New York: Free Press.

Lorenz, E. N. (1993). *The essence of chaos.* Seattle, WA: University of Washington Press.

Lubar, K., & Halpern, B. L. (2004). *Leadership presence.* New York: Gotham.

Lucia, A. D., & Lepsinger, R. (1999). *The art and science of competency models: Pinpointing critical success factors in organizations.* San Francisco: Jossey-Bass.

Lyubomirsky, S. (2007). *The how of happiness: A scientific approach to getting the life you want.* New York: Penguin.

Mackay, H. B. (2005). *Swim with the sharks without begin eaten alive: Outsell, outmanage, outmotivate, and outnegotiate your competition.* New York: Ballantine.

Magee, M. (2005). *Health politics: Power, populism, and health.* New York: Spencer.

Malloch, K., & Porter-O'Grady, P. (2008). *The quantum leader: Applications for the new world of work.* Sudbury, MA: Jones & Bartlett.

Marion, R. (1999). *The edge of organization: Chaos and complexity theories of formal social systems.* London: Sage.

Marriner-Tomey, A. (1993). *Transformational leadership in nursing.* St. Louis, MO: Mosby.

Marshall, H. (1972). *Mary Adelaide Nutting: Pioneer of modern nursing.* Baltimore, MD: Johns Hopkins University Press.

Martin, N. A., & Bloom, J. L. (2003). *Career aspirations and expeditions: Advancing your career in higher education administration.* Champaign, IL: Stipes.

Maslow, A. H. (1954). *Motivation and personality.* Upper Saddle River, NJ: Prentice-Hall.

Maxwell, J. C. (1998). *The 21 irrefutable laws of leadership.* Nashville, TN: Thomas Nelson.

Mayo, E. (1953). *The human problems of an industrialized civilization.* New York: Macmillan.

McGregor, D. (1960). *The human side of enterprise.* New York: McGraw Hill.

McNamara, C. (2009). *Field guide to consulting and organizational development.* Minneapolis, MN: Authenticity Consulting.

Melander, R. (2006). *A generous presence: Spiritual leadership and the art of coaching.* Herndon, VA: The Alban Institute.

Melnyk, B. M., & Fineout-Overholt, E. (2005). *Evidence-based practice in nursing and health care.* Philadelphia: Lippincott Williams & Wilkins.

Moore, T. (1992). *Care of the soul: A guide for cultivating depth and sacredness in everyday life.* New York: HarperCollins.

Moore, T. (1994). *Soul mates: Honoring the mysteries of love and relationship.* New York: HarperCollins.

Morrell, M., & Capparell, S. (2001). *Shackleton's way: Leadership lessons from the great Antarctic explorer.* New York: Viking.

Nanus, B. (1992). *Visionary leadership.* San Francisco: Jossey-Bass.

Neumeier, M. (2007). *Zag: The #1 strategy of high performance brands.* Berkeley, CA: New Riders

Nutting, M. A. (1926). *A sound economic basis for schools of nursing and other addresses.* New York: G. P. Putnam's Sons.

O'Kelly, E. (2008). *Chasing daylight: How my forthcoming death transformed my life.* New York: McGraw-Hill.

Ouchi, W. G. (1981). *Theory Z: How American management can meet the Japanese challenge.* Reading, MA: Addison-Wesley.

Patterson, K., Grenny, J., McMillan, R., & Switzler, A. (2005). *Crucial confrontations.* New York: McGraw-Hill.

Patterson, K., Grenny, J., McMillan, R., Switzler, A., & Covey, S. R. (2002). *Crucial conversations.* New York: McGraw-Hill.

Peters, T. J., & Waterman, R. H., Jr. (1982). *In search of excellence: Lessons from the best-run companies*New York: Warner Books.

Pfeffer, J. (1992). *Managing with power: Power and influence in organizations.* Boston: Harvard Business School Press.

Pitcher, P. (1997). *The drama of leadership.* New York: Wiley.

Porter-O'Grady, T., & Malloch, K. (2007). *Quantum leadership: A resource for health care innovation* (2nd ed.). Sudbury, MA: Jones & Bartlett.

Reeves, D. (2002). *The learning leader: How to focus school improvement for better results.* San Francisco: Jossey-Bass.

Reverby, S. (1985). *The history of American nursing.* New York: Garland Press.

Reynolds, S. (1998). *Thoughts from Chairman Buffett: Thirty years of unconventional wisdom from the sage of Omaha.* New York: HarperBusiness.

Rivers, F. (1997). *The way of the owl: Succeeding with integrity in a conflicted world.* New York: Harper Collins.

Rogers, E. M. (2003). *Diffusion of innovations* (5th ed.). New York: Free Press.

Rosenberg, M. (2003). *Nonviolent communication: A language of life.* Encinitas, CA: Puddledancer Press.

Rothert, M., Cranley, M., Keefe, M. R., & Martin, E. J. (2005). *Academic leadership in nursing: Making the journey.* Washington D.C.: American Association of Colleges of Nursing.

Roussel, L., & Swansburg, R. C. (2009). *Management and leadership for nurse administrators* (5th ed.). Sudbury, MA: Jones & Bartlett.

Schorr, T. M., & Zimmerman, A. (1988). *Making choices taking chances: Nursing leaders tell their stories.* St. Louis, MO: Mosby.

Secretan, L. (1999). *Inspirational leadership: Destiny, cause, and calling.* Caledon, Ontario, Canada: The Secretan Center.

Seligman, M. E. P. (2004). *Authentic happiness: Using the new positive psychology to realize your potential for lasting fulfillment.* New York: Free Press.

Senge, P. (1990). *The fifth discipline: The art and practice of the learning organization.* New York: Doubleday.

Sipe, J. W. (2009). *Seven pillars of servant leadership: Practicing the wisdom of leading by serving.* New York: Paulist Press.

Spears, L. C. (1995). *Reflections on leadership: How Robert K. Greenleaf's Servant Leadership influenced today's top management thinkers.* New York: Wiley.

Spencer, L. M., & Spencer, S. M. (1993). *Competence at work: Models for superior performance.* New York: John Wiley & Sons.

Stacey, R. D., Griffin, D., & Shaw, P. (2000). *Complexity and management: Fad or radical challenge to systems thinking?* London: Routledge.

Stogdill, R. M. (1974). *Handbook of leadership: A survey of theory and leadership.* New York: Free Press.

Strauss, W., & Howe, N. (1997). *The fourth turning: What the cycles of history tell us about America's next rendezvous with destiny.* New York: Broadway Books.

Sullivan, E. J. (2004). *Becoming influential: A guide for nurses.* Upper Saddle River, NJ: Prentice Hall.

Sullivan, T. J. (1998). *Collaboration: A health care imperative.* New York: McGraw-Hill.

Tessier, C., Chaudron, L., & Muller, H. (2002). *Conflicting agents: Conflict management in multi-agent systems.* New York: Kluwer Academic.

Tolle, E. (1999). *The power of now.* Novato, CA: New World Library.

Useem, M. (2001). *Leading up: How to lead your boss so you both win.* New York: Crown.

von Bertalanffy, L. (1968). *General systems theory.* New York: Braziller.

Von Oech, R. (2008). *A whack on the side of the head: How you can be more creative.* Business Plus.

Vroom, V. H., & Yetton, P. W. (1973). *Leadership and decision-making.* Pittsburgh, PA: University of Pittsburgh Press.

Watkins, M. (2003). *The first 90 days: Critical success strategies for new leaders at all levels.* Boston: Harvard Business School Press.

Wenger, E. (1998). *Communities of practice: Learning, meaning, and identity.* Cambridge, England: Cambridge University Press.

Wenger, E., McDermott, R., & Snyder, W. (2002). *Cultivating communities of practice: A guide to managing knowledge.* Cambridge, MA: Harvard Business School Press.

Wheatley, M. J. (1992). *Leadership and the new science: Learning about organization from an orderly universe.* San Francisco: Berrett-Koehler.

Wilson, C. K., & Porter-O'Grady, T. (1999). *Leading the revolution in health care.* Gaithersburg, MD: Aspen.

Yoder-Wise, P. S., & Kowalski, K. E. (2006). *Beyond leading and managing: Nursing administration for the future.* St. Louis, MO: Mosby.

Zachary, L. J. (2000). *The mentor's guide: Facilitating effective learning relationships.* San Francisco: Jossey-Bass.

Zander, B., & Stone, R. (2002). *The art of possibility: Transforming professional and personal life.* New York: Penguin.

Zimmerman, B., Lindberg, C., Plsek, P. (1998). *Edgeware: Insights from complexity science for health care leaders.* Irving, TX: Voluntary Hospitals of America.

INDEX